Dictatorship of Virtue

RICHARD BERNSTEIN

Dictatorship of Virtue

Richard Bernstein was the Hong Kong and Beijing correspondent for *Time* magazine and both a foreign and a national correspondent for *The New York Times*. He was given a Freedom Forum fellowship at Columbia University to write this book. He is currently a book critic for *The New York Times*. He lives in New York.

BOOKS BY **RICHARD BERNSTEIN**

From the Center of the Earth:
The Search for the Truth About China

Fragile Glory:
A Portrait of France and the French

Dictatorship of Virtue:
How the Battle Over Multiculturalism
Is Reshaping Our Schools,
Our Country, and Our Lives

DICTATORSHIP OF VIRTUE

DICTATORSHIP OF VIRTUE

OF VIRTUE

*How the Battle Over Multiculturalism
Is Reshaping Our Schools,
Our Country, and Our Lives*

RICHARD BERNSTEIN

Vintage Books   A Division of Random House, Inc.   New York

FIRST VINTAGE BOOKS EDITION, SEPTEMBER 1995

Copyright © 1994 by Richard Bernstein
Afterword © 1995 by Richard Bernstein

The Library of Congress has cataloged the Knopf edition
as follows:
Bernstein, Richard, [date]
Dictatorship of virtue : multiculturalism and the battle for
America's future / by Richard Bernstein.
p. cm.
Includes bibliographical references and index.
ISBN 0-679-41156-9
1. Multiculturalism—United States.   2. Pluralism (Social
sciences)—United States.   3. United States—Race relations.
4. United States—Ethnic relations.   I. Title
E184.A1B.128 1994
305.8′00973—dc20
93-39508
CIP
Vintage ISBN: 0-679-76398-8

Manufactured in the United States of America
10   9   8   7   6   5   4   3   2   1

In memory of my father

HERBERT BERNSTEIN

*who told me long ago that if you carry your own
lantern, you need not be afraid of the darkness*

Terror is naught but prompt, severe, inflexible
justice; it is therefore an emanation of virtue.

—Maximilien de Robespierre

Contents

DICTATORSHIP OF VIRTUE

Prologue

DÉRAPAGE

Loyalty to petrified opinion never yet broke a chain
or freed a human soul.

—MARK TWAIN

There is a school of French historians that uses the word *dérapage* to
describe the fateful moment when the Great Revolution of 1789,
the first monumental effort to break the chain, skidded from the
enlightened universalism of the Declaration of the Rights of Man and
Citizen into the rule of the Committee of Public Safety and the Terror.
Dérapage, which literally means a "skid" or a "slide," refers to the
way fanaticism and dogmatism swept the great upheaval from consti-
tutionalism to dictatorship, from eighteenth-century rationalism, inspired by the thinkers of the Enlightenment, to a dramatic
foreshadowing of twentieth-century totalitarianism, urged on by grim,
prim Robespierrean despots with a gift for demagogy who believed
they were serving the cause of Liberty, Equality, and Fraternity.

In 1794 Robespierre told the elected parliamentary assembly
known as the Convention that the Revolution aimed at such good
things—"to substitute morality for egotism, probity for honor . . . the
empire of reason for the tyranny of fashions"—that nothing, not even
reason, could stand in its way. Robespierre was an elegant maker of
speeches, an aristocrat of words. "Terror," he told the Jacobin assembly, justifying the ferreting out of enemies real and imagined, "is

naught but prompt, severe, inflexible justice; it is therefore an emanation of virtue."

I don't want to be melodramatic here. We are not reexperiencing the French Revolution, and we are not in danger of the guillotine or rule by a national-level Committee of Public Safety (though I think subsequent pages show the existence of rather smaller versions of that committee). But we are threatened by a narrow orthodoxy—and the occasional outright atrocity—imposed, or committed, in the name of the very values that are supposed to define a pluralist society. That is why that word *dérapage* has stuck in my mind as I have studied a movement gathering force in the United States during the past decade or so, aimed supposedly at a greater inclusiveness of all of the country's diverse component parts, that has somehow slipped from its moorings and turned into a new petrified opinion of the sort it was supposed to transcend.

I am speaking of multiculturalism, which is the term that has emerged to encompass a host of activities, a number of different ways of seeing things, a set of goals that ranges from teaching first-graders in Oregon about the achievements of sub-Saharan African civilization to racial set-asides and quotas at newspapers on the East Coast. Certain other words are being used as well, most common among them "inclusion" and "diversity," and these too are rhetorical crystallizations of the, as it were, diverse tendencies arising from the multiculturalist sensibility. A search of NEXIS, the electronic data bank with the complete texts of most of the major American newspapers, reveals that the words "multiculturalism" and "multicultural" appeared in forty articles in 1981. In 1992, the number had risen to more than two thousand, a fiftyfold increase in just eleven years.

Presumably, American society did not suddenly become fifty times as multicultural as it was before, so the increase in the use of the word "multiculturalism" suggests less an actual change than a discovery of something, perhaps a wish for it or, just as likely, a new trope used not so much to describe things the way they are but to try to make them conform with the way they should be. Certainly, the term is imprecise. It is used for everything from multicultural curricula to what one newspaper, referring to African motifs in the fashion business, called "multiculturally-aware wear."

What exactly is it?

I remember a scholar of China talking years ago about the Great Proletarian Cultural Revolution, which raged in that country in the late 1960s and early 1970s. Certainly, he said, the term referred to something momentous happening in China, but whatever it was, it was not Great, it was not Proletarian, it had nothing to do with Culture, and it was certainly not a Revolution. Similarly with multiculturalism. It does not have the kind of consistent or coherent set of ideas behind it to make it an ism exactly. That prefix "multi" is, yes, applicable in theory, but in practice it is often a mask for what would more accurately be called "mono." Most important, multiculturalism has no more to do with culture than the Cultural Revolution did.

Its most common usage seems to relate to things that happen at our schools and universities where offices of multicultural education and mandatory training in the "multicultural realities" of America are becoming nearly universal. Multiculturalism, and its rhetorical sidekicks, diversity and inclusion, represent, at least in theory, a sensibility of openness to the enormous cultural difference that has always existed in American life, but whose fullness has been suppressed by the might of the dominant European culture. The logical corollary of this is that the domination that white men have enjoyed needs to end in order to allow for full pride of place to other identities, especially those of women and people of color, who have been excluded or marginalized in the past.

In other words multiculturalism is good, unobjectionable, virtuous. It is like Liberty, Equality, Fraternity, like economic justice for the working class and an end to exploitation. It is a way of saying, "Let's be truly diverse, tolerant of difference. Let's give everybody in the gorgeous mosaic an equal shot at racial, ethnic, religious, or sexual pride and through that pride a genuinely equal chance at success." Multiculturalism in this sense would seem to be the logical extension of the civil rights movement of the 1960s, when the relative invisibility of people of color and women became, at least in theory, unacceptable to the political majority. And to be sure, in my travels I have certainly seen much that is rich and wonderful in the work of scholars, writers, artists, and journalists to bring to light previously neglected identities.

But is multiculturalism ordinarily, mostly, in the main, the logical extension of the civil rights movement? Or is it actually a cloak for a late-twentieth-century American *dérapage*?

There are clues to these questions among the self-proclaimed multiculturalists themselves. They rarely, at least as I have gotten to know them, know much about culture at all and even more rarely about somebody else's culture. There are interesting and worthy and certainly very well-intentioned people within the ranks of what I will call the ideological multiculturalists. And yet their lack of curiosity about the real cultural richness of the world, or their reduction of that richness to a few rhapsodic clichés, seems to confirm that culture is not really what is at issue in multiculturalism. At best, the ideological multiculturalists reiterate a few obsessively sincere phrases about the holistic spirit of Native American cultures or about how things are done in what they call the Asian culture or in the African-American culture. The Asian culture, it happens, is something I know a bit about, having spent five years at Harvard striving for a Ph.D. in a joint program called History and East Asian Languages and, after that, living either as a student (for one year) or a journalist (for six years) in China and Southeast Asia. At least I know enough to know that there is no such thing as the "Asian culture." There are dozens of cultures that exist in that vast geographical domain called Asia. When the multiculturalists speak, tremulous with respect, of the "Asian culture," it is out of goodness of heart, but not much actual knowledge.

My experience leads me to believe that insofar as culture is involved in multiculturalism, it is not so much for me to be required to learn about other cultures as for me to be able to celebrate myself and for you to be required to celebrate me, and, along the way, to support my demand for more respect, more pride of place, more jobs, more foundation support, more money, more programs, more books, more prizes, more people like me in high places, a higher degree of attention.

The paradox is that the power of culture is utterly contrary to the most fervently held beliefs and values of the advocates of multiculturalism. Multiculturalism is a movement of the left, emerging from the counterculture of the 1960s. But culture is powerfully conservative. Culture is what enforces obedience to authority, the authority of parents, of history, of custom, of superstition. Deep attachment to culture is one of the things that prevents different people from understanding one another. It is what pushes groups into compliance with practices that can be good or bad, depending on one's point of view. Suttee (the practice, eradicated by British colonialism, in which Indian widows were burned alive on the funeral pyres of their husbands) and female circumcision, as well as the spirit of rational inquiry and a belief in the sanctity of each human life, are products of cultural attachments of different kinds. Those who practiced suttee, or who believe that women who commit adultery should be stoned to death, do not believe there is anything bad about these practices, any more than those who practice rational inquiry under conditions of freedom think there is anything wrong with that.

The reality of culture is something that the ideological multiculturalists would despise, if they knew what it was. The power of culture, especially the culture rooted in ancient traditions, is anathema to the actual goals and ideology of multiculturalism, which does not seek an appreciation of other cultures but operates out of the wishful assumption that the unknown, obscure, neglected, subaltern cultures of the world are actually manifestations of a leftist ideology born out of the particular culture of American and European universities and existing practically no place else.

The point is that while multiculturalism is in some instances what it sounds like it should be, a fuller realization of American pluralism, it is for the most part a code word for something that, again, is not multi, or cultural, or even an ism. It is a code word for a political ambition, a yearning for more power, combined with a genuine, earnest, zealous, self-righteous craving for social improvement that is characteristic of the mentality of the post-1960s era in American life. The 1960s were the rebellion years. A new consciousness emerged, involving irreverence for standard beliefs and a sudden illumination of how our traditions were not the results of some irrefutable logic but rather servants of the holders of power, how our unexamined habits of mind perpetuated an unjust status quo. Out of the burning wish for betterment grew what has now become a kind of bureaucracy of the good, fighting battles that have already been won, demanding ever greater commitments of virtue from a recalcitrant population. This bureaucracy, made up of people who, like Robespierre, are convinced that they are waging the good fight on behalf of virtue, is the instrument of ideological multiculturalism whose effectiveness lies precisely in its ability to appear to be the opposite of what it actually is. It is an ardently advocated, veritably messianic political program, and, like most political programs that have succumbed to the utopian temptation, it does not take kindly to true difference.

Multiculturalism, in short, cannot be taken at face value, and that is what makes it so tricky. Nobody wants to appear to be against multiculturalism. Hence, the irresistible temptation of the post-1960s, radical-left inhabitants of a political dreamland to use the term "multiculturalism" as a defense against exposure or criticism and to bring into service a vocabulary to which multiculturalism has an almost salacious attraction, words like "racist," "sexist," "homophobic." To put matters bluntly: the multiculturalist rhetoric has the rest of us on the run, unable to respond for fear of being branded unicultural, or racist, or (to get into the trendy academic lingo) complicit in the structures of hegemony imposed by the Eurocentric patriarchy and its strategies of domination.

In such a way does multiculturalism limit discussion; it makes people afraid to say what they think and feel; it presents dubious and cranky interpretations and analyses as self-evident, indisputable truths. It often operates, not through the usual means of civil discourse and persuasion, but via intimidation and intellectual decree. It rewrites history. It sanctions a cultivation of aggrievement, a constant claim of victimization, an excessive, fussy, self-pitying sort of wariness that induces others to spout pieties. And that, in turn, covers the public discussion of crucial issues with a layer of fear, so that we can no longer speak forthrightly and honestly about such matters as crime, race, poverty, AIDS, the failure of schools, single-parenthood, affirmative action, racial preferences, welfare, college admissions, merit, the breakup of the family, and the disintegration of urban life.

Multiculturalism, in short, has reached the point of *dérapage*. It is a universe of ambitious good intentions that has veered off the high road of respect for difference and plunged into a foggy chasm of dogmatic assertions, wishful thinking, and pseudoscientific pronouncements about race and sex. At its worst, it is what my title suggests. It draws on the old Puritan notion of America as the city on the hill, a new moral universe, to impose a certain vision of rectitude. And, in this, the idealistic and good-hearted movement of inclusion and greater justice veers toward a dictatorship of virtue.

It is not easy to say these things, in part because one does not want to lose sight of all that there is to be admired in the sensibility that gave rise to the multiculturalist challenge in the first place. I am part of the broad liberal consensus that assumes the correctness of the values and practices that emerged from the civil rights movement of the 1960s, one of the most profound and truly liberating social upheavals of all of history, comparable, and indeed linked to, the great events of 1789 in Paris. But the movement known as multiculturalism is no longer that. Indeed, a single-sentence summation of my theme would be this: multiculturalism as it is commonly formulated and practiced is the *dérapage* of the civil rights movement.

As I have said, the guillotine does not await us at the other end of the *dérapage*. The dangers that do lurk on the dark side of the multiculturalist revolution are less than that, but they are nonetheless serious enough. Some writers before me have dwelled on one particular consequence of the multiculturalist impulse, deriving from its tendency to make a religion of "difference" and to exalt race, ethnicity, and sex as the sole components of identity. This, as the essayist Charles Krauthammer has said, is shoving us toward a "new tribalism," a splintering of the national culture and an intensification of our conflicts. After all, these writers have noted, we have arrayed before us in the pages of our newspapers the tragedies being played out elsewhere among people who have stressed their differences rather than their commonalities. There is the nightmare in the former Yugoslavia, for example. There are wars between Hutu and Tutsi in Burundi and Rwanda, and between Zulu and Xhosa in South Africa, between Armenians and Azerbaijani, Protestants and Catholics in Northern Ireland, Arabs and Jews in the Middle East, Abkhazians and Georgians in the former Soviet republic of Georgia, and a dozen other conflicts involving, not usually race, but an aggressive ethnicity demonstrating that human beings are just as likely to live in conditions of group animosity as in some harmonious ethnic salad. My own sense is that we are more likely to end up in a simmering sort of mutual dislike on the level of everyday unpleasantness than we are in full-scale Balkan warfare. But that is bad enough.

More alarming perhaps than the prospect of disunion is the possibility that multicultural doctrine will turn out to be a false promise to those members of our society who can least endure yet another false promise. After all, the pattern of assimilation, so easily dismissed by the champions of sweeping change, worked pretty well for millions of people and continues to work well for the many new arrivals who flock, legally and otherwise, to our shores every year. Now a certain racial militancy and small-group affiliation are encouraged by the multiculturalist missionaries on the grounds that these attitudes will help to break the vicious cycles of poverty and violence that are keeping millions of American citizens down.

Multiculturalism in this sense is a code word for an expanded concept of moral and cultural relativism. Originally, relativism deflated the imperial arrogance of Western civilization. By now, the *dérapage* has pushed us to the point where we are fearful of upholding any aspect of the Western way of doing things as better than other ways. It was perhaps inevitable in the liberal American culture that multiculturalism got conflated with an expanded version of a phenomenon that Daniel Patrick Moynihan has called "defining down deviancy." Moynihan was talking about the way our tolerant and forgiving liberal culture removes more and more bad behavior from the category of the delinquent, so that it can no longer be punished. My own belief is that the multiculturalist rhetoric has the effect of defining down many other forms of bad behavior. Teenage pregnancy is transformed from a cause of shame into one of many "diverse forms of the family." Violence in schools is not an offense but the teachers' ignorance of the "cultures" of a "diverse student population." Their pupils fail to learn, not because they do not study hard enough but because they have "different ways of knowing" or because they do not see themselves "reflected" in the curriculum. Anti-male, anti-white, and anti-Semitic bigotry at institutions of higher learning is coddled in the belief that it is the natural expression of the rage of the culturally dispossessed.

But what if this relativism turns out to be a fraud, perpetrated by mostly middle-class intellectuals, all of whom have jobs? What if the ideas coded in multiculturalism do not so much prepare people for real life as foster illusions about it, or, worse, provide a pretext for repudiating the values and behaviors that have traditionally led to success, such as objectivity and achievement, on the grounds that they are the values of the despised Eurocentrist group?

One of my own underlying theses is that, like it or not, there are certain cultural norms, certain things to know and do, a mastery of a certain discourse, that is most likely to get people on the great engine of upward social mobility in the United States. The multiculturalists contend that there are many different avenues to the same result. They promise, as we will see, that different "learning styles," these things vaguely tied to race and gender, will lead to success, which can no longer be defined in the masculine, Eurocentric way. They promise that the enforcement of a certain rhetorical code will address the real problems of inequality and prejudice that have bedeviled American society from the beginning of its history. And, in this, they would impose a certain conformity to their ideas, one originating in the concept of virtue and that puts the vast and ever-growing multiculturalist bureaucracy into the tradition of Robespierre.

Joseph Conrad wrote in *Under Western Eyes* that "in a real revolution the best characters do not come to the front. . . . The scrupulous and the just, the noble, humane and devoted natures, the unselfish and the intelligent may begin a movement—but it passes away from them." This, I believe, is true of multiculturalism, a humane and humanizing idea that has, somehow, gone wrong. It is nobility perverted. And those who are perverting it, not the scrupulous and the just, but the zealots and the tyrants, belong to a burgeoning bureaucracy that, like all bureaucracies, finds ways to perpetuate and aggrandize itself. Its members may not deliver on their promise to the victimized of our society. They will, nonetheless, not lose their jobs.

The plain and inescapable fact is that the derived Western European culture of American life produced the highest degree of prosperity in the conditions of the greatest freedom ever known on planet Earth. The rich and the advantaged of our society will survive even if they are taught to believe something different. But to teach the poor and the disadvantaged that they can ignore the standards and modes of behavior that have always made for success in American life is more than mere silliness. It is a lie.

PART I

Diversity

Whatever crushes individuality is despotism.

— JOHN STUART MILL

Chapter 1

ELEMENTARY DIVERSITY

In 1991, after bitter complaints by some reporters over what they called racism in an editorial about poverty in the inner city, the management of the Philadelphia *Inquirer* invited a professional "facilitator" to conduct "diversity-training" sessions for the entire staff, the purpose being to make all of the editors and writers of the venerable urban daily more aware of the feelings of those of different backgrounds. The meetings took place in the *Inquirer* building auditorium, a homely square room that manages, somehow, to be both austere and disheveled at the same time. Sandwiches and coffee were laid out on a table in the back of the room while participants in the meeting, a group of the *Inquirer*'s editors and reporters, photographers and columnists, clustered in the middle rows of blue plastic chairs, shyly leaving the first few rows empty.

The reporters and editors had gathered as part of what was called the Pluralism Plan at the *Inquirer*, a link in the Knight-Ridder chain of newspapers that had decided to make diversity a company-wide policy, the belief being, logically enough, that to cover a diverse society, a newsroom needs both a diverse staff and a receptive attitude toward the idea of diversity. At the *Inquirer*, however, sensitivity training, as the series of meetings with the facilitator came to be called, arrived at an unusual and conflictual moment.

On December 12, 1990, the *Inquirer* ran an editorial entitled "Poverty and Norplant: Can Contraception Reduce the Underclass?" It noted two separate developments: one was the dramatic increase in the number of black children, most of them born to single mothers, who live in poverty; the other was approval by the U.S. Food and Drug Administration of Norplant, a contraceptive that is put under the skin and can provide birth control for five years.

"No one should be compelled to use Norplant," the editorial said, also pointing out that the device can be taken out at any time if a woman who uses it decides she wants to have a baby. Meanwhile, the paper asked, addressing here one of the pressing social problems of our time, "What if welfare mothers were offered an increased benefit for agreeing to use this new, safe, long-term contraception?"

"All right, the subject makes us uncomfortable, too," the editorial concluded. "But we're made even more uncomfortable by the impoverishment of black America and its effect on the nation's future. Think about it."

The editorial caused an eruption of anger, not especially among readers of the *Inquirer*, who did not seem to take umbrage in significant numbers, but among the staff. Black reporters circulated a petition calling for the dismissal of David Boldt, the editor of the editorial page. The newspaper published a letter by one of its own reporters, Vanessa Williams, president of the Philadelphia Association of Black Journalists, assailing the editorial's suggestion as a "tacit endorsement of slow genocide." The outrage on the paper, the *Inquirer's* editor Maxwell King told me, was not that a sensitive and difficult subject involving race and poverty had been raised, but rather that the editorial had appeared to contain a subtle implication. As King put it: "A lot of people read that editorial and came away with the idea that the *Inquirer* was saying that the answer to the race problem was to have fewer black people," though, he added, "that is certainly not what the paper intended."

King, a bearded, friendly, approachable man who spent many years as a reporter himself, recounted that in the days after the editorial was published editors and writers deluged him and Boldt with requests for a meeting to air their views. The demand was so great that two meetings were held at which angry reporters, some but by no means all of them black, charged that Boldt and Donald Kimelman, Boldt's deputy and the actual author of the offending editorial, were racists and that the attitudes that had led them to publish the Norplant editorial showed the white-male biases rampant in American society. King, who presided at the meetings, told me that something bothered him about the confrontations, unprecedented at the *Inquirer*. It was not so much the charges of racism and white-male bias directed against Kimelman and Boldt, which, while certainly untrue, needed to be answered, King said. What disturbed him was something else.

"There were times when the tone and texture of the meetings became so combative that it felt to me that there was something potentially destructive there," he said. Specifically, there were the calls for the resignations of Boldt and Kimelman. "What was in the air was that somehow the answer would be to silence these people," King said. "That bothered me." The healthy aspect of the incident, he said, which was the candid exchange of views and the resulting greater awareness of differing racial perspectives, mingled "with some unhealthy aspects to it," namely what King called "intellectual intimidation."

The newspaper did not fire Boldt or Kimelman. But King did order an apology for the Norplant editorial. The apology ran in the paper on December 21. It called the view that Kimelman had expressed a "misguided and wrongheaded editorial opinion" that had been "fatally flawed," not by its actual ideas but by the insensitive way it had put things, especially its conflation of "race and contraception." The apology in turn caused a new round of complaints both from within and without the paper, this time that King, rather than boldly affirm the newspaper's responsibility to comment on difficult and controversial issues, had ceded to the thought police, the race censors, what he himself later called intellectual intimidation. Boldt argued in a signed article several months later that the original editorial had, in fact, been "tepid and tentative in tone," while the apology had involved "needless groveling." An important discussion of inner-city poverty had, in effect, been deformed into a separate and in this case largely irrelevant argument about racial sensitivity, an examination of the thought of those who were making the arguments. The need to be sensitive had, it seemed, taken priority over the need to discuss our social problems freely and openly.

Kimelman himself wrote a brief article in the *Masthead*, an editorial writers' newsletter, in which he gave the background to the incident. What happens normally, he said, is that editorial writers receive a new batch of grim figures on black poverty, following which they are expected "to decry the trend and propose a familiar litany of remedies—from prenatal care to job training." Instead, Kimelman said, the *Inquirer* departed from the usual script. It introduced something new into the picture, namely birth control, which, though routinely practiced by most middle-class people of all races and almost all religions, is what set off the storm.

And so the incident at the *Inquirer* showed the anger and the tension that threaten these days to boil over in American society, where the safeguarding of a group's image, the vigilance over the way it is portrayed in the media, often lead some to view the normal expression of opinion as racial affront. It showed the ferocity of the challenge to what is perceived to be white control over the images depicted in the media.

The editors of the *Inquirer* had several ways to respond to this. They could have supported the arguments of Boldt and Kimelman and defended the editorial. They could have assigned a team of reporters to investigate the attitudes of poor black and other people to the idea of using Norplant for contraception.* They could have published a page or two of different views and opinions on this difficult and sensitive subject.

In fact, except for publishing a few letters, the *Inquirer* did none of these things. Instead, it did what most newspapers these days probably would have done under the same circumstances, which was to invest new energy in its already existing Pluralism Plan. Following its apology for the editorial, the paper moved to make sure that nothing like the Norplant controversy ever again disturbed the domestic tranquillity by requiring that any potentially controversial statement, and especially anything involving race, be approved by the entire thirteen-member editorial board—in essence, as Kimelman put it, giving a veto power to the board's three black members. The Monitoring Committee was created to study the actual content of the *Inquirer* and determine whether there were biases in the paper's coverage. (Its first investigation was into charges that black criminal suspects were shown in photographs more commonly than whites. It found the charge to be untrue.) The Diversity Committee was set up to monitor minority hiring, to make recommendations on covering stories, and to look into such matters as spousal benefits for the partners of homosexual and lesbian staff members.

Around the same time, Maxwell King announced an ambitious

---

*They might have found, for example, that the people actually affected by the proposed program saw nothing racist about it. In Baltimore, a city with a black majority population and a black mayor, a plan to make Norplant available free at city school clinics was announced in December 1992, causing no outcry at all.

hiring policy by which half of the new employees would have to be members of minority groups; the other half would have to be women. In other words, a white male could, in theory, only be hired if, say, a newly engaged employee fulfilled two of the criteria at the same time—was, for example, female and black—thus leaving a space open for the nonfavored white-male category. And then there was the most generally applicable aspect of the Pluralism Plan, the holding of diversity-training sessions for every member of the newspaper's staff. For months, meeting in small groups, reporters and editors at the venerable daily munched their sandwiches and sat on those blue plastic chairs listening as a facilitator trained them in the realities of the new America.

The session I observed at the *Inquirer* took place late in 1991 after the program was well advanced, and it was an illustration of what might be called a mild diversity program, a nonconfrontational discussion about prejudice and stereotypes. It began with a kind of glimpse of the future provided by a twenty-minute videotape called *Managing Diversity*. The tape, which costs $600 ($450 for a nonprofit organization), is part of a series of videos entitled Valuing Diversity, produced by a San Francisco company then called Copeland Griggs Productions (later changed to Griggs Productions), whose materials are designed more for corporations than newsrooms. After some quite professional introductory graphics set to music, a narrator states the basic theme.

"Times have changed," he says. "Today for the first time in history white males are the minority in the workplace, only 46 percent. And, the U.S. Department of Labor projects that in the 1990s, 75 percent of those entering the workforce will be minorities and women."

The video continues by quoting a number of different people of different races, all of them agreeing on one point: people of different backgrounds and ethnicities, who will be entering the labor force in great numbers soon, are different by nature. "Because we're all equal, that does not mean we are all the same," says Gerald Adolph, identified as a consultant with Booz, Allen & Hamilton, a corporate consulting company in New York. "It just means that while we have differences and may come at things in different ways, those are of equal value." In a similar vein, but using her own metaphor, Daisy Chin-Lor, director of multicultural planning at Avon, the cosmetics giant, talks of human beings in the workplace as flowers in a garden.

The flowers are different. All of them are beautiful. But they each need their own particular kind of care, she says.

Then come some dramatizations illustrating how cultural misunderstanding, which is to say the failure to value diversity, can result in bad management. And, of course, bad management is bad for performance, bad for productivity, bad for profits. There is, for example, a woman executive who seems not to be taken seriously at all by her male colleagues. "One of the major concerns is that they are invisible," Chin-Lor explains, speaking of women in the workplace. "Most men don't recognize their existence and legitimate it."

The woman shown in the videotape is svelte and blond and dressed for success. She sits at a boardroom meeting with four men, and while she is given a chance to speak, her ideas and opinions are ignored. The men pause while she has her say but then continue to talk to one another as though she were not present. Somehow—though this is not explained in the videotape—the blond woman has attained a high executive position, which, presumably, includes high executive pay, but then she is turned into a nonperson, not because the men are actively antifemale, but because they simply have the reflex to form an in-group, to bond with one another and to take one another, and only one another, seriously.

So it is, for example, that when one of the men, the only one who is just a bit more sensitive to the woman's presence, offers up exactly the same idea that she had offered without eliciting any reaction a few minutes earlier, it is readily endorsed. Then, the meeting over, the men go out to lunch, failing to invite the woman to join them. Finally, after a few more scenes illustrating the way women are invisible, the woman executive takes another job, and the practical business point is made. The company has lost a valuable employee, not because of overt discrimination or hostility but because of habits of mind deeply ingrained in white males over the centuries, because of insensitivity to difference.

Another scene: a man of Asian ancestry is telling his boss that he would like a promotion to be the chief of a new research group that is to be formed inside the company. The boss tells the Asian man that he knows he has technical skills, but does he know how to manage a group? The employee never answers the question. He replies with statements about the accomplishments of the group, but he does not boast about his own abilities as a leader.

Asians, we are then told by the narrator, are culturally apt to behave in this way. They are modest, self-effacing people, unlike what are sometimes called Euro-American men, who would respond quickly and directly to the manager's question by stating their qualifications. We have to be aware of these cultural differences, especially in light of the demographic trends stated at the outset of the film, wherein the previously white-male enclaves of the American economy will soon take on all the hues of the rainbow.

The lesson here is shown in an alternative management approach. Rather than ask whether the Asian employee is capable of leadership, the manager is shown drawing him out beyond his culturally induced reticence. "What does Bill do in the group?" the manager asks, starting out by focusing attention on somebody else. "What about Harry? And [blandly, as if nothing but idle curiosity is involved] what about you? What do you do in the group?" This culturally sensitive, tuned-in manner of dealing with an Asian would be consistent, the video suggests, with valuing diversity.

There is more along these lines. A Native American woman is shown making a technical innovation in a factory workshop, but when she is publicly praised by a loud, white, Guy Smiley–type manager, she is deeply embarrassed. The manager is plainly of goodwill, but he failed to understand that Native Americans (a bit like Asians in this vision of the multicultural world) are shy folk who appreciate a more discreet, private approach, which is also shown in the Copeland Griggs video as an alternative to the direct, bombastic approach the boss takes initially. Rather than call attention to the worker's innovation in front of everybody else, he quietly tells her, in this alternative scenario, that he appreciates what she has done, and he shows her a note to that effect that he is putting into her personnel file. Before, the woman was embarrassed. Now, having been dealt with in this culturally sensitive manner, her face lights up with appreciation. "Thank you very much, Ted," she says.

All over America people are learning to "value diversity." The idea is that with the country changing as rapidly as it is, becoming less white, less European, more like the rainbow, a new way of living and working will have to be learned, starting in grammar school and continuing through adult education, and this way of living is something that must be taught. And being taught it is. NEXIS shows the phrase "sensitivity training" appearing in seventeen articles nationwide in 1981. In 1991, that had increased to 320, and in 1992, the number was more than 500.

The Valuing Diversity videotape series that I saw at the *Inquirer*, and a companion set called Going International, have been bought, in whole or in part, by about four thousand organizations, Griggs Productions says. The *Wall Street Journal* reported in August 1992 that "managing diversity in the workplace has become a full-time job." About half of the Fortune 500 companies now have "diversity managers," paid between $75,000 and $130,000 a year, one of whose duties is "to run sensitivity training programs for male and female employees." Colgate-Palmolive, for example, had just picked its first "cultural diversity manager" from among five hundred applicants, the *Journal* said, adding that the firm "needed someone to help managers integrate cultural diversity into their business practices."

The business of training people in the new American diversity is infused with the spirit of idealism and openness and goodwill and, at the same time, lightly redolent of 1960s-style teach-ins, of consciousness-raising, of group therapy, of remedial morality, beginning with the notion that the white-male point of view is going to have to be replaced with a more inclusive vision.

Many places besides corporations are adopting the practice. At schools and universities, special diversity-training courses are required for incoming freshmen or for students seeking special jobs such as dorm counselors. These sessions normally are run by members of the groups that feel sensitivity is lacking—black students' unions, sometimes the Anti-Defamation League or some other Jewish group, frequently the local gay- and lesbian-rights organization. At the University of Pennsylvania, starting in 1990, senior administrators, twenty-six of them in this case, were required to undergo what was officially called training in "managing diversity," described by a campus publication as "a three-day workshop to explore the effects of racism and sexism on individuals, groups and institutions."

In Madison, Wisconsin, two young women, Anne Ready and Maureen Rowe, advertised in a local newspaper for a female roommate to share their house. When they refused to accept a self-proclaimed lesbian who wanted the room, they were found by the local Equal Opportunities Commission of Madison to have violated the local equal-housing ordinances, which forbid discrimination on the basis of sexual preference. In a decision that was eventually reversed on appeal, the two women were assessed damages, fined the lesbian woman's legal fees, and ordered to attend a two-hour sensitivity-training session conducted by the United, Madison's gay-rights organization.

Because the decision was overturned, Ready and Rowe never did have to undergo sensitivity training. Others charged with insensitive behavior in Madison, however, have. One lawyer there, Ann Sulton, told me that she makes it a practice in civil cases not only to demand money damages for the mental anguish stemming from racial or other discrimination but to have wrongdoing corrected by mandatory education. "We want society to change," she told me, giving the practice of civil law a legislative purpose, "so what I have required is not only that they pay my clients money but that they go through racial-sensitivity training, or that they modify internal features to create a more sensitive work environment."

In one case Sulton handled a lawsuit on behalf of Cheryl Robinson, a black woman who lost her five children in a fire at home. "The police chief made statements to the press saying that they thought she wasn't home at the time of the fire, the implication being that she was therefore responsible for the death of her children," Sulton said. The policeman's claim prompted demonstrations led by local black clergymen against what was called "gross insensitivity." In addition, said Sulton, "We filed a lawsuit in federal court alleging that they had defamed her and caused injury. The case was settled about three or four weeks before trial, and the police agreed to pay six thousand dollars in costs, to change the training procedures for police and fire officers, to redouble affirmative action efforts, to hire more people of color, to change the citizen complaint process, and to issue a public apology to my client." All this was done because of one allegedly insensitive remark by a police officer. "They had to add a component of sensitivity training about the multicultural community and the training has to be done by nonwhites," Sulton said.

In what way was the police chief's statement discriminatory? "We alleged that if Cheryl Robinson had been a rich white woman he would never have made those statements to the press," Sulton said.

She did not refer to numerous newspaper reports appearing at the time in which Robinson's whereabouts in the period before the fire were hotly contested. There were some who said she was at home when the fire broke out and left to seek help. But the local *Capital Times* newspaper reported on police-radio recordings that indicated Robinson could not be found until an hour or so after the alarm on the early morning fire was sounded and that a witness told police he saw her at a local café at midnight, two hours before the fire.

Across the country, at Stanford University Medical School, where a woman neurosurgeon had spectacularly resigned from the faculty claiming an insupportable atmosphere of petty sexism—one of whose signs was the "old-fashioned" attitude about women held by the department chairman—weekend retreats for diversity and sensitivity training were organized for the entire faculty.

Michael Cowan, the director of the effort (and, despite her first name, a woman), told me, "They are two-day programs. They are on multiculturalism and included is racism, sexism, ageism, homophobism, and anything you want to name ism." The training was carried out by Equity Institute, a California sensitivity-training firm whose brochure, entitled *Turning "Isms" into "Wasms,"* promises to "empower individuals" via "an inclusive multicultural approach" that addresses a host of "issues," including "racism, anti-Semitism, heterosexism, classism, ageism and ableism. . . . Eliminating 'isms' from your organization is possible. . . . Harmony and understanding are within your reach."

Ms. Cowan's vocabulary indicated that she may have been influenced by a well-publicized effort at Smith College to encode the correct ways of thinking about difference. In 1990, the Office of Student Affairs at Smith, an old and revered institution of higher learning in Massachusetts, published a leaflet containing a glossary of terms to help students living in a diverse environment. The leaflet was distributed to all students during what were called "orientation workshops on community living" and was drawn from material produced by a national organization called SOAR (Society Organized Against Racism). This whole matter caused some embarrassment at Smith when the leaflet got national attention in the press. So to rebut charges that the university was sanctioning politically correct language, an official statement was issued explaining what was really at stake. The controversial leaflet, said the statement put out by Smith's press office, was meant to provide students with "information" that would prevent them from inflicting "unintentional hurt out of ignorance. . . . It serves an educational purpose, not a political one."

This entirely nonpolitical leaflet provided a list of what it called "specific manifestations of oppression," which included the information that "people can be oppressed in many ways and for many reasons because they are perceived to be different." It then gave a kind of catalog of forms of oppression, which included

Ableism: oppression of the differently abled, by the temporarily able.

Ageism: oppression of the young and the old, by young adults and the middle-aged in the belief that others are "incapable" or unable to take care of themselves.

Classism: oppression of the working-class and non-propertied, by the upper and middle-class.

Lookism: the belief that appearance is an indicator of a person's value; the construction of a standard for beauty/attractiveness; and oppression through stereotypes and generalizations of both those who do not fit that standard and those who do.

Sexism: stereotyping of males and females on the basis of their gender; the oppression of women by society in the belief that gender is an indication of ability.

It would have been interesting to engage the lexicographers who drafted this list in discussion, to ask them, for example, how long one is temporarily able, or who were the young who were being oppressed in what is called ageism, or what proof there was that what we find to be beautiful or attractive is constructed by society, not innate in human beings. But without any discussion or explanation of these matters, without an invitation to alternative views, the "informational tool and stimulus for discussion" moved on to list "factors of oppression in general" and gave definitions for each of several terms—"prejudice," "discrimination," "oppression," and "institutional power," this last defined as "access to resources and privileges within the dominant culture and its institutions." And it provided lists of "preferred te ns," from "African-American" and "European-American" (substituting for "black" and "white") to "bisexual," "gay," "lesbian," "differently abled," and "non-traditional-age student."

There was much bittersweet reaction to efforts like these, including parodies of politically correct terminology—referring to short people as "vertically challenged" became a common joke. One response to the mood came at the University of Arizona, where a secretary posted a survey form on the bulletin board of the physics department.

It invited people to fill out a "sexual harassment consent form" on which they could check sexual behavior that they would welcome. "Eye-to-bust contact" and "heavy breathing on the neck" were two of the possible forms of behavior on which women were asked to express approval or disapproval. It was supposed to be a joke, a dig, not at sensitivity but at oversensitivity and sanctimoniousness. The dean of the science faculty, Edgar J. McCollough, however, saw nothing funny in the effort. He ordered what the school's newspaper called "sexual harassment awareness workshops," not just for the irreverent physics department, but for all of the university's sixteen science departments, but the order was resisted.

Even the United States Navy has adopted the sensitivity-training route. In 1992, five career officers were demoted after a party at which Congresswoman Pat Schroeder was cruelly parodied, even though then President Bush and Vice-president Quayle were also the objects of satire at the same party. The lesson here was that a sensitivity seen as obligatory for women like Schroeder is not so obligatory when it comes to a man, even if the man is the commander in chief. After the famous 1991 Tailhook incident—in which a bunch of drunken sailors grabbed and groped at passing women officers, thereby drawing the attention of the national media—the navy announced that it would institute a full day of training on sexual harassment rules for all enlisted men and officers. The underlying assumption here was not that a few young men had gotten drunk and misbehaved terribly, which they certainly had, but that the socialization of the male of the species led directly to bestiality, necessitating universal inoculation. "Does anyone really need a day in a classroom to learn that it's wrong to grab a woman's breasts?" the *Wall Street Journal* asked in an editorial.

Polite as they are, most Americans, including the uncomfortable white males, who are subtly branded the ones who actually need sensitivity training, sit quietly through these sessions—but not always. At the Philadelphia *Inquirer*, the diversity-training workshops—which, while not mandatory, were seen by most on the staff to be highly recommended—aroused objections from some. One reporter said that he would have attended what he called the "pluralism meetings," but only if "I was given a guarantee that any sensitivity training include a serious seminar excoriating the heinous practice of white-male bashing."

Art Carey, an editor on the *Inquirer*'s Sunday magazine, told the Washington *Post* that "training in sensitivity and diversity legitimates and enforces a certain politically correct view of the world and the fashionable left-liberal orthodoxy of the *Inquirer*." Carey said that he felt an irony in the situation. He had been attracted to newspapers in the first place "because I believed they were true meritocracies that valued independence of thought and diversity—not only of people, but also of opinion, belief and political outlook. I don't believe that's the case now. There's a moral smugness and self-righteousness that pervades this place now. If you don't embrace the dictates of the Sensitivity Gestapo, you are, ipso facto, a racist."

Carey, though perhaps inclined toward a degree of verbal overkill, had had some experiences leading him to his view that sensitivity of the sort encouraged in diversity training endangered the unhindered exchange of ideas and opinions. Sometime before I met him, he had been asked by the *Inquirer*'s book review editor, Mike Leary, to write a review of *Illiberal Education: The Politics of Race and Sex on Campus*, by Dinesh D'Souza. The D'Souza book was a powerful assault on the coercive force of the reigning liberal orthodoxy in higher education and was viewed as a contemptible, reactionary tirade by many on the academic left. Carey agreed with the book's premises and wrote a favorable review. An editor on the book review noted it when Carey turned it in for publication, and he sent it up through the editorial bureaucracy, which, it seems, was worried that the favorable review of a book seen by many as an assault on multiculturalism could evoke the same kind of turmoil as the Norplant editorial a few months earlier. The newspaper's decision: to postpone Carey's review until the book could be sent to a reviewer who would write an unfavorable review. The result was that on page one of the *Inquirer*'s book review section, two reviews of the D'Souza book appeared, one of them favorable, the other not.

If that were a common practice, or even an occasional practice at the *Inquirer*, such a policy would seem entirely laudable, a marvelous way of allowing the reader exposure to a genuine diversity of opinion. The fact is that nobody seemed to remember another time when reviews had been paired in such a way. I asked King whether, in his view, the same thing would have been done if the initial review of the D'Souza book had been unfavorable. King had to admit that there would very likely have been no pairing in that situation. Diversity of view is imposed when a conservative point of view is expressed and needs to be balanced with a liberal view, which is odd given how rarely conservative views are expressed in the liberal *Inquirer* in the first place.*

A few at the *Inquirer* saw a link between diversity training and the newspaper's relentlessly liberal outlook, both of which seemed to belong to the same moral and political universe. Ralph Cipriano, an obituary writer, wrote an open letter to his colleagues on the day after the meeting at which staff members lambasted the editorial staff for its racism and its white-male biases. He complained that "one group has categorized 300 people in a newsroom, people of diverse religious, ethnic and cultural backgrounds, into several arbitrary categories. From what I heard yesterday, we white males are all identical slices in the same loaf of Wonder Bread.

"I applaud your attempts to diversify the newsroom," Cipriano (who is of Arab ancestry) continued, "but I reject your attempts to stereotype me. . . . What was supposed to be a plan to bring us together instead is pulling us apart by pitting one alleged group against another."

The meeting I attended was devoid of fireworks or sharp conflict, even though a couple of the journalists present did voice some feeling that the portrayals of Asians, Native Americans, and others were too pat, as if each of us wore a little label containing information about the accidental circumstances of our birth and that information were just about all we needed to know about one another's character. The videotape *Managing Diversity* creates stereotypes in the alleged effort to extirpate stereotypes. Some Native Americans are shy; some, presumably, are not. Some men of Asian ancestry might be too modest to talk of their qualifications for a new job; others would not be.

I know from my own experience that the very concept "Asian" encompasses such enormous diversity as to be meaningless. Are we talking about an Indonesian who might well be Muslim and speak a dialect of Malay? A Mongolian who would also be Muslim and who lives in a goatskin yurt on the grasslands, or a Hmong tribesman who

---

*After his review ran, Carey received a letter from an *Inquirer* colleague who said he was "appalled" by what Carey had written about the D'Souza book. His review, the letter said, exposed Carey's "racist, sexist, homophobic attitudes." The letter, and the newspaper's decision to pair his review with one taking the opposite point of view, struck Carey as an example of the very tendencies that D'Souza described—and that D'Souza's critics claimed did not exist.

practices animism and is a member of a group persecuted and despised by the ethnic majority in his own country (the lowland Lao believe the Montagnard Hmong to be only slightly more civilized than the neighorhood monkeys, so little do they value diversity)? And take it from me: generals in China's Red Army, in contrast to Copeland Griggs's Asian employee, are not shy about proclaiming their abilities to manage a group; neither are Khmer Rouge ideologues. There are no doubt men and women of Asian ancestry working for companies in the United States who are shy, but their cousins in Hong Kong were not too shy to build vast shipping, real estate, and industrial empires without benefit of diversity training for the ruling white male British colonialists. The plain fact is that the richness and unpredictability of genuine human diversity cannot be encompassed by a few caricatures, even if they are very well intentioned.

In any case, whatever its intellectual limitations, the diversity movement has in good capitalist fashion produced an entire new sensitivity industry. Right thinking about "difference" is being marketed like soap powder or computer software. Griggs Productions not only produces its two videotape series, it also holds five-day conferences (at a cost of $1,500 for corporations, $1,000 for nonprofit organizations) "designed for those who want to learn more effective ways to use their VALUING DIVERSITY films."

At these conferences, according to the brochure, participants enjoy many benefits. They will be better able to "handle tough questions about diversity" and to "deal more effectively with sexism, racism and other forms of prejudice." They will "more skillfully interact with people who are different from themselves" and "feel more confidence in their multicultural training activities." The brochure has a visual image of this new and exciting world of diversity. It shows an American woman wearing a sleeveless blouse and short pants and long loose hair, a camera slung over her shoulder, walking in what appears to be an Islamic country. Crossing her path is a man in an Arab headdress. Obediently walking behind him is a woman clad from head to toe in a black chador, the bottom part of her face veiled.

The picture makes one pause. What does it mean in the context of "valuing diversity"? Is it supposed to show two cultures congenially interacting with each other, the largely uncovered woman and the entirely covered woman both valuing diversity? Everybody knows that Islamic fundamentalism anathematizes Western secularism. Muslim fundamentalists do not value what they see as our promiscuous sexual comportment and our other satanic ways. We do not admire the diversity introduced into our world by Islamic societies when their members cut off the hands of thieves, as they do in Saudi Arabia, or execute female adulterers, as they do in Pakistan, or set off car bombs in crowded marketplaces to force the government to repudiate secularism, as they do in Egypt. Diversity is to be valued, but only to a point.

Perhaps the photograph reflects the insensitivity of the American woman, blithely exhibiting the anything-goes youth culture of late-twentieth-century America, unaware of the fact that to the Arab couple near her she incarnates precisely the immorality in dress and behavior that they associate with decadent infidels. Very likely, the picture is merely intended to show that we live in a world of varying and different cultures and customs, and that this is to be appreciated.

But if that is the case, the photograph illustrates both the good-heartedness of "valuing diversity" and also its naïveté. One wants to ask what the response of corporate managers and fellow workers would be if a rise in Islamic fundamentalism should suddenly create an influx of women in the workplace, several of them married to the same man, wearing the chador? Or if some African men tried to convince fellow workers of the benefits of clitoridectomy? Or if some workers demanded time off to smoke hashish or practice voodoo? That would be diversity for you, a wider and wilder sort than the narrow band, that very Americanized diversity depicted in the Copeland Griggs videotapes and likened by Ms. Chin-Lor to a harmonious garden. Valuing Diversity imagines a world of diversity in which, paradoxically, everybody will have more or less the same ideas, the same philosophy, the same vaguely liberal political convictions, the same notions of the equality of all peoples, all sexes, and all sexual practices, the same sanctimoniousness of that "nonpolitical" Smith College glossary, the same conception of America as a place where unfairness and inequality lurk behind every rock in every institution.

In short, Valuing Diversity is sadly misinformed about what real diversity in the world is like, not only the world of such dubious practices as the veil and suttee and female infanticide and where homosexuality is seen as an offense against God and Nature, a blasphemy punishable by death, but also the world of several centuries of political and social analysis.

There is, after all, a vast literature, from Edmund Burke to Shelby Steele, of profundity and merit in which certain conclusions are reached different from those considered more or less universal by our new bureaucracy of diversity facilitators. I myself would prefer to spend my time reading Burke's *Reflections on the Revolution in France* or Steele's *The Content of Our Character: A New Vision of Race in America* than listening to some feel-good social worker expatiate upon race, or upon covert racism, or upon internalized repression as he/she tries to get me to turn my isms into wasms.

The irony of diversity training is that it takes what are actually a few varieties of the Western tradition and presents them as the world of diversity. When they speak of the richness of our diverse world, diversity facilitators and multiculturalist militants confuse a few Westernized representatives of those cultures with the cultures themselves. In their attempt to open our minds to that great world of difference that they know exists out there, they unintentionally reaffirm their own attachment to values and practices that originated in the West and often exist in other parts of the world only insofar as they have been acquired, usually through cultural imperialism. When Daisy Chin-Lor, a woman who appears to be of Asian ancestry, speaks of cultivating her harmonious garden, she is casting a very Westernized eye on the American workplace. No Asian countries that I know of practice diversity training in the workplace. And when Chin-Lor complains about the "invisibility" of women, she is not speaking from the traditions of her ancestors, for whom the woman's place in the world was to be subordinate to her husband, to raise his children, to keep house, and to be obedient. Sexual equality is not an Asian invention.

One of the busiest diversity trainers on the East Coast is a man named David P. Tulin, a round, jowly, middle-aged, affable, energetic New Yorker who studied political science at Temple University in Philadelphia and was the head of the American Zionist Federation, where he did some work in Arab-Jewish reconciliation. After that, he went to work for the Fellowship House Farm, a nonprofit educational center dealing, as Tulin puts it, in "human relations and social change." Among other things, Tulin created "Adventures in Harmony." "We went into the schools," he told me, "did faculty training, brought Asian, black, white, and Hispanic students together and oriented them to what would be happening in an overnight retreat. Then, they spent two full days in Fellowship Farm where they dealt with conflict resolution skills, breaking down stereotypes, and leadership development."

In 1988, he started Tulin Diversiteam, Inc., having perceived the need to combat what he felt was a rising tide of racial and other prejudices washing over America. Why this rising tide just now? Tulin cites "the backlash phenomenon," which he sees as an unfortunate legacy of the Reagan years. Before Reagan, he said, "there was this phenomenon where the national, PC way of thinking and behaving was not to use racist or anti-Semitic expressions, not to laugh at people's differences, not to laugh at stereotypes that we've had from 'Amos 'n' Andy' and since." This civil contract was violated by the new president almost as soon as he came into office, Tulin believes.

"As soon as the Reagan era began, the national consensus that began with Kennedy seemed to be broken by a president who had press conferences telling stories about welfare queens in Cadillacs, and an attorney general talking about how homeless people wanted to be homeless, that they liked it. So, before you had many people who felt that they had to hide or change their prejudices. All of a sudden what happened is that the administration gave legitimacy and unstopped the dams to a lot of acculturated processes. The pendulum swung back and people said, 'Oh, finally I can tell jokes again. Finally, I'm a part of the power structure again.' "

Diversiteam, Inc.'s, flyer promises to combat this Reagan-era trend. It lists twenty-four benefits in all arising out of Tulin's services. Reduced conflict is one such benefit. Enhanced loyalty is another. There will be decreased absenteeism, better cooperation, an improved recruitment and promotion policy, even a better safety record. Among Tulin's clients have been chambers of commerce in Ohio, Texas, and Alabama. He has conducted training seminars for the Philadelphia police, the Pennsylvania Department of Agriculture, Florida Power and Light, the Loews Corporation, Southeast Florida Toyota, Coca-Cola Foods, and many others. He was also the facilitator at the first several sessions of diversity training at the Philadelphia *Inquirer*.

"What's happening," he told me, explaining the interest in his services on the part of corporations, schools, and other organizations, "is that the whole plan of improvement is impacted upon by diversity issues. People are now seeing diversity as a value-added component."

Tulin is a sincere and very likable man. He describes himself as a Jewish liberal, knowledgeable about the Holocaust and aware of its lessons both of hatred and of silence. He came of age in the idealistic 1960s, when blacks and whites were going to create a just, color-blind society by breaking down the barriers that existed between them and finding ways to be together. He believes in his work. When I called him once and asked how he was, his reply was "Hanging in there. Busy. Trying to make a difference." In a letter he wrote to a prospective client, he announced: "Those of us who attempt to facilitate planned change in the area of cultural awareness and valuing & managing diversity must ourselves be models of professionals who are continually working on our own issues related to diversity, racism, sexism & other forms of discrimination." Tulin is the sort of moral and good man you would trust to be the executor of your will or the guardian of your children. He understands that there is often resistance to the kind of thing he tries to do, especially among people who are not aware of the racism that encrusts the hearts of all of us. In one report that he provided to the *Inquirer* after conducting a diversity-training seminar there, he spoke a bit sadly of the existence of "a strong but small minority of white males resistant to diversity instruction."

Tulin distributes a flyer entitled *Whitelash: White Male Backlash in an Era of Down-Sizing & Layoffs* that describes this white-male resistance and attempts to counter it with "the facts." Among the facts, for example, is one adduced to counter white resentment of affirmative action. It is what Tulin describes as the existence of "an Affirmative Action Program in the USA for the last 200 years." The real culprit, he says, is that "racism, sexism and other 'isms' were, to varying degrees, force-fed into all of us at an early age." We have "prejudice bones," he says. And so when white males lose their jobs to women or members of minority groups, they find that "the classic forces of stereotyping and scapegoating offer simplistic and spleen-comforting easy targets." The antidote tastes awful sometimes, Tulin allows, but his company's nurturing of "basic diversity facilitation skills" can certainly help.

I met Tulin at the Marriott Hotel outside of Princeton, New Jersey, in the fall of 1991. He was doing what he called a quickie seminar at a convention of the New Jersey Judicial Staff College, which includes much of the personnel of the state court system, except for actual lawyers and judges. Tulin—friendly, large, voluble, a model of glad inoffensiveness—stood at the front of the room and made a ninety-minute speech to a group of fifty or so people, interspersing it with questions to members of the audience and a couple of episodes of role-playing in which the assembled court workers participated. Before the time was over he had learned the names, the particular jobs, and the personal backgrounds of perhaps one-quarter of the attendees.

"You might notice that I am a white male," he said, breaking the ice in a room that contained a sizable minority of black and Hispanic employees of the court system. Indeed, the minority group members had organized the session and were the ones who felt that it was necessary. Introducing Tulin as a man with a "win/win philosophy," a Hispanic woman organizer expressed the hope that at future conventions, diversity-training sessions would become mandatory, not, like this one, optional.

"We've been given the chance to change the system that has been impacted by racism and sexism," said Tulin after introducing himself. A lot of people's arms are crossed, he notes, looking at the audience, and identifies these crossed arms as body language signifying discomfort, resistance, the existence of prejudice bones. We're not racists or sexists in here, says Tulin, suggesting what is going on inside the minds of all those people with crossed arms. I'm not prejudiced. I don't need any Goody Two-shoes sensitivity trainer to introduce me to right thinking. Ah, but you do, says Tulin. In fact, he says, his voice milky with comprehension, we're all racists and sexists, even though few of us know we are.

"The man who says he hasn't got a prejudice bone in his body, I want to give him an X-ray examination," Tulin says. "The truth is that every person in this room has prejudice bones, but only when we become aware of them and how they work do they become something that we can do something about."

Tulin has an entire philosophy of the way good people absorb bad thoughts and make them their own. We start as children without prejudice, even resisting prejudice, but then in comes "all that acculturated stuff," he says. "We're all force-fed stereotypes; we're given a way of dealing with the world." One day Dad will be driving the car, and he'll be cut off by another car, driven by a woman. "Dad [wouldn't] say, 'There go those blond, blue-eyed white guys again,'" Tulin says. No, but he makes a derogatory remark about women drivers, thereby imparting a stereotype to his son.

"Society gives you ways to find people guilty until they're proven innocent," he says. "How many people have ever said, 'We've got to hire some qualified Jews here, some qualified white men.'" The subtle implication, of course, is that Jews and white men are somehow inherently qualified; others are not.

Tulin picks out people in the audience to show how stereotypes function. He is trying to show how they lead us to interpret differently behavior that is precisely the same, depending on who engages in it. First Tulin designates a white male, named Bill. "He's your manager," says Tulin. "He says he really needs that data at three o'clock. That behavior is seen as neutral, normal, good." Tulin next points to a white woman in the audience, finds out her name is Barbara, and says, "Now, Barbara is the manager. She does the same thing as Bill, but when she does it she's seen as a bitch, overbearing, trying to act as a man; her behavior is negative." Yolanda is a black woman. When she needs the data at three o'clock, she is, Tulin says, "uppity, has a chip on her shoulder, is confrontational." When the manager is Thomas, a black man, "he is seen as aggressive, hostile, militant."

Each and every one of us, Tulin tells his audience, belongs to two groups in our society. There are target groups and nontarget groups. The former are "traditionally targeted for stereotyping and discrimination and traditionally not empowered." The latter are "not traditionally targeted for stereotyping and discrimination and are traditionally empowered." "Targeted," says Tulin, "means that you're assumed incompetent until proven competent."

The permutations are infinite in this effort to determine people by the circumstances of their birth. A black man is "targeted" because of his race. This is obvious. But Tulin points to Charlie, a middle-aged white man sitting in the front row, and shows how he is both nontargeted and targeted. He is nontargeted because he is white, a male, and a Protestant. But he comes from a poor family and in this sense is targeted, given, presumably, the disadvantages entailed in coming from the lower economic strata. Tulin does not point out the rather large numbers of people in our history, from Abraham Lincoln to Ross Perot, who have climbed from modest backgrounds to great wealth and power. He quickly passes on to show that Charlie is a targeted person in a less obvious way than in his poor family background. Charlie's job is to make sure that prospective jurors are present for jury selection at the beginning of each trial, and he has been doing the job for about twenty-five years. In other words, he is not so young anymore. Tulin imagines a situation in which his middle age might make him a targeted person. What, asks Tulin, if a younger man with less experience suggests a new computer system for the office? Charlie doesn't think it's necessary to change. "Charlie has been here too long" is the resulting opinion spreading perniciously around the office, Tulin says. "He's too set in his ways. In other words, Charlie is not up to speed."

The black and Hispanic members of the New Jersey Judicial Staff College say that they experience insensitive treatment in the workplace, and this feeling on their part is not to be dismissed. Opening the meeting at the conference of the New Jersey Judicial Staff College, one of the meeting's organizers, a straightforward, friendly black woman, talked about "the need to help people manage their behavior.

"You wouldn't believe that a top manager allowed a new employee to be ostracized at a business function," she said, "that a top manager said to a woman that people didn't believe she graduated from an Ivy League institution, that a top manager referred to a 'boy' when he was talking about a black member of the office. These are true incidents. This is reality."

A numerical reality was also described at the meeting. In the decade after 1980, the percentage of the staff consisting of minorities went from 18.2 percent to 27 percent. In the latter period, 13 percent of the staff was black; 10 percent was Hispanic; 4 percent was Asian. Many of these people obviously feel that they are representatives of the changes in the racial demography taking place inside American society. They are convinced that for the country to be competitive, for it to be at internal peace, and for everybody to feel that they have a place of dignity, managing diversity is going to be essential.

The minority groups at the New Jersey Judicial Staff College were not declaring that they had a different culture from the white majority. They just wanted everybody to be aware of what Tulin discreetly termed their "unconscious prejudices." There was nothing militant or aggressive about these employees. They sat courteously, shyly, in the audience, making no angry demands, engaging in no racial confrontations. The organizers of the meeting wanted a little respect, nothing more, and Tulin was there to help them get it.

And certainly there is lots to be gained when different people openly discuss their feelings about one another, including their stereotypes, the "acculturated stuff." At the same time, diversity training, as it seems to be carried out in most places, is illustrative of much of the multicultural initiative.

Hiding behind the innocuous, unobjectionable, entirely praiseworthy goal of eliminating prejudice from the human heart lies a certain ideology, a control of language, a vision of America that, presented as consensual common sense, is actually highly debatable. By its very nature it thrusts the concepts of "racism" and "sexism" and the various other isms to the forefront, turning them from ugly aberrations into the central elements of American life and implicitly branding anyone who does not share that assumption to be guilty of the very isms that he feels do not lie in his heart. Diversity training is the corporatist counterpart to that obsession in university education summed up by the boilerplate phrase "race, class, and gender," whereby, for example, the study of literature is deprived of such considerations as the struggle for meaning, or character as tragedy, or mystery and ambiguity, and instead is cogitated over endlessly by literary "theorists" demonstrating through "texts" how attitudes toward race and sex are "socially constructed."

To be sure, no reeducation-camp atmosphere reigns in the mild diversity-training program of a David Tulin, who, as I have said, is an entirely reasonable man. Still, the underlying ideology that emerges, oh so gently, from a Tulin workshop incriminates whites, portraying them as the bearers of the chief defects of thought, while exculpating others from corresponding defects. It reifies (to use a popular New Age academic term) victim status. It erodes individualism, in that it presents people primarily as products of their racial and sexual identity, rather than as free, self-fashioning members of a democratic society who assume responsibility for themselves. It also detracts from the idea that when people come to the job, they have some duty to acquire the culture that will enable them to do the job well. The assumption of managing diversity is that companies have to train themselves to value the differences of diverse employees, not that the employees have something to learn as well. Writ larger on the multiculturalist tablets, it means more generally that assimilation to what is pejoratively branded the Eurocentric norm is unfair, too much to expect from those of other cultures.

I have thought about Charlie in this connection, the veteran of the Judicial Staff College who sat in on Tulin's workshop. Though white, male, and Protestant, Charlie was doing a small civil-service job after a quarter century in the New Jersey courts. To what extent has Charlie's nontargetedness determined his life? How much did he gain from being Eurocentric? In America today, many people of color, many women, gays and lesbians, and handicapped people, because they worked hard, had intelligence, talent, ability, because they showed determination and took initiatives, have had far more glorious careers than the presumably advantaged white male Charlie.

True, Charlie, especially given the generation he belongs to, no doubt did enjoy certain advantages from being white and male. He had the absence of self-consciousness that comes from being in the majority. For most of his life he could assume that nobody would discriminate against him. But during the last quarter of a century haven't certain advantages accrued to nonwhites and nonmales in a society whose leadership is striving to make the parts of the whole, as Bill Clinton has said, "look like America"? When it came time for promotion and Charlie did not get the nod, what did he think? That he wasn't qualified, or that the bosses were looking to promote blacks and women? That he had risen as far as his qualities would take him, or that he was being discriminated against?

In fact, for me at any rate, the biggest objection to diversity training is not even its content, but the fact that it exists at all, adding yet another coating of mandatory sanctimony to a society that already has trouble talking about things frankly and honestly. It is, quite simply, an attack on freedom and autonomy for people to be pressured, or required, to attend chapel and told what it is proper to think, to feel, and to believe. The whole point of the liberal revolution that gave rise to the 1960s was to free us from somebody else's dogma, but now the very same people who fought for personal liberation a generation ago are striving to impose on others a secularized religion involving a set of values and codes that they believe in, disguising it behind innocuous labels like "diversity training" and "respect for difference."

At least David Tulin and other practitioners of the mild diversity program have created schemes that allow for some free discussion and some complexity. As we will see in another chapter, there is also the more radical program, where lessons in our world of diversity are less nuanced, certainly less benign, far more tethered to a political program. And when education in the proper codes of moral conscience becomes a blunt instrument for ideological conformity, then we are in the domain of the dictatorship of virtue, or, to give it its end-of-century designation, political correctness.

Diversity training is one small part of the multiculturalist initiative. It has many other manifestations, which bring with them considerable confusion about who, exactly, we are, how worthy we are, and whether we have any things in common.

Chapter 2

PLACES OF MEMORY

Sometime before dawn on the clear, cold morning of October 21, 1892, the people of Chicago were awakened by a cannon shot booming under their dark windows from Lake Front Park. The noise, echoing across Lake Michigan, rattling the windows of the city's brick and masonry buildings, marked the beginning of a celebration billed by its promoters as the veritable Event of the Late Century, the commemoration of the historical episode that marked the division between the darkness of the old age and the light of the new, or between the American era in history and the pre-American era. The boom, as one newspaper put it, signified the establishment of the "Christian civilization under whose beneficent influences all nations are marching onward and upward, keeping step to the music of triumphant democracy."

The four hundredth anniversary of what was unabashedly called the discovery of America by Christopher Columbus took place all across late-nineteenth-century America, but Chicago's vast Columbian Exposition made it the epicenter of the national celebration. In contrast to the celebration of the same event one hundred years later, the 1892 event brought with it very little self-doubt, only a minor strain of moral anguish, and hardly any concern for ethnic diversity. The quincentennial, marked in 1992 ("celebrated" would be the wrong word for an event so full of ambivalence and conflict), was close to the inverse of the quatercentenary.

The dominant view in 1892 was that Columbus's voyage of four hundred years earlier was the starting point for a prolonged epic of freedom, progress, and, not incidentally, the subjugation of "savage tribes." There was much talk in newspapers and on podiums about the glory of the country, about Columbus as the herald of the age of republican freedom, and, as Chauncey M. Depew, the president of the New York Central Railroad and a future U.S. senator, put it, "the romance and reality of human development." The buzz in October 1892 was about universal Enlightenment, about love, truth, and faith, about industry and invention, education and civilization, of what Depew called the "flower and fruitage of this transcendant miracle," the United States of America. The Chicago *Tribune*, reporting on the festivities of October 21, 1892, thrilled to the spectacle of the mighty and the humble of the earth—"each man sovereign in the vested rights of the Republic." All were gathered inside the vast Manufacturers and Liberal Arts Building to "honor the great silent student of 400 years ago, who, in his way, was the pioneer of them all, who led the van of human thought and manly daring, and gave to the world a new continent and to posterity an imperishable reverence for Christopher Columbus."

It happens that in 1892, the United States was already, as the current term would have it, multicultural. The pageant of 1892 came at a time when new immigrants from a wide variety of evidently benighted places were upsetting the ethnic balance, and a brusque, brash, brutal (but unopposed) effort to assimilate them was taking place across the country. The historian John Higham has termed the drive for assimilation a "Crusade for Americanization" that would culminate during World War I in "100 percent Americanism," a great wave of distrust of the foreign, the different, the unassimilated, the Other. There were patriotic rituals of assimilation, great July Fourth festivities in which new citizens en masse swore fealty to their new culture; there were English and civics classes for the hordes of new arrivals, to which reverence for the country's Anglo-Saxon institutions was central. During the Columbian celebration it was repeated over and over again that Columbus was exactly the sort of universal, iconic figure who would "Americanize the Americans." The image lasted a long time.

"More than five hundred years after his birth," the celebrated Harvard historian Samuel Eliot Morison wrote in 1954, "when the day that Columbus first raised an island in the New World is celebrated throughout the length and breadth of the Americas, his fame and reputation may be considered secure for all time." Morison's tone, so enthusiastic, so nearly worshipful of the great explorer, seems mawkish and unsophisticated four decades later. "He had his faults and his defects," Morison says of Columbus, "but they were largely the defects of the qualities that made him great—his indomitable will, his superb faith in God and in his own mission as the Christ-bearer to lands beyond the seas, his stubborn persistence despite neglect, poverty and discouragement."

It seems strange by the standards of today to proclaim a faith in one's own "mission as the Christ-bearer" as an admirable quality. No doubt there are still those who see America as the embodiment of the divine will, but very few of them are distinguished professors at Harvard, where even the Divinity School has now become a radically transgressive institution.

Certainly Morison could have said the same things about the United States as he did about Columbus, particularly when he spoke of the faults that are the defects of the qualities that make for greatness. Those defects were on view in Chicago in 1892. There was the overweening optimism of that era, the self-satisfaction of a nation that had, after all, been built, in part, on the defeat and displacement of indigenous peoples (whose ultimate and final military defeat at the Battle of Wounded Knee had taken place less than two years earlier, in December 1890) and the enslavement of Africans, which had come to an end just twenty-nine years before. The greatness, or, perhaps more accurately, the power of the country, was embodied in the quatercentenary's very unreflective and energetic conviction that the best in history was being produced right then, at that time, in that place, and that it was a best that owed its origins to Christopher Columbus. And so, six decades later, Morison could believe (and how wrong he was!) that Columbus's reputation "may be considered secure for all time."

It is not even that there weren't in 1892 some whisperings of the themes that rose to a crescendo for the Columbian quincentennial in 1992 when the mood had dramatically changed. The very patriotic *Magazine of American History* even complained of a certain killjoy nihilism in the air. Some of the things being said transformed Columbus into "the poorest specimen of humanity who ever masqueraded as a hero or a discoverer," the magazine's writer, Mrs. M. J. Lamb, allowed, adding quickly: "If there is anything which I detest more than another, it is that spirit of critical historical inquiry which doubts everything; that modern spirit which destroys all the illusions and all the heroes which have been the inspiration of patriotism through all the centuries."

This unease seems to have been aroused by some efforts, pretty marginal to the overall festivity, that attempted to replace healthy nation-building myths with dangerous quests for the complicated truth. There was, for example, the Reverend Henry Van Dyke, who denounced Columbus from the pulpit of the Brick Presbyterian Church on Fifth Avenue and Thirty-seventh Street in New York on the grounds that he was "immoral and guilty of great cruelty, and was responsible for the West Indian slave trade that marks a dark spot in the history of the Old World." A few iconoclastic biographies of Columbus appeared in time for the quatercentenary, such as *Christopher Columbus and How He Received and Imparted the Spirit of Discovery*, by Justin Winsor. The book, according to a contemporary review, describes the discoverer of America as "a man of a paltry commercial and worldly spirit, feeble, cruel, an inefficient colonial administrator, a slave trader and a kidnapper."

Black people also dissented from the 1892 celebrations or largely boycotted the few token efforts made to include them. By 1892, of course, Reconstruction was over, and Jim Crow, which was to last for the next half century and more, was in full effect. Lynchings were common. Under the circumstances, it is not surprising that there was no black person on any of the commissions governing the Chicago fair, leading the New York *Age*, one of the country's earliest black-owned newspapers, to "advise the race to have nothing whatever to do with the Columbian Exposition."

Some blacks whose views made their way into the public record wanted to use the occasion to publicize to the rest of the world the plight of black Americans. Others feared that such an action would only increase white hostility. In the end, blacks simply stayed away. A decision to hold Colored People's Day at the Chicago Exposition was intended perhaps as an acknowledgment that black people existed, but blacks themselves saw it as a demeaning afterthought. Only about one thousand people showed up for the event.

The Chicago Exposition did have a section devoted to American Indians, but it was designed to show how much the native peoples had benefited from the white man's civilization. This provoked a protest from one Emma Sickles, who was on the staff of the committee that organized the Indian exhibition, which, she said in a letter to the *New York Times*, "has been used to work up sentiment against the

Indian by showing that he is either savage or can be educated only by Government agencies." A group of Sioux chiefs, probably unaware of Sickles's advocacy on their behalf, came to the opening ceremonies in Chicago, arriving just as the chorus began singing "America," and watching from the prestigious high point of the administration building.

Despite its handful of preacher troublemakers and scholar iconoclasts, 1892 in America was a year of adulation in which commonality was the supreme value and patriotism the means to achieve it. The faint noises of dissent were in the air in Chicago when a cannon shot at 4:00 a.m. served as a collective alarm clock, but they were lost in the thunder of self-congratulation.

In New York, a million visitors were on hand on October 12 for what one eyewitness called "the unique expression of a city's gratitude and patriotism." The great mansions of the city were "one great mass of color." The streets were festooned with garlands and palms and Chinese lanterns. Fifth Avenue was canopied for an entire mile with innumerable flags of every color. A parade took place, stressing military themes involving mounted police and some ten army divisions and fifty thousand uniformed men. There were elaborate floats representing the *Santa María*, the court of Queen Isabella, the marriage of John and Priscilla Alden (a foundational myth seen as related, albeit from a later century than that of Columbus's discovery), and even one demonstrating an early interest in multiculturalism. This was a scene showing Aztec warriors worshiping the genius of the sun while nearby a sacrificial victim perished at the foot of a smoking pyramid. Showing the harmony between science and happiness, there was a spectacular float called the Hydra of Lightning Controlled by the Genius of Edison. It was thirty feet long and was drawn by ten horses. It was illuminated by three thousand electric lightbulbs, some of them forming the giant head of the monster and another two thousand of them outlining a revolving disk on which stood thirty beautiful girls in metallic costumes. There was a display of American pluralism described by Mrs. Lamb of the *Magazine of American History*, who noted that marching behind ten thousand public-school boys was a throng of students from Catholic institutions of learning and behind them more students from the Hebrew Sheltering Guardian Society, then the Dante Alighieri Italian College of Astoria, and the Hebrew Orphan Asylum Cadets. There were members of the General Society of Mechanics and Tradesmen and the German Turn Verein societies.

There were noisy, cheering students from New York University and Columbia College and from the New York College of Dentistry, all of them gathered to listen to the rhapsodic Chauncey Depew declare: "This is an American night, an American week, an American month, an American year, an American allegory." The panoply led Mrs. Lamb to thrill to the spectacle of "the peoples of every nation marching under one flag . . . growing up to be American citizens no matter what might be their creed or their origin."

In Chicago that day, after that early morning cannon shot, the exposition's official inauguration took place in the biggest building ever built in front of the largest crowd ever assembled. Some one hundred thousand people waved handkerchiefs as the exposition opened and then listened to a five-thousand-member choir sing "The Columbian March," composed for the occasion by John K. Paine. At night what was billed as the biggest and most expensive fireworks display in human history took place. Three white ships representing the *Niña*, the *Pinta*, and the *Santa María* blazed into view before the astonished crowd, burning first white, then turning into blue and fading away in red. A wall of "colored fire" some six hundred feet high represented Niagara Falls, and, as a finale, some five thousand rockets and Roman candles were fired into the air simultaneously by means of electric batteries. This last display, costing twenty-five thousand dollars, which was a great deal in 1892, and mounted in front of three hundred thousand people, was given a name that pretty much summed up the national pageant. It was called the Columbian Bouquet.

A few months before Columbus Day a century later, a little-noted incident took place in New York City that echoed a larger national turmoil. It happened that replicas of Columbus's ships, the *Niña*, the *Pinta*, and the *Santa María*, which were on a tour from Spain to various capitals of the world, were due to arrive in New York harbor on June 25 in preparation for a great Hudson River parade of sailing vessels that took place that Fourth of July. A formal welcome by local officials was scheduled for that day, but it was canceled—and the three ships kept waiting outside the harbor overnight—when somebody figured out that June 25 was the 116th anniversary of the Sioux massacre of General Custer's troops at the Little Bighorn. The feeling was that in a multicultural society such as our own, sensitivity to native peoples required that no celebratory fuss be made about Columbus on a day of such historic importance.

It is worth drawing attention to the implications of this delicate judgment. Those who canceled the formal welcome and made the ships stand out of the harbor for an extra day were saying in essence that what had been, until recently, the founding figure of the American epic—our William the Conqueror, our Joan of Arc, our Alexander Nevsky—was seen as so potentially offensive to one of the component parts of the country that a celebration in his honor had, as it were, to be trumpeted softly.

Every country has what the French historian Pierre Nora has called *les lieux de mémoire*, "the places of memory." Nora, who edited a massive multivolume work on the French *lieux de mémoire*, defined them, at a time when he felt that France was losing its national memory, as "the most striking symbols" that give a people their identity, "the holidays, the insignia, the monuments and memorials, the objects of veneration, the dictionaries and museums." One of Nora's volumes examined the places of memory that gave the French republic (as opposed to the country's various monarchies and dictatorships) its common identity, including such symbols as the tricolor flag, the republican calendar, the "Marseillaise," and such less obvious historical moments as the anniversaries of the births of Voltaire and Rousseau, the funeral of Victor Hugo, the centennial observation in 1879 of the Great Revolution.

The places of memory are, in short, those events or the commemoration of those events out of which are formed the distinctive features of a people. They are manifest in the way some formative event is collectively remembered, as in republican France, for example, the drafting of the *Grand Larousse*, the vast encyclopedia published in 524 installments that, at a time when the Republic was shaky indeed, provided a broad foundation of knowledge that supported republican forms of government and became the standard reference work for France ever after.

The places of memory can reside in a speech, like the Gettysburg Address, or a book or a poem or in the way a battle is remembered (the photo of GIs raising the flag on Iwo Jima comes to mind). In America, where there are no common racial or religious bonds, no common origins or ancestry, commonality was devised out of the interpretations given to past events. In such a way were national features created, a shared mythology, a kind of unified origin bestowed on people who often had only one real feature in common, the fact that they were here.

French textbooks, even in colonial West Africa, are legendary for having begun with the phrase "Our ancestors the Gauls," a phrase that now seems the epitome of colonial education, designed to make the schoolchild in Saigon and in Senegal assume a French identity. Have the efforts made until now to create a common historical culture in America been a kind of colonial education? Plenty of people involved in the reassessment of Columbus, and in the broader movement of which that is a part, see a similarity. For decades, they feel, we have inculcated a culture that, while claiming to have universal value, actually served the interests of a protocolonial ruling class made up of the immediate progeny of Columbus, the white European settlers who expelled the Indians from their land and created an offshoot of European civilization.

This is the idea that lies behind the dramatically different way in which the encounter of Columbus with the New World was commemorated in 1992. By then, the very idea that that event was a discovery, or that it was even a historic good, had become untenable. Indeed, the challenge to the American places of memory marks a new era, one in which the assumptions and the definitions that held for many decades hold no longer. Old places of memory are under assault; new ones are being created, and both destruction and invention are part of the same process. They show what might be called the multiculturalist sensibility in action. More important is the extent to which multiculturalism has already emerged triumphant, becoming, even as it presents itself as a rebellion against domination, the reigning, the dominant ideology of the late twentieth century.

Items:

• The most elaborate event of the Columbian quincentennial was the exhibition at the National Gallery of Art in Washington called "Circa 1492: Art in the Age of Exploration." This exhibition—huge, ambitious, daring—presented a vast panoply of the world's arts and crafts, from Spain, where Columbus embarked on his voyage, to China, where he thought he was going. It included also West Africa and the Islamic world and, of course, the empires of the

Aztecs and Incas and the smaller West Indian cultures. The exhibition had everything from Hieronymus Bosch's *Temptation of Saint Anthony* to the bronze *Queen Mother Head* from Nigeria to the porphyry figure of Quetzalcoatl, the Aztecs' mythical feathered serpent, which brought civilization to mankind. It had drawings by Leonardo da Vinci, inlaid Koran chests from Turkey, landscape paintings from China and Japan, bronze Hindu sculptures of Parvati and Krishna, miniatures from western India, ancient woven cloths of the Incas, carved calendar stones from the Aztec empire.

"Circa 1492" was in this sense an ideal expression of the multicultural sensibility triumphant, in both the good and the excessive senses. It certainly showed broad-mindedness. It was mind-expanding. But it also raised the question in our multiculturalist age of what the proper balance should be between an appreciation of the Other and a willingness to accord greater historical importance to developments in a Europe that happened to be at the height of the Renaissance.

Jay A. Levenson, the curator of the vast exhibition, told me that "Circa 1492" reflected our late-twentieth-century mood by "illustrating a theme of globalism and hinting that perhaps there is more to understand and appreciate and to know about other peoples' cultures." But it did much more than show understanding and appreciation of other peoples' cultures, which, in any case, we have been doing in the West for a century and more (one has only to look at the British Museum or the Metropolitan Museum of Art to see just how much Western imperialism treasured the works of the Middle East, of China and Japan, of South Asia and Africa). "Circa 1492" went beyond appreciation to a kind of complete cultural relativism that refused to make any judgment about the greater historical significance of the West, even though it was the West that was, at that time (and by the evidence of Columbus's voyage), demonstrating itself to be the most dynamic and Promethean of the great world civilizations—and, moreover, that it was *our* civilization, the place where American values and institutions originated. History, in short, was being made in Renaissance Europe more than it was being made anyplace else. But in trying to impart the lesson that Europe had no claim to greater artistic or creative importance, "Circa 1492" partook of the sanctimoniousness of the multicultural era. It was, in short, a bold statement of political correctness and a timid statement about history.

• Press reports in 1992 showed how the Smithsonian Institution in Washington, D.C., that veritable repository of places of memory, has formed a committee of curators to bring about the "post-colonial museum." Many changes are envisaged. One involves the iconography of John Smith and Pocahontas. Smith will no longer stand heroically in the canoe while Pocahontas looks adoringly up at him, but the two will be shown in a more equal position.

• In history departments across the country something called the new history is being written, especially the "new" history of the American West. Others besides white males are being taken into account, the blacks, the Hispanics, the Asians, the women, the Jews, who played their previously neglected role in the westward expansion. Frederick Jackson Turner's once-dominant theory of the frontier, the line that divided settlement from wilderness and gave American history its particular rough-and-ready democratic character, has been scrapped, viewed as Eurocentric, making the whites the only genuine historical protagonists.

But the assault of the new historians goes further than that. Until them, there were plenty of critical writers who understood the enormous human cost of the westward expansion and, especially, the grievous burden it imposed on the Indians, but they nonetheless saw the whole adventure as, at the very least, an inevitability leading to a free and prosperous life for tens of millions of people. It was, at least in this respect, a triumphal progress.

The new historians, by contrast, stress failure. They are blazing a pioneer's trail toward an altered view of the moral status of America itself, a view in which the national faults and imperfections seem to outweigh the national virtues. One of the main figures in the new western history, Patricia Limerick of the University of Colorado, uses pictures of ghost towns to illustrate the essential feature of the westward expansion. She has a name for the overall approach: "failure studies," she calls it.

• In December 1987 the American Historical Association held its annual convention in Washington, D.C. The AHA, the main professional grouping of historians in the United States, is the kind of organization that, when I was in graduate school in the late 1960s, conveyed a certain ponderousness, or at least a link between ponderousness and seriousness. By 1987, the AHA was as ponderous and serious as ever, and yet it could hardly have been more different.

Most obviously, the historical subjects under discussion had changed dramatically. It was as though the preoccupation with great events and great figures had disappeared, replaced by what was called social history, the history of movements, of moods, of mentalities. More striking yet was the rise of a kind of special-interest history, so that one's scholarly activity seemed to derive directly from one's personal circumstances and affiliations.

When I studied China in graduate school, I had before me a subject far removed from me personally. At the AHA now everybody seemed to be studying what was closest to themselves, a fact that should have provided an early clue to the true nature of multiculturalism—it is not an interest in the other so much as an insistence that the other be interested in me. The organization was subdivided into a host of special interests. There was the women's interest section, the African-American section, the gay and lesbian section, the Marxist history section, and various others. Gone were what I thought of as the Grand Themes, the declines and falls of empires, the waxing and waning of civilizations, the struggles of competing armies, the achievements of Great Men and Women. The panels had titles like "Women's Definitions of Love Throughout Western History," "Sex, Gender and the Constitution," "Black Women in the Work Force," "Sodomy and Pederasty Among 19th-Century Seafarers."

Again, there was much in this that enlarged the mind, and much that seemed a cloying, guilt-ridden effort to make group affiliation the ultimate principle, race and sex the prisms through which the data from the past would be filtered. There should be no nostalgia for the good old days of the AHA, which, up to the mid-1960s or so, truly was a male and WASP club. But what the 1987 AHA meeting showed was that each group now had created its own closed club in which the advancement of its political program replaced even the ideal of disinterestedness.

The panels took place in an atmosphere of in-group complicity rather than scholarly debate. The unvarying underlying themes were the repressiveness inherent in American life and the sufferings of the groups claiming to be victims of that repressiveness. We lived in a vale of tears. The history of the United States was the history of suffering for all but the white establishment. For many historians, history had become advocacy, and this was justified because, they said, it had always been that way. The only difference was that in the past, white males, the patriarchy, the "heterosexy," had used their control of history to ensure their domination, espousing the ideal of disinterestedness to make their power seem to derive from a human universal. My own feeling was that the old white-male club, which was, after all, dominated by a group known as the progressive historians, who furthered the liberal ideal, was more open to challenge and to dissent than the various splinter groups that seem to dominate the proceedings today.

• At Yale University in 1990, the dean of the college, a re-nowned classics scholar named Donald Kagan, made a speech to the incoming class of 1994 suggesting that the study of the West should be the core of any American's liberal education. He was practically shouted down by the student body and unsupported by the liberal-arts faculty.

The *Yale Daily News*, the student newspaper, pointed out that Kagan was a "white male professor" who "has sent what could be perceived as a dangerous message to this community." In 1992, after a complicated series of incidents at Yale that had little to do with the newspaper's complaint, Kagan stepped down as dean. Even before that, however, there was no possibility that Yale could ever again require students to share a common culture based on the study of Western thought.

• The *New York Times* in June 1991 carried an op-ed piece by a high school junior named David Reich who had just taken the Scholastic Aptitude Test. His article, checked by the *Times* with the Educational Testing Service, which produces the SAT, noted the disproportionate number of questions that referred to blacks, other minority group members, and women, as though the ETS, guilty of having "silenced" these voices for so long, was now silenc-ing others, giving the previously excluded so much of a compensa-tory presence that a new imbalance had been created. Albert Einstein and Saul Bellow were absent from the test, but Richard Wright, Gwendolyn Brooks, Lorraine Hansberry, Jackie Robinson, Maya Angelou, August Wilson, Ralph Ellison, and Zora Neale Hurs-ton were present.

• In the late 1980s and early 1990s, helped enormously in 1992 by the film by Spike Lee, Malcolm X came to compete with Martin Luther King, Jr., as the most important iconographic black figure, the chief African-American place of memory. Malcolm, who spent most of his life in a group very marginal to black American life, the Nation of Islam of Elijah Muhammed, and who for years contended that the solution to the race problem was for the American govern- ment to pay for the transportation of blacks back to Africa, emerged as a transcendent figure whose "X" suddenly became the most fashionable image on the streets of black neighborhoods, in schools and on university campuses. The contrast between King and Mal- colm is striking. For most of their lives (indeed, until just shortly before Malcolm was assassinated by members of the Nation, with which he had broken), Malcolm and King represented the two poles of black political opinion. King, who refused to appear on the same platform as Malcolm X, stood for interracial brotherhood, integra- tion, and pacifism. Malcolm X represented racial separation, antago- nism toward whites, and the threat of violence as the means to obtain racial justice.

Columbus and Malcolm X are telling images of the move from pluralism to multiculturalism. The spirit of the age has made one the personification of the White Oppressor and the other the Oppressed Person of Color; one has become discredited, Eurocentric unicultural- ism, the other a validation of the rebellion against prevailing norms. In both instances, historical truth has given way to political and cul- tural need, involving an antimyth about one and a myth about the other. One is the occasion for the jettisoning of a place of memory; the other the occasion for the creation of one.

In the case of Malcolm X, the iniquities of white society are exaggerated, and so are Malcolm's virtues. Lee's movie, for example, shows Malcolm's father's house being burned down by the Ku Klux Klan. The historical evidence is that Malcolm's father burned the house down himself in order to collect the insurance.

In the case of Columbus, the motives of the new iconography are reversed: Columbus's iniquity is exaggerated; his virtues disappear. In the case of Malcolm X there was almost no journalistic zeal to investigate the truth about the man; there was an unspoken agreement in the press to allow the new myth to go unchallenged. In the case of

Columbus, there was a similar acquiesence as the antimyth took hold and became the new historical truth.

In 1991 the National Council of Churches readied its member denominations, thirty-two of them in all, representing forty-two million people, for an official position on Columbus, on his legacy, and, indirectly, on the nature of the United States of America. The purpose, as the NCC's general secretary, the Reverend Joan Campbell, told a representative conference of seventy-five people, was to enable the churches to "make their voices heard in all the hoorah." The idea, said Jim Wallis, the editor of *Sojourners* magazine, was to expose the Columbus myth as "a creation story" that "legitimates centuries of racial oppression. . . . The official celebration that we are about to endure will be a liturgy of empire, exercising the symbols of domination."

The governing board of the organization drew up a resolution announcing that "a celebration is not an appropriate observance of this anniversary," given, it said, that the consequences of the Columbian "invasion" were "genocide, slavery, 'ecocide' and exploitation of the wealth of the land." The resolution then listed separately in a kind of bill of indictment the specific horrors that were visited upon each of the various groups affected by the arrival of Columbus in the New World.

Thus, for the indigenous people of the Caribbean islands, "Christopher Columbus's invasion marked the beginning of slavery and their eventual genocide." For the indigenous people of Central America, an additional item in the bill of indictment was added: the result for them was "slavery, genocide and exploitation, leading to the present struggle for liberation." The indigenous people of South America suffered "slavery, genocide and the exploitation of their mineral and other natural resources." The result was similar, the National Council of Churches resolution said, for the indigenous people of Mexico.

The resolution, excluding nobody from its list of victims, argued that for the "people of modern Puerto Rico, Hawaii and the Philippines," Columbus's landing brought "the eventual grabbing of the land, genocide and the present economic captivity." For the indigenous peoples of North America, Columbus's arrival "led to their descendants' impoverished lives." For the people of the "African disapora . . . the result was slavery, an evil and immoral system steeped in racism, economic exploitation, rape of human and mineral resources and national divisiveness along the lines of colonizing nations."

As for the peoples from Asia who were "brought to work the land," they were "torn from their families and cultures by false promises of economic prosperity." The result for them was "labor camps, discrimination and today's victimization of the descendants facing anti-Asian racism." Finally, even the "descendants of the European conquerors" were given their fair dollop of victimization. For them, "the subsequent legacy has been the perpetuation of paternalism and racism into our cultures and times."

That might seem like a heavy load to place on the shoulders of one man who died nearly five hundred years earlier, but, lest it appear that the National Council of Churches resolution struck an unusually harsh tone, it should be noted that other pronouncements supported its overall conclusion, namely that the Columbian landing was far from the opening move in a glorious new history of the planet, but the beginning of the end of the possibility of a humane, nonracist, environmentally responsible society. The American Library Association, whose thirty-five thousand members work at state, public, school, academic, and special libraries in all fifty states, issued a statement in June 1990 bemoaning the official Columbus Jubilee's plans to "honor the achievement of Columbus" and announcing that the events of 1492 "begin a legacy of European piracy, brutality, slave trading, murder, disease, conquest, and ethnocide."

"Genocide and slavery was the real legacy of Columbus," wrote Manning Marable, a professor of political science and history at the University of Colorado. It is certainly true that the decimation of the Indian population and slavery were part of the Columbian legacy. That fact has not been disputed, even by Columbus's admirers, like Morison. My argument is not that there were no evil consequences to the Columbian arrival, but that between 1892 and 1992 the country swung from a mood that was not critical enough to one that was so critical that another part of the Columbian legacy seems to have been almost forgotten: the eventual building of the biggest and most prosperous democracy in world history.

It is certainly not surprising, in this regard, that American Indian organizations invoked the disaster that the Columbian landing entailed for the American indigenous peoples. The newspaper *Navajo Nation* said that twenty Indians died for every one that survived the

European invasion and seizure of the Americas. The National Congress of American Indians contended in a resolution in 1991 that: "The American Indian population stood at nearly 116 million people when Columbus arrived in North America in 1492, according to historians' estimates. By 1900, Native Americans were reduced in number to little over 250,000."

These elements in the picture are and should be invoked by historians and in school curricula. History is often a tragic process. It has countless times involved cruel fates for some, corresponding to the triumphs of others. What was unacknowledged during the collective breast-beating of the quincentennial was that Indian history, too, before the arrival of the white man, was replete with warfare and slaughter, scalp taking and torture. The Taino, who occupied the Caribbean islands that Columbus landed on in 1492, were at the time already under attack from the Carib peoples, who were cannibalistic. The Aztecs had just completed the consolidation of their empire via conquest, plunder, tribute, and large-scale human sacrifice.

The point is that the eradication of the Columbian place of memory seems to have been motivated by a moralistic need to portray the Europeans, not as one cruel, blood-lusting people among others, but as the embodiment of a special iniquity, that iniquity continuing to stain the American identity. It is in this sense typical that the historian and environmentalist Kirkpatrick Sale entitled his influential and critically acclaimed biography of Columbus, which appeared in 1990, *Conquest of Paradise*. Pre-Columbian America, he said in an interview with the Washington *Post*, was a place where "singing, dancing, laughing and sex" were the "regular components." Europe, he said in a television interview, was "a miserable, unhappy, unsettled place." The Indians, he continued, were "people who lived in as happy a state as we can imagine, with as much abundance and fertility as we can imagine," while we ourselves descend from a "desperately sick and inwardly miserable society" that was then and is still today "founded on a set of ideas that are fundamentally pernicious, and they have to do with rationalism and humanism and materialism and science and progress."

There seems to be a good deal of guilt, something akin to self-flagellation, in statements like these and many others made around the same time, such as that of Yale professor emeritus Benjamin Keen. He said that the Columbian era "brought about the greatest genocide in the history of the world." The *Amsterdam News*, a black newspaper in New York, published a kind of FBI poster for "Columbus the Thug." "Wanted," it said, "Christopher Columbus for Genocide, Exploitation, Theft and Slavery." It was as though the country, rather than celebrate a foundational myth in 1992, decided instead to seek absolution, the yearning for absolution, ironically, being part of the very Western heritage held responsible for the sinful acts for which absolution was being sought. It is as if the questioning and self-doubt, the belief in an inherent moral flaw in ourselves that emerged in the 1960s in America, particularly during the Vietnam War, were being extended backward in time, and the causes of that moral flaw were being found in the very first minutes of European-American history. The Taino, the Aztecs, the Incas, are analogous in this respect to the Vietnamese, the Laotians, the Cambodians. In our current retrospective look, Columbus becomes the combined Lyndon Johnson and William Westmoreland of the fifteenth century.

As the quincentennial approached, the very word "discovery" became an embarrassment. The National Council of Churches chose to use the word "invasion." The more common, more neutral term "encounter" replaced "discovery" in most official quincentennial pronouncements. The Washington *Post* reported on Fairfax County, Virginia, fifth-grade teacher Lillie Vinson's reaction when a small girl—answering the question "Who was Columbus?"—responded "He discovered America in 1492." The newspaper described Vinson's tone of astonishment and incredulity as she repeated the little girl's answer: "He discovered America?" Vinson stressed the word "discovered." The article continued:

> She nudged her class to think about that word, until a girl with red hair answered the teacher's probing.
> "He didn't actually discover it," the girl said. "It was already discovered by the Indians. He just sort of like came up there."

Vinson allowed that she approved of that answer.

Educators, the article continued, have come to believe that for many years Columbus was taught "simplistically," in a way that has "perpetuated myths and stereotypes of Indians as savages and Europeans as saviors." Correcting this mistake, the National Education Association, the major professional organization of teachers and administrators, principals and counselors, from high schools, colleges, and universities, resolved at its conference in 1991 to call on its members to present an "all-sided analysis of the Columbus landing" to pupils across the nation. "Never again will Christopher Columbus sit on a pedestal in United States history," an explanatory article in the NEA's journal, *NEA Today*, declared.

"Christopher Columbus brought slavery to this hemisphere," the article said. "The native American population was reduced from perhaps 60–70 million to a tiny fraction of that as a result of contact with Europeans," it said (giving a far smaller figure for the total Indian population than that cited by the National Congress of American Indians). These themes were developed by a national group of public-school teachers, administrators, and parents, called the National Coalition of Education Activists, which published a ninety-seven-page pedagogical guide for the quincentennial entitled *Rethinking Columbus*.

Chapter titles in this document include "We Have No Reason to Celebrate an Invasion," "Why I Am Not Thankful for Thanksgiving," "Helping Children Critique Columbus Books," "Once Upon a Genocide," "Struggles Unite Native Peoples," and "Maps: Taking Europe Off Center Stage." One chapter, called "George Washington: Speculator in Native Lands," details the founding father's real estate speculations beyond the Allegheny Mountains and his military expedition against the six tribes of the Iroquois Confederacy who fought on the side of the British during the Revolutionary War. ("The British used lies to trick some warriors from the Confederacy into fighting for them," the article says.) This selection, the booklet says, "is particulary useful to balance information given to students during Washington's Birthday celebrations in February." We wouldn't want our children to be unaware of the racist depredations and the capitalist-style greed of the father of our country.

Bill Bigelow, a member of the group who edited *Rethinking Columbus*, spent two years out of the classroom (he teaches American history in a Portland, Oregon, high school) traveling the country and giving workshops to school districts on ways of teaching the Columbus story. He told me that about three thousand teachers had participated in his workshops up to the summer of 1992. In *Rethinking Columbus* he described his own classroom methods in treating this topic. He said that he begins his class by stealing a student's purse. Then he described what happens when, as expected, his students contend that the purse doesn't belong to him:

> What if I said I discovered this purse, then would it be mine? A little laughter is my reward, but I don't get any takers; they still think the purse is rightfully Nikki's.
>
> "So," I ask, "why do we say that Columbus discovered America?"
>
> Now they begin to see what I've been leading up to: I ask a series of questions which implicitly link Nikki's purse and the Indians' land. . . .
>
> Students start with phrases they used to describe what I did to Nikki's purse: "He stole it; he took it; he ripped it off." And others: "He invaded it; he conquered it."
>
> I want students to see that the word "discovery" is loaded.

Late in 1991, the Los Angeles *Times* carried a story entitled "As the 500th Anniversary of the Fabled 'Discovery' Begins, Artists Are Exploring the Dark Side of the Story." The paper, in seeing fit to put the word "discovery" in quotation marks, struck a tone of agreement with the little red-haired girl across the country in Vinson's class in Fairfax County, who had learned well the lesson that Columbus had just sort of come up there.

Not for the Los Angeles *Times* either will Columbus ever again sit on a pedestal. The newspaper reported that while the official Christopher Columbus Quincentennial Jubilee Commission, created by Congress, was preparing one celebration, a host of artistic groups were preparing "a slew of counter-events" because, as the newspaper put it, these groups were "no longer willing to sit through what they see as the glorification of an invading slave trader and mass murderer." The result, the newspaper reported, is an "unprecedented amount of socially conscious creative activity." It also "reflects the reemergence in this country of the artist as social critic." These artistic groups, after all, have been the places where "political insurgency flourished," even when the insurgency was attacked by the right. Now the artists are "fighting back," and more than the quincentennial is at stake. The very "underpinnings" of our society are to be examined, the paper reported, such things as "colonialization as a system" and the "Eurocentric history" that the glorification of Columbus has always represented.

It is certainly noteworthy that the challenge to Christopher Columbus as a chief American place of memory is based on no new knowledge, no new information about Columbus himself or about his voyages or even what happened as a consequence of them. Nothing has been brought to light, no details of Columbus's biography, no new archeological findings, no discovery of previously unknown manuscripts, no uncovering of original diaries, journals, letters, or contemporary accounts. The change in our view of Columbus is analogous to the change in our collective view of ourselves. It is another aspect of the broader multicultural phenomenon that leads big-time capitalist entities to mandate diversity training for their employees, or impels school systems to alter the way the American places of memory are presented to children.

We will see more of this later. For now, it is enough to note that multiculturalism has already succeeded in making several basic changes in the nature of public discourse.

First is the elimination from acceptable discourse of any claim of superiority or even special status for Europe, or any definition of the United States as derived primarily from European civilization.

Second is the attack on the very notion of the individual and the concomitant paramount status accorded group identification. Columbus in the quincentennial became the prototype of the white race.

Third is the triumph of the politics of difference over the politics of equality, that great and still-visionary goal of the civil rights movement. Multiculturalism here is the indictment of one group and the exculpation of all the others. The attack on Columbus was a tactic, unconscious or not, in the furtherance of the cult of the victim, in which society is viewed as an arena of oppression exercised by the white majority over everybody else.

This obsession with the themes of cultural domination and oppression justifies one of the most important departures from the principal and essential goal of the civil rights movement, equality of opportunity. Multiculturalism insists on equality of results. "I dream of a day when my four little children will not be judged by the color of their skin but by the content of their character," said Martin Luther King, Jr., crystallizing in one sentence the essential ideal of liberalism. The multiculturalist phrase, by contrast, is: "Judge me by the color of my skin for therein lies my identity and my place in the world."

And then, of course, there is the *dérapage*. Much of the iconoclasm directed against Columbus is the sign of a remarkable health in American society. In 1892, Americans rigorously stamped out of public view the moral costs involved in nation building. By 1992, we were able to incorporate them into the picture. And then, it seems, the liberal mind became so passionate in its embrace of our iniquity that in many quarters it came to stand for the whole of our historical identity. That was visible in Columbus's moral crash landing on Western shores. It is also visible in some of the less benign forms of that new great American practice—lessons in the New View of the American nature, indoctrination into the more progressive state of sensitivity.

Chapter 3

ADVANCED SENSITIVITY

Imagine a freshman arriving at a prestigious academy, say the University of Pennsylvania, the venerable Ivy League institution in Philadelphia founded by that great questioner of orthodoxies, Benjamin Franklin. This freshman will be a boy or a girl of about seventeen or eighteen years of age whose main concerns are getting ahead, having some fun, being somebody, fitting in, and, perhaps, making the world a better place. Freshpersons (as they are called in "gender-neutral" language these days) are, variously, nervous, burdened with angst, with homesickness, depression, eating disorders, horniness, stress, loneliness, fear of failure, fear of success. They know nothing; they know it all. Boys especially often manifest that combination of idealism, dogmatism, unbearable anguish at the stupidity of others, and lack of true confidence in themselves that is characteristic of late adolescence. But even the white boys come to college already imbued with the standard values of American life, which, polls and research show, are placed equally on the notions of fairness and individualism. The open expression of racial prejudice has been socially unacceptable for most of these children for their entire lives. They did not for the most part grow up in households that taught them to hate. They may be ignorant of many things, including some of their own preconceptions, but most of them believe that racism, anti-Semitism, gay bashing, the rape and harassment of women, and other evils are . . . evils. A survey of more than 200,000 freshmen at 404 schools, conducted by the UCLA Graduate School of Education in 1992, shows that 85 percent of them disagree with the statement "Racial discrimination is no longer a major problem in America." Students live in a liberal culture. They want, if not actually to be good, to be seen as being good.

And yet, of course, educators have for years, and with reason, viewed the young people who enter their domains of higher learning as only partially civilized creatures. Since the beginning of time, they have felt that instilling a respect for certain values and ways of behaving—that is, the norms of the civic culture—was part of their job. For years, the best schools were religious schools, and inculcating religious conviction was a part of the civilizing mission. And even after that was no longer the case, compulsory chapel was seen as an essential part of the university experience. Country, work, and family were the primary values; neatness, sexual restraint, and honesty made up the principles of the code of behavior, even though the universities tended to be more flexible, rebellious, skeptical on some of these matters than the country at large. No visits to rooms of the opposite sex were allowed. Strict curfews for women were maintained. Homosexuality was invisible. There were genteel teas at which attendance was required; dorm mothers were part of the landscape. Jackets and ties, or dresses, were required at dinner. Colleges and universities were places where you not only got an education, but also became a good, moral citizen.

And so when, in the 1980s, the inculcation of civic virtue started to take the form of training in the world of diversity, a tradition was not being abandoned; it was, in a sense, being restored, though with a powerful political difference. The multiculturalist ideal, the elevation of respect for difference as the chief element in the new code of behavior, became the prime value to inculcate. And, certainly, there is nothing wrong with orienting the bright and idealistic young men and women who arrive as freshmen at the three thousand colleges and universities of the United States in the values of tolerance, and with telling them that they will be expected to live peacefully together in a world made up of many different types. And that, presumably, is what the universities, including the University of Pennsylvania, attempt to do as they create what are commonly called multicultural communities. What reasonable person could object?

The problem is that, as with much else in the multiculturalist initiative, the lessons imparted to students are difficult to separate from attempts to foster a radical political ideology, disguised by recourse to those constant refrains, diversity and tolerance. Orientations in multiculturalism have tended to follow a certain pattern as discussions of race, ethnicity, sex, and homosexuality have moved from the informal domains of the late-night dormitory to the formal arena of structured orientation.

Slowly these discussions have become mandatory in the way that attending religious services was once mandatory at American universities. They became an official part of university life organized by a growing multiculturalist bureaucracy, a heavy rank of assistant deans and assistant provosts, of diversity programmers and social equity directors and affirmative action officers, of educational consultants who give full-day seminars on "understanding differences," of people with master's degrees in psychology and social work whose vocabulary is chock-full of expressions like "internalized oppression" and "psychological captivity," of specialists in multicultural education, people who use words like "problematize" and use "impact" as a verb (as in "white culture and white identity negatively impact the lives of people"). Not all institutions are the same. Brigham Young University, the Mormon institution in Utah, is unlike the University of California at Santa Cruz. But there is certainly plenty of evidence that at many places discussions about diversity are not frank exchanges about race, class, gender, discrimination, affirmative action, and other difficult questions, during which the component parts of the American mosaic can learn to understand one another. They have become the moments when the holders of the dominant view on campus minister to captive congregations made up of the entire student body, and they use that opportunity to instill in the young minds their vision of society as a nightmare of isms. My own sense of foreboding comes not from discussing the diversity of American society and certainly not from airing views about relations among the races, which is a clear good, but from the way it is being done. It comes also from the evidence that multiculturalism and the battle against discrimination are used to turn the universities into therapeutic communities, places where psychological conformity is encouraged by a kind of happy-face total atmosphere.

Literally from day one—indeed, as we will see, from before day one—freshmen and freshwomen are introduced to a twin message. Its first part is: "You have just entered an institution that is deeply racist, sexist, patriarchal, unfair, unjust, and old-fashioned—an institution, in other words, that is a microcosm of the iniquitous society from which you came." The second part is: "Each of you is a member of a group involving race, ethnic background, and sexuality, and you will be seen, and you should see yourself, primarily as a product of the perspectives, the limitations, and the sufferings of those groups." Finally, students are told: "Your first responsibility, the thing that will designate you as a good person, will be to adopt the great cause of multiculturalism as your own."

In 1992, according to the *Wall Street Journal*, universities across the country were "reorienting their freshman orientations" in the multiculturalist direction. In some places the programs seemed entirely constructive. At Brandeis University in Waltham, Massachusetts, for example, all 775 entering freshman were asked to read *There Are No Children Here*, Alex Kotlowitz's account of two brothers growing up in the black ghetto of Chicago, and *The Dispossessed: America's Underclass from the Civil War to the Present*, and then to attend discussion sessions on these books when they arrived on campus. At Columbia, the required summer reading was *The Autobiography of Malcolm X* and *The Joy Luck Club*, by Amy Tan. Matters, as we will see, depend on how discussions are handled. The Malcolm X book could, of course, lead to a fascinating discussion about race and racism in America, or, of course, it could lead to an orgy of white-male bashing. Elsewhere, the political lessons imparted in orientation seem clear.

At Bowdoin College in Maine, in 1992, the assistant to the president hosted a brown-bag lunch for students called "Defining Diversity: Your Role in Racial-Consciousness Raising, Cultural Differences, and Cross-Cultural Enhancers." At Oberlin College in Ohio, separate orientation programs were arranged for Asians, blacks, Latinos, and gay, lesbian, and bisexual students.* At Harvard a few years ago there was a weeklong program of panels and workshops seductively called AWARE (Actively Working Against Racism and Ethnocentrism), whose purposes, the program notes said, were to "address people's denial about racism" and "to engage people in trying to understand racism." Participants heard very precise statistics: that 85 percent of Americans harbor "subtle racism" while 15 percent are "overt racists." One professor, Karel Liem, an ichthyologist, was quoted as saying: "The pain that racial insensitivity can create is more important than a professor's academic freedom." Another speaker said: "Overreacting and being paranoid is the only way we can deal with this system."

---

*These examples are drawn from Heather MacDonald, "Welcome, Freshman! Oppressor or Oppressed?" *Wall Street Journal*, Sept. 29, 1992, page A16.

One Harvard professor offered the dissenting view that haranguing white people about their racism is not the way to improve race relations, but the tone of the meeting seemed better represented by the comment of another speaker; referring to racial insensitivity, he said: "Never think you imagined it, because chances are that you didn't."*

The University of Pennsylvania is a kind of average place in this regard, a place still devoted to teaching and scholarship and where students, spread out on the lawn of the gracious campus, have that clean-cut, Ralph Lauren look of students of the 1990s. I talked to Terri White, the university administrator in charge of planning the four-day freshman orientation, and she asserted that Penn's program was designed to be moderate and ideologically open, different from the more radical programs she said she knew existed at other universities.

The freshmen arrive at the beginning of September, about two thousand of them. But even before that, minority group members have already been brought to campus for special orientations, the purpose being to give these students, more likely than whites to be the first in their families to attend a university, a bit of extra help in getting adjusted to their new environments, making them feel comfortable, overcoming the fears they may have. This is all to the good as universities cope with populations it is fashionable to call "differently prepared." But I have also been struck on campuses by the way in which a group of militant students seems to speak for the group as a whole. Why does there seem to be so little diversity of opinion expressed within the group? The answer is complicated, but part of the reason is that the university itself in effect sanctions as sole legitimate representatives of minority points of view campus groups whose members are by self-selection likely to be more militant than others. At this special advance orientation, in short, as one critic of the system put it, "the minority students are introduced to their leaders," that is, to the various minority student organizations and their faculty backers, who happen generally to belong to the multiculturalist ministry. And since the entire student body is encouraged to wage relentless struggle against the ever-present evils of racism and sexism, the official organs of that struggle have enormous power and prestige.

The themes of struggle and oppression saturate freshman orienta-

---

*A first-person account of this meeting by Robert R. Detlefsen, a postdoctoral fellow in government at Harvard, is in *The New Republic*, Apr. 10, 1989, pages 18–21.

tion and much else in freshman life. Students are encouraged to believe that if they do not feel racism and oppression personally, it is because they have engaged in internalized repression. For those who ask how it could be that the institution that admitted them, gave them financial aid, and officially encourages diversity education could be racist, there is an answer. It is provided in many places, one of them a little booklet entitled *Racism at Penn—Waddaya Mean?* Racism, the booklet argues, involves who gets to see themselves reflected in the curriculum, in the fact that Afro-American studies is only a program and not a full department, in the low numbers of tenured minority professors, in the racial "homogeneity in the composition of Penn's leadership," in the "alienating general atmosphere" for "students of color at our school."

Similarly a pamphlet put out by the Office of Student Life, entitled *Multicultural Experiences at Penn: What You Can Do*, begins with this sentence: "Institutions of higher learning across the United States are troubled by . . . proliferating incidents of racial and sexual harassment, bigotry and incivility." All of this verbiage is heaped on the minority students before they have even begun classes, before their fellow students who are white have even arrived on campus. Meanwhile, others are being prepared to deal with potential problems. The Department of Residential Living issues a written notice to all resident advisers, the graduate students and faculty who live in the undergraduate dormitories. It tells them not only to behave well but that even if they are "perceived" to harbor impure attitudes, they are ipso facto guilty of "an attitude of intolerance. . . .

"If you are *perceived* [emphasis added] to be racist, sexist, heterosexist, ethnocentric, biased against those with religions different from your own, or intolerant of disabilities, you must be willing to examine and change that behavior," the administration's notice says.

Before arriving on campus, all members of the entering class at Penn are asked to read one book, to be discussed in special seminars during orientation. The book for the class that arrived at the university in September 1992 was *The Narrative of the Life of Frederick Douglass, An American Slave*, the autobiography of the great nineteenth-century abolitionist and, by anybody's standard, a seminal work in both American literary and political history. The book could be the basis for thought-provoking discussion, but the administration makes its best effort to be sure that it is interpreted in a certain way, with the stress given to oppression, victimization, and identity politics.

Each of the discussion leaders in 1992 was distributed a five-page guide called *Strategies for Teaching Frederick Douglass' Narrative*, by Professor Herman Beavers of the Department of English. To those not familiar with current academic cant the importance of that word "strategies" might not be immediately clear, but it is one of those code words that signals membership in the academic club of the New Consciousness. A "teaching strategy" is, in effect, a plan for getting across a particular point of view, and Beavers's is not hard to discern.

At several points in this background preparation for the freshmen arrival at Penn, Beavers recommends that students be encouraged to see their own lives and worlds in terms of the Douglass narrative. "What you want to try to do here is to talk about the impact of oppression on those who oppress others," he writes of one passage. Of another: "You could use this as an occasion to explore class difference." Beavers goes on with more pedagogical strategies: "Or you could talk about the ways in which those who are disenfranchised in one segment of society are capable of being oppressive in another." He continues: "You could talk then about the ways in which men can oppress women. Or the ways that women of one class or race can oppress women of another class or race. The ways that heterosexuals can oppress gays and lesbians. Or the ways that we marginalize those who are HIV positive."

Just in case anybody might be concerned "about this turning into a PC discussion," Professor Beavers says, there is really no cause for worry. "This need not turn into any kind of polar [*sic*] discussion," he assures his readers. Adding non sequitur to malapropism, Beavers then says: "Douglass establishes very clearly that slavery, as a system, transforms people, and so white people are not inherently evil, just as blacks are not inherently good."

Beavers's "strategies" are only at the beginning of moral education at Penn. In addition to the discussions of the Douglass narrative, other meetings to talk about diversity are on the schedule, and the faculty members who will lead them—and who are required to undergo a half-day orientation themselves—have been provided with a *Facilitators' Guide* to help them help their students. For some years, the preparers of the guide asked the facilitators to read a list of "examples of racial, gender-related, religious, and homophobic incidents of harassment that have taken place at the University over the past few years." The examples supposedly show how deep the problems of racism and discrimination go at Penn, though others might see them, ironically, as evidence that there is, in fact, no pattern of racism, merely the occasional and rather aberrational unpleasant incident. There was, for example, the story of the man who walked a woman home after a party and "became extremely abusive and tried to make her feel badly for inconveniencing him" when she refused to sleep with him. There is the rare but blatant racist, anti-Semitic, or antigay epithet of the sort that, unfortunately, is going to happen in any group of ten thousand or more people. Among the more serious incidents read to students were these: (1) a white student punched a black student in the elevator; (2) "racial and sexist slurs" were yelled at a certain fraternity party when "African-American strippers" had been hired to entertain the members; (3) a lecturer "continually referred to African-American students in his class as 'ex-slaves.'"

Michael Cohen, a professor of physics at Penn, was moved to action when he noted that none of those three particular incidents had actually occurred, at least not as described in the *Facilitators' Guide*. The vice-provost for student life, he said, the very person who compiled the list of examples, had herself stated that there had been no report to her of a white student punching a black student in an elevator. The second incident had been investigated by the Fraternity/Sorority Advisory Board, which in its lengthy report made no mention of racial slurs (and also pointed out that the strippers had been both black and white). Incident number three was investigated by the Wharton School Academic Freedom Committee, which reported that in twenty-two years of teaching, the lecturer in question had not "continually referred to" African-Americans as "ex-slaves"; he had done so only once, and, on that occasion, he had referred to himself as an "ex-slave" in the same sentence.*

After reading this dubious list of examples of the supposedly rampant racism and bigotry on the Penn campus, the facilitators were then instructed to ask the students, "What is happening here and why?" Professor Cohen's comment on this: "In short, give the students a factually incorrect account of what is happening and ask them, on the basis of their 24 hours of experience at Penn and their profound knowledge of social psychology, to discuss *why* it is happening." He said: "It is not surprising that when the University gets into the business of indoctrinating rather than education, old-fashioned values like truth and factual accuracy get battered."

*See Chapter 4 for a fuller account of this particular incident.

That was in 1989. Administrators who responded to Cohen's charges in a campus publication claimed the examples were "composites or case examples that had been mixed up deliberately so that no particular person or fraternity would be identified"—to which Cohen countered that the students were not so informed. They were left to believe that these events had actually taken place. The vice-provost for student life then went on to argue that some "confusion" had emerged over whether the examples were "composites," but that whether they were or not, they showed "the climate of opinion" at Penn. In any case, the administration thought better of its list of examples in subsequent years, and it was dropped.

By 1992, freshman orientation consisted of a one-day program entitled Multicultural Experiences at Penn. It began with a meeting of the entire student body, its first-ever general assembly at Penn, which was followed by small-group discussions of case studies in what was called living in a multicultural community. At the initial assembly, one Jodi Bromberg served as a kind of mistress of ceremonies. Bromberg was the head of the university's Lesbian, Gay, Bisexual Alliance, and she clearly spoke on that basis, informing the new members of the freshman class that it was important for students to understand various things about gender, race, and sexual preference. "Not everyone is white," she said, "not everyone is American, not everyone speaks English, and, no, not everyone is heterosexual."

Bromberg introduced Sheldon Hackney, then the president of the University of Pennsylvania, who made a short speech, also stressing the diversity of the institution, reminding Penn's new crop of eighteen-year-olds—who are very likely unaware of the obsessions of their elders with race, gender, and sexual preference—that words such as "diversity," "pluralistic," and "multicultural" are not "as some commentators outside of the university seem to think" a matter of some politically correct ideology. They reflect "the reality of who you are and that you are more diverse than a class that sat in those same seats 20 years ago." Hackney stressed that whites and Christians are actually a minority in the world today, and that "we are all a multicultural community."

Next Bromberg introduced Pam Urueata, head of the United Minorities Council at Penn, a student organization, and she promptly told the freshmen "what the Penn catalogs don't tell you about." There is a "disturbing reality" at Penn, she said. For one thing, the university is "by no means as diverse as it should be." There are too few minorities, she said, in the student body, on the faculty, and in the curriculum. There are very serious problems, she said, especially (you guessed it!) "racism, sexism, and heterosexism" and also many instances of harassment based on race, sex, and sexual preference. "The minorities at Penn," Urueata said, "continue to be victims."

A half day is not much, and even if there is a bit too much harping on the isms rampant at the university, the sessions will not be a major part of any student's overall experience at Penn. Perhaps for that very reason, there is a yearlong series of continuing seminars offered to freshmen for course credit, and these often focus on oppression, even when the subject matter of the course would seem to have nothing whatever to do with it.

For example, in the 1991–92 listing there was a seminar on early American literature that "will call into question more traditional interpretations of the texts" and deal with such questions as "feminist challenges to early American patriarchy (or the absence of such challenges), national identity and who is included." And then there was Women, Feminism & Wide-World Changing. From the catalog description: "One of the main issues raised by African-American, Native-American, Asian-American and Latina women in these texts is the issue of racism: the forms of racism they experience as members of minority groups in the U.S.; how that racism affects them emotionally as well as economically and politically, and, finally, how racism creates barriers among women of color themselves, and between women of color and white women which prevent women from becoming effective allies for each other." There were readings from African and Arab women that "address similar issues, but from a broader angle: this is, how prejudices and misinformation on the part of Western feminists create barriers to mutual understanding and respect, and to building effective global alliances."

There were a group of writing seminars, not all but many of which have a clear ideological thrust. One was entitled Where Do You Come From My Lady? which, according to the syllabus, "will explore strategies for writing about the self in a multicultural environment." Or there was Writing About American Culture, in which, again according to the seminar description, "We will explore changing and enduring aspects of our American culture(s) by looking at the history and rhetoric of social protest movements, specifically concentrating on movements for equality involving Native-American Indians, African-Americans, union labor, and women." Another seminar was Art of the Narrative, which asked questions such as "How is a Sherlock Holmes story that takes place in England indebted to imperialism? What ties Walter Scott's romance *The Talisman* (1822) to the crisis in the Persian Gulf? As critical readers we must relate such literary works to complex issues of identity and domination."

Freshmen are also expected to participate in an ongoing series of seminars held inside residence halls that will continue their training in diversity even after their initial orientation. The Department of Residential Living, which is in charge of the dormitories, sends out a letter to every faculty member inviting participation in this program "on specific topics of diversity within the First Year Houses. . . .

"The specific program blocks that have been targeted are race and ethnic issues, religious issues, sexism, and issues of gay/lesbian and bisexual concern," the letter says, thereby presumably hanging out a DO NOT ENTER sign for any would-be counselors who do not happen to think that those are the main things freshmen ought to be talking about for an entire academic year. Attached to the letter are some pages of a brochure entitled *The Challenge for Change* that helpfully lists some of the specific suggested programs to be followed during the course of the year. The 1992–93 version of this attractively produced booklet had dozens of course offerings. There were Cultural Perspective and Discrimination; Race and Masculinity; The Roots and Manifestations of Racism; and Fear of Difference: The Importance of Racial Identity for All Students. To be sure, inserted here and there in this program of instruction were seminars being sponsored by independent-minded faculty members whose purpose was to question the more general assumptions of the orthodox view at Penn, such as Charles Alan Kors's Indoctrination and Intellectual Diversity, whose catalog description promises an exploration of the possibility that "the models of group diversity employed in diversity education constitute a threat to an authentic model of diversity, one based on individualism and intellectual diversity."

For the most part, however, Kors and a small number of others were numerically swamped in that political sameness that, paradoxically, uses the term "diversity" as its trademark. The program guide was full of boilerplate phrases and prefabricated concepts, such as "learn and appreciate how diversity enhances our everyday lives," and "ethnocentrism . . . is the soil from which racism, sexism, ageism, religious prejudice and other judgments of people germinates and is nourished," and "a better understanding of racism and its impact on the student community," and "the nature of prejudice and power as they impact on creating and maintaining 'isms' (e.g., sexism, racism, heterosexism, anti-Semitism, etc.)," and "an overview of issues of racism as it affects white women," and "the impact of homophobia and heterosexism on the women's community." Other seminar topics included Latinos and Bicultural Stress; Preventing Harassment: Everyone's Responsibility; Gays, Lesbians and Bisexuals in Protestantism; Gays and Lesbians in the Jewish Community; Who Is a Sexual Minority?—Everyone; Liberating Women Through Religion; Violence Against Women; Acquaintance Rape: A Workshop for Men; Lies I Use to Prove My Masculinity; and The Challenge for the White Male.

The University of Pennsylvania, like many universities, still, of course, offers its students a rich buffet table of courses and courses of study, from theoretical physics to semiotics, taught by a learned and distinguished faculty. Even those students I talked to who strongly felt that there was a good deal of attempted political indoctrination expressed great satisfaction with the education they received at Penn. But they also described a campus that, despite concerted efforts to make students sensitive and accepting of difference, is obsessed, mesmerized, driven by an unceasing battle between the various racial, ethnic, and sexual groups on campus. The campus, for one thing, is largely segregated. Black and white students tend to live in separate dormitories, beginning with the freshman year; they eat in separate portions of the dining hall; they belong to different clubs and campus organizations. There are, for example, virtually no black students among the three hundred or so who put out the *Daily Pennsylvanian*, the student newspaper, despite concerted efforts by the paper to recruit black students. Perhaps this is because the newspaper is deemed a "white" club; possibly it is because there are some twenty or so organizations for black students, and only about five hundred black undergraduates, 10 percent of the student body, to belong to them. Students also identify themselves by sexual preference, though this is complicated. There are, for example, three distinct, competing gay and lesbian organizations—one, the Lesbian, Gay, Bisexual Alliance (LGBA), the "mainstream" gay group, accused by another, QUIP, Queers Invading Penn, for being too conservative and too exclusive (meaning that it is mostly white). In this regard QUIP is supported by PEARL, Penn's Eagerly Awaited Radical Ladies, formed in 1988 because, its members felt, the LGBA was too male and not sufficiently lesbian in membership.

The student newspaper, which is central to daily life at Penn, is frequently accused of racism, or at least insensitivity to blacks. An accusation along those lines, for example, was made at the end of May 1993 by Houston Baker, the chairman of Penn's Center for the Study of Black Literature and Culture and a past president of the Modern Language Association. Baker, writing in the Philadelphia *Inquirer*, accused the *DP* of failing to present "the brute and brutal realities of African-American everyday life on Penn's campus," which, he continued, made it complicit in "the big white lie that drifts daily toward the most rancorous forms of bigotry that any of us who are black can imagine."

The *Daily Pennsylvanian* itself provides a steady diet of stories that show the mood of antagonism and the paramountcy given to identity politics. One day, there will be a long list of faculty and students, representing black organizations, signing a letter protesting the newspaper's "racism" and "insensitivity" in publishing a photograph of a black homeless man hanging out and drinking from a liquor bottle near the Penn campus. "Objectivity does not exist in journalism," the letter will say, echoing common multiculturalist themes, especially the notion, borrowed from poststructuralist literary criticism, that there is no reality, only representations, texts, signifiers. "The juxtaposition of images and words creates a particular and distinct system of meaning."

On another day, some white students write letters to protest a speech given by Del Jones, a black militant invited onto campus by a black residence hall, who voiced the opinion that AIDS and crack cocaine are elements in a white conspiracy aimed at exterminating the black race. On yet another day there is a notice of a series of five evenings of discussion, sponsored by a group called White Women Against Racism, which will "examine the impact of Racism on White Women and What we can Do about it."

The newspaper reports on other things, on some diversity workshops for Penn administrators that explored "the effects of racism and sexism on individuals, groups and institutions," or on Khallid Muhammad, the minister of information of the Nation of Islam, who came to give a speech on campus in which he spent a lot of his time addressing the Jews in the audience, telling them, among other things, to "correct what your elders and those who have come before you have set in motion" and "Just as we don't agree with the crimes perpetuated by Hitler against the Jewish people, we don't agree with the crimes perpetuated by the Jewish people against Palestinians."* The *DP* reports that these remarks were "punctuated by frequent applause from the audience." On another day there is a story on something called the Eracism Conference, a student group dedicated to combating the scourge of racism in America. There is a piece on an African-American student-leadership retreat held off campus, whose purpose, said Dan Scott Butler, administrative assistant for the Afro-American studies department, "is to teach leadership skills from an Afro-centric perspective."

Then there is the saga of the Romance languages department, also recounted in detail in the *Daily Pennsylvanian*. In 1988, the department instituted what the newspaper described as "mandatory sensitivity workshops for teaching assistants following an alleged racial incident last semester." Meanwhile, the university's administration was looking into creating a program on race relations for all faculty members. An alleged incident? The teaching assistants had to be given doses of racial awareness and the faculty instructed in race relations not because of a finding, but merely an allegation? So it seems. A student named Erik Williams brought charges of what the newspaper report called "racial callousness." Williams refused to give details, but he said that it was a case of "insensitivity," not "harassment." It was Williams who publicly proposed mandatory sensitivity workshops for the entire faculty, after which he circulated a letter congratulating the Romance languages department for being a pioneer in that area, sending the letter on to President Sheldon Hackney, whose assistant, Nicholas Constan, responding to Williams's suggestion, said that it was "a good idea"; it was "feasible"; it was "certainly being looked into."

Taken individually, none of these things seem terribly significant, but there is no doubt a cumulative impact from all of the separate evocations of racism and oppressiveness, daily instances where difference among groups is elevated from an important concern to an obsession. Relentless identity politics, moreover, and the consequent fragmentation of the university along the fault lines of small-group

---

*The *Daily Pennsylvanian* reports Muhammad using the verb "perpetuated" as he expressed the anti-Jewish crimes of Hitler and the apparently equivalent anti-Palestinian crimes of the Jews, though perhaps Muhammad actually said "perpetrated" in both cases.

antagonisms are abetted by faculty members and administrators themselves committed to the cause of Right Thinking.

I once visited the Women's Center at Penn, which is a branch of the provost's office created in 1968 as a place where women who have been the targets of harassment or sexual abuse can go for counseling and support. The director of the Women's Center is a native of Great Neck, Long Island, named Elena DiLapi, who was educated at Nassau Community College and the State University of New York at Stony Brook and got her M.A. in social work at Penn. On the wall of her wood-paneled office is the sign FEMALE AT BIRTH; LESBIAN BY GRACE. Another banner says, simply, LESISMOS. DiLapi's private choices, whatever they might be, are her own business, of course. Still, I did wonder about that somewhat provocative message on the wall of an office of the Penn administration, hanging there like a challenge to students who might disagree with its underlying sentiment.

A recent graduate of Penn, Katie Brant, once told me that, in her opinion at least, the Penn Women's Center was not about choice at all, and certainly not about a respect for diversity. "If you're not pro-lesbian and pro-choice, resentful of men and career oriented, you're not really a woman by their lights," she said. A pro-choice advocate herself, Brant told me that she once went to the Women's Center to get information about antiabortion groups on campus. She says that the receptionist curtly told her, "This office is pro-choice." Elena DiLapi used exactly the same expression when I visited her, and I asked her why it was necessary—indeed, if it was appropriate—for a branch of the university administration that supposedly served all tuition-paying students to take an official position on one of the most vexing and divisive issues in American politics.

"My position is that the pro-choice position is the middle ground," DiLapi said. "The middle ground allows for everybody to have their own personal opinion."

What, I asked, is on the other side, then?

"If you have pro-life saying there should be no abortion," she replied, "the opposite of that is that everybody should have an abortion. The middle ground is that everybody should decide for themselves. You cannot point to a program where I have said everybody should get an abortion. We don't support that."

This is like arguing that favoring the death penalty would put you in the middle position in the debate about capital punishment. If you are against the death penalty then you think that nobody should be executed. The opposite of that is that everybody should be executed. To believe that people should be executed only for certain crimes is the middle position. Perhaps it is a bad comparison; nonetheless, it did seem to me that DiLapi's discourse on abortion suggested a certain predominating tone at a center that is supposed to be for all of the diverse population of women paying the university's $22,740 in yearly undergraduate charges. It also suggested how disagreement might entail the exclusion indicated in that dismissive phrase, "We're pro-choice here."

Penn is the kind of place where, in 1989, an undergraduate on the university's planning committee for diversity education wrote a memo to her colleagues in which she mentioned "my deep regard for the individual and my desire to protect the freedom of all members of society." An administrator underlined the word "individual" in the student's memo and wrote back: "This is a RED FLAG phrase today, which is considered by many to be RACIST. Arguments that champion the individual over the group ultimately privileges [sic] the 'individuals' belonging to the largest or dominant group."

On one visit to Penn, I was handed a flyer calling on the members of a residence hall known as Community House to engage in a Gay Jeans Day, which was suggested as part of a larger activity known as Gay, Lesbian, Bisexual Awareness Week. The flyer, issued by Liz Golden, whose title is program assistant for diversity education, good-naturedly explained that "I have taken it upon myself" to ask all people to show their support for gay civil rights by wearing jeans on March 28."

Given that about 80 percent of college students these days wear jeans every day of the year, I wasn't sure how the supporters of gay civil rights would be distinguished from others who were simply wearing their usual jeans. Were those who did not wear jeans showing themselves to be the enemies of gay civil rights, or were their jeans simply at the laundry? Would they be excoriated? Would they feel pressured to wear jeans on that day so as to avoid embarrassment or conflict? Never mind. The real question was what right did an officer of the university have to set things up so that the option of doing nothing, of not participating in a political activity, was effectively eliminated? Universities certainly should take steps to ban antihomo-sexual discrimination and to require that gay men and women suffer no harm because of their sexuality. But will pressuring students into making an active show of support for gay rights a condition of good citizenship really achieve the aim of tolerance and acceptance of homosexuality, or will it breed resentment?

"The purpose of having an In-House version of this campuswide event is to personalize it and make it more visible both to those who do and don't support the notions of Gay pride and personal freedom," Golden joyfully declares in her flyer. So part of the purpose is to mark out those who do not support gay pride—and who, in the world according to Golden, would be showing that they are also against personal freedom! Very likely Golden does not intend that to be the only conclusion one could draw about those who did not wear jeans on Gay Jeans Day. Still, she adds a dollop of mandatoriness to her initiative. The week after Gay, Lesbian, Bisexual Awareness Week, says her flyer, "there will be a program to deal with what came up for House members in response to the Day. The program will be required for RA's [resident advisers], Managers and the Diversity Board Members."

So it is that the university begins with the commendable goal of fostering acceptance and tolerance of the gay members of the community, then moves to pressuring students to make some visible show of support for gay rights, and finally requires those in charge of undergraduate life to attend a meeting to discuss "what came up." It is worth pointing out that one year during Gay Jeans Day a few protesters stood near the gay and lesbian activists and held out a placard declaring: HETEROSEXUAL FOOTWEAR DAY—WEAR SHOES IF YOU ARE A HETEROSEXUAL and DON'T BEND FOR A FRIEND. This was officially branded an "incident of harassment" by the Penn administration and was put on the list of such incidents to be read at freshman orientation. In short, it is fine to pressure students into showing their support for gay rights but it is harassment to parody the effort.

I have strong feelings about certain things. I would like all university students and administrators to take mandatory courses in clarity of expression and to read George Orwell's "Politics and the English Language," which would be of considerable benefit to many, including, I suspect, Ms. Golden. I wish that everybody would wear Star of David lapel buttons on Israeli Independence Day to commemorate the victims of the Holocaust and to celebrate personal freedom for everybody. Those who do not wear the button would then conveniently make visible their indifference to the crime of genocide, their insensitivity to the feelings of the Jews, and their disregard for personal freedom. They would be prime candidates for workshops on religious-difference awareness. Of course, I don't have the power to require these things of students. Nobody should have the power. The plain fact is that Golden's initiative, which provoked no objection from higher university officials, intruded on the personal freedom she so values, namely the personal freedom to disagree with her opinions and to be left in peace, even during Gay, Lesbian, Bisexual Awareness Week.

In 1992, several campus organizations, including the Student Health Office, sponsored something called "Eroticizing Safer Sex Workshops" as part of HIV/AIDS Awareness Week at Penn (there are so many weeks devoted to awareness at Penn, it's a wonder anybody has time to learn anything of an academic nature). The program organizers broke the Penn community down into six different categories, each with its own separate program: there was the workshop for gay and bisexual men, one for lesbian and bisexual women, and another for straight women. Then there were workshops for men of color, for straight men, and for women of color.

It is perhaps not a very important matter, these "Eroticizing Safer Sex Workshops," but examine the underlying assumption: not only do gays and straights, men and women, have the need for separate sessions (I could certainly see a case being made for that), so too do white men and women and men and women of color. This classification entails so many fine questions. Does a gay Asian man go to the workshop for gay and bisexual men or to the workshop for men of color? Why weren't there separate workshops for gay or bisexual black, Asian, Hispanic, or Native American men and women? It seems unfair that they are herded into the catchall male homosexual group, while white men get divided into workshops for straight men (which, given the existence of a workshop for men of color, must mean white men) and workshops for gay men. Or perhaps the workshops for men and women of color are intended to include both gays and straights. But if that is the case, wouldn't the workshop for gay and bisexual men be for white men only? That would be unfair because it would exclude gay men and women of color. Come to think of it, there should be separate workshops for straight white men, straight men of color, gay and bisexual white men, and gay and bisexual men of color—and the same for women. That, however, raises the question of why gays and bisexuals should be in the same workshop, rather than separate workshops, since, after all, a bisexual person is presumably equidistant from one who is exclusively heterosexual and one who is exclusively gay. And what of Hispanics? Should Hispanics, who as Catholics might have different ideas about sexuality than their fellow students, have their own "Eroticizing Safer Sex" workshops? And the Jews?

I wanted to know what Martin Dias, the head of the Black Student League at Penn, thought of all these things. Dias, when I spoke to him in the fall of 1992, was a twenty-one-year-old majoring in economics. He was an assertive, athletic-looking, slightly defensive young man who said he wanted, after graduation, to go into banking. My main question was whether Penn was racist and, if it was, how this racism was manifested. As he answered, Dias mingled a certain hipster's slang that he did not learn from his professors with the vocabulary of victimization and oppression that he probably did not possess before he began his Ivy League education.

"Policies don't have to overtly exclude you," he said, for a place to be racist. I observed that, by contrast with the past, black students were no longer barred from the university, that they were eagerly sought after in what is a national effort to increase their proportions at universities across the country. Didn't that, I wondered, indicate that the common phrase "institutional racism" was too strong?

"They no longer have to say, 'We do not let blacks in,'" Dias said, "because [the black students] understand that if you subscribe to certain ideologies, if you subscribe to the norm, which is a white norm because it's a white country, you will do certain things which will get you in. But you can have a very, very intelligent student who will subscribe to an Afrocentric or an African way of learning who will do very poorly with the standards that have been set up by American society.

"Because the way of African learning is very different," Dias said. "I mean in many ways an African sense of learning is a people sense of learning. It's a spiritual sense of learning. It's not a learning, necessarily, about machines or learning about ways to destroy people or ways to make things more efficient."

Dias was decidedly not wedded to some rigid theory of racial difference and racial separatism. He had been accepted to both Dartmouth and Penn, the only two Ivy League schools he applied to, along with Boston University and Union College in upstate New York, where he was accepted also. I told him that I myself, growing up in a small, rural town in Connecticut in the late 1950s and early 1960s, never even thought to apply to the Ivy League, since my parents couldn't have afforded to send me there, and, anyway, we had a habit of thinking a bit small in my surroundings. And yet here he was assuming almost as a matter of course that the Ivy League was open to him, and still he talked about "institutional racism." How, I asked, given all this, could that expression be justified? Was Penn really racist?

"If you think that just somebody walking by and saying 'nigger' is the only way that overt racism is manifested, then probably no, you wouldn't see a lot of overt racism, because that doesn't happen an awful lot," Dias said. "But if you think that when you walk into a building and the only black people you see have brooms and mops and have, you know, maid's gear on and you feel that that's overt racism, then, yeah, there's plenty of that. If you think that in a city which has a very sizable black population and there's not a whole lot of black people at this school, if you find that as overt racism, then, yeah, that's something overt.

"You know, if you disrespect other people's curriculums and other people's cultures through books and the way people learn and the classes that you take and the level of respect that certain populations get over other certain populations, then, yeah, that's something overt too."

Dias referred to a local campus dispute having to do with the annual observation of Martin Luther King Day. Some professors, he said, give quizzes on that day, which is contrary to the general understanding that the entire university will celebrate a kind of semi-holiday. Classes will be held as usual, but no major exams will be given or papers called for.

"That for me," he said, referring to the quizzes on Martin Luther King Day, "is a perfect example of institutional racism, because I as a black person cannot celebrate myself, and that's a problem. That's a very big problem. And if you don't think it's a problem, well, I think you might need to reevaluate your sensitivity level, because I think my not being able to be me in a social context where people are supposed to be celebrating diversity, I think that's a very big issue."

I felt that Dias, despite his rhetoric, did appreciate his chance to attend a great institution of higher learning and that his presence in the heart of what was once the exclusive breeding ground of the white elite did signal to him an important change in American life. He didn't say it, but I assumed that he wanted to finish school and make some money, which may involve accepting the "white norm," as he called it. There was, I think, something just a bit rhetorical about his state-ment of a multiculturalist philosophy, which was based on the idea that mere access to the goods of society is not enough, particularly if that access was conditioned on acceptance by him of those supposedly white norms.

But Dias would not yield to my argument that racism is no longer the social norm in American life, even though I thought that his own experience was powerful testimony to that fact. He felt, apparently, that he had to defend the multiculturalist propositions on this point, even if he never used the word "multiculturalism" himself. For him, the prevalence of what he called white norms was synonymous with a racist culture. White norms in the world today accomplish the same task that was begun several centuries ago when, he said, whites robbed African people of their identity, of their names, their religion, their dress, their language, their very personhood.

"When I say control," he said, "I mean basically that the power class wants to maintain control over the entire society, and right now control mechanisms can include financial institutions, banks, credit, little things that make sure certain groups of people aren't getting into business as much as other groups. You can also include education, indoctrination through the teaching of history through a very Euro-centric perspective. It can be simple things like propaganda through TV, so that little black girls don't want to play with little black dolls."

Progress toward racial equality is not, he said, "mutually exclu-sive" with institutional racism. "Just because the university passes all these laws doesn't mean, one, that racism is going to diminish, or, two, that they even believe that it might diminish. When Lyndon Johnson signs a civil rights bill, he may not necessarily even believe that it's going to be successful. All he's got to do is sign it because he was put in a certain situation where he really had very little choice.

"Look, if I give you a loaded gun right now and tell you to go outside and you can go live your life, or whatever, and I know full well that as soon as you step outside twenty police are going to shoot you dead, I'll give you that gun! I'll say, 'Sure, here you go. Take it. Go outside. Do your thing. Go ahead. Go. You know, start a revolu-tion, 'cause I know you're going to die as soon as you go outside.' "

There was a touching delicacy to this young person, despite this cynicism, a disarming frankness about his own vulnerabilities. He spoke movingly during our conversation of what he called his fear of desperation, his sense, which he said was common among blacks, that the good life hangs by a single thread, which can break at any time, and that, in the end, is what explained his attachment to his conditioned sort of skepticism.

"I think desperation is the thing I fear most in life," Dias said. "I don't fear dead people. I don't fear darkness. I don't fear too much of anything except desperation: not having a way out, being very dependent upon one individual. It makes me feel . . . it scares me a little bit.

"Desperation is something that blacks really have to deal with, because a lot of times it is just, you know, that one job, or a lot of times it is just that one hope or that one chance. And, you know, those feelings of desperation aren't always brought out positively, or externalized positively, but you can understand where they're coming from.

"And, I'm not sure exactly how that relates to desperation, but I think one of the things I like most about learning about African tradition is my sense of security that I have. It helps me. It helps me learn, because I feel more secure, and if you have any kind of insecurities, it really is a detriment to your study habits. But also it just makes me feel good about myself and where I come from, and it takes away some of those desperate feelings."

Martin Dias is a sample of one, but nonetheless a good sample of the depth of feeling that lies behind a racial experience and a racial identity. No mood of general satisfaction, no belief that things, finally, are turning out right, will automatically come to the collective mind just because the universities become more diverse. There will be the normal expressions of higher expectations, of pride and defensiveness, of ideology and desperation. That is a given. To deal with it and to ensure that everybody gets the kind of education that will equip a person for success in later life (which does mean some immersion in "white norms") are the paramount challenges of any university these days. And because college kids cannot be counted on to be reasonable, the task of creating an environment welcoming of both group expression and community peace will require a combination of sympathetic understanding and firmness. The universities need good sheriffs, Gary Cooper figures, who will be friendly and dependable but who will stand in front of the jailhouse door and tell the angry mob that he is the law in this town and anybody who wants to take the law into his own hands will have to deal with him first. Instead, there is a reflex toward sanctimony, an impulse toward appeasement, even when things get truly out of hand. The plain fact is that students like Martin Dias know that they have the universities on the run.

"Students today," said Glenn Loury, an economist at Boston University, "can take over the university by much more subtle means than picking up weapons. Rather than controlling people's bodies with guns, they control their minds with . . . politically correct epithets. It's much more satisfying to be able to claim that anything your opponent is saying is racist and actually hound them off campus, than it is to take guns and threaten to kill people. It's a much greater exercise of power."

Showing in part how Penn encourages the very atmosphere described by Loury is this text of a printed form sent to a student accused of a violation of the university's official Code of Conduct by the office charged with prosecuting such violations:

In accordance with the agreement, you are to:

Participate in a comprehensive program on sexual harassment, except for the time you are attending classes for which you have registered at the university or are reporting for employment. Said programming shall include weekly assignments which must be performed during each week in which classes are in session through the Spring 1992 term. You will be required to present written evidence of completion of assignments and a satisfactory performance must be documented by Ms. Elena DiLapi, Director of the Women's Center, or her representative before your transcript can be released.

There are several things to say about this document, addressed to an individual whose identity will remain secret. The statement represented a proposed agreement sent to a student who had not yet been convicted of wrongdoing, but who was being offered an alternative to an official hearing and a possible guilty finding against him. If he agreed to participate in the "comprehensive program on sexual harassment" outlined in the proposed agreement and lasting through the spring semester, and to which he would be subject at any time he was not attending classes or reporting for employment, then the charges would be dropped.

We have already been introduced to the person who would judge his performance, Elena DiLapi, known for her strong views. When that fraternity at Penn held the party at which there were some black striptease dancers, DiLapi was among the members of White Women Against Racism who signed an open letter arguing that "the fact that the participants were men and the strippers were women makes it sexist; the fact that the participants were white and the strippers were black makes it racist." It was a "symbolic rape," the letter said, and it "reflects the racist sexual exploitation of black women by white males throughout American history." On another occasion, when some students and faculty at Penn argued that the speech codes put limits on free expression, DiLapi was quoted in the student newspaper as saying that these arguments amounted to an attempt to "keep racism and sexism alive and well on this campus." DiLapi, of course, is absolutely entitled to her opinions and the expression of them. She certainly makes Penn a more interesting place, and many women on campus clearly adore her. But does she have sufficient emotional detachment to be a fair judge of somebody's performance in a punitive program on sexual harassment?

I called DiLapi and the vice-provost, Larry Moneta, to whom the judicial inquiry officer reports, to ask about the apparent efforts by the university to offer a kind of plea-bargaining arrangement to those accused of violating the harassment rules. DiLapi said that she would not comment on any disciplinary proceeding, though she added that she did not know of any printed form on which her name appeared. When I told her that I had a copy of just such a form in front of me, she again said that she had no comment. Moneta reiterated that disciplinary matters were kept entirely confidential, largely for the protection of the accused, but that each case was handled individually, and the kind of plea bargaining suggested in the document I had obtained would at most have been an isolated instance. My requests, made both by telephone and in writing, to interview Sheldon Hackney, who was at the time the president of Penn, about this and other matters went unanswered.

Then early in 1993 came a case that received national publicity, the so-called water buffalo incident in which an Orthodox Jewish freshman named Eden Jacobowitz was accused of racial harassment when he shouted "Shut up, you water buffalo" to a group of black women making a lot of noise late one night outside his dormitory. Jacobowitz readily admitted to the campus police, who came to the dormitory to investigate the women's complaint of racial insults, that he had uttered the fateful words "water buffalo," thinking that he had done nothing wrong and had nothing to hide. Jacobowitz was interrogated twice by the police. He was then questioned by the university's assistant judicial inquiry officer, Robin Read, who, when confronted with his claim that "water buffalo" had no racial connotation, asked Jacobowitz whether he was entertaining any "racist thoughts" when he shouted out the epithet.

It turned out that Jacobowitz, who was born in Israel and went to a Hebrew day school, had unconsciously translated a Hebrew word, *beheymah*, usually used by one Jew to chastise another, as "water buffalo." Still, the Judicial Inquiry Office pursued the charges against Jacobowitz for the entire semester, until, after a barrage of negative stories on the incident had appeared in the national press, the five women plaintiffs (accompanied to at least one hearing by DiLapi) dropped the charges, claiming that Jacobowitz was getting out his side of the story while they had to remain silent. (In fact, once Jacobowitz talked to the press there was no rule preventing the five women from doing the same thing, but, until their press conference, they refused even to allow their names to be released.)

It is hard to know whether the dropping of the charge had anything at all to do with the fact that just as the water buffalo case was getting national publicity, Sheldon Hackney was named by President Bill Clinton to be the head of the National Endowment for the Humanities (NEH), the federal agency that gives $150 million a year to support research, documentaries, and exhibitions in literature and history. In any case, before the charges were dropped, Jacobowitz too was offered a settlement from the assistant judicial inquiry officer, Ms. Read. In a letter to him, Read specified that Jacobowitz's case would be dropped if he agreed to several terms, among them that he write a letter of apology to the complainants "acknowledging inappropriate behavior" and that he present a "program for living in a diverse community environment." The letter also specified that the notation "violation of the code of conduct and racial harassment policy" would be put into his transcript, "to be removed at the beginning of your junior year."

Jacobowitz refused to sign, telling reporters, "I may be young but

I'm not stupid." Instead, he and history professor Alan Kors, who served as his faculty adviser, assembled witnesses who would testify to his behavior on the night of the incident and to the absence of racial connotations in the epithet he used, but the university postponed the hearing on the grounds that the plaintiffs had been assigned no faculty adviser. By the time a second hearing was scheduled, most of Jacobowitz's witnesses had gone home for the summer. Still, he was ready to go ahead to have his day in court, when his accusers dropped the charges against him. Meanwhile, Kors had lunch with a deputy counsel of the university, and he asked whether agreements like the one offered Jacobowitz were common. Kors says the deputy counsel told him, "Oh yeah, I sign off on lots of those. I have lunch with Elena DiLapi every other week."

As if to prove the existence of the semisecret plea-bargaining practice, the Judicial Inquiry Office had been engaged in yet another case involving the offer of a settlement with a student in exchange for the nonprosecution of a complaint. Every year, the *Daily Pennsylvanian* has a single conservative columnist, the position during the 1992–93 academic year held by a young man named Gregory Pavlik. Pavlik wrote several particularly controversial columns. One argued against celebrating Martin Luther King Day on the grounds, Pavlik said, that King was an adulterer and a plagiarist. Another was critical of affirmative action, which, Pavlik wrote, went contrary to the American principle of equal treatment for all.

One day Pavlik received a call from the Judicial Inquiry Office during which he was informed that he was under investigation for racial harassment because of the opinions he had expressed in his columns. But, he was told, the charges would be dropped if he would agree to a meeting with the thirty-one students who had accused him. Pavlik rejected the settlement. Eventually, and apparently at Hackney's urging (the student newspaper said that Kors, again serving as Penn's defender of free speech, called him and warned him that it would look very bad to prosecute a student for columns written in the newspaper), the Judicial Inquiry Office dropped its threat.*

Meanwhile, in protest against Pavlik, a group of black students confiscated and destroyed the entire pressrun of the *Daily Pennsylva-*

---

*The *Daily Pennsylvanian* in its accounts of this case reported that Catherine Schifter, the judicial inquiry officer who called Pavlik, denied offering to drop the charges if he would agree to a meeting with his accusers. But, the paper said, she "admitted telling Pavlik that if a meeting could be worked out, the deal would be 'very possible.' "

nian, arguing rather remarkably that Pavlik's columns were racial harassment while their action was a legitimate protest protected by the rules of free expression. That morning, when campus police noticed the theft of the newspaper being carried out, a few of the black students were arrested, a couple of them in handcuffs, and one, who physically resisted arrest, was struck by a policeman's baton, though not injured. The students were quickly released, but they claimed harassment at the hands of the police. President Hackney made a much-quoted statement: "Two important university values, diversity and open expression, appear to be in conflict." His remark played directly into the hands of critics and commentators who saw in it an acknowledgment that a double standard was in force. Racial diversity yes, ideological diversity no, seemed to be the implicit message.

The denouement of the newspaper theft provided powerful evidence of the existence of Penn's quite extraordinary effort to accommodate the diversity part of the picture, the sensitivity component over the free-expression component. Following the incident, Hackney, as the nominee for the NEH post, went before the Senate Labor Committee for his confirmation hearings. There, he denied press reports that no punishment of the black students was being contemplated. "That is a misperception," Hackney said. "Those students involved will face disciplinary procedures when they return to campus in the fall." Meanwhile, he created the Public Safety Task Force to look into the confiscation of the newspaper. Its members were named by the chief of the university police and by the vice-provost for university life, one of Penn's most visible pro-diversity advocates. It issued its findings the very day after Hackney was approved by the Labor Committee by a vote of 17 to 0. The report left the question of discipline to the Judicial Inquiry Office to determine. Meanwhile, it said that the university police, dispatched to the three sites where the paper was being confiscated, should have known that the action was "a form of student protest and not an indicator of criminal behavior." The report agreed with the black group that their treatment at the hands of the police amounted to harassment.

The Public Safety Task Force issued a three-day suspension, without pay, of the officer who had struck a student with his baton the morning the papers were stolen. It said that he had acted "unprofessionally." Other police officers received "written or oral warnings." The police, the report found, should have summoned open expression monitors, administrators who normally oversee student protest to make sure that the university's official *Open Expression Guidelines* are being observed. (As one student columnist observed, the "protest" took place at a time when these open expression monitors are at home sleeping, not at their desks drinking coffee.) The report recommended that the students who took the fourteen thousand copies of the *Daily Pennsylvanian* should be given copies of the university's *Confiscation of Publications on Campus Policy*. Henceforth, the report went on, the campus police should maintain data on handcuffed detainees, recording their race and sex and the reasons for their detention, and this data should be analyzed regularly "to determine if the policy has an adverse impact on any groups and if the policy is applied in a consistent, non-discriminatory manner."

In the fall, the Judicial Inquiry Office chose not to prosecute the black students who took the copies of the newspaper. And so the only people reprimanded for the theft of the newspapers were the police who apprehended the thieves. One can only speculate what the university's response would have been had the theft been carried out by white students and the objects stolen a black students' publication. Somehow, it seems highly unlikely that the Public Safety Task Force would have come to the conclusion it came to in the case that actually occurred. "What kind of message does this send to the University especially when we are told to respect the diversity of opinion that exists within our community?" the *Daily Pennsylvanian* asked in an editorial. "Whatever happened to stopping a crime while it occurs?"

" 'Keep Your Rosaries off Our Ovaries' and 'Hey Hey What D'ya Say, Born Again Bigots Go Away' and 'Spread Your Legs for Christ,'— Christians have to see these slogans on T-shirts all the time," said Alan Kors. "Moderate black students are taunted with being Uncle Toms or Oreos." There is no judicial punishment against those free expressions of opinion.

Penn, of course, is not the only place where diversity training becomes an exercise in the advancement of a radical political ideology. Indeed, I chose Penn because I thought it would prove to be fairly typical of the atmosphere prevailing on many university campuses these days, where overzealous diversity bureaucrats exercise their inclinations toward social engineering via 1960s-style group therapy. It is as if they want to transform the universities into successful versions of one of those rural communes that failed in the 1960s and 1970s. Diversity training reeks of the yearning for that place of perfect virtue where goodness reigns and the wicked get their comeuppance.

Certainly this seems to have been the case at another Ivy League institution a few hundred miles from Penn in the hilly country of New York State—Cornell, where the effort to mold the moral mind turned truly tyrannical.

You wouldn't call Timothy Gregory a conservative, certainly not a conservative ideologue. He is a medical student at the State University of New York who graduated from Cornell in 1992, a practicing Catholic from a working-class family in Erie, Pennsylvania, whose basic political position is infused with notions of tolerance and openness. He espouses support for gay rights; he believes in equal opportunity for all, regardless of race, creed, sex, or national origin. He is not a member of the WASP establishment. No silver spoon was in his mouth at birth. He is a dark-haired young man of medium height, modest in demeanor, polite, respectful of authority, a kind of average guy in many ways, certainly intelligent but not pyrotechnically so. There is a solidity to him, an aura of old-fashioned salt-of-the-earth reliability.

Tim Gregory seems, in short, a good candidate for the job he wanted in his junior and senior years at Cornell University, that of resident adviser in an undergraduate dormitory. In a family of five children, all of them having gone or preparing to go to college, he had to earn some money on his own to help his family send him to Cornell, where tuition plus room and board was, during his time there, around twenty-two thousand dollars a year.

And so Tim applied to be an RA, was accepted, and then, in August 1990, went to Ithaca for a nine-day session of training, repeating more or less the same procedure the following year when he got the RA job a second time. The training, which is a kind of sensitivity- and diversity-training course writ large, is required of all RAs. It began with sociable sundaes and a tie-dying party on a Thursday night; it included seminars on multiculturalism, sexual harassment, something called "Issues of Oppression," attitudes about homosexuality, and conflict mediation; it ended with a session on alcohol and drug abuse. Tim was somewhat surprised when he found himself quickly labeled, not, Tulin-style, as a member of a nontargeted group, but more simply and bluntly as a "privileged person." The others occupied various rungs on the ladder of the "oppressed," meaning gays and lesbians, the physically handicapped, all women and all members of racial minorities.

"In the first year, 1990," Tim recalled, "during the 'Intro to Multi-culturalism' workshop, we played a little game. First, we were broken up into groups, which were in turn subdivided into two other groups, group A and group B. Group A forms a tight little circle and does not allow in members of group B. Then the people in group B are asked to say how it felt to be excluded.

"In the second year this was even more obvious. Everybody lined up for a game of Simon Says. The leader would say, 'All whites take two steps forward; all people of color take two steps back; white men take one step forward; gay blacks take one step back. White men take one step forward; white women one step back; black women two steps back.' Then they would say, 'This is how things work. The privileged people advance to the front of the line; people of color are in back.' "

Tim had qualms about the underlying ideology of RA training, this determination of everything by group categories. He was no doubt aware, for example, that there were black kids at Cornell who came from families far wealthier than his, who went to exclusive prep schools whose interior he had never seen, so the phyla "oppressed" and "privileged" seemed a bit obsolescent to him, to represent a schema that no longer existed in American society. That, of course, is a matter that could be discussed. What Tim soon learned at Cornell RA training is that there is no discussion, at least not of that subject, and that is what particularly upset a young student who expected that at a great American university a full airing of views, genuine debate in an atmosphere free of belligerence and coercion, would be the very lifeblood. In fact, on the sensitive subjects, opinions different from those of the trainers were not tolerated. Resident-life training at Cornell, like so much of multiculturalism in practice, proclaims the richness of difference when difference is a matter of race, sex, and sexual preference, but suppresses difference of opinion. Tim knew, however, that he had to pass muster with the sessions' leaders in order to get the RA job, so he rarely voiced his misgivings.

Once during the "Issues of Oppression" workshop, a fellow trainee (she happened to be black) asserted, as Tim remembered it, that white men have life handed to them on a "silver platter." They just "slide down the glistening sidewalk of life," she said. Tim responded to this. He did not mean to downplay the disadvantages of people of color, he said, but he came from a rural part of Pennsylvania where many white people lived lives of dire poverty, so it did not seem to him that all whites automatically have lives of great privilege and ease.

"I was screamed at so severely by the other RAs and RHDs [resident hall directors] for espousing such 'racist' views that I almost quit on the spot," Tim said. Later that same day, he attended a small-group session with other trainees where he was required to explain why he had made his offensive comment. During that conversation fellow trainees made some dubious remarks. One criticized the decision made by the New York City St. Patrick's Day Parade to exclude gays, saying of the parade bosses, "They're just a bunch of drunken Irish anyway." Tim is of Irish descent. Another student said that white males had no culture.

"The double standard is so blatant," Tim said. "If an 'oppressed person' says something offensive to somebody in a privileged group it's just a reflection of his plight. But if I say something that is construed to be offensive, I have to explain myself. And naturally if I'd said something like 'Blacks are just a bunch of stupid watermelon eaters' (not that I would want to say anything like that), I would definitely have been fired."

On the first Sunday of the training program Tim told his group leaders that he wanted to go to mass. He was told that he would not be allowed to go, since that would mean missing a training session. When he observed that his own diversity was not being recognized, he was told that his accusation was unfounded. "They said that they wouldn't be allowing anybody to go to services, because then they'd have to allow Muslims and Jews to go to services too, so I was being treated fairly because it was the same rule for everybody. I told them that in my religion it's considered a sin not to go to mass, but they said, 'You have to be at RA training and that's all there is to it.'

"That day was gay day," he continued, "and they brought in members of ZAP, which is the gay, lesbian, and bisexual group. They were very nice people," Tim said, "but in the end they showed us explicit sex movies, first one of lesbians and then one about gay men. The gay movie was really triple X. They showed everything, fellatio, oral-anal sex, mutual masturbation, and heavy wet kissing.

"While it was playing, two people went around taking pictures of the RAs' reactions." This apparently was done to examine facial expressions to make sure that nobody was harboring any homophobic squeamishness while watching the film. "One of the people taking pictures was an RHD who was a declared lesbian," Tim said. "The other was a programming assistant from one of the dorms. Afterwards we were asked what we thought of the movies. Now, I had been at a dorm for a couple of years at Cornell, so I knew about gay rights, but I didn't know that it was so in-your-face. I also couldn't understand that instead of going to church, I had to watch a movie that is against my religion. Any kind of pornography is against my religion, and I don't want to see it. Those were the sorts of things that were going through my mind, but I didn't say anything.

"My RHD was married," Tim said, giving an example of political correctness in action at Cornell, "and when another RHD who was a declared lesbian came into her apartment, she accused my RHD of heterosexism because she displayed pictures of herself and her husband. So my RHD took the pictures down."

This version of political correctness extends to other areas of what might be called traditional life. I have heard students say that in order to put a Christmas tree in the lobby of their college dormitory, they had to get signed statements from every dorm resident asserting that they had no objection. Tim was forbidden to put a MERRY CHRISTMAS sign on the outside of his door (though this order was countermanded after the prohibition got some publicity in a student newspaper). "In their opinion," he said, referring to the groups that run RA sensitivity training, "the Bible is a document that promotes wife beating and slavery. Marriage is on the way out, they say."

If corporate America offers what might be seen as courses in elementary sensitivity, sponsored by the likes of David Tulin and guided by Griggs Productions videotapes, the universities are arenas of advanced training, where sensitivity is instilled by sledgehammer. In corporate America, one suspects, some of the training is done as a legal formality to forestall lawsuits charging discrimination or holding the company responsible for sexual harassment. It is relatively anodyne, gentle, the stress not so much on cultural differences (though these are certainly present) as on the bottom line, the financial benefits of a diverse workplace.

In many universities, by contrast, sensitivity training is undertaken in earnest. And the earnestness, a natural trait of human beings of student age, is nourished by sympathetic faculty members and midlevel social-work bureaucrats who see the beatific visions of the 1960s simultaneously junked by society at large and embraced in those buffer zones known as institutions of higher learning. Meanwhile, in many places, no efforts to attenuate the rapier thrusts of ideology are made by administrators who live in fear that the black students or the feminists or the gay and lesbian group will occupy their offices, post a list of demands (one of which is frequently what is called mandatory racial-sensitivity training), and accuse the university of institutional racism or sexism, thereby drawing the attention of the newspapers and local television stations.

Sensitivity training is perhaps a small concession, given the pressures at the universities, and what many administrators seem to have done is allow this domain to be controlled by multiculturalist ideologues, whose assumptions are well represented in the written materials that are sometimes distributed as part of training. One widely used device was created by the American College Personnel Association and revised by Michael Whaley of Central Connecticut State University. It was, for example, given to Tim Gregory and his fellow RA trainees at Cornell. It is called the Identity Awareness Model and consists of a multipage questionnaire that each trainee is asked to fill out, only there are separate questionnaires for separate categories of people. One set of questions is called "Group Survey for Oppressed Persons" and the other "Group Survey for Privileged Persons." In each case, the trainees are asked to strongly agree, agree, disagree, or strongly disagree with twenty statements. For the "privileged persons" the statements include these:

- Our common history as Americans is what makes us all similar.
- I know that I have some prejudices against some oppressed persons and that is not always bad.
- I have been the victim of reverse discrimination.
- Discrimination that is based on race, sex and sexual orientation is a thing of the past.

Among the statements for the "oppressed groups" are:

- It is up to the oppressed group to define its own sense of identity.
- I have never been the victim of discrimination from a privileged group.

- I would not join any oppressed group organization that focused on totally oppressed group concerns.

Each of the responses that the student gives has a numerical equivalent. For example, if you agree with the statement "Our common history as Americans is what makes us all similar," you get a lower score than if you disagree with that statement. The tests thus provide a score that tells the "identity awareness" of each person; the higher the score, the more "aware" you are. An explanation consisting of several photocopied pages elaborates the stages of identity awareness. The score that the privileged persons receive on the "Group Survey for Privileged Persons" identifies their level of "sensitivity to their own identity and to the concerns of oppressed persons." It shows, in short, where each person is starting from and how far he has to go on the difficult course leading to enlightenment.

The explanation even provides a list of the standard beliefs and the kinds of things that people say at their particular stage of development. Privileged persons usually begin in the contact stage. At this primitive level of consciousness they have "a naive curiosity about culturally different people." Encountering somebody from a different group can be a "minor crisis." Privileged persons at this state naively "believe in the melting pot theory of assimilation." Those at this point on the darkening hill we all have to climb give themselves away by saying things like this:

- "When I talk to you, I don't think of you as black."
- "I don't care who you sleep with, but why do you have to wear it on your sleeve?"
- "Some of my best friends are Jewish."
- "Why are all the Hispanics sitting together at lunch?"

From this point, the privileged persons enter the disintegration stage, which marks a healthy disturbance of their ignorant complacency. For the first time they "acknowledge that prejudice and discrimination exist," and they are "forced to view themselves as members of a privileged group." (This is what Timothy Gregory refused to do when he suggested that maybe poor whites were not all that privileged after all.) From the disintegration stage it is an arduous climb to the reintegration stage, wherein "the person of privilege tends to focus on how they [sic] have been socialized in a world of privilege." At the fourth level the privileged person enters the pseudo-independence stage. Here, he/she "becomes interested in understanding racial, cultural and sexual orientation differences." Finally, at the summit of right thinking, is the autonomy stage, which is "characterized by the person becoming knowledgeable about racial, cultural and sexual orientation differences and similarities." At this stage, the truly good people "seek opportunities to involve themselves in cross-cultural interactions." In the spirit of Griggs Productions, they "value diversity" and they are "knowledgeable about cultural differences." They are likely to say things like:

- "I am actively involved in fighting racism."
- "I am a recovering sexist."
- "We're all members of the same global community."
- "Discrimination against any group has a negative impact on us all."

Whaley says that when the Identity Awareness Model first came into use, most of the privileged persons were in the first stage, namely the contact stage, and they move up from there. There is a parallel coming to awareness for the members of the oppressed groups at Cornell, who also receive a score based on their answers to the "Group Survey for Oppressed Persons." Here the progression is from the acceptance stage, which, Whaley said, is where most minority group members begin. It involves "limited self-awareness about differences and dependence on privileged groups for a sense of worth," up to the internalization stage, wherein "the New Identity is incorporated and the individual can renegotiate with those in privilege." The intermediate stages are called the resistance stage ("a significant event creates receptivity to a new identity") and the redefinition stage, involving "the destruction of the old identity and a glorification of the new identity."

During the gestation of this New Man or New Woman there are, as with privileged persons, certain statements that indicate the person's level of awareness. An oppressed person in the acceptance stage, for example, is prone to say things like "We're all just people," or "Women are superficial." In the resistance stage, a black person might say, "I've discovered that my being black makes a difference to whites," or someone might comment, "I met a man who was proud to be gay." "Black is beautiful" and "Only gay men can be sensitive" are statements associated with the redefinition stage. But once the nirvana of the internalization stage is reached, people make such wise statements as:

- "I can learn from both men and women."
- "I'll never change his mind and I can't control his attitude."
- "To be liberated as a black man I must confront my own sexism."

Can this be dismissed as the normal idealistic silliness of college students, encouraged by the legions of social workers and diversity facilitators and residence-life coordinators and social equity directors who earn their livelihood with this sort of thing? Should we perhaps even value such sensitivity training as a way of making people think about inequality, which, after all, does exist in our society, and thereby making them think about the practices and attitudes they have complacently taken for granted? After all, to be black in American society is, outside the arranged environments of the universities, more difficult than to be white, and whites are often unaware of the many ways that this is true. It is on this basis, of course, that the powerful drive to introduce students into the realities of American racism is promoted. And even if white students are forced to endure certain slights on the basis of their race, perhaps that will indeed make them more sensitive to the concerns of people of color.

Whaley avers that the use of the Identity Awareness Model has truly helped to promote understanding. It is, he says, "a nonjudgmental, intellectual way to address these issues, not hitting a lot of emotions and raw nerves as much."

Isn't it true, in any case, that in the past other ideas predominated at the universities, an unreflective patriotism, for example, or, alternatively, an exclusive white-male, private-club mentality, an exclusion of others achieved so effortlessly that it was not even seen as exclusion but merely the existence of the world the way it was? For Tim Gregory the nine-day orientation was only a brief passage. He did get the RA job. He did finish at Cornell and go on to medical school. And even if the RA training annoyed and dismayed him—not least because short shrift was given in training to other matters, such as dealing with severe depression, suicide attempts, illness, and academic failure, which he felt were more urgent and immediate problems for undergraduates than the evils of heterosexism—he held on privately to his views.

I doubt in any case that sensitivity training will have much effect on the dyed-in-the-wool insensitive. On relatively open-minded and tolerant people of the sort generally found at institutions of higher learning like Cornell, the procedure's aura of radical indoctrination could lead more to irritation than to the dissolution of antagonisms in some magical potion of mandatory goodness. Even if nobody ever died from a dose of sensitivity training, the method will have at best mixed results if it is deemed (and it is hard to deem it otherwise) an attempt, backed by the heavy artillery of political correctness, to foster an eccentric and dubious view of America as a matter of undebatable consensus.

University life in particular should be about discussion. Questions and opinions, especially provocative, controversial questions and opinions about other people's orthodoxies, should be asked and held with no intimidation from those given authority over students by the institution. Sensitivity training may be justified by the existence of racism, including racism on campus, but, as it is often practiced, it is the *dérapage* of a good idea.

And even if students find the world described to them strange and irrelevant, even if they repudiate the view of the world presented to them as the sole correct view from their very first day, the terms of the debate have been set, the language has been imposed, and, as the bearers of the new consciousness never tire of saying—and in this they are correct—to control the language is to hold power.

Chapter 4

NOTEBOOK

What is the value of an anecdote? People advocating one position in the ongoing culture wars accuse their critics of circulating the same few stories and falsely proclaiming that they make concrete an otherwise abstract description of American life. An incident of racism is all that is needed for the bearers of the New Consciousness to proclaim the inescapable iniquity of American life. At the same time, every outrage perpetrated in the name of the battle against racism and sexism is used to discredit the entire battle, rather than seen as an isolated instance of slippage, of excessive zeal in a good cause.

A list of instances of that slippage is offered below in the theory that, unlike the anecdotes told and retold by the fervent advocates of multiculturalism, they are not isolated episodes, not aberrations, but reveal an essential element of the *dérapage*. At the very least, they show the tendency of the politically correct to lurch into a kind of goody-goody ridiculousness. At worst, they show a movement of good intentions torn from its rootedness in the moral sense and becoming a grab for power.

Jacques Derrida, the French philosopher who is the founding father of deconstruction, has talked of the exterminating gesture, the attack that does not point out a fault lying among virtues but, in the interests of a superseding virtue, aims at total destruction. The exterminating gesture can come from any part of the political spectrum, and, certainly, in American history, it has more often come from the right than the left. These gestures still do come from the right, but more and more they come from the quarters that most suffered from them in the past. That is the collective moral of the stories that follow. It is not to demonstrate that political correctness is a worse problem than discrimination or prejudice, but to show that the movement of liberal minds that led the fight against those evils is in danger of being captured by the very forces of intolerance of difference and narrow-mindedness that were once the preserve of the racist and sexist right.

Guilty If Charged

In the fall of 1993, the administration of the University of New Hampshire in Portsmouth put up a series of five dramatically large posters that spelled out five isms against which war would be waged. SEXISM HAS NO PLACE AT UNH, one poster said. That was the headline. Underneath it was the entirely praiseworthy sentiment: "We seek not only to be a diverse community but a caring one." And then beneath that in boldface print was some instruction in caring: "Tell someone. File a complaint," the poster urged, providing telephone numbers by which students and faculty could inform on their colleagues and peers. Other posters of exactly the same format urged combat against racism, homophobia, discrimination, and religious persecution.

Needless to say, none of these evils should have a place at the University of New Hampshire or anyplace else. And yet, to some at UNH, the advertisements seemed just a mite Big Brotherish, a tad fanatical in their urging members of the university community to rat on others. The posters came at the same time as a campaign, led by the university's Affirmative Action Office, to have the faculty adopt one of the more draconian speech codes in the country—deliberations over which were still going on at this writing. The code would have banned any speech that "disparaged" persons on the basis of their race, sex, religion, or sexual orientation. At one point in the debate, a physics professor, Chris Balling, who opposed the code on the grounds that it would likely punish merely unpopular speech, asked the head of the Affirmative Action Office, Chris Burns-DiBiasio, for an example of the kind of thing that the code would punish.

"In the classroom," Burns-DiBiasio said, "a faculty member repeatedly comments that women are not cut out to be scientists because they do not have the motivation to succeed as men do." Balling's belief is that such a comment, while he would not be inclined to make it, would be an expression of opinion, not harassment. "The fact is," he told me, "there are very few women in physics, so one could say, 'Women just can't do physics,' but if I did say that, I could be brought up on harassment charges."

All of this is by way of background, an effort to make explicable the otherwise inexplicable story of J. Donald Silva, a tenured English professor of thirty years' standing at UNH and, as it happens, the pastor of the Congregationalist church on Great Island, near Portsmouth, convicted of sexual harassment. It happened this way:

Early in the spring term of 1992, Silva, who teaches a course in technical writing for students in the two-year Thompson School of Life Science, made two questionable remarks. Explaining the concept of "focus," which he deemed important for a writer, Silva noticed in one class that, as he put it, "the students just weren't getting it." To capture their attention, he said, he would explain the concept using a sexual image.

"Focus is like sex," he said. "You zero in on your subject. You seek a target. You move from side to side. You close in on the subject. You bracket the subject and center on it. Focus connects experience and language. You and the subject become one."

A couple of days later, he was explaining the concept of simile to the same class. Long ago, it happens, he had read, of all things, a booklet on belly dancing, and for years he had been using a line from that booklet as his example: "Belly dancing is like Jell-O on a plate with a vibrator under the plate," he said.

Some women students took serious offense at these two remarks, saying such sexual references made them extremely uncomfortable. A few of them went to a class taught by a faculty colleague of Silva's, Jerilee Zezula, the head of the animal science program at the Thompson School, and they told her what Silva had said. Zezula, according to her own notes of her meeting with the students, told them that they had a "legitimate complaint" and asked them "how far they wished to go with this." Almost within hours, eight women had filed formal "To Whom It May Concern" letters describing what they felt was Silva's offensive behavior, which they sent to Neil B. Lubow, the university's associate vice-president for academic affairs. The matter was quickly reported to the university's Sexual Harassment and Rape Prevention Program (SHARPP), a very active and prominent campus advocacy group created in 1988 by the administration, and one of whose several duties is to receive complaints of mistreatment from women on campus.

On March 3, five days after Silva's second classroom comment, an informal hearing was held in Lubow's office, at which Silva was confronted with the evidence of what now was being called sexual harassment, all of which was provided in the letters submitted by the eight female undergraduate students. The letters illustrate that the women were indeed angry at Silva, and perhaps with some reason. But they also show the way in which what might be called the normal offenses of everyday life are, in the hothouses of ideological aggrievement cultivated in our institutions of higher learning, transformed into acts of viciousness and criminality that must be handled, not by argument and discussion, but by unleashing the machinery of judicial vengeance. (The letters also show how much the students needed remedial writing instruction. They are riddled with mistakes, preserved intact in the citations that follow.)

One woman, Holly Alverson Woodhouse, who submitted three letters altogether over a period of ten months, said that she felt "degraded" by Silva's "vocabulary and insinuations" in class. "If he wants to make a point that we'll remember, certainly a Proffessor of English can find enough vocabulary to draw from without needing to use the visualizations he chooses," she wrote. Another of the women, Rachel Powers, said, "There is a border of what is tasteful and what is unacceptable and offensive Don since has greatly crossed this border."

Another student, Robyn Ferreira, recounts an argument she had with Silva immediately after his remarks in class, which she termed "very unappropriated and also very affending."

> Well then he went back to the bowl of jello and the vibrator and that he knew allot of people who used it to massage there muscles and that he was one of them. I told him that he was wacked because there are allot of other little massages their that do the same thing.

Some of the women accused Silva of harassment outside of class also, most of it occurring on what appears to be a single day in the library. Woodhouse, for example, recounts how she was there with Silva and several other students. One of them, Nicole Libbey, talked about getting started on an assignment and said, "I guess I'll jump on a computer before someone else does." Woodhouse reports: "Don Silva smiled and said, 'I'd like to see that!.' We all laughed a bit uneasily & wandered off."

Woodhouse goes on to say that later, still in the library, "I was on the floor in the card indexes looking up books. Don Silva stopped, saw me on my hands and knees pulling out a floor level card index. Kate & Nikki heard him say to me, 'You look like you've had a lot of experience on your knees.' " Silva, who does not deny having spoken to Woodhouse, remembers his words as: "You look like you've had a lot of experience doing that."

Two other students, Jamalyn Brown and Denise Kohler, wrote a joint complaint, accusing Silva, apparently, of implying that the two of them had a lesbian relationship. According to the students, Silva asked them, "How long have you two been together?" Silva remembers saying, "How long have you two known each other?"

Yet another letter is from Kimberly Austin. She and a male student overheard Silva administering a spelling test to a third student. "Myself and the male student went into his office and there heard him using sentences with Sexual Slants," Austin writes. "I don't remember the *exact* words. One out of every three sentences had a sexual slant."

Those were the reported actions of Silva, perhaps tasteless, certainly interpreted by the women as sexual double entendres, perhaps only the gestures of a middle-aged man doing nothing more insidious than trying to banter with his students, to be hip. But from the beginning, the UNH administration chose to see Silva's remarks in exactly the same way that the women students saw them, as unmistakably sexual in content and as instances of harassment. In March, Brian A. Giles, the dean of the Thompson School, who seems to have conducted no formal investigation of the charges, wrote a letter informing Silva that his "pattern of sexual remarks in and out of the classroom has created an intimidating, hostile, and offensive academic environment that has substantially interfered with [the students'] educational experience." The proposed punishment involved several things, most important that Silva undergo a year of "weekly counseling sessions" with a "professional psychotherapist approved by the university." Silva was also required to reimburse the university for $2,000 to cover the cost of setting up an alternative section of his course to accommodate the students who could no longer study with him. Finally, Silva was required to apologize, in writing, "for creating a hostile and offensive academic environment."

Silva told me that he was willing to apologize to the women for any offense he had given them, but he denied committing sexual harassment. Others at UNH reasoned that even if Silva had suffered a lapse of judgment in his remarks in class, those lapses had not created an "offensive learning environment" and should have been protected by Silva's academic freedom.

"What you have here," Balling said, "is a professor who probably exercised poor judgment in searching for a way to grab students' attention. I don't know anyone who doesn't think it was a mistake, but I don't see how one can construe it as sexual harassment. The classroom remarks were not directed specifically to the individuals who complained. He said them each once. He was not warned that these particular students took offense. He was just immediately hit by a formal harassment charge. Yet, to harass somebody you have to go at someone more than once, it has to be individually, and you have to know it is offensive and yet keep on doing it."

Certainly, several important details in the sexual harassment charges suggest that overzealousness was in the air. For example, the student who was going to jump on the computer, Nicole Libbey, was not the one who filed a complaint against Silva. Holly Woodhouse, who overheard Silva's comment to Libbey, reported it as an instance of harassment. As for Woodhouse's complaint regarding Silva's remark to her when she was on her knees at the card file, she acknowledges that she was informed of it by two other women; she did not hear it herself.

So too with Kimberly Austin's report of overhearing Silva's spelling test. The person who actually took the test did not complain about it. In addition, the male student who was with Austin at the time, Robert Wardleigh, testified at Silva's hearing later that he heard nothing with a "Sexual Slant." Yet nearly a year later, when a formal hearing took place, all three incidents remained prominent in what were called "findings of fact," the conclusion of the university apparently being that one can feel harassed even when the harasser is talking to somebody else.

Silva, despite this, rejected Giles's reprimand, and thus in June, Giles, who had still not conducted an investigation, suspended Silva, a tenured full professor, from teaching. The suspension was short-lived, because Silva appealed it to a faculty grievance committee, which found in his favor, forcing the university to reinstate him and to go through the formal procedure that exists when accusations of sexual harassment are concerned. The first step in this procedure involved a formal complaint from the women in Silva's class, seven of whom wrote to Lubow in November 1992:

"In light of the seriousness of the initial offense and his behavior since then, we would like to see Mr. Silva's position and tenure at UNH terminated," the women wrote, adding a demand that they seem to have taken directly out of the multiculturalist bureaucrat's handbook. "We feel it is imperative that the University implement mandatory Sexual Harassment/Assault education for all incoming students, not just freshmen, as well as for all faculty."

The main event of the university's procedure is a hearing before a sexual harassment hearing panel, whose five members are chosen and trained by Burns-DiBiasio of the Affirmative Action Office, the same person who led the administration's effort to draft a new, expanded policy on harassment the spring following the Silva affair. Burns-DiBiasio is recognizable as an example of a new type of specialist at many universities. She has never been a member of a faculty but has made a career in what she calls "equity issues," meaning, she told me, explaining and implementing Title VII and Title IX of the Civil Rights Act, the provisions involving discrimination and harassment. DiBiasio got a master's degree in education from Montana State University, worked on "equity issues" for the Department of Health, Education and Welfare during the Carter administration, and has headed the UNH Affirmative Action Office since its creation in 1989.

Burns-DiBiasio told me that she maintains a "pool of people," proposed to her informally by various campus organizations, from which harassment hearing panels will be chosen. She then chooses the specific members of each pool and presides over their training, which, she said, involves briefings on recent court cases and the current state of the law governing discrimination. In other words, a member of the same university administration that had already moved to suspend Silva from teaching prosecuted the case before a panel of five judges, chose those judges, and instructed them in the law.

The panel drawn together to hear Silva's case on February 2, 1993, involved two associate professors, a data analyst, and two undergraduate students. The chairperson was one of the students. At the hearing, the student complainants were represented by a SHARPP counselor, Jane Stapleton, who led each of them through a lengthy recitation of Silva's offenses. Lubow, Giles, and Zezula testified against Silva, even though none of them had ever actually witnessed anything that Silva was accused of doing. Five students, including

Libbey and Wardleigh, testified on Silva's behalf; another student, Danielle E. Foley, submitted a sworn statement describing Silva as a "thoughtful lecturer" who "makes a point of speaking with his students in an informal and pleasant manner" and who never "conducted himself in a manner that could in any way be construed as sexually harassing." Nonetheless, the panel's written judgment was that "a reasonable female student would find Professor Silva's comments and his behavior to be offensive, intimidating and contributing to a hostile academic environment."

A few weeks later, an appeals board was convened, whose members, three from the faculty and two students, were appointed, again, by the same university administration that had already found against Silva. This second hearing was an emotional affair, lasting nearly thirteen hours, until about 1:00 a.m. on March 30. At one point, according to both Silva and Thomas Carnicelli, an English professor who served as his counsel during the appeal, one of the women, Kimberly Austin, who had overheard the questionable spelling test, suddenly pushed herself up from the table, heaved herself toward the door, and fell toward the floor. Another young woman supported her, and the two of them staggered out of the room together. At another point, Holly Woodhouse said that it's not your ordinary household that has a bowl of Jell-O and a vibrator. Silva—unwisely, perhaps—muttered "especially Jell-O" into Carnicelli's ear, his private remark surely the aggrieved sarcasm of a man who felt he was being persecuted and needed to vent his sense of the ridiculousness of it all. The representative of SHARPP, however, jumped to her feet and accused Silva of having said that every girl ought to have a vibrator. With that, several of the women complainants said they heard the same thing, and so did one of the members of the hearing panel. Carnicelli says that Silva spoke so softly that even he did not hear what Silva said. But the incident made it clear to him that the impulse to ferret out the sinfulness of every one of Silva's gestures was going to prevail over a commonsensical examination of the evidence.

The appeals panel found against Silva, citing him for "repeated and sustained comments and behavior of a sexual and otherwise intrusive nature [that] had the effect of creating a hostile and intimidating academic environment." The panel imposed a penalty more severe than the one specified in the university's initial reprimand. Not only was Silva required to "begin counseling sessions at his own expense, with a licensed and certified counselor selected by the University," he was also suspended without pay for "at least one year." His office and even the carrel assigned to him in the library were taken away.

How could so harsh a punishment be meted out for so ambiguous an offense? It is important to note that throughout all of this, there was not a single charge against Silva of physical contact with students, no invitations to cozy rendezvous with women after class, no fixed staring, no pubic hairs found on Coke cans (as in Anita Hill's famous accusations against Clarence Thomas). Nobody alleges that there was a single private encounter between Silva and any student, ever. In what they called their "findings of fact," the two hearing panels accepted the women's interpretations of Silva's words and actions as though the mere fact that the women felt the way they did was proof of harassment. There was no attempt to grapple with any of the underlying issues, particularly whether the two offending remarks made by Silva in class would be so disturbing to a "reasonable woman" that his academic freedom could justifiably be overridden.

I called several people in the UNH administration to try to find out how they justified their handling of the Silva case. Lubow, the associate vice-president for academic affairs, said that I should realize that the law's definition of sexual harassment specified that it could occur with mere words that created a "hostile environment," that action was not required. However, he said, he could not discuss the Silva case, much as he would like to, because the university policy forbade comment on disciplinary matters. Giles, the dean of the Thompson School, refused to discuss the Silva matter with me at all, referring me to the university's general counsel. This person, Ronald Rodgers, reiterated the university's confidentiality requirement. Burns-DiBiasio spoke to me about harassment in general but not much about the Silva case in particular. She did say that there were elements of the Silva case that I apparently did not know about, specifically a problem with Silva's behavior in the past, which is what led to the harshness of the penalty levied against him.

Burns-DiBiasio would not say what these earlier misdeeds on Silva's part had been, but Silva himself had already told me that in 1990, four women had complained against him for telling sexual stories and making racist remarks in class. In a speech class, giving an example of rhythm and cadence in poetry, he had read aloud Vachel Lindsay's "The Congo," which by today's standards could certainly be seen as a racist poem. Another time, he made a joking reference to an Ann Landers column about a man who tied his wife to the bed and then knocked himself out playing Batman in an effort to leap to her from atop the dresser. Upbraided by Giles at the time, Silva apologized to the entire class for any offense that he had given. That may have been a mistake, since his decision not to contest the charges was treated as an admission of guilt, which became part of Silva's permanent record. Then, the university used his record to kick him out of the classroom.

And so the question remains: How could the "reasonable people" of the hearing panels have found Silva's behavior so egregious as to warrant suspension?

I don't know. Certainly it has to do with the rise of an intensely motivated bureaucratic clique whose methods, it is not too much to say, bear a chilling resemblance to those of true dictatorships. There was, for example, the idea that Silva should undergo psychotherapy, to be cured, as it were, of his sinfulness, as though to have a different vision of life and of language than the diversity bureaucracy were a mental disease. Need I mention that in the old Soviet Union, they used to send dissidents to psychiatric hospitals?

And then there was the secret nature of the judicial proceeding. Silva's livelihood was taken away for a year and his reputation was so badly damaged that it was hard to imagine him ever returning to UNH to teach, or, at the age of fifty-eight and with the label "sexual harasser" attached to him, ever getting a job anyplace else. He was not just penalized for his foolishness; he was destroyed for it, at an institution that, according to those posters, wants to be "not just a diverse community but a caring one." And how was this destruction effected? Silva was not allowed to have a lawyer representing him. He was not judged by a group chosen by his peers. He was put on trial in what amounted to a kangaroo court, in secret. Was that secrecy to protect him, as the university maintains, or was it to shield the upholders of virtue from public scrutiny?

"The meaning of the Silva case," Carnicelli told me, "is not that a bunch of zealots got together and packed the hearing. The meaning to me is that a perfectly decent group of people, because of the climate, or the way they were trained, or something, made this incredibly unjust decision. Even the good people can't see clearly anymore."

Or, as Nicole Libbey, the student supposedly harassed by Silva but who actually served as a character witness for him during his two hearings, put it: "Those women who made the complaints have gone on to live their own lives, and they haven't been affected by this at all. But they practically ruined a man's life."

Censorship and Double Standards

In 1989 no issue more provoked the cognoscenti to talk than the decision by the National Endowment for the Arts (NEA), a government agency funded by Congress, to withdraw grants from a few artists whose work had been attacked as obscene or pornographic by conservative and religious members of American society. The grants in question, generally involving small sums, had been approved by the peer-review committees that are set up in each of the subdivisions of the arts and whose judgments had, until 1989, been more or less rubber-stamped by the NEA's executive board.

The artists, or the activities, denied grants tended to use sexual images and body fluids to get their points across. Most famously, there were the homoerotic photographs of Robert Mapplethorpe, one of which showed a self-portrait of the photographer himself with a bullwhip inserted into his anus; another showed one man urinating into the mouth of another.

A major object of attack from the conservatives—most important, Jesse Helms, Republican senator of North Carolina, supported by fundamentalist Christian groups like the American Family Association in Tupelo, Mississippi—was Andrés Serrano's *Piss Christ*, which depicted a crucifix immersed in what the artist said was his own urine. The performance artist Karen Finley, the beneficiary of previous grants, was deprived of the grant to which she had grown accustomed because she did things like smear chocolate pudding over her body to symbolize the degradation of women in American society. Another performance artist, Annie Sprinkle, who, among other things, used to invite members of the audience to examine her vagina with a gynecologist's instrument, was another artist commonly mentioned in the controversy.

In general, newspapers followed the lead of the artists themselves in declaring the withdrawal of the grants to be censorship. Newspapers like the Atlanta *Constitution*, *Newsday*, the Seattle *Times*, the Boston *Globe*, *USA Today*, and many others editorialized against restrictions on NEA funding. The proponents of restrictions were called "self-righteous windbags" who "argue that they know what is good for the rest of us to read, look at and listen to." Finley said that she felt she no longer lived in a free country. Artists made headlines turning down grants awarded *them* by the NEA. Universities debated doing the same thing, the idea being that the money had been morally tainted by the agency's censorious actions regarding certain others.

In other words, there was, as usual, no true debate but only posturing in America, and it is too bad, because the whole question of government funding for the arts raised difficult questions. There was the clash of two principles: the right of the artist to create freely and the right of taxpayers to protest when they see their money going for purposes that are offensive to them. But anybody who tried to grapple with the issues was soon obscured by all the others who were only pinning badges of political identity on their lapels, the right striving to score points with its constituency on the morality front, the left presenting itself as victimized by censorship and struggling for artistic freedom.

The NEA imbroglio provided a point of comparison when, three years later, there was a similar withdrawal of funds by another government agency, the National Institutes of Health. In 1992, the NIH, which is also funded by Congress, overturned a decision to subsidize a scientific conference on heredity and criminal behavior at the University of Maryland. The decision to give the money was made by the peer-review committee. But there were complaints from some, especially a psychologist from Maryland named Peter Breggin, that the conference was part of an insidious "Federal violence initiative" whose goal was to target blacks as the main instigators of genetically induced violence. The NIH's director, Bernadine P. Healy, citing "unanticipated sensitivity and validity issues," froze the funds. The conference was canceled.

The episode was fascinating because it was exactly parallel to the incident at the NEA. In both instances, grants were being withdrawn in contradiction of peer-review judgments, the committee in the NIH matter having praised the conference organizers for the "superb job" they had done in "assessing the underlying scientific, legal, ethical and public policy issues." In both cases, too, opposition had come from private citizens and groups, with some support from Congress— Jesse Helms in the NEA matter, members of the Black Congressional Caucus on the NIH. In one instance, alleged obscenity was the issue; in another it was racism. *The Chronicle of Higher Education*, a large-circulation weekly devoted to coverage of academic life, paraphrased one member of the Committee to Stop the Violence Initiative, founded by Dr. Breggin, as saying that the conference "would encourage the government to charge, try, and convict black people for being criminals before they have committed any crimes."

"It is clear racism," the committee member Samuel F. Yette said. "It is an effort to use public money for a genocidal effort against African-Americans."

In short, in both cases, opponents of a particular piece of government spending, both of them perhaps just a bit too touchy, had spoken out and succeeded in curtailing what was, to them, objectionable use of taxpayer money. There was one big difference between the two cases, however. The NEA controversy brought loud cries of censorship and denunciations of the opponents of the NEA as troglodytes. There were a few voices who saw in the NIH matter a similar, perhaps even worse, censorship of free scientific inquiry. *The New Republic*, the Washington *Times*, and the Hartford *Courant* all felt that consistency required being disturbed about both instances. But, in general, the same press that had turned the NEA matter into one of the big stories of the year passed by the NIH issue with nary a whisper.

I asked a number of editorial-page editors of newspapers that had spoken out harshly on the NEA why they said nothing on the NIH.

"As to why we editorialized on [the NEA] and not NIH," said Mindy Cameron of the Seattle *Times*, "it was unconscious, and that's what makes it interesting." She continued: "Maybe we are much more comfortable and much more conversant about issues relating to the arts and to censorship than to matters of science."

Tom Benet of the San Francisco *Chronicle*, asked why his newspaper said nothing about the NIH incident, said: "I honestly don't know why we didn't. I honestly don't. We discuss a great many issues. I have a feeling it may have come up, but I can't put my finger on it."

"That was last month?" asked Loretta McLaughlin of the Boston *Globe*, when asked why her newspaper had not editorialized about the NIH. "I can tell you why," she went on. "We've been very short of staff." She continued: "The issue was only raised peripherally."

At *USA Today*, Karen Jurgensen explained: "I wasn't here during the NEA controversy, and NIH didn't come up."

In fact, neither case involved censorship. Nobody has a right to a government grant to express themselves or to discuss scientific matters, while taxpayers do have the right to protest when public money is used for purposes they do not like. Despite what sounded like evasion of the issue by the editorial writers, the reason for the difference in approach is easy to figure out. The NIH case involved the extraordinary force of the accusation of racism, even though the charge was untrue. There is and never was any "violence initiative" as described by Dr. Breggin and his allies, no plan to arrest black people before they commit crimes, no public money being used for a "genocidal effort." A paranoid accusation was enough to force the government to "censor" scientists, and, in contrast to the attempt to "censor" artists, almost nobody complained.

There is another big difference in the two cases. The conference on genetics and crime was canceled for lack of funds. That effort at scientific inquiry and exchange was indeed stopped dead in its tracks. Meanwhile, the artists whose work was "censored" by the NEA became celebrities; the prices of their photographs soared; they became folk heroes, champions of free expression; their performances—for example, Karen Finley's two-night show at Lincoln Center's Serious Fun Festival in New York—were sold out.

In American society, it seems, to be accused of pornography only enhances your reputation; to be accused of racism, even falsely, ends the discussion.

Virtue at the U of Penn

Also accused of racism was Murray Dolfman of the University of Pennsylvania, a senior lecturer in legal studies who, until he got caught in the nasty gears of racial politics, had taught for twenty-two years without untoward incident, indeed, with what one investigating commission called "uniformly outstanding" evaluations from students.

In fact, the accusations of racism against Professor Dolfman only took place after a strange delay. On February 13, 1985, an angry rally of black students at Penn was held to denounce him for an allegedly racist statement he had made the previous November, three months before. Despite the unexplained delay, the statement seemed extremely offensive. Dolfman, the accusation went, harassed and insulted black students in his class by using the term "ex-slaves" to refer to them during a session on constitutional law.

The news of Dolfman's amazingly clumsy alleged remark convulsed the campus for weeks. There was a series of protests by the Black Student League, a petition signed by 109 black faculty and administrators, an eight-hour vigil held on the lawn in front of the house of the university's president, Sheldon Hackney. Hackney, along with Provost Thomas Erlich, met several times with students from the Black Student League, and, after that, they joined with the Wharton School dean, Russell E. Palmer, and the chairman of the legal studies department, Frederick Kemprin, to "reprimand" Dolfman. Hackney called for an investigation into the charges and began asking deans to promote "discussions of racial concerns."

Meanwhile, about two hundred black students disrupted a large lecture class that Dolfman was teaching. When he tried to move to a different lecture room, the students disrupted that class as well. Such action is specifically forbidden by the university's code of conduct. But rather than punish or even reprimand the black students, Hackney summoned Dolfman to his office. "We discussed the whole incident, and he said to me, 'I want you to write something up that we can use in the form of an apology,'" Dolfman told me later. "So I went back to my office and wrote up something. There was a second meeting a couple hours later. He asked me not to talk to the press or anyone about it. 'We'll keep it in the university.' A few days later, my sisters in Miami and Los Angeles are reading about the incident in their local papers."

On February 18, Hackney released a statement informing the student body that in a direct talk with Dolfman he had "emphasized the seriousness with which I regarded the incident in his class" and told him that "a public apology from him was in order." Dolfman's apology was appended to Hackney's statement.

It might seem odd that the president of a great Ivy League institution would ask for an apology even before receiving the results of an investigation that he himself ordered. The fact is that pressures on campus were intense, and Hackney must have feared an explosion of unrest if he didn't slake some of the thirst for revenge against the egregious Dolfman. The Black Student League, encouraged by faculty members, had presented a list of demands to the university administration, and Hackney was apparently trying to give the impression of doing something while not acceding to everything right away. The demands were the dismissal of Dolfman; mandatory racism-awareness workshops, university-wide; an increase in hiring of black faculty.

The administration did not fire Dolfman—at least, not right away. But it kept up the concessions. *Almanac*, the university's official newsletter, reports that within one week of the first student demonstrations, a special Council of Deans agreed to sponsor what were called awareness programs. Hackney "offered his 1985–86 lecture series as a forum for issues of race and ethnicity." The president, in a public letter of February 21, said "we are grateful" to the students who had "brought forward sharply and clearly a number of real concerns on this campus." Hackney did not mention the black students' disruption of Dolfman's class as something to be grateful for. Meanwhile, Erlich, the provost, publicly declared of the Dolfman affair: "The remarks that were attributed were wholly inappropriate." One student quoted in the school newspaper said that Dolfman was not only racist, he was sexist as well, though the student gave no particulars.

Still, the students and their faculty backers remained unsatisfied. A delegation from the Black Student League stormed out of a meeting with President Hackney and other senior administrators because their demand for Dolfman's immediate dismissal was not being met. The next day, about two hundred students occupied Hackney's office for an hour or so to protest the administration's "insensitivity to student demands." Dolfman's remarks, the students said, were "the latest in an unrelenting series of assaults on the self-esteem of black students. . . . There's been an attempt to convince us of our inferiority." Word circulated around campus that Dolfman had repeatedly called black students ex-slaves. In fact, it was a renewal of that offensive behavior that, students said, had produced the round of protest that February.

Outraged, Houston Baker, the well-known scholar of black literature, declared at a rally: "It seems a great deal of bullshit has occurred on this campus lately. We have people here who are unqualified to teach dogs let alone students and they ought to be instantly fired." On another occasion, Baker told students: "This is no longer just a black struggle. We are in the forefront because some asshole decided that his classroom is going to be turned into a cesspool." (The *Almanac*'s bowdlerized description of this event: "Dr. Houston Baker delivered and expanded on BFA's [Black Faculty Association's] February 20 statement, charging insensitivity among University leaders.")

Near the end of February, ten professors, including the chairman of the sociology department and the graduate chairperson of the Department of Religious Studies, signed a letter calling for Dolfman's suspension, with pay, pending an investigation. About a month after the initial accusations, the university council, the group of faculty, administrators, and students that advise the president, took a straw vote on Dolfman. It was 15 to 4 in favor of requiring his immediate suspension. Robert E. Davies, the Benjamin Franklin and university professor of molecular biology and the person who proposed the vote, told the campus newspaper that, though the charges should be investigated, Dolfman's actions were serious enough to warrant suspension.

"I believe in due process," Professor Davies said, "but it doesn't mean you cannot take immediate action."

There are those, of course, who believe that due process means exactly that you cannot take immediate action. Due process means that you need, for example, to make sure that an accusation is correct before taking immediate action, normally by giving the accused a chance to defend himself before his accusers, rather than allow a lynch mob to take the law into its own hands. But UPenn had nobody to stand up to the mob. The constituted authorities, instead, appeased it. Indeed, hardly anybody at Penn—there were one or two exceptions—seemed to find anything at all amiss in the incident, except for Dolfman's alleged behavior. Nobody, not even Professor Davies, the proponent of immediate action, asked why there had been a three-month delay between Dolfman's alleged remarks about "ex-slaves" and the first public complaints about them. If Dolfman's behavior had been so utterly heinous, so "wholly inappropriate," why had the Black Student League waited so long to complain about his "haranguing and harassing"?

Come to think of it, did Dolfman actually make the remarks attributed to him? What was the context? What, exactly, would he have meant? Their conspicuously political handling of the matter did not allow President Hackney and Provost Erlich, or Dean Palmer and Chairman Kemprin, along with Professors Davies and Baker and the various others demanding Dolfman's suspension, to investigate the charges, to talk to other students in the class and to Dolfman himself before "reprimanding" him or calling for his immediate dismissal. These questions became—or, more properly, should have become—more pertinent when, finally, on March 28, 1985, the Wharton School Committee on Academic Freedom and Responsibility issued the report of its investigation into Dolfman's actions in class.

The report affirmed that in his twenty-two consecutive one-year teaching appointments, Dolfman's course evaluations could not have been better, that he "has been and remains an extremely popular teacher," and that "competition has been keen among students to get into Mr. Dolfman's sections of a course that is regularly taught by other professors." The report also indicated something about Dolfman's teaching style. He "routinely singles out students for questioning and often asks them to repeat recitations or readings." The report said there was no evidence that Dolfman had referred to black students in his class as "ex-slaves" except on that one occasion in November 1984.

As for that incident, the report said this: "Mr. Dolfman asked the class what Constitutional Amendment related to the concept of involuntary servitude. There was no response. Mr. Dolfman observed that if anyone should know the answer, it would be the black students. He then asked the black students in the class, individually and seriatim, if they could recite the 13th amendment. When none could do so, Mr. Dolfman asked one black student to stand and read the amendment out loud.

"Mr. Dolfman then expressed surprise that while he, as a Jew and a 'former slave,' celebrated Passover, the black students, whom he likewise called 'former slaves,' or 'ex-slaves,' did not celebrate the passage of the 13th amendment."

So, for the first time, it became clear what had happened. Dolfman did, no doubt, single out black students for special attention in that particular class, and that could certainly be seen as a lapse of judgment. But the report also makes clear that Dolfman had, as it were, made common cause with the black students by referring to himself and to them as "former slaves" or "ex-slaves"; second, he routinely does with other students what he did that day with the black students; third, he only used the phrase "ex-slaves" once; fourth, when approached by several black students immediately after that one time, he had recognized his indiscretion and apologized for it on the spot—and was no doubt surprised that the demand for his dismissal only came three months later.

The outcome: Dolfman was suspended by Dean Palmer for one semester, his return to the university conditional on his attending what were called "sensitivity and racial awareness sessions," after which he would be on probation, with "appropriate monitoring by the Legal Studies Department." President Hackney commended the dean for his decision, terming it "fair in substance," and concurring in Palmer's finding that "this conduct by Mr. Dolfman was not acceptable and must not be allowed to continue."

The moral of the story: in the era of political correctness and craven university administrations, the charge of racism, unsubstantiated but accompanied by a few demonstrations and angry rhetorical perorations, suffices to paralyze a campus, to destroy a reputation, and to compel an administration into submission.

Whatever happened to:

• Houston Baker, who spoke against Dolfman at student rallies? He was soon thereafter named to the search committee for a new dean; he then became head of a brand-new Center for the Study of Black Literature and Culture; in 1991, he was elected president of the Modern Language Association. In 1993, he was appointed to the search committee for a new president of the university.

• Robert E. Davies, who demanded Dolfman's suspension before there was an investigation? He became chairman of the faculty senate. When he died in the spring of 1993, he was eulogized as a champion of free speech and academic freedom.

• Provost Thomas Erlich? He became the chancellor of Indiana University in 1992.

• Sheldon Hackney, who stood by as a member of his faculty was smeared, vilified, and suspended, and who failed to protect his academic freedom? He was named chairman of the National Endowment for the Humanities by President Clinton in 1993 and confirmed by the Senate in that post by a vote of 77 to 22.

• Murray Dolfman? He finished his suspension and his racial-awareness and sensitivity seminar and returned to the classroom at Penn. In 1992 when his seven-year contract expired, the Wharton School, citing budgetary reasons, opted not to renew it. In such a way did Dolfman's career at Penn come to an end after twenty-nine years of distinguished teaching. He is practicing law in Philadelphia.

Wellesley Shows How It's Done

It is a commonplace of Afrocentrism, as that view is propagated across the country, that Western civilization was stolen from Africa by the Greeks. I first heard this eccentric idea in 1987 when I was covering a debate at Stanford University over a proposed elimination of a mandatory freshman program on Western civilization and its replacement by a kind of global-studies approach stressing the works of "women, minorities and people of color." I was interviewing the head of the Black Students' Association at Stanford, who told me that the failure to teach certain subjects was racist. I asked him for examples of the things not being taught.

"Well," he replied, "for example, if in ancient history courses they don't teach how Plato and Aristotle got a lot of their ideas from Africa, that's racist."

"Plato and Aristotle got a lot of their ideas from Africa?" I asked. I was assured by the young man that such was indeed the case.

Unknown to me at the time, there was already a well-developed cottage industry, a chief product of which is the theft of Western civilization from Africa.* In April 1993, for example, Mary Lefkowitz, the Andrew W. Mellon professor in the humanities at Wellesley College, wrote in the *Wall Street Journal* of a speech given at Wellesley by Yosef A. ben-Jochannan, a leading Afrocentrist writer. The occasion was the annual Martin Luther King, Jr., Memorial Lecture. Lefkowitz is a distinguished scholar of the ancient world. She reported that ben-Jochannan "assured his young audience that Greek civilization dates from only 1000 B.C." Ben-Jochannan, Lefkowitz went on, argued that Socrates was a figment of Plato's imagination. Plato himself, ben-Jochannan said, studied in Egypt for eleven years, and he asserted that "Aristotle sacked the Library of Alexandria and stole his philosophy from the Egyptians."

Professor Lefkowitz has the expertise necessary to address these claims. Thus, she wrote: (1) that Greek-speaking peoples occupied the Greek mainland for at least half a millennium before the date given by ben-Jochannan, (2) that Socrates is mentioned by several other contemporary writers, such as Aristophanes and Xenophon, so he could not have been an invention of Plato, (3) that it is "very unlikely" that Plato ever traveled to Egypt, (4) that the Library of Alexandria "was not built until after Aristotle's death and there is no evidence that Aristotle ever went to Egypt, much less stole his philosophy from there."†

Lefkowitz reported further: "When a colleague and I asked Mr. ben-Jochannan to identify the ancient sources on which he based his assertions, he declined to answer. When we pointed out one or two errors of fact, he accused us of arrogance and insolence. One student apologized to the speaker for our rudeness and walked out. After the

---

*This will be dealt with more fully in Chapter 8.

†*Wall Street Journal*, Apr. 7, 1993, opinion page.

lecture, other students surrounded us, saying: 'You think you know the truth, but *he* is telling the truth. What you learned is wrong.' "

Lefkowitz is a tenured professor and not in any danger of losing her income whatever her position on Afrocentrism. Nonetheless, her arguments did cause her some grief. Well before her *Wall Street Journal* article she wrote a long piece detailing the Afrocentrists' errors of fact in *The New Republic*, for which she was criticized by her dean, who argued that her article insulted another member of the faculty, Anthony Martin, who teaches the course Africans in Antiquity in Wellesley's Department of Africana Studies. Martin himself in a speech before the faculty senate accused Lefkowitz of persecuting him. Martin, as it turns out, taught a course on African-American history in which one of his texts was *The Secret Relationship Between Blacks and Jews*, published by the Historical Research Department of the Nation of Islam.

The Secret Relationship Between Blacks and Jews is well established in the canon erected by certain, thankfully small, black groups. It has been promoted by the rap-music star Ice-T as a book that everybody should read. I myself saw copies of it for sale at an Afrocentrists' conference I attended in Atlanta. It is carried around and proclaimed as the Previously Untold Truth by the likes of Khallid Mohammad as he does his college speaking tours. The book is a remarkable work of hate, which purports to prove, using "Jewish sources," that, for example, "the most prominent of the Jewish pilgrim fathers used kidnapped Black Africans disproportionately more than any other ethnic or religious group in New World history."

Jewish pilgrim fathers! Did they come over on the *Mayflower*?

"Though scattered throughout the globe by political, economic and religious circumstances," the book goes on to say of the Jews, "they would reunite later in an unholy coalition of kidnappers and slave makers." Columbus himself, the anonymous authors of this book write, "took a group of Jewish refugees with him to the New World" where Columbus's "brutality against and enslavement of the native population was financed by Jewish investors." Then: "The history books appear to have confused the word *Jews* for the word *jewels*. Queen Isabella's *jewels* had no part in the finance of Columbus's expedition, but her *Jews* did."

The authors of *Protocols of the Learned Elders of Zion* did not do better than this claptrap, which has been denounced by black scholars as well as white. Its appearance on a reading list at Wellesley College, one of the country's premier institutions of higher learning, spurred anger, especially among Jewish students, and considerable discussion around campus. Unlike the events at Penn, when some questionable words used in class led to a witch-hunt and an exorcism, the response of Wellesley to Professor Martin's presence was close to exemplary.

Martin himself wrote what he called *Broadside Number 1*, which he printed and distributed himself. He argued that *The Secret Relationship* "is an excellent study of Jewish involvement in the Transatlantic slave trade and African slavery." The persecution of blacks by Jews did not end with slavery, Martin wrote. He gave several examples of this, all on the paranoid side, including, for example, this nugget: "Ted Koppel and other Jews on ABC's Nightline program . . . hinted broadly to Mandela [during the visit of the South African leader Nelson Mandela to the United States] that he had better succumb to Jewish pressure or risk losing U.S. support."

Martin also attacked Mary Lefkowitz in *Broadside Number 1*. "Anti-semitism has also become a clever smoke screen for a burgeoning Jewish intolerance of truly Stalinist proportions," he wrote. He continued: "Last year my esteemed College colleague Mary Lefkowitz, Andrew Mellon professor (the same one who did not know that Herodotus had referred to the doctrine of the immortality of the soul; the same one who recently insulted our Martin Luther King, Jr., memorial speaker, Dr. Yosef ben-Jochannon, in the college chapel) launched into a sudden and unprovoked attack on my 'Africans in Antiquity' course.

"This type of mindless intolerance is clearly not acceptable. Despite their recent victories, Jews have nothing to gain in the long run from picking fights with an aroused and conscious African American population. They must realize that slavery has ended."

One is tempted to ask Houston Baker of Penn whether he, had he been at Wellesley, would have demanded the immediate dismissal of this person turning his classroom "into a cesspool," this person who isn't fit "to teach dogs." At Wellesley, normally a great citadel of political correctness, the administration and the students did the right thing. They fought offensive speech with the best weapon available— more speech. The chairman of the Africana studies department said that *The Secret History* is not worth the effort needed to read it, since the Jews' role in the slave trade was "too minimal." Whereas the Penn

Academic Council voted for the immediate ouster of Murray Dolfman (against whom the charges were false), the counterpart organization at Wellesley made a statement outlining the principles of academic freedom, saying that Professor Martin had the right to use whatever he saw fit in his classes, but those choices were subject to criticisms by others, and Martin violated the spirit of scholarly life when he responded to those criticisms by false and ad hominem attacks on the motives and character of the critics.

And so while charges of anti-Semitism against Martin would have been true had they been formally lodged, they were not in fact lodged. He continues to teach his course and, probably, to rant about the "mindless intolerance" of the Jews. One wonders nonetheless what would have happened if a white teacher at Wellesley were found using William Shockley's theories about the supposed intellectual inferiority of black people. There is no reason to believe that this person would not have received the same treatment at Wellesley as the offensive Professor Martin. Certainly, at other universities, those found guilty of incorrect positions on race or sex have not found their academic rights nearly as well protected.

A Philosophy of the Boudoir

Alison Jaggar is a leading feminist philosopher who teaches women's studies at the University of Colorado and was chair of the American Philosophical Association's Committee on the Status of Women in the Profession. She and several other women in philosophy, including Sandra Lee Bartky, a member of the committee, have for several years engaged in a war of words with a leading critic, Christina Hoff Sommers of Clark University in Massachusetts. In 1991, when *The Atlantic Monthly* was considering an article by Sommers critical of feminist philosophy, Bartky (whose "philosophy" is neatly summed up in her description of "that complex process whereby bisexual infants are transformed into male and female gender personalities, the one destined to command, the other destined to obey") wrote to the editors of *The Atlantic* to urge them not to use Sommers's article, but to commission one from her instead.

The Chronicle of Higher Education reported on Bartky's initiative, which she at first denied ever having taken. Confronted with the actual text of her letter to *The Atlantic*, Bartky had to admit that she had indeed tried to head off Sommers's piece. "I wouldn't want a nut case who thinks there wasn't a Holocaust to write about the Holocaust," she said by way of justification for her effort.

Sommers may be a nut case to Bartky. To others, she has been an effective critic, not just of feminist philosophy, which is devoted to the overall task of "making philosophy responsive to feminism," but to the legitimacy of that overall task itself. Feminism, she believes, is a political movement, not a scholarly one. Philosophy involves informed speculation about truth and is not to be manipulated to serve anybody's particular ends. At the very least, Sommers objects to the position taken by Jaggar that academic feminism is "the intellectual arm of the women's movement." Otherwise, Jaggar said, "we have betrayed our trust."

To Sommers the trust is betrayed when scholarship is subordinated to political purposes. Her skill and persistence in pressing this view has made her a kind of bête noire of the feminism establishment in philosophy, which, as in other areas of scholarship, is considerable. Once, in 1991, Sommers published a four-page letter in the *American Philosophical Association Proceedings* in which she accused the profession of "monitoring philosophical discourse in a manner that inhibits or silences dissent."

Sommers's accusations included, among others, the Bartky effort at *The Atlantic*. She mentioned a time when she and another philosopher had written articles containing opposing views on the family. The *APA Newsletter on Philosophy and Feminism*, which is distributed to all eight thousand APA members, published the other philosopher's article but not Sommers's rejoinder. Sommers concluded that "the dearth of dispassionate appraisals of basic feminist positions" is "due in part to the reluctance of skeptical philosophers to face the kind of ad hominem opprobrium and political censure that feminist philosophers too often mete out to their critics."

The response to this letter, which consisted almost entirely of denials that her accusations were true, gave a startling demonstration of just how accurate was her description of that "ad hominem opprobrium and political censure" that chills real debate. The *APA Proceedings*, in two issues, published a total of forty-four pages of responses to Sommers's letter, all but a few pages negative. Only in a third issue of the *APA Proceedings* did a few friends of Sommers come to her defense. Meanwhile there had been nearly forty-four pages of hostile responses to Sommers's letter, from writers who claimed that nobody did exactly what, in writing those letters, they were doing!

One of the letter writers (her letter alone was nine pages) was Jaggar. Jaggar and Sommers, as it happened, had clashed before. In 1991, *Forbes* magazine published an article by Dinesh D'Souza summarizing some of the positions that Jaggar had taken, these summaries apparently drawn from Sommers. Jaggar wrote a letter to the magazine complaining of the "distorting and misrepresenting" of her views and arguing that these "irresponsible attacks" against her in the *Forbes* article "exert a chilling effect on scholarship that challenges received opinions."

What Jaggar understands by the term "received opinions" remains unclear. What is not unclear is what Jaggar has said and written, despite what she claims to be distortions and misrepresentations of her views. Sommers's crystallization of Jaggar's writings were distilled down to a single sentence, namely that Jaggar "denounced the traditional nuclear family as a 'cornerstone of women's oppression' and anticipates scientific advances enabling men to carry fetuses in their bodies so that child-bearing responsibilities can be shared between the sexes."

This citation is important because it exposes the most intellectually vulnerable aspects of the radical feminist position, namely that it is (1) not just pro-woman but anti-male and (2) that it stems from a frustration with reality itself. The rage of the gender feminists, as it appears in this summary of Jaggar's writings, stems from the fact that the world was not made the way certain feminists would like for it to have been made, and they insist, damn it, that it is actually different. But could Jaggar really have talked about a sharing of childbearing responsibilities? Does she really see the traditional nuclear family as a "cornerstone of women's oppression"?

Jaggar's book, *Feminist Politics and Human Nature*, does indicate that she has written exactly what Sommers says she has written. It is a wonderful example of what the academic multiculturalists solemnly call the "new scholarship" that is so broadening the collective horizon.

"Socialist feminists," Jaggar writes in this work, "see this family structure as a cornerstone of women's oppression: it enforces women's dependence on men, it enforces heterosexuality and it imposes the prevailing masculine and feminine character structures on the next generation."

As for the biological requirement that women be the childbearers, with its implication that some degree of sex-role differentiation is embedded in nature itself, Jaggar writes: "The sexual division of labor

must be eliminated in every area of life . . . so men must participate
fully in childrearing and, so far as possible, in childbearing."

The difference between socialist feminists and plain liberals, Jaggar writes, lies in the aim of the former to go beyond "psychological
androgyny to a possible transformation of 'physical' human capacities,
some of which, until now, have been seen as biologically limited to
one sex. This transformation might even include the capacities for
insemination, for lactation and for gestation, so that, for instance, one
woman could inseminate another, so that men and nonparturitive
women could lactate and so that fertilized ova could get transplanted
into women's or even men's bodies."

Perfumed Pollution

Special note: Many people who attend the University or work at it
are seriously impaired by Environmental Illness. The large number
of pollutants, chemicals, sprays, perfumes, soaps, carcinogenic
agents, etc., affect immune systems to such a degree that many
are unable to function. Severe congestion, headaches, fatigue and
blackouts are frequent problems.

In classrooms such as ours, with no windows which open (!) and
only back doors through which fresh air can circulate, your awareness of this problem becomes especially critical. Minimizing the use
of strongly scented soaps, perfumes, etc., *really* helps folks.

—Introduction to Feminism, course description, Fall 1989,
University of California at Santa Cruz—which, it should be noted,
is set amid verdant and well-ventilated redwood groves
overlooking the Pacific Ocean

The Puritans at Nicolet High

The Nicolet High School district in suburban Milwaukee is one
of the nation's richest and most favored. In 1992, the Wisconsin
Association of School Boards suggested a sexual harassment policy for
the entire state, and Nicolet, with some small changes, adopted it.
The policy requires what the Nicolet school board calls an "inservice
on harassment" for every new employee plus "at least one harassment
inservice annually," presumably for all employees. The school board
decreed that any teacher, employee, or student at Nicolet High
School who engages in harassment or who attempts to retaliate against

anybody who has reported on harassment "is subject to immediate discipline, up to and including discharge or expulsion, as the case may be."

According to the code adopted by the school board, harassment at Nicolet "can include, but is not limited to" such obvious forms of behavior as "physical or mental abuse" and "racial, ethnic or religious insults or slurs." Harassment is also defined as "requests for sexual favors used as a condition of employment or student evaluation." These are things the rules say can lead to discharge or dismissal, and who would argue with that? Any teacher or administrator who demands sexual favors as a condition of employment or good grades ought to be fired.

The definitions of harassment that can lead to discharge or dismissal include some other actions suggesting a certain *dérapage* in the formulation of the harassment policy, a skid—deriving, it would seem, from radical feminism—from a concern with genuine harassment to a labeling of practically any sexual interest as illegitimate, including:

- unwelcome sexual advances or touching.
- sexual comments, jokes, stories, or innuendoes.
- referring to another person as a girl, hunk, doll, babe or honey.
- intentionally standing close or brushing up against another person.
- inappropriate staring.
- asking personal questions about another person's sexual life.
- repeatedly asking out a person who has stated that he or she is not interested.

The Puritans at the Modern Language Association

Much has been said about sexual harassment against women, and much has been done to combat it. The 1991 summer newsletter of the Modern Language Association reported that the Committee on the Status of Women in the Profession has discovered a new offense— not harassment of women, but what the MLA called "anti-feminist harassment," that is, special forms of harassment that target not all women but only feminist women.

"Anti-feminist harassment is on the increase," the newsletter said. "Threatening and intimidating behavior by teachers, students and other academic workers leads to censorship and self-censorship of feminists." The specific offenses are as follows:

- Easy dismissal of feminist writers, journals, and presses
- Automatic deprecation of feminist work as "narrow," "partisan," and "lacking in rigor" (Goodness! What reasonable person could find anything partisan in feminist writing?)
- Heckling of feminists at conferences and in classes
- Malicious humor directed against feminists
- Racist, sexist, and homophobic slurs directed against feminists
- Defacement of feminist books, posters, and offices
- Physical threats

The MLA newsletter gave no figures on the frequency of such things as malicious humor, heckling incidents, book defacement, or physical threats, though, if my own experience at academic conferences is any guide, these things do not happen very often. Indeed, the MLA conventions that I have been to were saturated with feminism. Feminism of the doctrinal kind is like a religion at the MLA; it is the Dominant Discourse, the Hegemonic Ideology. It is hard to imagine anybody engaging in antifeminist harassment at the MLA. Still, the newsletter said that the Committee on the Status of Women in the Profession is concerned about these "escalating incidents of antifeminist harassment in the academy." It is planning a volume of essays: "Topics include an introductory historical overview of the current backlash; freedom-of-speech issues; sites of power; the publishing and reviewing process; destructive conflict within specific cultural or ethnic communities; prejudices that interlock with antifeminist harassment, such as racism, ageism and antilesbianism; women harassing women; and resources and strategies for change."

Legislating Diversity

In 1992, the board of directors of the National Association of Black Journalists (NABJ) made several decisions. It rejected Orlando, Florida, home of Disney World, as the site for its annual convention on the grounds, the group's secretary explained, that "there's a perception out there that Disney—from Japan around the world—is racist." It put the Voice of America on a list of government agencies, already including the CIA and FBI, banned from exhibiting at the convention job fair, because of the VOA's "similar history" of "misinformation."

When the *New York Times* ran an editorial on then mayor David Dinkins's need for help from all ethnic groups in New York and headlined it "No Black Magic in the Mayor," the NABJ protested the "insensitivity" of the headline, promoting an apology from the *Times*'s editorial-page editor. When a columnist for the Boston *Globe*, Mike Barnicle, a white man, said in print that he knew "more about being black, being under seige in this city than any other black writer or black TV person that you can name," the NABJ granted him its annual Thumbs Down Award, his remarks having been deemed "vain, arrogant and an insult to all of our members."

In short, the NABJ has a point of view, to which, of course, it is perfectly entitled and which is, indeed, not objectionable that I can see. It is the largest of several groups—others include the National Association of Hispanic Journalists, the Asian American Journalists Association, and the Gay and Lesbian Journalists' Association—whose purpose is to advance the interests of members of that particular group who are journalists, and to complain to newspapers when that group is portrayed in an offensive way. Most of the organizations have annual national conventions and job fairs, to which many major newspapers and broadcast stations send their recruiters, hopeful of finding talented young minority reporters to hire.

In 1991, the NABJ was invited to be on the Accrediting Committee for the American Council on Education in Journalism and Mass Communications (ACEJMC), which seven years earlier had adopted what came to be called a diversity standard—otherwise known as Standard 12—that all journalism schools need to meet in order to pass muster. The 1984 standard required the schools to "recruit, advise and retain minority students and minority and female faculty members and to include in the curriculum information for all students about contributions to journalism and mass communications made by minority and female practitioners from early America to the present." In 1991, eight of the twenty-three journalism programs investigated were found lacking in this regard; six others were given provisional accreditation for the same reason.

The following year, the diversity standard was supplemented so that the schools were now required to submit "written plans . . . on which to base their efforts to recruit, retain, and advance women and minorities" and to "document the number and percent of minority students currently enrolled."

The NABJ is doing what any lobbying and advocacy group does, and it does its job with energy and skill. The question is the extent to which its views become prevailing orthodoxy in a profession whose main stock-in-trade is critical distance from all advocacy groups. The idea that any accrediting agency should have a "diversity" standard is itself highly debatable. Indeed, this issue is being fiercely debated as other accrediting agencies have moved from advocating "diversity" to making it a condition for accreditation. The argument in favor of the diversity standard is, in essence, that institutions controlled by white males—even white males with the best of hearts—will reflexively and unconsciously perpetuate the patterns of the past unless they are made, somehow, to look hard beyond the groups they naturally feel most comfortable with.

The argument against the diversity standard is that it erodes intrinsic quality and worth by erecting rigid quotas—that it requires schools to make decisions not regardless of race or sex but because of some social engineer's beliefs about the proper racial and sexual representativeness of what is taught and by whom. Take, for example, that language about "contributions to journalism and mass communications made by minority and female practitioners from early America to the present." The diversity advocates will say that these contributions will be neglected unless a determined effort is made to bring them to light. The skeptics (and I am among them) will wonder if contributions will have to be exaggerated or invented and history thus rewritten in order to accommodate political desire. Similar arguments involve the diversity requirements in recruitment of students and in hiring of faculty, which could also be subordinated to politics at the expense of quality if the more radical diversity advocates have their way.

My own point of view is that a certain commonsensical approach could and should prevail. Special efforts to be more inclusive need to be made—and, indeed, given the faddishness of the diversity drive these days, it is not surprising that they are being made all across the country. It is when something called diversity is made a condition for accreditation that the fears of the skeptics are realized. Until Standard 12 was modified in 1992, the journalism program of at least one traditionally black college was denied accreditation because it did not have any whites on its faculty. The black college felt that its mission was to give the best education it could to its students and to hire the best teachers it could to that end, and if they all happened to be black, it would be their quality as teachers, not their blackness, that should count for accreditation. The same, of course, could apply to departments that had too few minority faculty. Indeed, what guarantee could the Accrediting Committee give that, in requiring some arbitrary racial balance, it would not actually reduce the quality of instruction, rather than improve it?

The point is that Standard 12 was put in to improve racial representativeness, a political goal that might or might not have educational value. Dubious as it was for the ACEJMC to adopt that standard in the first place, more dubious was its invitation to the lobbying and advocacy group NABJ, to play a formal role in the accreditation decisions. Both moves show the way in which the desire for more diverse news staffs actually plays out in practice. In the name of diversity, genuine diversity of opinion is discouraged, since any school that has nonorthodox views on racial preferences will, quite simply, not get accredited. At the same time, the tenets of ideological multiculturalism gain acceptance as fundamental principles by the very establishment that should be safeguarding journalism's independence.

When, for example, Standard 12 came under some criticism along the lines suggested above, Lee Stinnett, executive director of the American Society of Newspaper Editors (ASNE), publicly supported the standard. So did the American Society of Newspaper Editors, which is the national group to which the heads of most newspapers belong. In 1987, the ASNE board unanimously resolved to urge the Accrediting Committee "to faithfully examine, constantly monitor and strictly enforce the spirit and letter of Standard 12."

Whitemale

As a Jew and the son of poor immigrants, I am as aware as the next guy of the historic advantages held by white Protestant men. And yet, of course, things have been changing rapidly in the past twenty or thirty years. Take, for example, those former preserves of WASP power and prestige, Harvard and Stanford universities. The freshmen arriving at Harvard in September 1993 were 37 percent minority group members and 44.6 percent women. Across the country at Stanford, the numbers were 45.2 percent and 49.9 percent respectively. And the classes at Harvard and Stanford are as good an indication of the nature of the future overlapping directorate of the American elite as anything could be.

In fact, you would have to invent a whole new social calculus able to take into account all of the rapidly changing variables in order to figure out exactly who has how much advantage in American society today. This does not mean that whiteness and maleness are not advantages. But the picture here is very complicated. How many companies, universities, law firms, and newspapers are eager to promote blacks, women, and other minorities these days? And to what extent does that eagerness provide a comparative advantage over the historic advantages of white maleness? I have mentioned the Harvard Club, whose fine oil portraits suggest the era when some of the men in authority did not think that Jews, blacks, and other social or intellectual inferiors were suitable subjects for a Harvard education. Those portraits have such a fusty, obsolete quality to them. They come across like the advertisements of brand-new products you see in old magazines, looking now so old-fashioned that it seems kind of funny that these same products were once viewed as the height of style.

If organizations like the American Newspaper Publishers Association and the state university system of California have established formal goals for hiring so that the workforce will mirror the representation of each group in the society, then it is inevitable that minority group members and women will be treated unequally—that is, more favorably—than white men. Perhaps that is justified by the requirements of historical social justice. Most reasonable people, myself included, are willing to accept a degree of favoritism to black people and others who have been kept out in the past. The point is that this question of privilege and advantage is not easy to figure out these days. One study by the National Opinion Research Center in 1990 found that one in ten white men has been injured by affirmative action.* Sometimes the drive for redressment (and the moral absolution that comes with it) is stated with refreshing candor. In 1993, seventy-five supervisors in New York's Human Resources Administration were passed over for promotion because they were, one official was quoted as saying, "too white and too male."

And yet precisely that deep collective guilt about the unequal legacy of history, that need for absolution, are largely responsible for

*Frederick R. Lynch, "Tales from an Oppressed Class," *Wall Street Journal*, November 11, 1991, Section A, page 12.

the acceptance of a new stereotype, even as stereotypes in general have never been more thoroughly and widely condemned. This is the stereotype of what is called the white male, sometimes spelled as a single word, "whitemale," suggesting a narrow-minded, uptight bigot, either of the Archie Bunker type or of the Harvard Club oil-portrait type. The very commonness of the expression "white male" suggests something almost biologically predetermined about this particular species, as though it were a zoological category. The trope, which would be correctly seen as an entirely malicious impulse if applied to any other racial or sexual category, is not innocent. It has no doubt fewer real consequences than other stereotypes, but it is a stereotype, and it is manufactured for the same reason as others—to serve as a weapon in racial and sexual combat.

Indeed, it is a remarkable proof of the explosive growth of multiculturalist ideology to see just how widely accepted this subspecies known as the white male has become, just how legitimate it is as a term of description and analysis. Its first major appearance to my knowledge was at those supposed domains of clear and serious thinking, the universities, where the derogatory term "dead white European males" emerged as a way of denigrating the geniuses of Western literature and philosophy. The works of the DWEMs were going to be balanced by what Stanford University called "works by women, minorities, and people of color."

The "dead white males" concept reached a conceptual apogee at Georgetown University, where the faculty decided to give a new literature course, English 112, the name White Male Writers. The justification, according to Valerie Babb, the assistant professor of English who originated the course, and providing a good illustration of the wishful thinking that passes for scholarly analysis these days, was: "This is just one small group within a large body of literature, so let's title it that. Just as we say Native American writers, just as we say black women writers, these are white male writers."

Certainly the "canon" of great works needed to be redefined, even if it is difficult to see the white-male contribution to literature as the products of "just one small group." How many eighteen-year-olds these days are really going to be turned on to the pleasures of high thought by reading Saint Thomas Aquinas? Still, there were many things that were objectionable in the formulation "dead white European male," not least of all the erroneous impression that the seminal figures of Western thought were, somehow, conservatives.

In fact they were the very figures of courage and rebellion against the received ideas who laid the groundwork for the demand for the inclusion of the Other that is so central to multicultural thinking.

A second fault was that the DWEMs were pictured in the same way as those famous stone megaliths of Easter Island staring out to sea—as Jacob Bronowski pointed out, what is impressive about them is not that they are big or that they must have been very difficult to transport to their particular positions, but that they are all the same. The third was the idea related to the attack on the DWEMs, which is that the curriculum needs an affirmative action component, too, with choices of "great" books made not regardless of the race or sex of the author but because of them.

These last two elements need each other. The idea that the creators of the canon were all pretty much the same, or that they shared the essential characteristic of their white maleness, was necessary for the idea that followed, namely that reading lists had to be ethnically, racially, and sexually representative, rather than based merely on pure brilliance. It's a good thing that basketball teams are not governed by the same criteria.

The point is that "white male" becomes synonymous with the hunger for power, with imperialism, with ruthless capitalist exploitation, while all others belong to the camp of the meek and the beautiful. The white male is the symbol of inclusion, while all others are, by definition, seeking to be included against white-male resistance. Hence, hiring policies based primarily on race or sex are justified without any thought to the variations that take place within each group. I myself, for example, would be quite happy to see a subcategory of the white male created, one that would differentiate white-ethnic males of immigrant parents from scions of the WASP establishment. Some white males have had it easy; they were practically born into their privileged positions. Others, many others, are just emerging from centuries of penury and discrimination themselves. They were born of parents who took in laundry so that they could go to the university. When they arrive there, having studied hard at their public high school, they find some black students whose parents were rich and sent them to Choate, and who then benefit from racial preferences that apply across the board to all nonwhites. Similar contrasts are evident between lower-class white males and upper-crust women, gays, lesbians, Hispanics, and Asians.

When the racial formulas inherent in multiculturalism are stated in too blatant a fashion, they are often, it is true, branded unacceptable or ridiculous, as when Professor Leonard Jeffries, chairman of the black studies department at the City College of New York, elaborates his theories about the "ice people" and the "sun people." The whites, he argues, were forged in the Ice Age and thus bred for cruelty and aggression; blacks come from tropical climes, which made them intuitive, loving, and nice (like Jeffries himself perhaps). These ideas, rejected when they come out of the mouth of a Jeffries, enter the mainstream when given a bit of faux scholarly gloss.

We have, in this regard, already met Professor Houston Baker of the University of Pennsylvania, he who led a part of the attack on his faculty colleague at Penn, Murray Dolfman. Baker, the director of the Center for the Study of Black Literature and Culture, and, for one glorious year, the president of the Modern Language Association, was invited once to speak at the Madison Center in Washington, D.C. Baker is one of those who has reduced the term "white male" to the single word "whitemale," as in: "What seems certain is that an unchallenged sense of global, Western, whitemale superiority, or beauty, or authority has 'had its chance,' and we are now engaged with the dynamics of the articulate ascendance of *others*."

Baker approvingly cites the play *The Slave*, by Amiri Baraka, for showing that "the introduction of love, truth, and beauty into the world has never been the preoccupation of white leaders and bosses of the West," whose goals have been "power, money, and lordship over subject peoples." It is "the newly emergent peoples" who are "attempting to show the hierarchical superiority of their beauty."

These "newly emergent peoples" moreover are all people but the whitemales, Baker says. They are, he specifies, "African-Americans, gay and lesbian spokespersons, Chicano and Chicana critics and artists, Asian-American theorists and activists, Latin American commentators, recent scholars of postcolonial discourse and postmodernism, and all others who are seriously interrogating formerly unquestioned Western hegemonic arrangements of knowledge and power."

Professor Baker's description of the world is not very convincing. It is true that the white leaders and the bosses of the West have not been preoccupied by truth and beauty. Neither have the leaders and bosses of the East, or of the South. Poets and painters, philosophers and scientists, of all colors and both sexes have shown their preoccupation with truth and beauty. This is not a preoccupation that is the monopoly of any one group. "Men are cruel, but Man is kind," said

Rabindranath Tagore. Still, because we feel kind of guilty and we sense that commentary like Baker's doesn't really do any harm, we let most of it pass unremarked, even though, on this point, Jeffries and Baker are intellectually pretty much the same.

At Columbia University in 1992, the comfortingly named Committee on Race, Religion, and Ethnicity, a group whose goal is to promote understanding and tolerance among the races, sponsored a workshop entitled "White Culture and White Identity." The suggestion that there is some definable white culture and white identity is probably defensible, even if the separate identities of white people are so diverse as to make very dubious any attempt to associate general personal qualities with whiteness. That did not stop the group at Columbia from agreeing with Baker by attributing a number of ignoble habits of mind to white people, who are prone

- to have negative stereotypes about others
- to take a paternalistic/patronizing attitude toward the targets of racism
- to secure what we can do for ourselves without concern for others who may have less than we do
- to blame the victims of racism/people of color for the realities of their lives

In other words, white people are selfish, uncaring, egotistical, paternalistic/patronizing, and inconsiderate. Well, no doubt some are.

What has become the normal use of the term "white male" suggests resentment, the belief, also contained in Baker's morphology of the historical world, that the white males have lorded it over the rest of us long enough, imposing their "point of view," their "structures of knowledge," their racist and sexist hegemony, all of which was somehow the work of a very small number of the members of this curious species. Typical of this was the speech of the headmaster of George School in Newtown, Pennsylvania, who declared to his youthful charges: "The country they're going to graduate to [sic] is no longer dominated by a few white males, and our students need to be equipped for that."

The idea here is that the world was created according to white-male specifications, and, as we become more diverse, that world will necessarily change, no doubt for the better. "We need to find new heroes and myths for our society," said Jose Rivera, author of the acclaimed play *Marisol*. "The God we know now is a right-wing white male corporate God in whose world racism, sexism and political injustice are rampant."

Or here is Marie-Claire King, a distinguished geneticist at Berkeley, proudly telling an interviewer that her mentoring was especially directed toward those whom Houston Baker would list among the Others. "I was in this business for years and years before I had a straight white male graduate student," she said.

The interesting thing would be to engage in a substitution of terms and ask whether a newspaper would even have published the quotation that would have resulted. If Jose Rivera had said that Africa worships the gods of superstition, tribal massacre, clitoridectomy, and Mobutu-ism and needs the civilizing influence of Western-style democracy, he would have had a hard time getting a hearing for his view. If Professor King had expressed a preference for heterosexual white males and an implicit disdain for the others, she would, rightly, have been branded a racist and a sexist.

Here is Roscoe C. Brown, president of the Bronx Community College and director of the Bronx Hall of Fame for Great Americans, a now somewhat-neglected monument that at a certain time attempted to enshrine the great figures of the country, and whose membership is, not surprisingly, given the actual facts of our history, far more white and male than otherwise.

"If it's a monument to anything, it's a monument to the sexism and racism of the elite white males who dominated in the first half of this century," Brown said, drawing no complaints with his automatic association of racism and sexism with white maleness. If Mr. Brown had been speaking of an African hall of fame, which had few women and no gays, and declared it to show the sexism and homophobia of the traditional African culture, he would have been clobbered.

Writing with Breast Milk

By writing with and about that which was once unmentionable— menstrual blood, breast milk, wombs, vaginas, the lips of the clitoris—woman's language writes the body. The woman's body, no longer idealized, conventionalized, as in men's writing, is apprehended in all its physical difference and is able to disrupt discourse as we know it. Personal and open, the language of woman . . . seeks to achieve the fluidity it writes about by making the meanings of words elusive.

—Temma F. Berg et al., eds.,
Engendering the Word:
Feminist Essays in Psychosexual Poetics

After all, didn't Renoir once say that he painted with his penis?

Women Profs

Equality of opportunity does not necessarily involve equality of result. The major newspapers often seem to forget this.

One Sunday in January 1993, for example, the *New York Times* published a page-one article entitled "Rare in Ivy League: Women Who Work As Full Professors." The article reported that only about 11.6 percent of full professors nationwide are women. Some major schools, like Harvard's dental school, have no women full professors at all (the article did acknowledge parenthetically that six women were currently on track for tenure). There is more at stake, the article said, than "the obvious issues of equity. . . . If minority students and women have trouble identifying with professors they may hesitate to consider becoming professors themselves, thereby prolonging the shortage." In fields like math and science, where women and minorities are particularly underrepresented, "their absence is seen as doubly troubling."

The newspaper gave several reasons for this unfortunate trend. Women are "worn down by subtle discrimination and suspicion about their abilities." University departments are controlled by "senior professors in academic departments, who are sometimes averse to change." But, the paper concluded, "the bottom line, many Ivy League women say, is that the all-male tradition of the Ivy institutions still haunts them. Until women are in senior positions, and able to influence choices about hiring, they say, many areas of academe will remain hostile to women." Above all, the article said, "change has come slowly."

The *Times* presented all of this as established truth rather than the debatable propositions that they are. And yet there is certainly a widespread feeling at the universities, and a good deal of evidence, that to be female or dark-skinned these days often confers a certain advantage. At the University of Wisconsin in 1992 a faculty investigation on salary discrepancies, commissioned by Donna Shalala, later to be secretary of Health and Human Services in the Clinton administration, found that men were paid roughly 1.6 percent more than women doing the same jobs and showing the same merit. An unintended consequence of the study, however, was to show salary differentials by race and by age as well. It turned out that the gap between whites and blacks was higher than that between men and women, with blacks earning 2.9 percent more than whites. And while men were ahead of women in absolute amounts, the amount of the merit increases going to women in recent years was 3 percent higher than the amount for men.

Nobody would dispute the fact that women have gotten to high positions far less than men, in the universities and elsewhere. Discrimination was surely part of this, though it was probably a discrimination linked to economic necessity. Until recently, the level of economic and technological development allowed only wealthy families the luxury of two-career households. Work was outside of the household, except on farms. There were no laborsaving devices, no cars, no day care, no disposable diapers, no ready-made foods, and you had to have five children in order to end up with two or three surviving descendants. Somebody had to stay home to take care of the children, and that somebody tended to be the person who gave birth to them and nursed them. And so in 1970 it was not that surprising that only 13 percent of all Ph.D.'s went to women. This means, it should be noted, that the percentage of full professors now, just under 12 percent, is pretty close to the number of women getting Ph.D.'s two decades ago. And since it takes twenty years or so to rise up the academic ranks to be a full professor, the representation of women at that level does not seem, contrary to the *Times* report, to be due to obstacles to advancement. It has to do with the fact that few women embarked on academic careers in the first place.

However, in 1990, 43 percent of the Ph.D.'s awarded to American citizens went to women. No doubt that increase will show up in larger numbers of women full professors fifteen to twenty years later. Meanwhile, the increase in the numbers of women in certain fields has been astonishingly rapid. Women faculty in the humanities went from a total of 10,800 in 1977 to 20,800 in 1989. While 10,000 more women joined the university teaching ranks in that twelve-year period, the number of men went up by 7,800, suggesting that if there is discrimination at all, it is probably against males.*

In law schools, according to the American Bar Association, full-time tenure-track positions held by women increased from 1.7 percent in 1967 to 16 percent in 1987, while women faculty in general went up from a 1972 total of 7 percent to 25 percent in 1990. There were only 3,916 female business and management graduates in the country in 1960; there were 116,377 thirty years later, according to the National Center for Education Statistics. There is a similar pattern in medicine. In 1974, the number of women applying to medical school was one-fourth the number of men, though a modestly higher percentage of the women was admitted (38.9 percent versus 34.4 percent). By 1991, the total number of medical students had dropped. Still, just under 7,000 women were admitted, compared with 3,400 in 1974. The number of men admitted declined by about 1,000.

The very day after the *Times* article, Shirley M. Tilghman, a professor of molecular biology at Princeton, wrote on the op-ed page of the newspaper that "the percentage of women receiving science, medical or engineering degrees increased dramatically" between 1966 and 1988. Professor Tilghman's statistics showed that science Ph.D.'s going to women went from 9 percent of the total to 27 percent between 1966 and 1988, a threefold increase in roughly a generation, which does not suggest that "change has come slowly."

Professor Tilghman, to be sure, goes on to complain that women are not in "leadership positions," that the increase has been far faster in the life sciences than in math or the physical sciences, and that "cultural biases" are important reasons for the continuing disparities in the careers of male and female scientists. Tilghman appreciated that there has been remarkable progress, but it has not, in her view, been remarkable enough. The *Times* article, by contrast, with its claim of astonishingly low female representation, would make you believe that the changes were insignificant or, where they have taken place, uncharacteristic.

A tripling in the percentage of total science Ph.D.'s going to women is a big change. In psychology, women get more than half of all Ph.D.'s awarded. In biology they get half of the bachelor's degrees. Since the white male professors who hold the full professorships are

*These figures are from the National Research Council Office of Scientific and Engineering Personnel, Doctorate Surveys Office.

not going to disappear suddenly, it is understandable that women can only step into their shoes gradually. Still, given the sharp increase in the number of women getting graduate degrees and entering the academic ranks, there can be no doubt that there will be many more full professors very soon. Even the *Times* article reported that at the levels of assistant and associate professors, women are already about one-third of the total. Remember that argument to the effect that since women and minorities will have trouble identifying with their white male professors, the shortage will be prolonged? And yet by the newspaper's own evidence, the shortage is rapidly being made up.

The *Times* article, in fact, might have represented the true situation with a lead paragraph like this: "Women, who were hardly represented at all on major faculties two decades ago, now hold nearly one-third of all faculty positions, a rapid change from the past that promises to alter the traditional culture of higher learning."

Newspapers, of course, are supposed to catch trends and report on them, which is why the *Times*'s stress on discrimination, rather than on the far more striking trend toward rapid change, is all the more puzzling. But, of course, the *Times* was not so much reporting on as reflecting a different trend in its story on women professors. This is the trend to claim victimization. When a claim of discrimination against women is made, critical reason often seems to melt away in favor of a soggy sort of credulity, even when the evidence about revolutionary change is so striking that it would seem almost impossible not to notice it.

Consciousness-Raising by the Numbers

If you teach, say, freshman composition, you can always make your contribution to human enlightenment by asking students to write essays about the Silencing of the Other. But what if you teach a subject matter less conducive to political content? John Kellermeier, an associate professor of mathematics at the State University of New York at Plattsburgh, shows how he teaches statistics with what he unabashedly calls a "hidden curriculum" of multiculturalism.

For example, you can pose a problem in statistics using red and green balls in an urn, in which case the "overt curriculum" would be statistics, and the hidden curriculum red and green balls, or you can pose it like this:

In sixty-five percent of all rapes, the victim knows her assailant. If we interview twenty women who were raped, what is the probability that no more than four of them were raped by strangers?

In such a way does the teacher serve two purposes at once. He/she can teach statistics and encourage social awareness at the same time, and this is a good thing to do, Professor Kellermeier explains, because, "We live in a society in which diversity is used to marginalize people, a society in which power and privilege are based on a 'norm' or standard of rightness. To balance this, there is a need to celebrate and expand acceptance of diverse people and cultures." Also, he says, "The inclusion of issues of race, class, and gender breaks down the image of areas such as math and science as white-male domains."

Professor Kellermeier gives other examples of performing good works via the teaching of statistics. You can make up problems in sampling and probability with women's literature, getting in references to stories by writers like Hisaye Yamamoto and Guadalupe Valdes Fallis. You can show "diverse cultural settings" by making up problems about people with names like Haji, Consuela, and Kyoko. You can draw attention to social problems by using statistics about the number of black children who live with their mothers and the numbers who live with their fathers. You can slip in a problem based on the incomes of African-American single mothers, about the percentages of people who are bisexual, or the representation of women in the armed forces.

Here's a problem made up by Professor Kellermeier that will be particularly helpful to religious students in need of consciousness-raising:

The number of seconds required to perform a six-week vacuum aspiration abortion was recorded for a sample of six such abortions. The results were as follows:

84, 100, 80, 85 and 84

For this sample, find:

a. The mean and the median.
b. The range, the variance, and the standard deviation.

Professor Kellermeier's invaluable suggestions appear in a journal called *Transformations*, which is published by a state-funded group in New Jersey whose goal is to "integrate scholarship on gender, race, class and ethnicity into core curricula." Other people writing for *Transformations* have other ideas. In fact, the journal is a small repository of all of the received ideas of ideological multiculturalism. There are articles about the "feminization of the teaching of writing," for example, or about how one teacher raised consciousnesses in Rutgers University's course Homosexuality and Society. She avoided "the potentially oppressive or ideologically rigid modes of operation within a classroom dynamic" and created a "politicized pedagogy," she proudly wrote.

What is brilliant about Professor Kellermeier's suggestion is its use of subliminal messages to create good consciousness. After all, here is a way to impart political points of view without bothering to have to defend them or discuss them. The program of the tenured revolutionaries can be introduced as if it were established truth. I was reminded of China during the Cultural Revolution when teachers teaching children to read used the selected quotations of Chairman Mao as a text. Calligraphers copied only the Great Helmsman's poems. That too was combining an overt curriculum and a hidden curriculum, even though the hidden one wasn't really very hidden.

I wondered, reading Professor Kellermeier's virtuous problems in statistics, how he would feel if some colleagues in his department decided to introduce other political concepts into their lessons. Here's a suggested problem to solve:

Recent studies show that among women who have abortions, 27 percent later come to feel that abortion is equivalent to murder. The same studies show that 17 percent of all women have had abortions.

    a. If we interview 20 women who have had abortions, what is the probability that no more than 2 of them will come to feel that they murdered their own child?

    b. What is the probability that all of them will come to feel that way?

More Monkey Trials in Tennessee

At the end of 1991, all the members of the faculty of Middle Tennessee State University who taught in the general studies department received a questionnaire from a previously unknown committee called the Advisory Committee for Curricular Transformation, which was examining the general studies courses for the possibility of gender bias by seeing how often and in what ways women were included in the curriculum. There were questions like these:

- How often were the pronouns "she" and "her" used?
- How often were role titles male-related (e.g. "chairman")?
- How often did the examples relate only to typically male experiences or use only males in examples [*sic*]?
- Did the reading assignments include materials covering differences between the positions, power, and/or perspectives of men and women?

There were eighty-six questions in all, covering four pages, and besides asking doctors of philosophy to go through textbooks and count pronouns, they got into a level of tediousness remarkable even for the halls of academe. Question sixty-nine, for example, asked whether women and men mentioned in the course material were

- a. treated separately and not compared
- b. described both separately and comparatively
- c. described both separately and comparatively, stressing interrelationships
- d. described both separately and comparatively, stressing interrelationships and changes over time.

The senders of the questionnaire urged all faculty to take the time to respond to it, saying that doing so "gives you a chance to look carefully at your course in terms of gender bias, which is, in many cases, a by-product of the historic attitudes toward the roles of males and females."

Tennessee, of course, was the state where in 1925, still within the memory of many people living today, a teacher was put on trial for insisting on teaching the theory of evolution. Fundamentalist Christianity had forced its way into the classroom and required teachers to toe the line on the Bible. The fundamentalists at that time had the support of the state, whose legislature forbade the teaching of evolution.

In the more recent case, the Tennessee Board of Regents had

issued the report *The Status of Women in Academe,* and it had man-
dated the formation of the Advisory Committee for Curricular Transformation, which, in essence, was attempting to forbid the teaching
of materials that contradicted feminist beliefs in the general studies
curriculum.

"I find these sorts of questions intrusive and offensively moralistic," a latter-day Clarence Darrow, a sociologist named Dan
McMurry, wrote in a letter to his faculty colleagues. The committee,
he said, "puts itself in the position of monitoring conformity with the
ill-defined ideas of certain fashionable academic activists who have set
themselves up to investigate the moral purity and/or political rectitude of our course offerings." Our brave advocate asked the key
question: What if the fashion changes? What if patriotism, family
values, or the rights of the fetus were in fashion, rather than race,
class, and gender?

The questionnaire could have asked, for example, (a) whether
patriotism and family values were treated separately and not interrelated or (b) separately and interrelated and, if interrelated, (c) stressing comparisons or (d) stressing changes over time. The justification
for such questions would not be hard to find: "For a society to be
independent and self-governing, patriotism and family values must
remain strong. This survey gives you a chance to see if your course
contains materials subversive of national unity or destructive of the
nation's fundamental unit, the family."

In the case of integrating scholarship on women, it is hard to know
exactly what solutions the committee would have suggested if gender
bias had turned out to be severe at MTSU. If there weren't enough
women writers, would a few simply be added irrespective of intrinsic
merit? Dostoyevsky and Flaubert pushed out to make room for gender
equity?

As it turned out, however, this did not appear to be necessary.
The questionnaire revealed that there was no gender bias against
women in the general studies courses. The Committee for Curricular
Transformation had come too late—the curriculum had already been
transformed without it. A summary of findings of the questionnaire
was dated February 2, 1992, though, strangely, it was not made public
until the following fall. The report shows that the pronouns "she" or
"her" were used "sometimes" or "about half" the time in 79 percent
of the cases. Male-related titles like "chairman" were found in only
one-third of the materials. Women appeared in two-thirds of the

photos and illustrations. Men were "sometimes" shown in domestic roles in more than half of the materials. Twice as many of the films and videos used in class featured women rather than men.

Female authors or coauthors were cited 79.6 percent of the time, compared with 81.2 percent for male authors and coauthors. "Womanless" readings—with no mention of women at all—occurred 11.1 percent, compared with 5.7 percent for manlessness. Class behavior had some surprises also, since it is a feminist platitude that men are more aggressive than women and are therefore both more likely to participate in class discussion and more likely to interrupt others when they are speaking. "Male and female students were seen as equally likely to comment and/or ask questions," the report concluded. So much for the "chilly climate for women." It was slightly more common, moreover, for men to be interrupted than it was for women.

The climate, in short, was getting warmer all the time. And it was not the younger, newer members of the faculty who seemed better than the older ones, or the women better than the men. Overall, two-thirds of the respondents to the questionnaire had been teaching at MTSU for six or more years. Thirty-eight percent of the respondents were women and 62 percent male (overall at MTSU, women made up 36 percent of the faculty).

In other words, the unanticipated evidence of the survey was that the feminist revolution had already taken place before the campus feminists arrived on the scene to make it. What to do? A committee had been formed. The study done. Could the committee simply say, "The situation is fine, no further action needed"? Of course not.

Like a locomotive with no brakes, the process of curricular transformation continued apace at MTSU, as if the situation discovered in the survey did not exist. Indeed, a second survey was carried out aimed at discovering the same evidence of bias and exclusion that the first survey had been unsuccessful in uncovering. In the fall of 1992, portions of the faculty not asked to fill out the first questionnaire received a newly designed one consisting of fifty-eight questions covering much the same ground as the earlier document.

In March 1993, the vice-president for academic affairs was still sending out notices for "Curricular Transformation" workshops. "Special emphasis will be given," the memo says, "to the question of feminist pedagogy."

"Sexist" Language in the Media

P. J. Corso, a former reporter who now teaches communications at Hunter College in New York City, eager to make her contribution to the store of knowledge about the prevalence of sexism, has her students round up examples of sexist language that they find in press clippings. They are so numerous, she says, that the students "have either worked overtime" to gather them or "sexist language is as easily spotted in print today as Volkswagen Beetles were on the highways in the 1960s." It is always a good idea when somebody is claiming the prevalence of one or another of the isms that afflict us to see whether the evidence adduced actually matches the claim of prevalence. Corso listed her most dramatic findings in an October 1991 article in *Editor & Publisher*, the trade journal of the newspaper business. Among them:

- *USA Today*'s article on the first female college baseball player says she was a reserve "first baseman" for the team.
- The Pittsburgh *Press* calls one of the candidates in an election a "housewife" and, in a second reference, calls her "Mrs."
- The San Francisco *Chronicle* uses the term "sister ship" to refer to the . . . what? sister ship of the *Voyager 2*.

"The first example is a clear-cut case of ignoring a female," Corso writes of the first basewoman. "The second example stirs up memories of the notorious marriage vow, 'I now pronounce you man and wife,'" she continues. Regarding the third example, she asks: "Must the inanimate object being fired be personified as a sister?"

The atrocities adduced by Corso and her class, which, she seems to feel, indicate the extent of women's degradation in American society and prove as well the complicity of the media in this degradation, are not the only instances cited by the vigilant Professor Corso. Never mind that she has to go back to a long-defunct magazine in order to find it. What she calls "one of the worst sexist violations in print" is "a *Look* photo essay explaining how the ocean liner *Titanic* was 'steaming through the North Atlantic when an iceberg slashed a 300-foot gash in her starboard side.'" This is "one of the worst," Corso explains, because by "assigning a gender" to the ship, "the journalist writing about the *Titanic* has recreated an act of violence against a female, not a luxury liner."

Oh.

Et Tu, Beethoven?

Beethoven's symphonies add two other dimensions to the history of style: assaultive pelvic pounding . . . and sexual violence. The point of recapitulation in the first movement of the Ninth is one of the most horrifying moments in music, as the carefully prepared cadence is frustrated, damming up energy which finally explodes in the throttling, murderous rage of a rapist incapable of attaining release.

—Susan McClary, *Getting Down Off the Beanstalk: The Presence of a Woman's Voice in Janika Vandervelde's Genesis II*

Dallas Baptist U Too

Finally, there is this tale from Dallas Baptist University, a religious institution where, one might think, the waves of political correctness would not reach. Bible study and prayer are big parts of life for the 2,700 students and 60 full-time faculty. And so when David Ayers, an assistant professor of sociology and criminal justice, published an article, "The Inevitability of Failure: The Assumptions and Implementations of Modern Feminism," it was rather surprising that the feminist ax fell on his neck as quickly as it did.

In the spring of 1992, Ayers was asked to be a last-minute substitute for a canceled speaker at a regular faculty colloquium. He decided to give a précis of his article critical of feminism. Some members of the faculty, learning of this, put out word to boycott the lecture. The academic vice-president, Edward Pauley, seeking to avert strife, called him up to ask that he say at the beginning that he was not opposed to equal rights for women or to women teaching at DBU. Ayers felt that to make these disclaimers would imply that he was denying something that he had previously said, but he had previously said nothing that needed to be denied, so he refused. He also did not feel it was appropriate for anybody to tell him what to say. After all, he was a speaker, not a ventriloquist's puppet.

Ayers gave his talk. Another talk was organized to refute his ideas, and this talk was given by a new member of the English department named Deborah McCollister. After McCollister's talk, Ayers, questioned about what had become a noisy controversy on campus centering on him and McCollister, distributed to his classes both his own talk and that of McCollister. At one point, he jocularly referred in one of his classes to McCollister's paper as "the razor-sharp edge of the assassin's sword."

Ayer's remark, which was pretty mild compared with what the campus feminists were saying about him, was reported to the administration, which suspected Ayers of defaming a faculty member and disclosing the content of a private faculty colloquium. The president of the university, Gary Cook, formed a committee to investigate. Ayers was summoned by telephone to appear before the committee the next day, which he refused to do on the grounds that the summons was peremptory, giving him no time to know the charges against him or to prepare a defense.

Eventually, after much talk and considerable controversy on campus, the idea of the committee and a hearing of the case against Ayers was dropped. Instead, Pauley, the vice-president for academic affairs, announced in a memo to the faculty that he was asking John Jeffrey, the dean of Ayers's college, to look into the situation—that is, to determine if Ayers had maligned McCollister and revealed what had happened at a faculty colloquium—and to report his findings back to him. Pauley rather remarkably specified what he expected the results of this investigation would be if, indeed, it turned out that Ayers's remark about the assassin's sword could be seen as a personal insult to McCollister.

"As far as an outcome of this inquiry is concerned, I believe an apology to Professor McCollister from Professor Ayers is in order," he wrote, adding that that is the way things should be resolved among "Christian brothers and sisters."

Ayers was untenured and thus defenseless. So was Jeffrey. Nonetheless, Jeffrey sent a long memo back to Pauley saying that even if the charges against Ayers were true, "none would represent any perceivable wrongdoing in light of our Faculty Handbook, and the AAUP [American Association of University Professors] Guidelines." No wrongdoing, therefore nothing to investigate, was Jeffrey's brave conclusion. He also said that he was recommending to Ayers that he seek legal counsel.

One week later, both Ayers and Jeffrey received letters at their homes informing them that they were being dismissed. The notices were signed by Pauley, who made no mention of the controversy surrounding Ayers and gave no reasons for the firings.

The men were paid for the remainder of the academic year and for all of the next year. It seems that the administration was so terrified of feminist wrath at Dallas Baptist University that they preferred to pay Ayers and Jeffrey full salaries to do nothing rather than have them around and risk further debate about the feminist ideology.*

The question is: Why are these things happening now? Why have the forces of good intention become so ill mannered and churlish? As we will see, the reasons usually given for the advent of multiculturalism now are wrong. The reasons for the *dérapage* are mysterious, but they lie in the recent history of our era and, in particular, at that moment when a certain elite vision of America tipped toward disillusionment, and we came to see ourselves as representing a set of values and beliefs whose historical superiority we were no longer prepared to defend.

*I have drawn on Joseph S. Salemi's reconstruction of the incident at Dallas Baptist University in *Measure*, Aug.–Sept. 1992, modifying it somewhat in light of my own interviews.

PART II

Reasons

Men commit the error of not knowing when to limit their hopes.

—MACHIAVELLI

Chapter 5

OTHERNESS IN QUEENS

The borough of Queens, one of the five boroughs of New York City, is a laboratory of mingled and changing populations. Queens's nondescript streets, its neighborhoods of modest, practical apartment buildings, its block-long rows of attached houses with little plots of grass in front and one-car garages underneath, are sites of the American demographic revolution, and the revolution is ongoing. There are Indian gas-station owners (often the descendants of Indians who went to Guyana on the northern coast of South America a generation or two ago), Korean manicure salons and fresh produce stands, Colombian bodegas, Chinese real estate developments, Bangladeshi groceries, Jamaican beauty parlors, Dominican nightclubs, Russian bakeries, Pakistani newsstands. There are mosques and Hindu temples and Buddhist temples and synagogues just down the streets from Baptist and Pentecostalist and Spanish Catholic and Greek Orthodox churches in districts with unglamorous names—Astoria, Jackson Heights, Woodside, South Jamaica, Corona, Flushing.

The newspapers, providing illustrations of the borough's diversity, talk about School District 24, encompassing Elmhurst, Corona, and Sunnyside, where 27,000 students are said to speak eighty-three languages. One-third of these students are not fluent in English, leading to one of the most ambitious bilingual-education programs in the country. Queens has 127,000 immigrants from 167 countries enrolled in city schools. The largest number, 23,000, come from the Dominican Republic; they range downward from there: 10,000 from Jamaica, 8,000 from the former Soviet Union, 7,000 from Guyana, 7,000 from

China, 6,000 from Haiti, 4,800 from Trinidad, 4,200 from Mexico, and smaller groups from many other places.

And so Queens is a good place to study the more diverse population of the American future, the one that, the multiculturalists say, will bring to an end the requirement that all Americans, especially new ones, assimilate to an essentially Western common culture. Queens has another advantage in that at other times in its history something transpired similar to what is taking place there now. Many cultural Others from many different places of origin have dwelt in the borough, whose major advantages are that housing is relatively cheap and that it is a quick subway ride to Manhattan on the other side of the East River.

I am personally acquainted with the historic case of one Gizella Braun, her two husbands, her seven children and other relatives. Gizella and her first husband and five of her children arrived with their modest life savings from a small town called Kishvarda, Hungary, in about 1920, near the end of the giant tide of immigration that washed over America for three decades. Gizella was a delicate, brown-haired woman with large eyes and a sad sort of beauty. She looked like the young Virginia Woolf. Her first husband, Herman Braun, was round, mustached, and clever. In later years, Gizella used to tell her grandchildren that Herman would have become a great tycoon, if only misfortune had not struck.

Herman was a grocer in Kishvarda who felt that the usually nonviolent but underlying anti-Semitism of Hungary would prevent him and his children from attainments that matched his ambitions. As was the case with many energetic men in that era, Herman's main goals were to get rich and to provide well for his children, who ranged in age from two to eight. He had a brother already living in Queens, so he booked passage for the entire family on a liner sailing from Trieste to New York; then without ever explaining why, he changed the bookings to a different ship. It was a small decision with very big consequences. When the Brauns stepped off the ferry that took them from the Brooklyn dock to Ellis Island, where all but first-class passengers were brought to clear immigration and customs, they learned that the other ship, the one they would have been on but for Herman's fateful change, had filled up the quota for Hungarian immigrants. They were going to be deported.

Deeply chagrined, the Braun family waited on Ellis Island for passage back across the Atlantic. It was a cold, damp fall. The family lived in a drafty dormitory and spent their time gazing across the gray waters of New York Harbor at the unreachable skyscrapers of Manhattan less than a mile away. The Statue of Liberty visible just across the water in the opposite direction seemed an ironic emblem of their bad luck as it thrust its torch of freedom into a lead-colored sky. In December, the Brauns were, in a manner of speaking, lucky. They were the beneficiaries of an unexpected Christmas amnesty accorded all the would-be deportees on Ellis Island by President Warren G. Harding. But by the time they passed the fateful barrier of immigration control and took the ferry to Lower Manhattan, the drafty weeks they spent on Ellis Island had begun to take a toll, and most of them were sick.

The Braun family went directly from Manhattan to Astoria in Queens, just across from the Upper East Side of Manhattan where Herman's brother Amiel Brown (he had already Anglicized his name) had a dry-goods store. Soon after they arrived, one daughter died of pneumonia. Then two more of the children of Gizella and Herman died too. Herman was stricken with grief and with remorse for having, he felt, put his family in harm's way by bringing them to America in the first place. He managed to start a hardware store on Astoria Boulevard and Fourteenth Street, just a few minutes' walk from Amiel's shop, going into partnership with his grown nephew, Morris Reichman, who had been in America since he was thirteen. But then Herman too fell sick. Within a year he was dead, leaving Gizella with two children, a six-year-old boy and a two-year-old daughter, and no apparent means of support.

In the Orthodox Jewish tradition, when a husband dies, his unmarried brother, if he has one, is supposed to marry his widow. Herman had no unmarried brother, but he did have his nephew and business partner Morris, who was just a couple of years younger than he was. Herman called Morris to his deathbed and asked him to marry Gizella so he could take care of her and her children.

It would be hard to say that Gizella and Morris loved each other romantically. Not that Morris had no qualities. He was a good-looking man with rugged features, and he had plenty of ability and charm. He was also stubborn and difficult, intolerant, narrow-minded, and untender, though also strongly attached to his adopted family. In any case, Gizella was too stricken by her terrible losses to be capable of loving anybody. It didn't matter. Morris could speak English. He knew the ropes. He could run the hardware store. Gizella rejected

Amiel's advice, which was that she take her two surviving children and return to eastern Hungary, where she had parents and eleven brothers and sisters. She married Morris, who proceeded to make a living while she took care of her children, kept house, and coped with her grief. It would be impossible to say, though she lived for sixty more years, that she ever really overcame it.

It could be said that the Reichman family represented an early multicultural challenge in Queens. Except for Morris, they spoke no English; none of them were highly educated; they knew very little about their new country. They were not Western Europeans, not Anglo-Saxon Protestants or even Irish Catholics, but Central Europeans and Orthodox Jews—and Jews in those days were seen as extremely Other. They probably were just as different from the majority in place as the Others arriving in these last years of the twentieth century. Certainly they felt themselves very different, these Hungarian Jews, and if the statements of the time are to be believed, they were seen as very different as well.

Gizella received no help from the city or the state. There was virtually no public assistance then. There were no booklets printed in Hungarian, no multilingual ballots or cash machines, no bilingual education for her children, no driver's license exams given in twenty-two languages (which now include Farsi, Cambodian, Albanian, Laotian, Serbo-Croatian, Vietnamese, Turkish, Romanian, and, yes, Hungarian). Certainly there was no multiculturalist ideology encouraging Gizella and her children to value their own culture or telling them that, as immigrants and minorities, they were the victims of a dictatorship of the white, Anglo, patriarchal, non-Jewish majority that would use the school system to force their children to adopt the dominant discourse as their own, while systematically excluding the Hungarian Jews from the curriculum and thus depriving them of self-esteem and inflicting on them what at least one bilingual-education advocate calls identity eradication. The only option available to the Braun-Reichmans was assimilation, to become "100 percent American," as the slogan of the time put it. They had their problems and their tragedies, but they never saw the pressure to conform to be one of them.

Assimilation did not mean joining the Episcopalian church. Assimilation in America has always come with greater or lesser degrees of qualification. The members of the Braun-Reichman family maintained their difference. The children went to public school during the day and to Hebrew school at night and on Sunday. The boys (including two that Gizella had with Morris) were bar mitzvahed. All the children were made to understand that they would marry in the faith, and all of them did. At the same time, Gizella's children learned English in school by the immersion method, and they learned it quickly and extremely well. They then taught the language to their mother, who soon cultivated the habit of living a cultural life in English. She went to the public library, which was only a few doors down from the hardware store. She read the *Saturday Evening Post, Reader's Digest, Ladies' Home Journal.* She listened to "Philco Radio Time" and the "Wrigley Review" and, later, to "The Eddie Cantor Show," to "Burns and Allen" and "Amos 'n' Andy." At a certain point, perhaps a decade or so into her American life, Gizella and her family stopped speaking Hungarian at home altogether.

Meanwhile, Morris did well in the hardware business. He invested in AT&T stock. Gizella's oldest son went to Peter Stuyvesant High School, one of the three public schools in New York reserved for those who do well in a competitive entrance exam (Stuyvesant's enrollment is now more than half of Asian ancestry), then to the university, and finally to dental school. After serving in the U.S. Army during World War II, he started a practice in Jackson Heights, which he continued almost until his death in 1989. The two boys of Gizella and Morris followed similar patterns, one of them becoming a hospital administrator, the other a psychiatrist (a choice that the old-fashioned Morris noisily abhorred). Only Gizella's daughter was not sent to college, though she later enrolled after her own children were grown and got her B.A. and M.A. degrees. Before the war, the family moved from the apartment above the store in Astoria to one of those Queens two-story brick attached houses, with four bedrooms, a separate dining room, a garage, and a finished basement, in Jackson Heights.

After the war, Gizella sent money to the very few members of her family back in Hungary who had survived the Holocaust. One of them, a nephew, came to New York eventually, and after a considerable struggle with the foreign language, bad health, and terrible memories, became a prosperous architect in San Francisco. After the Hungarian uprising of 1956, Gizella helped other relatives make their way to America, where they followed the pattern of that part of the Hungarian-American clan, which by then were all pretty much "100 percent American" and who, except for the elders, didn't even speak Hungarian anymore.

And so, the question is this: In what way is the family of Gizella Reichman different from families arriving in the present wave of immigration? It is true that the Brauns were white and European, and that makes them different from the majority of new arrivals who are Asian, black, and Indian. But are the new immigrants really culturally more different from the population already in place? Do they have different ideas about assimilation? Different goals for themselves? Does their presence require an American redefinition in the way that the Hungarian Brauns' presence did not? Are they different from their immigrant predecessors, or is it the culture in place that has changed, becoming less sure that it has the right to demand cultural assimilation as the price of entry?

The question is relevant because of the answer most commonly given to another question, the most basic one about the multiculturalist fad: Why is it happening just now? The standard answer to that question invariably has to do with two interrelated factors: one is demographic change, the idea that the population is becoming more diverse and therefore the culture needs to reflect that diversity; the second, that the traditional racism of America, which resists this change, needs also to be overcome through a different sort of education.

The racism charges will be dealt with in the next chapter. This chapter will be devoted to the argument of demographic change, which strikes me as a reversal of the actual order of things. It is not that we need to be multicultural because the population is becoming more diverse. It is that we see the population becoming more diverse because we experience the need to be multicultural. We have been diverse all along, sometimes more culturally diverse than we are now. What has changed is our attitude toward ourselves, our unwillingness to see the American identity as worthy enough to expect newcomers to adopt it as their own.

The multiculturalists in this sense commit the error of solipsism. They assume that because their own creed represents virtue, it will naturally be the creed of those with whom they wish to make common cause—the oppressed, who, in the multicultural worldview, are naturally virtuous. But in reality there is nothing in the experience of new arrivals in this country, or others who are causing our demographic change, that pushes them to reject the standard icons and values of American life. Nor is there anything leading them to adopt the liberation theology that is taken as simple common sense by the middle-class bureaucrats and education entrepreneurs, the guilty white liberals and aging flower children of the 1960s who most aggressively press the multiculturalist agenda. The idea that we are becoming more genuinely diverse because we are ethnically more varied may be true, or it may not be. Whatever the case, it does not at all follow that the particular brand of liberalism that is flavored by resentment of American global success and upheld as virtuous by the New Consciousness will prove useful or valuable to those newly striving to make it in America.

In 1988, a dramatic finding about the population of the United States was reported by the Hudson Institute, the research organization situated in Indianapolis, Indiana, and specializing in evaluations of the future. Press reports of the study, which was commissioned by the United States Department of Labor and issued under the name *Workforce 2000*, indicated a remarkable change in the composition of the American people.

The main conclusion was that twenty-five million new workers would enter the American labor force in the next dozen years. Of these technicians, teachers, lawyers, computer programmers, travel agents, used-car salespersons, and neurosurgeons, a full 85 percent will be women, minorities, and immigrants. This meant, as Leonard Silk of the *New York Times* announced, that "native white males, who now constitute 47 percent of the labor force, will account for only 15 percent of the entrants to the labor force by the year 2000." Or as the *Workforce 2000* report itself said, "The cumulative impact of the changing ethnic and racial composition of the labor force will be dramatic."

The expected change in the population away from white Europeans and toward nonwhite non-Europeans made multiculturalism, in its late-twentieth-century version, seem not only natural and desirable, but inevitable. "We are becoming a different people," said Thomas Sobel, the New York State education commissioner in October 1989, speaking in support of the changes in education that he envisaged for New York's public school students. "Our country is becoming ethnically, linguistically and culturally diverse," he said.

"We must prepare for a 21st century dominated in number if not power by non-western peoples," wrote Clayton Carson, a professor of history and African-American studies at Stanford. Manning Marable

of the University of Colorado, arguing in favor of mandatory multiculturalism courses at universities, specified an exact year when people
of color would exceed the number of white people. This would happen, said Marable, in 2056. "The future of the U.S. lies in people of
color," he said. Similarly, the National Council for the Social Studies,
a group that provides materials for social studies teachers nationwide,
published its "Guidelines for Multicultural Education" in September
1992, arguing for major changes in the curriculum because "one out
of every four people who live in the United States is a person of color
and one out of every three people will be a person of color by the
turn of the century."

If, demographically speaking, European whites, and especially
white men, have reigned supreme in our culture until now, their
decline to 15 percent of the entrants in the workforce would certainly
seem to presage an end to that domination. Moreover, if you suppose,
as many do, that demographic changes are going to lead to the incor-
poration of a far wider array of cultures than the country has ever had
before, the shift in the population will entail a shift in the way the
nation identifies itself and conducts its everyday business.

In one follow-up article on the Labor Department report, for
example, the *New York Times* quotes Barbara Jerich, whose title at
Honeywell, Inc., is director of work-force diversity. She spoke of the
way *Workforce 2000* underlined the importance of "understanding
and valuing difference." The article also cited Roosevelt Thomas, the
director of the American Institute for Managing Diversity, which is
situated at Morehouse College in Atlanta, claiming that the new diversity is not a matter of social responsibility or morality. Affirmative
action, he said, "was considered a social, moral and legal responsibility." By contrast, "managing diversity is a business issue." Large
companies that do not "manage diversity," the *Times* reported, "will
find themselves at a competitive disadvantage."

The *Workforce 2000* figures seem to be the ones cited in those
Copeland Griggs Valuing Diversity videotapes when the narrator says
that 75 percent of the new entrants to the workforce will be minorities
and women. (The Labor Department figure was 85 percent, but that
included immigrants, who are not mentioned in the Copeland Griggs
videotape.) The conclusions of *Workforce 2000* "were more than just
conventional wisdom," said one magazine analysis. "They were gos-
pel." The magazine, *Government Executive*, continued: "Magazines
from *Fortune* to *Industry Week*, to, yes, *Government Executive* relied

on Workforce 2000 for dire warnings about the need for better work-force planning."

Conclusions based on *Workforce 2000* went well beyond the world of business. *Time* magazine, in April 1990, ran a cover story called "America's Changing Colors," asking "What will the U.S. be like when whites are no longer the majority? . . . In the 21st Century—and that's not far off—racial and ethnic groups in the U.S. will out-number whites for the first time. . . . The 'browning of America' will alter everything in society, from politics and education to industry, values and culture." In 1991, the very wealthy Ford Foundation, the largest grant-giving institution in the United States, announced that it was giving $1.6 million to several universities as a first step in its Race Relations and Cultural Diversity Initiative. The grants, a news release said, are aimed at "ensuring that college curricula and teaching keep pace with the rapid demographic and cultural changes underway in American society."

The *New York Times* in 1992 published an article under the head-line "As American as Apple Pie, Dim Sum or Burritos," the message of which was that the very definition of the word "American" is changing because of the new diversity of the population. It is interesting that ethnic food inspired the headline because the article, even in sug-gesting that an influx of new cultures was unsettling the complacent American landscape, to the point where the meaning of "American" was no longer clear, did not specify any important cultural changes, except for the gastronomical one. It did point out that the 1990 census found that there were 19.7 million foreign-born people in the United States and that more of them—far more of them—were born in Asia than in Europe, and more were born in Mexico than in Asia. "The number of Asians, which doubled in the last decade to 7.3 million, will double again in 20 years' time and will triple, to 21.5 million, by 2020," the *Times* reported.

Or here is David Louie, president of the Asian American Journal-ists Association, arguing why newspapers need to have a "plan for diversity." Interviewed by the magazine *Quill*, Louie does not only urge that more minorities be hired in newsrooms because that would be fair, just, and lead to better reporting. His reasoning, which is widely accepted by newspaper executives, is that a more diverse staff is needed to address the needs of the demographically changing readership. "Audiences," he said, "are becoming increasingly non-white, and newspaper staffs do not reflect that diversity."

It is difficult to understand exactly what people mean when they intone that word "diversity," though the assumption that seems to lie behind those statements is that different groups have different cultures and thus "mainstream culture" has to accommodate these differences. It is assumed that multiculturalism follows as the night the day the alteration of the population itself, which is due in large part to a new wave of immigration and to the higher birthrates of the nonwhite portions of the population. This is, of course, true, just as it is true that newspapers ought to have reporters that reflect the communities they are trying to serve. They will be much better newspapers if they do. Yet nobody at American newspapers advocates finding some way to appeal more to, say, religious readers, and especially not to fundamentalist readers, even though such people make up a far greater proportion of the population than, say, Asian-Americans. That would be the kind of diversity that multiculturalism abhors. In any case, it is not at all clear that demographic change today is all that different from demographic change in the past, except that more races and ethnicities are involved in it.

To listen to the multiculturalist discourse, you would think that population change is something new, when, of course, it is as old as American history. The United States has had proportionately larger waves of immigration before. In the first decade of this century, 8.8 million immigrants passed through Ellis Island and other ports of entry. In the decade of the 1980s, 8.5 million people arrived at Kennedy International, Los Angeles International, Miami International, and other airports. Most of those who came as immigrants early in the century were from southern and Eastern Europe as well as Ireland, so they were European, which the large majority of immigrants in the 1980s and 1990s are not.

Still, the total foreign-born percentage of the population is far from the highest it has ever been in American history. In 1990, those 19.7 million foreign-born people in the United States, while an impressive absolute number, represented less than 8 percent of the general population. In 1920 when the Brauns arrived from Hungary, the foreign-born population was 13 percent of the population as a whole, nearly twice as high as it was in 1990.* The figures for New York City, which include our test borough of Queens, show a far higher percentage of foreigners in earlier decades than now. In the mid-seventeenth cen-

---

*Jeffrey S. Passel and Barry Edmonston, *Immigration and Race in the United States: The 20th and 21st Centuries*, Urban Institute, Washington, D.C.

tury, twenty or so years after New York was founded, there were already eighteen languages being spoken in the city. In 1890, around the time the country was celebrating the four-hundredth anniversary of the Columbian voyages, fully 80 percent of the population of New York City were foreign-born or were the children of foreign-born parents.* The 1990 census showed New York with just over two million foreign-born residents, or about 29 percent of the total, which is about the same as the figures of fifty years before, in 1940.†

Because the new immigrants are "brown" rather than white, they supposedly present a cultural challenge far vaster than earlier waves. This is a complicated issue, since there probably is something that could be called the European culture, linking Finns and Sicilians, Irish and Germans, and the numerous other quarrelsome nationalities of Europe. They were all variations on Judeo-Christian culture. And, of course, there is no denying that being white in America is a different experience from being nonwhite. Still, it is not at all certain that arrivals from Asia or the Caribbean islands today are less familiar with the mainstream American culture than their European predecessors were. And certainly there is no sure measure indicating that Asians or Mexicans now feel more different from the mainstream than Hungarians or Sicilians or Polish Jews felt when they arrived here—or, for that matter, that they are viewed as somehow more alien, less easily assimilable, than those earlier immigrants were.

There is a good-hearted but fallacious inclination to make exotic anthropological specimens of the newest Americans, to attribute to them a kind of cultural impermeability that ignores the existence of a worldwide culture made up largely, and not necessarily for the better, of American icons. What this good-hearted vision ignores is that the newest immigrants come from a global village that did not exist in the seventeenth century or in the 1890s or the 1920s. A very large number of earlier immigrants were illiterate peasants and workers who had never left their fields and villages before, which is the case for a far smaller percentage of today's immigrants, most of whom have, figuratively, already voyaged far from home, if only by watching American television and the movies and listening to the broadcasts of the Voice of America.

*Daniel Patrick Moynihan and Nathan Glazer, *Beyond the Melting Pot* (Cambridge: MIT Press, 1963), pages 223–226.

†Department of City Planning/New York City, *The Newest New Yorkers: An Analysis of Immigration into New York City During the 1980s*, pages 5–6.

It is easy to imagine Sicilians or Jews of the late nineteenth century never having heard of William McKinley or Teddy Roosevelt. It is difficult to imagine Koreans or Jamaicans arriving in Miami or New York today unable to identify George Bush or Bill Clinton—or, for that matter, never having heard of Arnold Schwarzenegger and Michael Jackson, *Time* magazine and *Reader's Digest*, Madonna and Eddie Murphy, Woody Allen and Mohammad Ali, and the Cable News Network. Thomas Friedman, my colleague at the *New York Times*, tells in his book *From Beirut to Jerusalem* of driving through a military checkpoint in southern Lebanon once and, apparently as a result, being pursued by Shiite militiamen brandishing automatic weapons. When finally Friedman and another journalist were captured and, they feared, about to be shot, they were stunned to discover why their fundamentalist Islamic pursuers had chased them down. "Who shot J.R.?" they wanted to know.

When they were still back in their native places, newcomers to America today wore blue jeans and used Clairol shampoo and Vicks VapoRub. They saw Anita Hill accuse Clarence Thomas of sexual harassment and watched, on live television, as the Dream Team won the gold medal in the Barcelona Olympics of 1992. The whole world is swamped in an English-language culture. In China hundreds of millions of people watch "Dynasty" on their color televisions or listen to the Voice of America and the BBC on their radios, and outside every hotel there are clots of young people waiting for tourists to come out so they can practice their English with them. In Beijing, when student protesters demanded democratic reform, they hauled into Tiananmen Square a plaster statue modeled on the Statue of Liberty, which they called the Goddess of Democracy, a concept that did not come from Confucius. That image galvanized an entire generation. It is, in fact, the Communist tyrants in China who rail against the intrusion of global cultural influences, calling them examples of "spiritual pollution" and "bourgeois liberalization." It is the dictators who want the people to stay culturally impermeable, even though, ironically, the dictators themselves embrace another Western dogma, Marxism.

In Russia, before the collapse of communism, a pair of blue jeans on the black market would fetch the price of a few nights in the best hotel. Underground rock groups playing Japanese-made electric guitars subverted the authority of the Communist party. In refugee camps on the coast of Malaysia in the late 1970s, Vietnamese boat people, who spoke excellent French or English, talked in the language of human rights when they explained their attempt to escape to the West. For decades already, Korea, Taiwan, Hong Kong, and Singapore have been building modern industrial and high-tech economies dependent on their ability to react to changes in the global marketplace, techniques that their best students learned at Harvard, Wharton, and MIT.

If the degree of exoticism of immigrants today is overestimated, that of immigrants of yesteryear is given short shrift, this underestimation of difference a product of the ideological multiculturalists' confusion of race and culture. When, in the seventeenth century, Catholics and Protestants from England managed to live side by side in newly founded Maryland, it was a revolutionary development for people of such deeply different and incompatible beliefs to do so. Those descended from England did not think that the masses of Irish who came in the middle of the nineteenth century were culturally similar, and the Irish believed that the Sicilians and the Germans came from utterly different cultures. The nativist political movement known as Know Nothingism that flourished in the 1850s, helping to reshape political formations in the country in the years leading to the Civil War, was provoked by a reaction among native-born American Protestants against the influxes of Irish Catholics, who were viewed as immoral, in favor of slavery, and prone to drunkenness. In 1893, the *New York Times* editorialized negatively about the "long-whiskered descendants of Abraham, Isaac, Jacob, and Judah on the Lower East Side," feeling that these people were a menace, because their customs were just too different for them ever to be absorbed into the American mainstream. "A writer," the newspaper solemnly declared, "might go for a week reciting the abominations of these people and still have much to tell. One of their greatest faults is that they have an utter disregard for law." Similarly, in 1911, the most popular textbook in American schools, David Saville Muzzey's *An American History*, asked: "Can we assimilate and mold into citizenship the millions who are coming to our shores, or will they remain an ever-increasing body of aliens, an undigested and undigestible element in our body politic, and a constant menace to our free institutions?"*

Immigration, demographic change, has thus always brought with it the challenge of difference, a challenge that is no greater today than

*Frances FitzGerald, *American Revised* (Boston: Little, Brown and Co., 1979), page 78.

it was one hundred years ago. What is different is less the immigrants themselves than the attitude they find waiting for them in this country. The Asians and the Mexicans and the Caribbeans who have replaced the Jews, the Irish, and the Italians as the biggest immigrant groups still come for the same reasons as their predecessors. They have, after all, chosen to come to the United States, and part of that choice involves a willingness to adopt different ways. It is the American elites already in place who have lost their collective will to require, as a price of admission to the benefits of American life, the acceptance of a common culture, a price that the immigrants are perfectly willing to pay. And this fact flows inevitably from multiculturalism, since, after all, the idea of diversity negates the very existence of a common culture valid for all of us who are already here.

This is a remarkable change from a past in which difference was viewed as a grave threat to nation building, and assimilation was assumed to be not just desirable but an enforceable necessity. In the 1890s, the Irish were successfully threatening the political hegemony of earlier immigrants, and millions of others speaking Italian, Yiddish, Hungarian, Russian, and Greek were flocking to our shores. In the cities there were related worries about blight, poverty, labor agitation, alcoholism, prostitution, violence, incompatible cultures. The response, even though all of this immigration was Eurocentric, varied between fear and rejection to an easy acceptance. At times, as John Higham has pointed out in his classic study *Strangers in the Land*, there was "a confident faith in the natural, easy melting of many peoples into one." During some periods in the nineteenth century, America did not practice the enforced assimilation, the discouragement of native languages, the suppression of particularisms that were the rule in such other ethnic mosaics as the Austro-Hungarian Empire. This changed by the 1890s when the prospect of an unassimilable mass led to a conscious national effort to Americanize the foreigners. As Lillian Wald, the pioneering social worker, put it, the challenge consisted of "fusing these people who come to us from the Old World civilization into . . . a real brotherhood among men."*

To some extent this was an effort stemming from the chauvinism of such groups as the Daughters of the American Revolution and the Society of the Colonial Dames, representing an attitude of racial and cultural superiority that has happily disappeared. More conspicu-

---

*John Higham, *Strangers in the Land: Patterns of American Nativism, 1860–1925* (New Brunswick, N.J.: Rutgers University Press, 1955), pages 238–239.

ously, the pressure to assimilate was the response of liberal Protestant America to the large-scale immigration of that period. The YMCA organized English and civics classes for immigrants. Frances Keller wrote an exposé of the exploitation of immigrants in the tenement districts of New York, and she campaigned for a national policy of services and help "to make of all these people one nation." The Boston North American Civic League sponsored patriotic lectures in foreign languages in the evening schools. In 1915, Henry Ford, responding to accelerating pressure for Americanization and the demand for loyalty to the country on the eve of its entry into World War I, set up the Ford English School and compelled foreign workers to attend it. The first sentence they learned there was "I am a good American." One ceremony at the school is described in Higham's *Strangers in the Land* (pages 247–248):

> A great melting pot (labeled as such) occupied the middle of the stage. A long column of immigrant students descended into the pot from backstage, clad in outlandish garb and flaunting signs proclaiming their fatherlands. Simultaneously from either side of the pot another stream of men emerged, each prosperously dressed in identical suits of clothes and each carrying a little American flag.

There was something called the National Americanization Committee that, among other things, turned the Fourth of July into Americanization Day, during which large and festive receptions were held for newly naturalized citizens. The American Defense Society held public meetings in immigrant neighborhoods to spread war propaganda. A climax of sorts was represented by the concept "100 percent American," which was aggressively pursued by a vast collection of agencies, "100 percent American" being, as Higham describes it, the effort "to stampede immigrants into citizenship, into adoption of the English language, and into an unquestioning reverence for existing American institutions. Immigrants were pressured to abandon entirely their Old World loyalties, customs, and memories. The advocates of Americanization used high-pressure, steamroller tactics. They cajoled and they commanded."

Matters today are different, and how could they not be, given that reverence for American institutions is seen in many places as a device of narrow-minded Eurocentrism? Is it possible to imagine in our age of bilingual education and multicultural curricula anybody urging us to melt our diverse parts into one nation? The underlying assumption of ideological multiculturalism is that demographic change is the same as cultural change. It is that the immigrants will join with the people of color already in place and together forge a new identity. Moreover, the corollary assumption is that to demand assimilation to what are called white and Eurocentric norms is unjust. It will prevent people of different cultures from succeeding in American life and thus achieving equality. This idea, as we will see, is particularly strong among advocates of progressive education. And yet it is strange, in light of these assumptions, that among the people who by any measure are doing the best in America these days are those who are culturally most different. The Asians are the example here, the children of Vietnamese boat people, the numerous newcomers from China, the Hmong from Laos, who, one would think, are as different from the culture in place as it is possible to be. The plain fact is that for centuries, American life has been quite good to newcomers, like the Brauns, who, certainly by the second generation, started their rapid climb up the ladder of mobility. What makes the ideological multiculturalists feel that people of color today are not able to accomplish the same thing, especially when the Asian, Jamaican, Haitian, and other people of color are proving them wrong every day?

In the early winter of 1992, the school board of District 28 in Queens, one of those ethnically diverse areas in the western part of the borough, held a meeting to discuss the *Children of the Rainbow Curriculum*, a 443-page guide to multicultural education put out by the New York City Board of Education, avidly supported by Mayor Dinkins and Schools Chancellor Joseph Fernandez, and representing the views of a "diverse" group of educators. About two hundred parents came to the meeting, which was held in the auditorium of Van Wyck Junior High School, to express their opinions to the local school board. The main item for discussion was the section of the *Children of the Rainbow Curriculum* subtitled "Fostering Positive Attitudes Toward Sexuality," which called on teachers, starting in the first grade, to "include references to lesbians/gay people in all curricular areas" and generally to encourage respect for homosexuals.

Other Queens school boards were not happy with the curriculum. The board of District 24, that ethnically most diverse part of Queens, the one with eighty-three different languages, had already formally rejected the entire *Rainbow Curriculum*—and then, as a result, had been suspended by Chancellor Fernandez. So had neighboring School Board 29. Now the parents of School Board 28 were assembled to engage one another in discussion over the issue.

Sitting on the wooden chairs in the badly lighted auditorium was the great American rainbow, the rainbow presumed by ideological multiculturalism to carry, apparently, within the pigmentation of its component parts, ideas remarkably similar to those of the multiculturalists themselves—political liberalism, a desire for multiculturalism, a feeling that the imposition of an alien, white, Eurocentric identity will deprive them of self-esteem and pride of place, and, above all perhaps, a sense of common feeling with all the other presumed oppressed peoples of the country. About three-quarters of the audience was black or Hispanic or of East Indian origin; about 25 percent of it was white.

As it turns out, a large majority of the people of color who are immigrants to this country today, including those from Asia and the Caribbean, are Christian; or they are Muslim or Buddhist or Hindu, and, like the Catholics and Protestants, they hold tight to very traditional family values. So it was with these parents who represented true diversity, not the kind that is envisaged in the universities or the diversity-training workshops of Equity Institute, but the real kind, where people are stubbornly different, not so much from each other but from the models of New Age enlightenment they supposedly represent. With very few exceptions, the Hispanic, black, and East Indian parents were angrily against the new curriculum, and especially the lesbian/gay component of it. Most did not voice opposition to homosexuality per se (though there were a couple of strong homophobes in the crowd), but they were almost all against teaching that homosexuality was a normal alternative in the schools. This is diversity.

Diversity, after all, means that some among us are homosexuals who suffer from discrimination and also fight against it. Gay activists, as everybody knows, have a certain political influence in New York, enough to ensure that the provision for teaching respect for homosexuality was included in the *Rainbow Curriculum* in the first place. Others among us are people who believe, in accordance with what they take to be the Judeo-Christian tradition, that it is a tyranny of the minority, a dictatorship of virtue, if the "correct" attitude about homosexuality is taught to children in the public schools, that "correct" attitude formulated by the gay activists themselves. They believe that that would be to deny diversity, which is diversity of opinion and of religious conviction. It is the same kind of diversity manifested by the Irish, the Italians, the Poles, and the Jews who sat in those same seats in Queens and sent their children to the same schools a generation or two ago, and who would also have opposed teaching about homosexuality to their first-grade children.

The consistent belief of black and white, Hispanic and East Indian parents at Queens School Board District 28 was that the Board of Education, in trying to engineer social change, was usurping the family's role in imparting values. The District 28 parents did not present themselves as victims of racism or of Eurocentrism or of sexism or of any other ism. They did not feel sorry for themselves. They were forceful, often eloquent, bold, straightforward, unembarrassed about their views, and they did not need anybody else to tell them who they were or what they should believe. A lack of self-esteem did not seem to be their problem. When one black woman who was in favor of the proposed new curriculum said, "We shouldn't discriminate because blacks have been discriminated against since we've been in this country," she was essentially shouted down by an audience apparently not interested in the philosophy of victimization. When a white woman argued, "There's no reason why my kids can't learn that [homosexuality] is OK," others in the crowd shouted out, "You teach them."

The parents used words like "brainwashing" and "indoctrination" to describe the *Rainbow Curriculum*. They said that there were guns in the schools, that children were failing in basic subjects like reading and math. "And," said one black mother of two boys, "you're worried about somebody being gay? Give me a break." Of the twenty-eight parents who spoke at the meeting, twenty-two of them were against the *Rainbow Curriculum*, six were in favor.

I should point out here that I am not expressing agreement with these people from Queens whose attitudes about homosexuality and religion are not at all the same as mine. My point is only that the good-hearted stereotypes created around them by the ethnic militants who lobbied for the *Rainbow Curriculum* in the first place are just that—stereotypes, bearing no more resemblance to reality than any other set of stereotypes. If there was any sentiment among these parents for a basic change in the American identity, it did not come through in their comments.

"We will not have any of this taught in our schools because we think it's wrong," said a black minister. "This country was founded on the Judeo-Christian manner of serving the Lord. We came here saying that God created Adam and Eve, not Adam and Steve."

A Hispanic member of the group, and a mother of three children, brought the audience to its feet when she said she wanted Christianity, not homosexuality, in the classroom. "We are a Christian nation," said one black woman, also to applause, agreeing in this respect with Mississippi governor Kirk Fordice, whose comments along those lines in 1992 were treated with such ridicule and protested so adamantly by the elites that he apologized for them. Some other remarks from the heart of multicultural Queens:

A black woman: "By sending my children to public school, I don't feel that I give up the right to teach them the morality that I believe and the things I'd like them to hold important."

Another black woman: "Let me talk about tolerance. Tolerance is not something a school should teach. It's something that has to come from the home. . . . I believe our schools can't teach students how to read, to write, and to do mathematics. I fail to see how any representative or any group . . . is going to get a program going that's going to help students, parents tolerate homosexuality or whatever else there is. . . . Tolerance is a thing that I find insulting because whether you like me or not, I don't really care. I'm here. If you have a problem with me, it's a condition that you have to resolve for yourself."

A white man: "Is sexual preference a culture? What about other sexual preferences, are they cultures also? The gay activists were highly involved in the creation of this. The campaign to impose their homosexual values on our school system shows consistently contempt for our parental rights. . . . Remember that the *Children of the Rainbow* specifically tells teachers that in all subjects they are to mention the gay and lesbian lifestyles. This means that in math, reading, and writing, our children will have to hear about this. And remember, this is the first grade. Teaching this style five hours a day, five days a week amounts to indoctrination."

A black man: "I love all mankind and all womankind. But we are about to lose the war. If we permit our young ones to be taught a lifestyle that God does not support, then we are going to lose the war."

A Hispanic woman: "We love our gay and lesbian sisters and brothers, but at this point, we have the right to ask as parents what's being taught to our children."

A black woman: "I took the opportunity to go down to the school board and read the curriculum. They want not only to teach our children about gay, lesbian lifestyles. They want to teach our children about gender-appropriate behavior, meaning that your son or your daughter will not be able to tell whether they're a girl or a boy. You have to read this curriculum. It's more dangerous than we even suspect."

A white woman: "What they're trying to do is take our children and form them into their ideal perfect society. So what if in ten years from now or twenty years from now they have a different ideal perfect society? And who's going to be raising our children's children? Us? Or the schools? These are our children."

Not that it matters, but, just for the record, it should be pointed out that there has been in all of the talk about *Workforce 2000*, and especially in the idea that white Europeans will become a minority by the end of the century, a considerable exaggeration. True, demographic change is occurring, and since it is impossible to predict with certainty either future birthrates or rates of immigration, it is simply not possible to know how much the "color" of the population will change in the decades ahead. Projections at the end of 1992 made it appear that nothing quite as rapid or as portentous as the change predicted by that *Time* magazine cover story will take place. Certainly, however, we will, as Clayton Carson predicted, be ever less white and ever more brown.

One study by the Census Bureau, which assumes that the immigration and birthrates will continue unchanged for the next century, shows the total nonwhite population of the United States at about 25 percent of the total in the year 2040, roughly a half century from now.* A study of the Urban Institute puts the total minority population in that year at about 40 percent of the total, minorities here including Hispanics, many of whom are white.† Some geographic areas—

---

*Gregory Spencer, *Projections of the Population of the United States, by Age, Sex, and Race: 1888–2080* (Washington, D.C.: U.S. Department of Commerce, Bureau of the Census), page 10.

†Passell and Edmonston, *Immigration and Race in the United States*, page 11.

Queens being one of them—already have nonwhite majorities. In-deed, in New York City as a whole, whites are the largest single group, but they are less than half of the total population. Still, nationwide, it is reasonable to believe that for the next half century at least, even if the immigration from non-European countries stays at its current rate, the United States will continue to have a considerable majority of people who are white and European in origin. (The current zeal to define people by race and ethnicity leads us to forget that Hispanic roots lie in Europe.)

This in and of itself is not very important. Still, the multiculturalist argument has made so much of the supposed dramatic change in the nature of the American population that it seems important to describe these changes more accurately than is often done. The real question is not how quickly the white majority will disappear, but what is the significance of the slow but steady growth in the numbers and in the percentages of people whose ancestors did not come from Europe?

There are those who began to feel in the early 1990s that these newcomers were a serious problem. The argument, being made in some conservative publications, was that cultural difference does mat-ter, some cultures being far more prone to economic failure, welfare dependency, and poverty than others, and some consideration should be given to closing the door to these groups.* These conservative, anti-immigration arguments share a striking common assumption with the arguments of the more strident multiculturalists: neither has much faith in the power of assimilation.

The conservatives want to reduce the number of certain groups of immigrants, those, they say, whose cultures are most prone to economic failure, welfare dependency, unemployment, criminality. The multiculturalists want us to change the mainstream culture so as to make the newcomers feel better without undergoing the ordeals of assimilation. Both put the newcomer into an exotic and unassimilable category. Both accept the idea that the deepest aspect of identity is race and ethnicity, and both in this sense stand well outside the liberal tradition, which values the inherent capacity of the individual to make himself or herself, shedding in the process the Frenchman de Crèvecoeur's "ancient prejudices."

But the ideological multiculturalists take this point of view to a sentimental extreme. While the conservatives feel that assimilation is

*The most influential of such pleading was Peter Brimelow, "Time to Rethink Immigra-tion?" *National Review*, June 22, 1992.

essential, and worry because they feel that different cultures and different races cannot shed "ancient prejudices," the multicultural ideology, disillusioned with the Eurocentric culture, maintains that having all those different cultures sharing the same territory should be the antiassimilation model of the future, the salad, as some put it, rather than the melting pot. The underlying belief here, based on the anodyne view of diversity presented by, say, those Copeland Griggs videotapes, is that all cultures are of at least equal value. How else, for example, to explain the fervent advocacy in schools of education that teachers must adapt their lessons to the different learning styles of culturally different pupils—some of whom, as Annette Kolodny, the dean of students at the University of Arizona, put it, "reason by analogy" rather than using "linear logic."

This is a warm and fuzzy concept that gains support because of its closeness to the American reflex toward toleration and the Western belief in cultural relativism. Of course, it is true that all cultures have value and are worthy of respect. But the idea that all cultures are equal in all respects, and particularly in their ability to prosper in a modern industrial economy, ignores most of the serious thinking about the correlation between culture and results done over the last century—ever since Max Weber adduced the intimate connection between the Protestant ethic and the development of capitalism.

If I was hoping that my daughter could have the same access to a career in physics as my son, I had better hope she learns some linear logic, even if Kolodny thinks that some other culturally formed mode, such as "reason by analogy" (whatever that is), is to be equally valued. Clearly, those people who learn "linear logic," who do well in school, who learn English, and who function in the common culture of the public arena are the ones who will do well in the America of the future. That is assimilation. The misty-eyed belief that all cultures are equal in all things is just nonsense, an encouragement of cultures of failure, an abdication of the responsibility to think clearly about what immigrant and nonwhite children need to know in order to succeed.

The question is not what color the population will be, or what will be its origin. Everybody knows that there already are and will be in the future more blacks and Asians present on what was, until a couple of decades ago, an all-white scene. Eventually, probably before the end of the next century, whites of European origin will be the largest plurality in the United States, but no longer the majority. There are more blacks and others in newsrooms, conference rooms, classrooms, and boardrooms than ever before as civil rights legislation has taken effect and the once-discouraged presence of nonwhites has come to be encouraged both by a change in attitude and by programs aimed at including them. The conspicuously high numbers of Asians being admitted to the best schools is often cited as an indicator of the national shift away from its European origins. In the Ivy League these days nearly one-quarter of the entering classes is of Asian origin. In California by the year 2000, half the population will be Asian, black, or Hispanic.

It is this part of the picture that is easily visible throughout Queens, and even in Astoria, in the neighborhood of Morris Reichman's hardware store.

When the Braun-Reichmans lived there, Astoria had sizable Jewish, Italian, and German populations. The size of the population has changed very little since then, but the composition of the district has. In the 1960s and 1970s it became one of the biggest Greek neighborhoods in the country. In more recent years, there has been an influx of the same groups that have settled in other parts of Queens. I stopped by the attached house on Seventy-sixth Street in Jackson Heights where Gizella and Morris moved their family from the apartment above the hardware store, and an elderly Asian gentleman opened the door. He seemed flustered by my attempts to speak with him and quickly went back inside his house, so I never found out who he was or what country he came from. My assumption was that his children, like Morris's before them, were going to medical school.

Just up Astoria Boulevard from Morris Reichman's former hardware store is a stretch of Broadway, not to be confused with the more famous Broadway of Manhattan. This is the unglamorous Broadway of Queens, a portion of which is now Astoria's main commercial district and where the true ethnic variety of the neighborhood is most conspicuously visible. Here on the short stretch between Thirty-fourth and Thirty-third Streets are a Greek gift shop called Panelliniou and the Pan Asiatic Travel Service. Nearby are a branch of the Chase Manhattan Bank and the El Greco superette, advertising "specialities from around the world," especially Greek coffees and olive oils. Then there is a Greek pastry shop and beyond that the Romeli Taberna, and near that is Gossips Saloon and Restaurant (billing laser karaoke every Sunday—"We provide lyrics, background music and back-up and you perform live"). There is Neil's Health Foods and the First Choice Meat Market with signs in the Cyrillic alphabet in the window. Further down is Brighton Cleaners, Rapid Medical Care, and Beatrix Books and Pictures, and beyond that at the end of the block is the Mun Loy Restaurant, specializing in a multicultural mix of "Cantonese, Szechuan & Spanish Cuisine."

At the corner of Thirty-third Street is the Mowchuk Grocery and Deli, advertising an even more culturally eclectic mixture—BANGLA DESH, INDIA AND GREEK, says the sign. TEA COFFEE CANDIES CIGA-RETTES. The store is owned by a group of five partners, all recent immigrants from Bangladesh, including the Mohammed brothers, Farooque and Majibur, both from Dhaka. Here is a latter-day version of the Braun family saga, separated by seventy-five years or so and about twenty city blocks. It is remarkable the extent to which the Brauns and the Mohammed brothers share a similar experience.

Majibur Mohammed came to North America in 1985, he said. "I was twenty-four or twenty-five. There's no opportunity in Dhaka, so I applied for a visa. I got a visa." The visa was for Canada, where Majibur first came. Herman Braun arrived without a valid visa and was able to enter the United States as a Christmas present from Warren Harding. Majibur paid two hundred dollars to a smuggler and got across the American border near Seattle clandestinely. He boarded a Greyhound bus and traveled straight through to New York, where inside of a few days he had gotten a five-dollar-an-hour job on a construction site. He worked there for a few weeks. Then he found he could make more money, about seventy dollars a day, as a delivery boy for a takeout restaurant. He did that for a while, and then he worked in a garment factory for more than seventy dollars a day. In 1988, he was able to get working papers and a green card, which regularized his status. After that he got a job working in the faculty club of the Columbia University Medical School.

"I work seven days a week in the last seven years," Majibur said. "No days off. I don't have a life." He sends much of his earnings to his family back in Dhaka, where he got married on one of his annual trips home. A couple of years after he arrived, Majibur sent money for his younger brother Farooque to join him. Back in Dhaka his wife gave birth to a baby girl, his first child. "My wife is not here so I feel very bad, but I can't afford to have my wife here because the rent is too much, and if I bring my daughter it's very hard for me," he said.

Majibur saved his money. He shared an apartment in Queens with other immigrants from Bangladesh who, like him, had traveled to the United States without their families. Eventually a group of them pooled their resources and for about seventy thousand dollars bought an existing grocery store on Broadway in Astoria that catered mostly to South Asian immigrants.

The store is not chic. It has the shabby look of a similar establishment back home. In the entrance are large sacks of rice, rice from India, rice from Thailand, rice from Alabama. There is a rack of Bengali newspapers, three of which are published in New York. The Mohammed brothers sell lottery tickets, cigarettes, music cassettes, condoms, candies, inexpensive generic cosmetics. In a large cardboard box standing unevenly on top of some burlap bags of rice is a jumbled shipment of bright yellow plastic piggy banks. The store rents movie videos in Bengali, Hindi, and Urdu, the dominant languages of, respectively, Bangladesh, India, and Pakistan. There is a shelf of items for ninety-nine cents—cosmetics and baby oil, shampoo, plastic bowls, and dishwashing liquid. Inside is a freezer with ice cream and whole frozen fish. The Korean stores put fresh produce in front and durable goods in back. In this Bangladeshi establishment these items are in reverse order, so that meats and poultry and fresh fruits and vegetables are in a storeroom in back (whence they are fetched by a store employee).

Majibur is darkly handsome, tall, taciturn. He has thick eyebrows and black hair and a nascent middle-aged girth. On one Sunday morning I watched as he tended his cash register. He wore a green-print shirt and gray cord pants and had a gold watch (fake gold or real gold, I could not tell) on his wrist. A small but steady stream of customers came in, most of them Bangladeshis, Indians, and Pakistanis. These, I thought, are people who do not get along very well back in South Asia, but there seem to be no open conflicts among them in Astoria. Majibur spoke in Bengali with the Bangladeshi customers, English with the Indians and Pakistanis.

They bought eggplant and frozen fish, cigarettes, whole plucked chickens, garlic, cumin powder, green beans, rice, Hostess cupcakes, chili peppers. People returned videotapes rented from the night before. One Caucasian woman came in and bought a carton of cigarettes. A Korean came in and asked Majibur if he had ice, saying that she would come in for it later. Another Asian man, perhaps also Korean, came in, looked around, and walked out again. Perhaps he was casing out the competition. Outside on the sunny street, elderly ladies with blue-gray hair helped each other climb from the curb to the sidewalk. A swarthy man in a turban walked by holding the hand of a brown-skinned little girl. Diagonally across the street the Greek restaurant, Uncle George's, a neighborhood classic, was opening for lunch. I asked Majibur how business was.

"We don't have enough money and we can't get credit to expand," he said. But he allowed that the income from the store was enough to cover the expenses of all five investors and for all of them to have begun the process of getting papers for their families to join them in New York. In short, Majibur and his business partners were slowly establishing themselves as new Americans.

It would be glib and facile to say that I could really understand Majibur—not any more than he could have penetrated to the interior life of Gizella and Morris Reichman had he spent a day or so with them in their hardware store down the street. A part of the unknowable stems from the fact that Majibur is a Muslim from Bangladesh while I am a Jew born in New York. We are different. But are the Mohammed brothers more different from me than Gizella and Morris were from the American-born of 1920?

Whatever Majibur's mysteries, there is certainly much about him that remains within the time-honored pattern of immigration and that links him to such earlier arrivals as his neighbors of another era, the Braun family from Hungary. As a native of a former British colony, he spoke English before he left Bangladesh. He came, not from a poor peasant family as did so many earlier immigrants to America, but from an educated, middle-class clan that included some wealthy businessmen and professional people. "My cousin has a big factory," Majibur told me. "I worked as his production director. I made three hundred dollars a month, which is a lot of money. All my cousins, all my relatives, are very rich, but my family is the poorest, so we think of coming here. But all of my family is educated. We have one doctor in my family. My grandfather and my father both died, but they were well educated. My uncle has an M.A. I went to college, but I failed the graduation exams."

A member of the global village, Majibur had seen American movies and American sitcoms and met Americans back home in Dhaka before he set foot in North America. "When I was in my country I met American people. Very nice, very gentle. I read about New York. It's the biggest economic city in the world. My dream: if I could make money there I could take care of my family." It was the same aborted dream of Herman Braun.

Majibur's major surprise and his major chagrin did not stem from the fact that he has to work very hard on Broadway and Thirty-third Street in Astoria, Queens. He expected that. What shocks him is the insecurity of life in Astoria and other parts of New York, the terrible rates of crime, the prevalence of muggers, the fact that he knows people from his homeland who had survived floods and typhoons and poverty and been killed in robberies on the streets of America.

I asked him what kind of education he wanted for his daughter once she arrived in this country, and he replied that he would send her to a regular American school, perhaps a boarding school if he can afford it. "I hope that she has an American education but I want her to keep her own culture too," he said. How will you do that? I asked. Majibur did not answer right away. "It is very difficult," he said, finally. "Maybe I'll send her back to Bangladesh when she is in the tenth or eleventh grade so she can have a year of schooling there."

One of Morris Reichman's disappointments was that none of his sons or grandsons studied for the rabbinate. I thought of that as I wondered what kind of life Majibur's daughter would have. Working for the *New York Times*, I have interviewed other children of newly arrived Muslim immigrants and listened to their stories of tensions between the anything-goes secularism of American life and the customs of their conservative parents. They resolve it in different ways, but everybody that I talked to was interested in upward mobility, in good schooling, in lives in business or in the professions. Even those who chose to hew closely to religious practice, even the women who wore veils and never had a date with a young man until they were ready for marriage, wanted fulfilling and interesting careers. They were not interested in reproducing the lives of their ancestors. They wanted assimilation into the public sphere of American life even as they preserved in private lives a separate South Asian or Muslim culture.

Whatever happens to Majibur's daughter will be a combination of several factors: her native culture, her parents' influence, the experiences she has in the United States, and her own temperament and personality. The daughter will not be an empty vessel into which her father or some social engineer can pour whatever he wants and create a cultural type. Freed from the restraints of conservative group determinism, she will exhibit the same stubborn particularity of other American children. She will be free to be an individual, and, try as they might, the multiculturalists will probably not succeed in imposing a racial and ethnic identity on her.

But note that Majibur is ambitious for her, even though she is a girl. This in itself is a departure from a certain South Asian tradition, which sees women as subordinate to men, certainly in the world of work. He is a modern man, Westernized, probably closer in his expectations and values to his new country than to his old one. Majibur is, in short, close enough to the American mainstream already to allow him to be successfully multicultural in his new country. He and his daughter and his future children will, in short, surely engage in their own version of what Norman Podhoretz has famously called the "brutal bargain" that newcomers have always made with their adoptive American home. In exchange for the blessings of American life, he and his family will shed the more obvious trappings of the past, particularly the languages, customs, and mores that might prevent assimilation into the American mainstream, while, in their private lives, they will reserve whatever degree of ethnic identity that they wish for themselves.

In 1992, an article in the *New York Times* described how a San Francisco hospital was adapting to the new "diversity" of American life. In San Francisco, where one-third of the population is now of Asian descent, doctors and nurses at General Hospital were taking greater note of some of their patients' traditional beliefs—for example that women who have just given birth should not eat vegetables. Why? Because, according to yin-yang cosmology, vegetables are a cold food and in the period immediately after the birth of an infant, women are especially vulnerable to cold energy. Thus, the doctors' advice: eat vegetables but cook them with ginger, which is a hot food and thus to be desired.

The article was a small illustration of the breadth of the belief in a new, unprecedented degree of diversity requiring adaptations. Most of the doctors and nurses at the hospital, the article reported, "argue that knowing the beliefs of Asian patients is essential to good care." What they really mean is that they need to know their patients' superstitions, and perhaps they do. But the article, which made much of the fact that some patients are elderly Indo-Chinese refugees and illiterate Hmong tribesmen, described a well-intentioned group engaging in that good-natured orientalism, in which vestiges of the exotic are made to stand for the entirety of a rapidly changing and much modernized culture, that of Asia. This seemed especially strange given the milieu of the doctors and nurses, San Francisco, which did not wait for Vietnamese refugees to arrive before becoming acquainted with exotic medical beliefs. Even today, after all, among third- and fourth-generation Americans, haven't there been all sorts of fads and ideas about alternative medicine, much of it, like the utterly unscientific belief in the wondrous properties of acupuncture and herbal medications, coming from Asia but receiving a credulous reception among millions of "Euro-Americans"?

There is, in fact, a lightly racist tinge to the idea that the superstitions of Asians have to be accommodated in a hospital that would, presumably, not be so multicultural in its attitude if the superstitions resided in the minds of white folks. Well before Hmong tribesmen started building communities in the United States, we were already a country where advanced scientific rationality coexisted with a great profusion of superstitions, where health spas for corporate executives have resident astrologers and subcontinental gurus to help with meditation, and where millions of people nurture obsessions about negative and positive spiritual energy, obsessions unsurpassed in their absence of scientific basis by the beliefs of any of the Cambodian rice farmers cited in the *Times* article.

The *Times* reported in October 1992 that the most successful cable-television program aimed at selling things to viewers was Dionne Warwick's "Psychic Friends Network," which urges people to call psychics on a 900 telephone number. A few weeks earlier the paper printed a long account of a woman who had made millions acting as the medium for a fifty-thousand-year-old Cro-Magnon man named Ramtha who gave advice to individuals in the here and now. There was no indication that either the woman, J. Z. Knight, described by the *Times* as "perhaps the most popular of the New Age spirit-channelers," or her clients were Hmong tribesmen. Knight's ex-husband, Jeffrey, was suing her, claiming that she had used Ramtha to bully him into accepting a meager divorce settlement.

And yet somehow the suggestion is rife that new Asian immigrants present a cultural challenge and a degree of diversity that the nation has never seen before. The *Times* article about the San Francisco hospital usefully quoted one doctor, notably of Asian ancestry, who dissented from the prevalent multiculturalist view. Peter Ng, a pediatrician, declared: "There are 20 zillion cultures out there and there's no way you can know every quirk." What is essential, he noted, was merely the common sense to be sensitive to the individual, to be curious, "to ask, and then ask again."

I wonder if any of the good-hearted doctors and nurses attentive to the odd cultural characteristics of Asians understood the deeper cultural and political context lying in the ancestral backgrounds of their patients' lives, the way their respect for exoticism was actually unwitting complicity in a repressive tradition. They might, for example, take a look at the works of Lu Xun, China's greatest twentieth-century writer. Lu Xun is credited by many Chinese with having forged a new consciousness for the youth of his era, a consciousness of the sclerotic injustices of the conservative past in which superstition, including medical superstition, served the interests of the holders of power. One of his most famous essays is a brief autobiographical introduction to a collection of stories called *Call to Arms*. In it, Lu recalls how, during the sickness of his father, he was sent regularly to a pawnshop, where he got a few coins in exchange for yet another increment of his family's possessions, which he would then use at the pharmacy to buy what his father's doctor, an "eminent" physician, prescribed—"aloe roots dug up in winter, sugar-cane that had been three years exposed to frost, original pairs of crickets, and ardisia that had seeded."

One of the most powerful of Lu Xun's stories is called "Medicine" and concerns a character named Old Shuang, who tries to save his sick son by spending his last silver coins on a "guaranteed cure" for consumption—a steamed bun dripped in warm human blood.

Needless to say, Lu Xun's father died despite the eminent physician's treatment with whole crickets and frosty sugarcane. Old Shuang's son was not saved by costly human blood. Fortunately, there is no evidence that most Asian immigrants, coming to us in the decades since Lu Xun wrote his stories, remain tyrannized by ignorance and superstition—and that is how Lu Xun saw these aspects of his culture, as a tyranny, as a set of utterly unrational and unscientific beliefs that bolstered the authority of a traditionalist ruling class. In most of Asia, Western-style medicine has been the norm for decades, with perhaps some ginseng root harmlessly thrown in for placebo effect, in much the same way as Americans take vitamin C tablets or deodorized garlic pills as general tonics. If the good doctors and nurses of San Francisco, with the notable exception of the Asian Dr. Ng, actually think that

in Canton and Shanghai, Seoul and Phnom Penh, doctors rely on
something other than what their counterparts in America rely on to
treat disease, they are very much mistaken. True, in Taipei near
the Lungshan Temple, middle-aged men drink fresh, raw snakes'
blood mixed with spirits to keep them potent, and, probably, if they
think the potion works, it actually does work. But when they really
get sick, they go to the doctor who was educated at the Taiwan
National University Medical School or, perhaps, Yale, and they get
the same treatment, grounded in the same Western science, that you
and I get.

Queens again has something to tell us about this. Flushing, a
district to the west of Astoria that was once full of modestly middle-
class Jews, Italians, and Irish, has been settled now by new Asian
immigrants and transformed into New York's second Chinatown. Most
of the new arrivals are from Korea, Taiwan, and the People's Republic
of China. You cross into Flushing over the William Prince Bridge,
which goes past Shea Stadium, and the Asian influence is immediately
apparent. The big sign on the Champion Billiards Hall is in Korean.
The Power Christian Center is marked in Chinese characters. Beyond
is a forest of exotic writing, a not-so-little Hong Kong intermingling
with a little Seoul.

I visited Pauline Chu, the head of the Chinese-American Parents
Association, who is herself a good illustration of the nature of Chinese
immigration. Chu was born in Nanjing on the Yangtze River in southern China. She went to Taiwan in 1948 when the Communist revolution was about to succeed on the Mainland. She came to the United
States to be a graduate student in educational psychology at the University of Minnesota, and if some doctor tried to cater to her belief
in the yin and the yang as part of his way of treating her, she would
probably find the gesture racist and condescending. In 1986, having
come to Queens, she founded the Chinese-American Parents Association that, as she put it in her very American way, using a vocabulary
that would have been quite foreign to her ancestors in China, "helps
parents become aware of their rights and responsibilities in the
schools."

She gave a capsule history of the Asian settlement of Flushing,
responding to my request for the reasons Asians settled in this particular part of New York City. In the 1970s, she said, a Chinese real estate
developer made an effort to attract Asian settlers to properties that

he owned in Flushing. "A lot of the newcomers at that time were from Taiwan, where the language is Mandarin. In Manhattan's Chinatown, Cantonese is the main language and the Taiwanese don't understand Cantonese, so a lot of them took the number-seven subway line to Flushing."

Many of the immigrants from Taiwan, like Chu herself, are a far cry from earlier waves of Chinese immigrants who came without their families to build the railroads, or, for that matter, earlier waves of Irish or Italian laborers. "Many of them are lawyers, doctors, accountants, self-employed people," Chu said. "In the 1960s especially, the typical immigrant was a scholar. He had to have a pretty good education in order to pass the exam to come abroad in the first place. Eighty to ninety percent of them were students. A lot of them got master's degrees and Ph.D.'s, and now they are professors at universities or they work in research institutes. A smaller number of them became businessmen."

A study by the Asian-American Center at Queens College found, after new immigration laws allowed a first large influx of Asians into New York, that 20 percent of them were "professionals, already trained in Western-style urban occupations in Asia." Many of them already spoke English. Most, the study indicates, were Christians. Many had been engaged in small businesses when they arrived, making it easier for them to establish small businesses here. Many from Taiwan, Hong Kong, Southeast Asia, and China came to study at American universities, and they stayed behind after their studies were complete. As of 1989, the Chinese in Queens had set up thirty Protestant churches, one Catholic church, and "a scattering" of Buddhist temples. In 1987, when the Flushing Merchants and Business Association announced that it was breaking from a decades-long tradition and would not put up Christmas decorations, the Flushing Chinese Business Association stepped into the breach, raising money so that the Christmas decorations could continue.*

What does this mean for multiculturalism? Pauline Chu had some observations to make on that subject that are perhaps representative of other Chinese immigrants. Children, she said, need to learn to "respect all cultures, especially in Queens, where there are so many of them." At the same time, the only way to succeed in American life is "to enter the mainstream." She said that many Asian parents have

*Chen Hsiang-shui and John Kuo Wei Tchen, *Toward a History of Chinese in Queens* (New York: Queens College, CUNY, 1989).

a great deal of difficulty with at least one multicultural program, bilingual education.

By and large, Asian parents, she said, don't want to have their children taught in bilingual classrooms because that suggests an incapacity to succeed in the regular classrooms. There have been incidents in which school bureaucrats, eager to gather together enough bilingual students to meet the minimum number for a program, have put Asian youngsters into bilingual classes against the wishes of the parents.

"The district sends every Korean student, including some American-born students, into bilingual ed," Chu said, "and every year there are protests."

While we were talking, her son came into her office with a schoolmate. Both were students at Syracuse University on summer vacation. Both were carrying racquetball rackets and wearing warm-up suits and Reebok shoes. The son was there to give his mother his American Express bill to pay. He spoke English like any other young American of his social class and age. "When he was in sixth grade," Chu said, "he was reading at a ninth-grade level, so I sent him back to Taiwan for one year to learn Chinese. He came back in the eighth grade and caught up again quickly."

There are gangs in Chinatown, gangs organized along the lines of the ancient Chinese secret societies, just as Italian gangs took the methods of the ancient Sicilian order known as the Mafia. There are sweatshops where Chinese capitalists exploit illegal immigrants. There are prostitution rings and gambling dens; there are clan societies and benevolent associations, just as there were in the Old Country. There are fortune-tellers, geomancers, theaters where kung fu movies play, and painting studios where children learn the ancient arts of calligraphy. There are dozens of family-name associations and regional associations where people with the same surname or who come from the same country or province in China can get some help if they need it. And there are tens of thousands of Chinese like Pauline Chu and her son Jeffrey who know all of this and speak the ancient languages and at the same time are perfectly at home in American society.

Like the wise Dr. Ng said, there are too many cultures out there for all of them to become a part of the national curriculum. There always have been. Nothing is new except that we are newly reluctant to demand the brutal bargain as the price of entry into the national club. But even if we are too sensitive to demand it, the immigrants will continue, willingly, to make that bargain whether the rest of us ask it of them or not.

The Queens College study of the Chinese in Queens talked of a famous incident in New York City's recent history. In January 1988, the *New York Times* published a front-page photograph of eleven students from the Benjamin Cardozo High School in Queens, all of whom had become finalists for the Westinghouse Science Prizes. All eleven were Asians or of Asian ancestry. There was much speculation in the press and in private conversation thereafter about what it was about Asians that made them so successful.

One explanation was that they came from stable, two-parent homes. Another was that their culture already emphasized hard work. A third was that failure in their culture was commonly attributed to the individual, rather than to "the system," and so, knowing that shortcomings would be attributed to them, they worked very hard to succeed. The students from Cardozo High School wrote a letter of their own protesting these attempts at generalization, illustrating how each of them was different from the others.

The students said they were all proud of their ethnicity. "But," they continued, "we are concerned that whenever a group of people such as ours is given wide attention and scrutiny, there is a danger of losing the individuality of each person in that group. Such labelling leads to stereotyping, which in its most extreme form is the root of prejudice, a disease than can never be cured by science."

Chapter 6

THE SEARCH FOR SIN

The city council of St. Paul, Minnesota, is a liberal group in a liberal town, proud of its progressive record on matters of racial justice. And so, in 1982, when some anti-Semitic graffiti was scrawled onto the walls of a St. Paul synagogue, it was well in character for the city council to take firm measures against crimes motivated by prejudice. It unanimously passed the Religious, Racial and Ethnic Acts of Malice Law, which required harsher penalties for crimes committed because of bias or hatred.

The law, as modified, also unanimously, in 1990, encompassed any behavior that could be "reasonably understood as communicating threats of harm, violence, contempt or hatred on the basis of race, color, creed, religion, or gender" and its passage, its sponsors said, came as a way of combating what they saw as an increase in crimes of hate, bigotry, prejudice, racism, and anti-Semitism, all of it intolerable for a society of the late twentieth century.

In fact, the St. Paul law was hardly unusual. Some thirty states have passed laws enhancing the penalties for bias crimes, and many colleges and universities have enacted regulations that get students or faculty into deep trouble if they make hateful remarks about somebody else's race or sex, national origin, handicap, or, in at least one case, what was called "Vietnam veteran status." No voices of protest were raised in St. Paul when the authorities used the new ordinance to prosecute a number of crimes.

In one instance, some young thugs broke into the Hillel House at Macalester College in St. Paul, drew swastikas, defecated in the kosher kitchen, and destroyed some property.

"They were prosecuted under the bias-crime enhancement provision, since the crime was done as an act of racial or religious hatred," Tom Foley, the Ramsey County district attorney, told me, making the case that the law was justified and effective. "We've found that people are willing to plead to a more serious crime rather than admit that they are racists or bigots."

Then in the predawn hours of June 21, 1990, a white teenager named Robert Viktora, acting together with a few friends, taped together two broken chair legs in the form of a cross, planted it in the yard of Russell and Laura Jones and their five children, who lived across the street, and set it on fire. In so doing, Viktora made legal history. He was prosecuted and convicted of committing a "bias-motivated assault" under the St. Paul hate-crimes ordinance. He appealed his conviction. The case went to the Supreme Court of the United States, which overturned it. The Court, whose decision provoked loud protests from such organizations as the Anti-Defamation League of B'nai B'rith and the National Association for the Advancement of Colored People, ruled in essence that the ordinance put an unjustifiable limitation on the First Amendment.*

The decision received national coverage and produced anger and dismay in St. Paul. Mayor Jim Scheibel was quoted in the local press saying that the city needed a law "that will not tolerate these crimes." District Attorney Foley told reporters, "This is obviously a setback for local and state governments that are attempting to curb the massive increase in hate crimes."

The real problem, as Foley's comment about a "massive increase" indicates, was that hate crimes were on the rise and action was needed to combat the trend. The figures told the story. The local press reported statistics published by the Minnesota Bureau of Criminal Apprehension, which since 1989 had been required by law to amass data on hate crime, showing that throughout the state, 425 such offenses had been reported, a disturbing 38 percent increase over the year before. In all, there had been 333 racial-bias crimes in 1991, up from 255 the year before, so in two years the increase in this type of offense was close to 50 percent.[†]

---

*A few months later, the Supreme Court upheld another bias-crime conviction, this one of a black youth guilty of an assault against a white in Wisconsin. The court said that the Wisconsin law aimed at conduct, while the St. Paul statute had aimed explictly at expression, hence the constitutionality of one and the unconstitutionality of the other.

[†]News release of the Minnesota Department of Public Safety, Apr. 9, 1992.

American racism is on the rise. The country is in the midst of a "massive increase in hate crimes."

There is a certain commonsense wisdom, a matter of everyday experience, indicating that these statements cannot be true. It is sadly the case, of course, that there are plenty of bigots, organizations based on racial hate and the ineradicable myth of white superiority. And yet despite its faults, the United States, which once bore a close similarity to South Africa in its treatment of black people, has probably never been less racist—and for that matter less sexist and homophobic—than it is now. Indeed, the case could certainly be made that the movement for civil rights effected a genuine social revolution in smashing the barriers to opportunity that once clearly existed for those who were not male, heterosexual, and, especially, not white.

Yet the idea that the country is mired in racist iniquity lies behind more than efforts to legislate against prejudice. What the writer Heather MacDonald has called the "promiscuous" use of the word "racism," the easy recourse to that term to describe the essential and most important qualities of American life, is a major, explicit element in the broad multiculturalist initiative. It is commonly offered as an explanation for why multiculturalism is happening just now. It spurs sensitivity training and university speech codes, changes in the curricula of elementary and high schools, demands for the mandatory study of the "excluded groups." It determines, perhaps most important, a great deal of the tone and style of the multicultural initiatives, giving them the moral urgency that cannot stem from mere advocacy but must be connected with the fight against the most powerful and insidious forces of darkness.

The data bank NEXIS shows how commonplace has become the idea that bigotry is on the increase. I searched the full data bank for appearances of the phrases "increase in hate crimes" or "rise in hate crimes." In 1980, the furthest back that NEXIS goes, those phrases do not appear at all. In 1985, the two expressions appeared in a total of only 14 articles. In 1990 the number of articles with one or the other of those phrases in them had leaped to 254, and the year after that the figure had gone above 400.

This, of course, is a difficult topic. Bigotry, being no laughing matter, is bound to cause a powerful response, especially among those who belong to groups that have been wholesale victims in the past

and who still live with discrimination. We are a country whose constituent parts include Aryan Nation and Holocaust revisionists, the Ku
Klux Klan and the White Citizens' Council. Slavery existed here for
close to three hundred years, and we are very far from being free of
the heritage of that evil institution. Indeed, my argument here is not
intended to diminish the significance of race or of racism in American
life. I think I have an appreciation of the extent to which race consciousness permeates our existence, of the ways in which race contri-
butes to the sum total of resentments, discomforts, and hatreds that
we experience. Despite what they might say against racial preferences
or affirmative action, few whites would want to change the color of
their skin; and few blacks have reason to be confident that they
will be judged, in a majority-white society, by their character and
their ability alone and not at all by their race. But precisely because
racism and other evils of prejudice are so powerfully present in our
history and social fabric, a bit of care is necessary in the use of the
racist label and its application. My own feeling is that the reckless,
heedless, and glib use of certain words, "racism" above all, but "sexism" and "homophobia" closely following, is a major flaw in standard
multicultural discourse. It is one of the reasons that there is so much
more striking of poses than honestly discussing and grappling with
problems in the United States of America today. The easy multicultural distribution of vile accusations is the main reason that we don't
talk to one another as much as we hurl insults.

Is it really true that racism and other evils are on the rise? The
Minnesota case, just one among many, exemplifies the tendency to
transform exception into rule, a common phenomenon, as we will see
below. The statistics released by the Minnesota Department of Public
Safety, cited by the local press and by the town fathers of St. Paul,
do indeed seem to prove that there is an alarming increase in bigotry.
And yet a closer examination of the reporting on those incidents
reveals not so much a pattern of systematic oppression as more avid
reporting on what amounts to isolated instances of individual deviance
from a socially accepted norm. The experience of Minnesota is part
of a larger pattern. Study after study, report after report, are produced
by those who have something to gain from exaggerating the extent of
racism and other forms of bigotry. The press, unwilling to appear soft
on those issues, lends them full credibility. And yet look at them
closely, and, in almost every instance, the very material of the study
fails to support its conclusion. These studies do show that there is a

great deal of invective in the air, a lot of angry group politics, which, I believe, is more a consequence than a cause of multicultural doctrine. But they also demonstrate something other than what they purport to demonstrate about the extent and ferocity of racism and related evils.

The Minnesota Department of Public Safety's 1991 compilation of bias crimes, the ones that, according to the district attorney, Tom Foley, marked a "massive increase," are broken down into 17 categories. In 1991, for example, there was one cross burning (compared with 7 the year before); there were 4 episodes of what is called "swastika," 77 of "oral abuse," and 118 instances of "simple assault," defined as an attack causing no broken bones or wounds requiring stitches. There were "hanging in effigy" (one incident in 1991), "criminal sexual conduct" (one case), and "arson" (no cases reported in 1991, 2 reported in 1990). The most serious offense associated with bias that takes place with some frequency is "aggravated assault," of which there were 44 reports in 1990 and 33 in 1991.

Do these cases represent a "massive increase" in bigotry? Perhaps if you are among the victims, it would be natural to think so. But overall the 425 cases reported in 1991 represent a fragment of a fraction of the total number of crimes reported each year in Minnesota—roughly 0.002 percent of the total of 203,107 reported crimes, or about one in every 500. Put another way, that is about one bias crime committed for every 8,800 Minnesota residents, and, if the less serious categories "simple assault" and "oral abuse" are taken out, it would be roughly one bias crime per 16,000 residents. In 1991, by contrast, there was one rape per 2,440 state residents and one robbery for roughly every 1,000 people, so the figures on bias crimes themselves do not seem to indicate a state that is rife with racism and bigotry. Four swastikas drawn on public buildings in a year is four swastikas too many, but, assuming that the four were drawn by four different people, that would be one swastika drawer per 1.2 million Minnesotans.

No doubt, some bias crimes go unreported. Many incidents do not get to the attention of the police. Still the situation described in the press as so alarming seems more likely to be a matter of a certain, perhaps even irreducible, racial friction, combined with a small and, unfortunately, very likely irreducible amount of genuine bigotry and racism, but that is nonetheless a minor element in the larger Minnesota context. In the two years covered by the latest Minnesota report there were no murders related to bias, this in a state that had 245 murders during that period. So the "massive increase in hate crimes" is really a phrase out of the handbook of well-intentioned hyperbole. To stress bias crimes as the most alarming problem shows the way the ideologically correct position can dramatically distort priorities. I am not against enhanced penalties for bias crime, but I would like to see enhanced penalties for unbiased murder also, including the black-on-black murder, the brothers killing brothers, which seems to have a vastly more devastating effect on minority communities than bias.

"The whole business of bias reporting is an attempt to get hard data, but it's built on sand," I was told by Bruce Mead, a sergeant in the Department of Public Safety who, until 1992, compiled the reports of incidents that came from beat officers.

"There's so much subjectivity involved. What happens is that a police officer takes the report of an incident, and he has to make a judgment, based on the victim's impression or his impression, whether bias is involved. Sometimes it's obvious. If you have somebody painting graffiti on a black person's home that says 'Kill niggers,' then it's pretty easy to see that bias was the motivation. We have a lot of Hmong in the state, and they have problems where their homes are damaged, and they think it's because of their ethnic origins, and I'll report that as bias because that's the way they feel about it.

"We've been keeping data only since 1988, so obviously we'll see some increases in reporting in the early years," Sergeant Mead continued. "People talk about a big increase in bias cases, but I don't think people are more intolerant or less intolerant. It's a two-edged sword, diversity. People are going to have more contact with each other so there's going to be more understanding and there's also going to be more conflict."

I asked Sergeant Mead about Tom Foley's argument of a "massive increase" in bias incidents. "He has to be reelected" was Mead's reply.

Many are seeking to be reelected, or just to gain attention, or to build a program or merely to have a point of view accepted. There is a sizable industry of exaggeration that combines with a fear of appearing complacent about racism to create a misleading impression of American life. It is misleading, not because it describes the existence of the ancient evils of bigotry and discrimination, but because it holds those evils to be endemic and intensifying, not as disapproved and diminishing. And it is misleading because it confuses the genuine article, the actual bigotry and intolerance that exist, with almost anything that rubs against the moralistic grain.

Certainly, the studies that pour off the presses make a powerful accumulative impression. In 1992, the Anti-Defamation League (ADL) of B'nai B'rith reported that anti-Semitic incidents had increased 11 percent in a single year "to a record total of 1,879," the highest number ever reported in the thirteen years that the organization has conducted its annual Audit of Anti-Semitic Incidents. A year later, the ADL commissioned a poll that found young white adults more likely to hold antiblack views (such as the belief that blacks are more prone to violence than other races) than members of the baby boom generation. The poll found that 31 percent of whites between eighteen and thirty years old held views that were very prejudiced against blacks.

In 1991, the Boston *Globe* reported: "Incidents of racial and religious harassment or intimidation have skyrocketed." There were local reports such as the one about the 50 percent increase in hate crime in two years in Minnesota, and academic hypotheses to the effect that a subtle form of "symbolic racism . . . more indirect, more subtle, more procedural, more ostensibly nonracial" was replacing the blatant racism that, most agreed, was on the wane. The theory of symbolic racism holds that certain generally conservative beliefs, especially opposition to more social programs, are a disguised racism, flourishing precisely because undisguised racism has become socially unacceptable. Racism, in other words, has been driven into the zone of ambiguous expression, double entendre, covert meanings. Or, as one group of scholars has characterized the theory: "Persons who dislike blacks need only declare that they oppose government assistance to blacks not because they dislike them but because they believe in self-reliance."* The point is that conservatism in general, and especially the belief in what have come to be called traditional values—work, family, individualism, self-reliance—are dismissed, with a dazzling flourish of political-science jargon, not just as wrong, but as subtly and therefore insidiously racist.

---

*Paul M. Sniderman et al., "The New Racism," *Journal of Political Science* 35, no. 2 (May 1991): 423, 424.

There is in the search for proof of the depths of racism a common tendency to concentrate on the way things are, rather than the degree to which they have changed. The press, for example, gave wide coverage in 1991 to the results of a very interesting study by the Urban Institute, in Washington, D.C., which showed, in the words of the institute's report, "widespread and entrenched" discrimination against blacks in the workplace. The study, which the Washington *Post* called "a timely reminder of how deeply ingrained racial and social hang-ups are," sent pairs of equally qualified black and white candidates off to apply for jobs listed in the *Post* and the Chicago *Tribune*. One in five of the blacks ran into discrimination. Reports in the press indicted that the whites got further in their applications three times more often than blacks.

Other studies done in recent years across the country show a similarly persistent pattern of racism in the courts—from the racial slurs made by lawyers when they think nobody is listening to the frequency with which the death penalty is meted out to black defendants. In 1991, *Newsday*, the Washington *Post*, the *Wall Street Journal*, and the *New York Times* all reported that the courts in New York were "infested with racism," a phrase that all of the newspapers picked up from the official press release on a report of a special judicial commission formed to investigate the problem.

In 1991, the Carnegie Foundation for the Advancement of Teaching found a "breakdown in civility" on college campuses. *Time* magazine and many other publications that year reported on a finding of the National Institute Against Prejudice and Violence, a group in Baltimore that has monitored bigotry at the universities since 1986. "More than 250 colleges and universities, including top schools such as Brown, Smith and Stanford, have reported racist incidents, ranging from swastikas painted on the walls to violent attacks and death threats," the magazine said. "Virtually every minority group finds itself under fire. . . . Many campuses seem to distill the free-floating bigotries of American society into a lethal brew." In January 1990, the president of Occidental College in Los Angeles, John Slaughter, announced that many blacks studying in predominantly white colleges "face a level of hatred, prejudice and ignorance comparable to that of the days of Bull Connor, Lester Maddox and Orval Faubus."

Belief in an intensification of racist feeling has produced a host of writings, particularly among academics, that stress the worsening nature of the problem, the oppressiveness of American life for those who are not white, and the numerous advantages of whiteness. Derrick Bell, the first-ever tenured black professor of law at the Harvard Law School, in his 1992 book *Faces at the Bottom of the Well*, describes a racial situation that his own position at Harvard would seem at least partially to belie. Bell, who got national attention by resigning from Harvard over the university's failure to hire a black woman to a tenured position on the faculty, insists on the very first page of his book that "Racism is an integral, permanent, and indestructible component of this society." The racism of white America is so powerful that any progress made by black people is more illusory than real, he maintains. Indeed, there has been no progress; things for black people are just as bad as they have ever been, Bell writes. "Even those herculean efforts we hail as successful will produce no more than temporary 'peaks of progress,' short-lived victories that slide into irrelevance as racial patterns adapt in ways that maintain white dominance," he says.

Or here, codifying Bell's opinion into a kind of pseudosociology, is a portion of a booklet put out by the University of Cincinnati called *Combating Racism on Campus: A Resource Book and Model for the 1990s*:

> Racism is the power individuals and groups of one race use to systematically oppress those of another race. The power bases through which this oppression takes place are government, corporations, educational systems, and other institutions such as churches and the judicial system.
>
> Racism is also defined as the assumption that psychocultural traits and abilities are determined by biological race and that races differ decisively from one another in this respect. This assumption is usually coupled with a belief in the inherent superiority of a particular race and its right to dominate others.
>
> According to these definitions, the United States would be considered to have a racist society. For example, the power bases listed above are controlled primarily by white males. (In this sense we would also consider the U.S. to be a sexist society.) The majority of these white males make "power decisions," unconsciously or consciously, which benefit white people.

As long ago as 1973, the National Education Association, the twenty-five-thousand-member teachers' union that did so much to advance the cause of multicultural education during the Columbian quincentennial, grandly proclaimed: "All whites are racists." The NEA said: "Even if whites are totally free from all conscious racial prejudice, they remain racist, for they receive benefits distributed by a racist society through racist institutions."

In Pennsylvania at a conference of the United Ministries in Higher Education, definitions of "racism," along with examples of it, were distributed to each participant. There is, the conferees learned, both "personal racism" and "organizational racism." In the former category: "Discouraging inter-racial dating and marriage" and "Reluctance or refusal to discuss racism when an ethnic minority labels an incident racist." In the latter: "Premature negotiation to avoid conflict" and "The absence of a definitive and effective affirmative action plan with specific steps regarding implementation and evaluation." So it is that the ugly word, "racism," is applied to an omission, a failure to accept a controversial social program.

In 1989, Wellesley College, reporting the results of its Task Force on Racism, concluded that, in fact, "instances of overt racism at Wellesley are rare." But, the report went on, "a more subtle form of racism does exist here." Wellesley, the report said, "unintentionally fosters racism because it does not self-consciously, or sufficiently, challenge taken-for-granted and unconscious habits of prejudice and discrimination." There is, the report said, an "unconscious whiteness" in "norms and practices" that prevail on campus as well as a "climate of gentility and civility in which complaints and conflicts are deflected and defused."

Racism, in short, is everywhere, if not overt, then covert, subtle, symbolic. It can be manifested in an increase in overt acts such as cross burnings on lawns, or, more generally, in what the Minnesota Bureau of Criminal Apprehension calls bias crimes. It can even come about because of a "climate of gentility and civility." It doesn't seem to matter in some views of this matter if you are a member of Aryan Nation or the National Council of Churches. If you are white, you are racist. As Molefi Asante of Temple University put it, white supremacy is inherent in the "structure of knowledge of the western world. . . . If you accept the dogma that reason begins with Europe and with white people and with the Greeks—which, of course, is a false dogma—if you accept that, then you can only reproduce racist thinking regardless of whatever else you do in terms of Asians or Africans or Latinos."

Or here is a brochure for parents distributed by the Milwaukee public school system and containing the official working definition of "racism":

> Racism is a mental illness of some groups of persons/institutions induced by greed and fear that systematically oppresses another group of people by suppressing their history/truth, their culture, their identity, and their speech and by controlling their socialization, their education, and their wealth and by means of unjust laws enforced segregation/apartheid thereby giving credence to the notion of genetic superiority of oppressor.

From definitions and statements like these it is but a short step to a companion notion dear to the multicultural ideology, which is that opposition to the full range of programs, from curriculum revision to hate speech codes, is yet another manifestation of the subtle racism that is allegedly on the rise. The common use of the terms "antiracist" and "gender neutral" to describe the new multicultural curricula in public schools underscores the link between multiculturalism and the fight against racism. It suggests, not very subtly, that only multiculturalism confronts the racist scourge, so that any opposition to the multiculturalist thrust in school texts (that, for example, some parts of it are factually incorrect or present an excessively negative image of American history) is a sign of, at the very least, unconscious cultural superiority—or, if this opposition comes from a person of color, of "internalized oppression."

If you are the target of a racial slur, or if you, like Russell and Laura Jones of St. Paul, Minnesota, have had a cross burned on your lawn, you might very well feel that what happened to you reflects something deeper than an occasional outburst of some dark impulse. And yet to think that American society is more racist than ever before—or even that the status of nonwhites, nonmales, nonheterosexuals, and others has not improved at all—is to forget where we have come from. Can John Slaughter of Occidental College really believe that black kids attending a university these days face hostility anything like that represented by the aforementioned Maddox, Faubus, and Connor, figures who emblematized a day when black kids could hardly go to mainstream, predominantly white universities at all and who, as John Leo of *U.S. News and World Report* has put it, "used police, axes, clubs, dogs and water hoses to abuse or exclude blacks"? Is anybody, Leo asked, doing any of that to black students today? The hyperbolic use of the word "racism" impels one to state the obvious: Theophilus Eugene ("Bull") Connor, who jailed Martin Luther King, Jr., in Birmingham in 1963, was long ago tossed onto the historical dustbin, where he belongs; the nation celebrates as a national holiday the birthday of the man he put in jail (and from which he then electrified the country with one of the most seminal essays ever written in American history).

But historical forgetfulness is only part of the puzzle here. Behind it lie all of those investigations, dutifully reported in the press, that prove beyond any doubt that the evils described by the ideological multiculturalists are not exaggerations. Then how about all those studies and claims, carried out and made by the most reputable and mainstream institutions of our society, which conclude that racism as well as sexism and other evils are on the rise? How can they be explained?

Early in 1992 most of the major newspapers across the country, including the *New York Times*, the Washington *Post*, the Los Angeles *Times*, the Boston *Globe*, and the San Francisco *Chronicle*, put on their front pages a dramatic report issued by the American Association of University Women, which concluded that girls were "shortchanged" by discrimination and bias in the school system. The study, *How Schools Shortchange Girls*, issued in the name of the AAUW, was carried out by the Wellesley Center for Research on Women.

"Bias Against Girls Is Found Rife In Schools, With Lasting Damage" was the *New York Times* headline. "Gender Bias In Schools Is Still Shortchanging Girls, Report Says," the Houston *Chronicle*'s read. The lead paragraphs in the stories of the two newspapers were almost identical. "School is still a place of unequal opportunity, where girls face discrimination from teachers, textbooks, tests and their male classmates," said the *Times*. According to the *Chronicle*, "School remains a place of unequal opportunity, where girls face discrimination from teachers, textbooks, tests and their male colleagues." An editorial in the *Christian Science Monitor* credited the report with identifying "what might be called a glass ceiling in American education—the invisible barriers and biases that keep girls from achieving their full potential in school."

Other articles on subsequent days showed right-thinking people already moving to remedy the grave problem identified in the report.

Under the headline "Easing Bias In Classrooms: Tips From Teachers On How To Help Girls," the Boston *Globe* quoted various classroom teachers who were, it said, trying to remedy "gender bias" and "level the playing fields in American classrooms." The Atlanta *Constitution* announced that the "landmark study" by the AAUW, which "cataloged the ways schools shortchange girls," was already leading to changes. The newspaper reported on an Atlanta forum in which everybody "from bankers to principals to parents to TV producers, pledged to take concrete steps to give girls a better shot at equal education."

What happened, in short, was that the conclusions of the Wellesley study undertaken for the AAUW became conventional wisdom. The strange thing, however, was that the very conclusions stressed in press reports about bias, discrimination, and inequity were in key instances not supported by the body of the report itself, and in some important cases they were contradicted by it.

The actual content of the study on girls, for example, showed some elements about the situation of girls difficult to square with the systematic "shortchanging" claimed on their behalf. It said, for example, that "girls generally receive better grades than boys, regardless of race or socioeconomic status." It reported that "gender differences in mathematics achievement are small and declining." It said that "gender differences in the number of science courses students take are small." It revealed that far more girls go on to college these days than boys and that girls of all racial and economic groups were less likely to drop out of school than boys. How, the newspapers might have asked, if "gender bias" were as serious as the press reports indicate, do so many girls manage to do so well? But very few of the newspapers asked that question.

Had reporters dug further—and the *New York Times* reporter did dig a bit further—they would likely have found some additional information to undercut the AAUW's conclusions. They would have found, for example, the rapid increase in the numbers of women attending law school, medical school, business school, and graduate school in both the arts and the sciences. In some instances, a bit of extra research would have revealed some rather hasty conclusions in the report, or some one-sided explanations. Among its findings, for example, was that boys traditionally score about 50 points higher in math than girls do on the Scholastic Aptitude Test. The report accounts for this difference by adducing an old argument—that the tests are biased in favor of boys, and that nothing has been done in our sexist society to correct this bias. In fact, this issue of alleged bias in testing has been intensely scrutinized for decades, though you would not know that reading the AAUW report. For years, the Educational Testing Service has tried to formulate a mathematics test in which the scores of boys and girls would come out roughly the same—and this, presumably, would then be a test free of bias—but it has persistently failed to achieve the desired result. Given the attempts to equalize matters, a bias against girls does not seem to be a factor, or to prove that it is a factor, the report would at least have had to examine the contrary evidence.

To some extent, the newspaper coverage of the AAUW report merely shows what might be called press-release journalism. Reporters, who suffer more from deadline pressure than from ideological predisposition, often simply do not have time to digest a long text. And so they rely on a summary or on a press release, their assumption being that these will provide accurate synopses of the full texts. In the case of the AAUW report, journalists were the targets of a state-of-the-art publicity campaign.

A press kit arrived at newspapers across the country in the form of a handsome brochure containing the report itself, a press release outlining its conclusions and offering handy quotations from "experts." All of this was sent out so that all reporters would get it on the same day, the only day that they had to work on their stories, forcing most of them no doubt to rely on the press release for their overall conclusions, the press release that stressed "shortcomings" in the system and made no mention of the contents of the report that contradicted that conclusion.

Still, the absence of skepticism shown toward the report on girls was remarkable even for journalists operating under deadline pressure. The organization that actually carried out the study was not some neutral institution with an unimpeachable record of disinterested scholarship on the status of women. The Wellesley Center for Research on Women, while not perhaps widely known to reporters, might by its very name and location have suggested a certain partisan attitude on subjects central to feminists' concerns. And, indeed, it is a group, operating out of a lovely old Victorian mansion just across the street from the Wellesley campus, that takes very clear, pro-feminist, pro-multicultural positions.

To put this another way, if the American Enterprise Institute in Washington, D.C., known as a serious, conservative research organization, had put out a report saying that there were no remaining inequalities between boys and girls, the conclusions would have provoked the critical distance usual in journalism. The institute would have been identified as a conservative group. Feminists likely to oppose its conclusions would have been contacted for comment.

Strangely, a report put out by an unabashedly and outspokenly feminist group, namely the Wellesley Center for Research on Women, did not produce the same reflex. None of the press reports identified the Wellesley Center as feminist. Few of them (with the *New York Times* again an exception) sought any opinions contrary to those in the report. Again, this may not be a product of ideological favoritism. It could be due simply to the fact that remaining inequity between boys and girls makes a better story than hard-won progress. The lead paragraphs on the AAUW report could have stressed, not the shortchanging of girls, but the remarkable progress made in a very short amount of time. But as John Leo observed, "That story would have wound up in the back of the weekly education section. But, by pressing the bias victimization button . . . the story catapulted to page one."

The result was millions of dollars of free, uncritical publicity for a point of view that is far from disinterested. The Wellesley Center represents a particular type of feminism, the characteristic boilerplate of which was heavily interspersed through the report for anybody who cared to notice it, though only a few did.

"We must address the degree to which violence against women is an increasingly accepted aspect of our culture," the report says, asserting as established fact the highly debatable proposition that violence against women is "increasingly accepted." It goes on to state what are other, clearly recognizable elements in the radical feminist agenda, particularly the notion that the central experience of women is their brutalization at the hands of men. "School curricula must help girls to understand the extent to which their lives are constrained by fear of rape, the possibility of battering, and the availability of pornography," the text declares.

The Wellesley study also provides a few conspicuous examples of the idea, also peculiar to the boilerplate of a certain branch of feminism, that girls and boys have different cultures, that they learn differently, that gender bias lurks in the very vocabulary used by school systems and textbooks. "In the upper grades especially," the report asserts, "the curriculum narrows and definitions of knowing take on gender-specific and culture specific qualities associated with Anglo-European male values." What is offered as an example of these Anglo-European male values? "Current events and civics curricula," the report explains, "which take up topics from the news media, tend to focus, like their sources, on news as controversy and conflict. Much of the daily texture of life is ignored in most current events classes."

In other words it would be more wholesome for children learning about current events to study the "daily texture of life," rather than war, revolution, perhaps the collapse of communism in Eastern Europe, maybe the Tiananmen incident in China, an interest that, it would seem, reflects "Anglo-European male values." This verbiage led *Fortune* magazine to identify the report as "a movement document masquerading as scholarly research," but few other publications either noted the ideology that lay behind the report or pointed out its consequences for educational philosophy. One writer, Cathy Young, noted in *Newsday* that the feminism of the Wellesley center is not "a feminism of equal opportunity and freedom of choice but an ideology that views relations between the sexes solely in terms of power and oppression."* The study *How Schools Shortchange Girls* is thus an excellent illustration of the necessary connection between a hyperbolic racism or sexism and the multiculturalist demand for redress and special attention in a society of relentless oppression.

The AAUW report contained forty recommendations, all of them having to do with more attention paid to resolving inequities in gender, which, as the report itself indicated, were in any case already narrowing rapidly without the AAUW's forty recommendations.

Mentioned only in passing in the report, and entirely absent from press accounts of it, were some figures on a far more alarming inequity in the educational system. A far larger gap than that between American boys and girls exists between American students of both sexes and the students of many other countries, both boys and girls, in math and science. At age thirteen, according to studies of twenty countries by the National Center for Education Statistics, Americans were thirteenth in science and fifteenth in math; among the countries that ranked higher in both subjects were Korea, Taiwan, Switzerland, the Soviet Union, Israel, Slovenia, Canada, France, and Hungary.† What is needed is not more feminist ideology in the schools telling girls that they are

---

*Cathy Young, "The Real School Scandal Hurts Kids of Both Sexes," *Newsday*, March 25, 1992, page 79.

†News release of the United States Department of Education, Feb. 5, 1992.

victims of violence and oppression and have different ways of knowing. What is needed is better, more rigorous education for everybody.

The issue before us, remember, is not whether racism exists in America. Of course it exists. The question is the direction of the society, its overall tone, whether racism is endemic and worsening (and must therefore be attacked by the heavy artillery of multiculturalism), or whether it is mostly a matter of deviance by individuals who do not obey the prevailing norms. What then of those studies that show alarmingly high incidents of racism? Aren't they impressive evidence that the standard multicultural description of the society is correct? There was, for example, that study by the special judicial commission to investigate discrimination in the New York court system, the one that concluded the courts were "infested with racism." The phrase, which appeared in the press release accompanying the commission's five-volume, two-thousand-page report, but not in those five volumes themselves, was reproduced in just about every newspaper article about the report.

The *New York Times* editorialized on the findings of the commission, not bothering to examine rigorously its underlying assumptions or to comment on its seventy-six recommendations (including, inevitably, "cross cultural sensitivity training for judges and other court workers"), but proceeding to commend the commission for "giving New Yorkers of all races ample reason for outrage." "Courts of Shame" was the headline atop the editorial, making it sound as if the *Times* felt that the courts of New York were the same as the kangaroo courts of dictators giving a gloss of legality to the incarceration of dissidents. Actually, the editorial stressed the dilapidated physical condition of the lower courts, where the litigants are more likely to be black and Hispanic than white—hence "race has something to do with the disparity."

In this sense, the editorial was typical of statements about racism in the justice system in that it scrupulously failed to mention that a disproportionate amount of the crime is committed by Hispanic and black youths. It also was unable to provide any substantiation for its implication that if it were the case that most defendants were white, the courts would be nicer. The plain fact is that lower courts and jails are pretty terrible even in places that have only one race. (In another context, a common complaint, supposedly proving the racism of society, has to do with the frequent failure of taxi drivers to stop for black people. A "Primetime Live" report on television once gave a dramatic demonstration of this, showing on the air a taxi passing a black man and stopping just ahead for a white one. The scene was Washington, D.C. The documentary failed to inform its viewers that 85 percent of the crime against taxi drivers is committed by blacks. It also failed to say that the vast majority of the drivers who fail to stop for black passengers are also black.)

Not surprisingly, the reporting on the report on the courts stressed the idea that racism, rather than the effort to combat it, was the overriding characteristic of the courts. A columnist in New York *Newsday* wrote: "A two-tier structure, which showers white defendants with mercy and reserves strict punishment for blacks, must be overhauled." The *Times* quoted one commission member, Judge Ivan Warner of the state supreme court in the Bronx: "It's a little naive to suggest that we can have a proper court system in the State of New York when the entire United States is a racist society."

A five-volume, two-thousand-page document written by lawyers and judges is not easy to read, but reading it does give a different impression than either the press release or the news reports would indicate. True, there are racist reflexes (such as the time court police put a choke hold on a black lawyer, thinking he was a defendant), and there are studies that show a historic pattern of different sentencing for whites and blacks, which is not the same thing as "showering whites with mercy." But much of the content of the report details tremendous and sustained efforts to rectify these problems. Indeed, after the initial stories on the commission's findings appeared, there were follow-up stories on how the report had not gone down well with some officials of the courts, who felt that the press release was exaggerated.

A letter written by a group of twelve judges from the Supreme, Criminal, Civil, and Housing Courts to the *New York Law Journal* provided a far better lead paragraph, one that balanced remaining problems against the record of improvement, than the hyperbolic and one-sided leads used by most of the press. "There is no doubt that there has been improvement in minority representation and sensitivity to discriminatory practices in recent years," the letter said. "However, there can be no serious disagreement with the essential message of the report, that racism is still a significant problem in our courts." Another judge, Milton Williams, deputy chief administrative judge for the New York City courts, told a City Council hearing that "the court system is not infested with racism" because minority judges (Judge Williams is black) would not stand for it.

"Men and women of good will acknowledge that racism exists throughout the United States," William C. Thompson, an associate justice of the New York Court of Appeals, wrote in a letter to the *New York Times*. "However, anyone knowing the press release without having perused the report would be left with the impression that our court system is entirely racist. Nothing is further from the truth. Those of us who know better ought to counter this impression."

These kinds of remarks, coming from people who could not be ignored, did lead the press to correct its first impressions, informing readers that there were controversy and disagreement about the press release, and pointing out that the five volumes of the report itself painted a different picture of the extent of racism in the courts. This is not done in many cases, however, where the conclusions regarding studies of racism are hyped. It was certainly not the case with the reporting on those lists of incidents compiled by the National Institute Against Prejudice and Violence, or on that experiment involving paired black and white job seekers in Chicago and in Washington, D.C. As with the Wellesley study on girls, these other studies and reports show a remarkable willingness to believe and to report the worst about ourselves, even when the data actually contained in them support quite different conclusions. The employment experiment and the compilations of racist incidents, in fact, provide evidence, not that racism and discrimination are worsening or even that they have remained the same, but that they are decreasing.

The most commonly remembered elements of the Urban Institute study, in which matched pairs of blacks and whites applied for the same jobs, were these: that discrimination was "widespread and entrenched"; that three times as many white job seekers were well treated in their applications as blacks; and that one in five black applicants ran into the wall of discrimination.

In all, the study was based on applications by the matched pairs of blacks and whites for 476 entry-level positions. The overall conclusion of the Urban Institute's study was that in 80 percent of those job searches, there was no discrimination against the black applicants. In 20 percent of the cases, the white applicant was offered a better job than the black candidate, and in 7 percent of the cases the situation was reversed, the black did better than the white.

That means, as *The New Republic* pointed out, that in 73 percent of the cases there was no discrimination at all; in 27 percent of the cases there was—most of it against blacks, some of it against whites. Does that mean that discrimination was "widespread and entrenched"? That is a judgment call; yet it is hard to believe that the discrimination encountered by the Urban Institute's paired job seekers was more widespread and entrenched than it would have been a decade or two before. Meanwhile, the finding that three times as many whites were placed in jobs as blacks—which made up the lead paragraphs in stories on the study in both the Los Angeles *Times* (page one) and the Washington *Post* (page A3)—is an illustration of innumeracy, of bad arithmetic, not of endemic racism.

What the report said was that in 20 percent of the cases, whites advanced further than blacks; in 7 percent blacks further than whites; while in all the rest of the cases, namely the aforementioned 73 percent, the experiences of the two races were the same. This shows, perhaps, a significant statistical advantage for whites, but, given equal treatment in 73 percent of the cases, it certainly does not show three times as many whites as blacks doing well. What it demonstrates is that in the minority of cases where there was discrimination, three blacks were discriminated against for every one white who was discriminated against. Or, put another way, the Urban Institute study found that blacks fared as well as or better than whites in 80 percent of the cases, while whites ended up in as good or better shape than blacks 93 percent of the time. That may, again, be a meaningful difference, but probably not one justifying the expression "widespread and entrenched" in describing discrimination in the job market.

"What are we to make of this relatively low level of bias?" *The New Republic* asked in an editorial commenting on the study. "We don't know, of course, exactly what a similar report would have found, say, in 1961, because such a report did not exist. But it doesn't take much agonizing to recognize that 73 percent fairness represents something close to a transformation in racial attitudes in a matter of decades. There are caveats, of course; 27 percent bias is still 27 percent too much. But the visceral, structural, overwhelming injustice of not so long ago has been dramatically reduced."*

More alarmingly and avidly reported in the press was another study regarding racial and other bias, this one having to do with the

*"In Black and White," *The New Republic*, June 10, 1991, pages 7–8.

universities. The group most active in collecting figures on campus "ethnoviolence and related forms of conflict," as it calls bias crime, is the National Institute Against Prejudice and Violence, in Baltimore. This is the organization that provided the figures used by *Time* magazine and other publications as they repeated those phrases about the increase in racial hostilities. *Time* said in 1990, for example, that 250 colleges and universities reported "racist incidents." It sounds serious and certainly it is cause for concern. But does it mark the growth of intolerance, or is it a kind of unfortunate normal disharmony? A close look at the claims of ever-intensifying racism strongly indicates the latter explanation.

Those *Time* magazine statistics adduced to call attention to a serious problem could actually indicate something close to the opposite. There are, after all, more than three thousand accredited institutions of higher learning in the United States. If 250 of them in a single year reported instances of hate crime, that means that in well over 90 percent of them there were no such reported instances. The figures presented by *Time* as alarmingly large seem, in context, to be exceedingly small, too small, indeed, to be credible. Given the propensity of human beings to get into ethnic conflict, it would be very surprising if some sort of racial incident did not take place on every campus across the country. Put two thousand or five thousand or sixty thousand young people of different races and creeds in the same small community, and there will always be expressions of bigotry. Collecting figures on their total numbers does not prove the alarming increase in hatred so commonly reported. It only proves that the United States has not reached that state of perfection in which all racism and all racial conflict are eliminated.

The National Institute itself, led by a former professor of social psychology named Howard J. Ehrlich ("I marched in my first civil rights picket in 1959," he announces in the preface to one report. "I'm still marching"), makes no secret of its belief that the years of Republican administration are to blame for our sorry state of affairs, or that campus racism reflects the inherent racism of the surrounding society.

"The fact is that prejudice, racism, discrimination, conflict and ethnoviolence have been institutionalized within the larger society," a 1990 report of the institute says. "The campus is not isolated from the pathologies of the larger society," which trace back in large part to the complacency of Republican leaders. "The net effect of the

Reagan era," the institute states in its 1990 publication, "has been to delegitimize minority demands for equity and social justice."

The report continues: "In such a context, an anti-minority agenda becomes viable again. It is in this political climate that most college students have come of age." Among the major recommendations offered to counter what it calls "institutional discrimination," the group proposes the standard solution: "Self-assessment in the context of a commitment to multicultural education is both the starting and ending point for any program," it says. Ehrlich himself declares his goals quite plainly: "What we can do is promote the facts of social justice, egalitarianism and cultural diversity in the curriculum and in the corporate structure of the university."

The problem is that the supporting material produced over the institute's monitoring of ethnoviolence fails utterly to describe an "anti-minority agenda" or even anything more than scattered instances of ethnoviolence. True, the institute, in a study it did of a branch campus of the University of Maryland, found that one in five minority students had "been the victim of ethnoviolence." Most of this, the institute says, was "psychological, entailing harassment, name-calling and other forms of verbal abuse." One in every four people belonging to that 20 percent of the minority population "had been harassed on more than one occasion," the report says, concluding overall that "the number of college students victimized by ethnoviolence is in the range of 800,000 to one million students annually."*

On the face of it, something seems not right here. First of all there is the language used, the word "ethnoviolence," as well as phrases like "institutional discrimination" and the "campus atmosphere of prejudice and discrimination" that also appear in Ehrlich's publications, are themselves psychologically loaded. "Ethnoviolence," with its implications of physical menace, is not exactly a neutral word. It is a word chosen for emotional impact. It suggests something more than "name-calling and other forms of verbal abuse," even though that, Ehrlich says, is what ethnoviolence usually is. But as used in the publications of the National Institute Against Prejudice and Violence, "ethnoviolence" covers everything from an actual bodily assault accompanied by racial epithets to an article in the campus newspaper raising questions about affirmative action. If some crank, perhaps from outside the university, paints a swastika on the

---

*Howard J. Ehrlich, "Campus Ethnoviolence . . . And the Policy Options," Institute Report no. 4, National Institute Against Prejudice and Violence (March 1990), pages 12–13.

wall or scrawls the word "nigger" on a mirror in the bathroom, does that mean that every minority group member who sees it has "been the victim of ethnoviolence?" Of the million estimated victims of ethnoviolence, how many of them have merely seen a swastika painted across a poster, how many have been taunted once or twice by some drunken frat boy on a Saturday night, how many have been truly humiliated in class by some bigoted professor, or denied an academic opportunity, or actually been physically assaulted?

The institute's extrapolations, aimed at exposing the iniquity of the society, really show nothing more than that eight hundred thousand to one million students have at least once experienced some form of denigration, which is certainly unfortunate, but it does not at all prove that ethnoviolence is dramatically on the rise. Moreover, some of the institute's own research belies its usual suggestion that ethnoviolence stems from racism and other forms of classical prejudice. In 1989, the institute undertook the National Victimization Project, in which it telephoned 2,078 people across the country and asked them whether they had been "victimized by various types of verbal and physical violence or abuse during the preceding twelve months." Among the findings: "White respondents reported ethnoviolent victimization at approximately the same frequency as Black respondents."*

Insofar as there is evidence in the institute's lists, which are compiled from press clippings of some five hundred newspapers, it tends to support the idea that the more trivial incidents are vastly more numerous than the weightier ones. Each year, the institute publishes a list of incidents of what its staff members regard as "ethnoviolence and related forms of conflict," giving a short summary of each one in an annual report. The incidents supposedly prove that the universities are gripped in a vicious cycle of racist and sexist discrimination and violence.

"It is easy to be depressed by these reports," the institute says in an introduction to its 1989 study, "but activists and educators should take this document as a springboard for programs."

Actually, on close inspection, the lists of incidents prove something close to the opposite of what the National Institute says they prove, not a depressing pattern of pervasive ethnoviolence, but a rather heartening context in which racist violence is sporadic at most and always deeply disapproved by vast majorities at just about every

*Joan Weiss et al., *Ethnoviolence at Work*, Institute Report no. 6, National Institute Against Prejudice and Violence (Winter 1991–92), pages 22–23.

university. They reveal a predominating antiracist ethos on campuses, administrations eager to assuage the anger of minority students, and a society mobilized to combat racism, not to take comfort in it. Sometimes they show the power of political correctness at the universities to squelch debate or to intimidate into silence students who challenge the prevailing orthodoxies. The National Institute's report for 1989, which disclosed "reports of ethnoviolence" on 109 campuses (about 3 percent of the total of more than 3,000 colleges and universities in the country), contained almost as much news of marches against racism and of administrators instituting racial-awareness seminars and vowing to hire more minorities as disclosures of actual acts of unmistakable racism, sexism, anti-Semitism, or homophobia.

What is striking, first of all, is that even very large campuses generally have a very small number of reported incidents. At the University of California in Los Angeles, for example, an institution that has about thirty-five thousand students, the institute lists a grand total of three incidents for all of 1989. None of them indicate a very pervasive pattern of racism or bigotry.

The first incident, dated March 17, involved a protest march of some five hundred students ("most of them minorities") on behalf of an Asian-American professor who was denied tenure in the Graduate School of Education. The next item, dated spring, shows the professor finally being granted tenure, after "a campus committee found 'widespread irregularities' and 'biases' during his first review." Also in the spring, the Armenian Student Association "continued its nine-month effort to get the Undergraduate Student Association to condemn a history professor for failing to accept Armenian accusations of genocide by Turks." That was the third and last incident of "ethnoviolence and related forms of conflict" at UCLA in 1989. Surely other unpleasant events occurred at UCLA in 1989, but none of them major enough to be reported in the local press.

In the view of the National Institute, and in the view of many campus activists looking to start new programs, an incident is never an isolated incident. It is always seen as evidence of a growing tide of racial hate. Moreover, every incident is seen as showing prejudice and discrimination, even when other explanations seem just as plausible. There are, for example, scattered through the 1989 report, references to Jewish protests against campus appearances by the Reverend Louis Farrakhan of the Nation of Islam and his various "ministers,"

Farrakhan not being very popular with Jews since his reported remark that Judaism was a "gutter religion." When Princeton University asked the Black Students' Association to pay extra security costs of about eight thousand dollars for Farrakhan's appearance, the black students charged that the "ridiculous security requirements and costs" were a way for the university to censor Farrakhan. Was this ethnoviolence, or was it something else, an illustration perhaps of the climate of heightened racial awareness, defensiveness, suspiciousness, and antagonism that prevails in most institutions and that is probably encouraged, not assuaged, by the ideological multiculturalists?

At Oberlin College in 1989, the institute reports, a speaker, Kwame Toure, denounced Israel and Zionism as immoral, prompting about fifty students to stand and turn their backs on the speaker, which, in turn, prompted some black students to give the speaker a standing ovation. Is this ethnoviolence? Racism? Anti-Semitism? Or is it two groups in rather unpleasant disagreement? The institute's compilation makes no effort to answer these questions.

In no incident among the several hundred that compose the 1989 report was there a single instance of serious physical harm done to anybody as a result of some racist assault, even though there were some nasty physical assaults. More commonly, the incidents that do show the ugly face of racism involved graffiti or shouted insults—these more often than not followed by large campus demonstrations against racism. For example, there was this brief item from Indiana University in Bloomington:

October 30

Over 500 students attended an anti-racism rally in response to a recent verbal assault against an African graduate student.

This apparently followed this incident:

October 22

An African graduate student was standing outside a university building when three White men jumped out of a car and shouted racial slurs. The White men called the student "nigger" and "Black bastard." This was the third racial assault experienced by this student during the past year.

Finally, on December 13, there was this incident:

> An African graduate student who was verbally assaulted in October
> met with his attacker. The meeting in the dean of student's office
> was arranged so that the perpetrator could apologize to the student.
> The assailant, who was an alumnus of the university, had already
> apologized by letter.

Five of the six incidents listed under Indiana University for 1989
involved this same African graduate student. The other involved a
panel discussion of hate crimes, after a campus report that there had
been "seventy-five incidents of racial harassment and six incidents of
harassment of gay students" during the course of the year. There are
thirty-six thousand students at IU.

I certainly do not want to make light of incidents like the eighty-
one reported at Indiana, which were surely upsetting to many people,
especially those on the receiving end of the abuse. The standard
slogans of bigotry—"Nigger go home," "Faggot," "Kill the Jews"—
are distressing, and efforts by university administrators to take clear,
strong positions against this sort of ugliness are entirely correct and
laudable. But are racist incidents increasing? Are they so pervasive
as to characterize university life, requiring an entire new multicultural
curriculum, mandatory sensitivity training, and new admissions standards to combat them? Or are they the work of the few bigots who
always lurk among the vast majority of good people? Certainly, the
pattern outlined by the National Institute's 1989 report shows students and faculty highly responsive to reported racist outrages.

It reports, for example, on the "march and rally against racial
harassment" at the University of Louisville in Belknap, Kentucky,
sparked by "a Black female student's report that she had received
anonymous notes containing racial slurs which said she should move
out of her dormitory." At Miami University in Oxford, Ohio, a march
across campus was held to protest three "racist acts" that had taken
place on campus, one of which involved the word "nigger" written
across a poster advertising the appearance of a well-known black
person who was coming to speak on campus. At Clark University in
Worcester, Massachusetts, the Task Force for a Pluralistic Community was formed after somebody painted KKK ALL THE WAY on a
campus wall.

At the University of Arizona in Tucson, the university president promised to increase minority enrollment and representation, to increase the number of black students by 10 percent, and to raise the graduation rate of black students by 50 percent by 1995 (exactly how this was to be accomplished was not disclosed), following "an anti-racism sit-in by about 80 students, who blocked the front of the administration building for several hours." The only "racist incident" reported at the university involved the suspension of three black students accused of a series of ten random attacks on whites around the campus. "The defendants claim that they were provoked by racial slurs," the institute report avers.

The institute report explains why even small incidents are seized upon and translated into demands for more ethnic studies courses, more recruiting of minority students, mandatory racial- and sexual-awareness training—because the demands are satisfied so quickly.

At California State University in Northridge a student editor was suspended from the school newspaper for printing a cartoon critical of affirmative action. Suspended! The National Institute's summary of this incident makes no mention of protests at the administration's apparently overzealous response to an expression of political opinion that on the face of it should be protected by the First Amendment. It did, however, report on one other student who wrote an opinion article criticizing the university for suspending the first student. He too was suspended! So much for free speech on the subject of affirmative action, criticism of which, apparently, is viewed as ethnoviolence by the administration of Cal State.

Some of the incidents listed show a readiness to label just about anything an incident of "ethnoviolence and related forms of conflict." Here are the complete texts of some of the summaries presented by the National Institute to prove the pervasiveness of ethnoviolence and the way the universities illustrate the "pathologies of the larger society":

Augusta College (Augusta, Ga.)
May 30

The president of the Black Student Union said, "We have an administration treating Black students differently than other students." He cited a double standard which prevents Black students from utilizing telephones, copy machines and other services that White students routinely have access to. White professors have also skipped chapters in textbooks that deal with Black history.

Bloomsburg University (Bloomsburg, Pa.)
February

Following a speech on campus by an assistant to Reverend Louis
Farrakhan, a Black student, who defended his appearance on campus in the student newspaper, received a vulgar letter from a White
student charging that Farrakhan is a bigot.

Brigham Young University (Provo, Utah)
February 23

During a basketball game against the University of Wyoming, one
of the Wyoming players allegedly told a BYU player to "Get off the
floor and quit crying, you bleeping Mormon." The Wyoming student
admitted that he did say to get off the floor, but that he never cursed
or referred to religion.

University of Chicago (Chicago, Ill.)
February 10

A law firm was suspended for one year from recruiting at the law
school after one of its recruiters made racist and sexist remarks to
an applicant. The Black female law student was interviewed by a
senior partner of Chicago's Baker & McKenzie law firm. He asked
her how she would react to being called a "nigger" or "black bitch"
by adversaries or colleagues.

University of Florida (Gainesville, Fla.)
October

An article in the campus newspaper contained the following statement: "To put it bluntly, many Black students gained entrance into
universities they were neither qualified nor prepared to attend."

Yale University (New Haven, Conn.)
November 1

About one hundred people held a rally outside the office of the
university president to protest the October 27 arrest of nine men
over a sexually explicit poster. The President formed a committee
to investigate the incident.

Is this the stuff that led *Time* magazine to report on how the
universities "distill the free-floating bigotries of American society into
a lethal brew"?

We are a vast and complicated country with a long history of cathartic violence, vigilantism, frontier justice, protest, idealism, pacifism. We have the Quakers on one side, and we have the fortunately less numerous Aryan Nation and the American Nazi Party. We have had slavery, Jim Crow, the Ku Klux Klan, Red scares, McCarthyism, periods of painful superpatriotism and nativism, of antiforeign Know-Nothingism, and the America First Committee. We are a nation of immigrants from many places, and, as noted, the total number of immigrants, especially nonwhite immigrants, has never been higher. At the moment, moreover, we are reading news of terrible occurrences in Europe, of the rise of far-right anti-immigrant political formations in Denmark, Belgium, and France, and of the emergence of a vicious, violent neo-Nazism in Germany. And yet in the United States, a country that, in the view of the ideological multiculturalists, is afflicted with endemic, imperishable, ever-intensifying, and, yes, more covert racism, we have virtually nothing of the organized nativism, none of the strident anti-immigrant sentiments or of the overtly racist formations springing up in Europe. All of that is in our past, where, we can hope, it will remain. Not even David Duke of Louisiana, former Nazi, former Ku Klux Klanner, 1991 candidate for governor of his state, exposed his true colors in public. He did not vaunt his past; apparently he felt that in order to win election, he had to deny it, and he lost anyway because of it.

And so why is progress in racial matters inevitably left out of the vocabulary of ideological multiculturalism? Why is it that the rhetoric has become far angrier now that matters are better than it was when matters were far worse? The answer is that the exaggeration of the national fault and an encouragement of the culture of victimization are necessary components of ideological multiculturalism, indispensable to its self-justification. The National Institute Against Prejudice and Violence and the Wellesley Center for Research on Women do not really aim at neutral and scientific tabulations of ethnoviolence or sexism. They want to add their doses of Miracle-Gro to the trendy rage of the allegedly oppressed and the guilt of the alleged oppressors. Under Comrade Stalin, the evils of capitalism were relentlessly exaggerated (or invented) so that those with doubts about collectivization or the rewriting of history could be convicted of complicity in the strategies of capitalist exploitation and of being out of the flow of history. In somewhat the same fashion, the promiscuous use of the word "racism" helps sustain the righteous fury that is the chief pose of the multiculturalist enforcers, and it disarms everybody else.

Multiculturalism is a demand for a radical change. It says, in essence, that the slow progress toward equality and toward civilized and enlightened attitudes that many Americans saw as fruits of the civil rights movement are illusory. We cannot just continue along the same paths, but must make many new departures. The demand for something entirely new and different can only justify itself if the prevailing post–civil rights movement ethos can be seen to have failed, to have made no real difference in the status of the Other in America. And what more devastating, unanswerable argument can there be—given what would appear to have been at least a degree of modest progress—than that racism remains the bedrock of white society, reimposing what former Harvard professor Derrick Bell called "white dominance" on those herculean efforts to change?

Racism does not explain multiculturalism, but hyperbolic race thinking does explain why ideological multiculturalism functions in its peculiarly unidimensional fashion. Perhaps there are some at the universities, or in curriculum-revision programs, or in newspapers who are calling for a genuine diversity of voices, but these seem to be few in number. Nobody, for example, calls for greater study of the contributions of fundamentalist Christians to the American culture or of Hasidic Jews or, for that matter, of Jews at all. There is no clamor to have conservative viewpoints represented in the curriculum or on the editorial boards of newspapers that are striving to encourage multicultural perspectives—even though the conservative tradition of Edmund Burke and Alexander Hamilton is an important one in American history. No angry students are occupying university administration buildings so that the views of pro-life feminists, or women antifeminists, or anti-affirmative-action black writers can be heard.

Conservatives like Midge Decter or Jeane Kirkpatrick, though women of obvious accomplishment and importance, are more likely to be hooted off the stage at women's studies meetings than invited to be on faculties, and black figures like Thomas Sowell and Glenn Loury, though articulate and thoughtful representatives of diversity among black people, are rarely invited to speak at universities. When in 1988, in a book called *Lovesong*, Julius Lester of the University of Massachusetts made some unflattering remarks about James Baldwin, he was forced out of the university's black studies department, even though it could persuasively be argued that he, as both a black and a Jew, stood for a real, and rare, diversity of viewpoint in his department, meaning that he alone had what could be called an unconventional, dissenting point of view.

Louis Farrakhan and various members of his cohort, or feminist legal scholars like Catherine MacKinnon, are far more popular speakers on the college circuit, and far more likely to be interviewed on television or to have their essays published in mainstream magazines, than Lester or Phyllis Schlafly or the Reverend Donald Wildmon of the American Family Association in Tupelo, Mississippi, who is not invited to be on that circuit at all. There does not seem to be a great yearning to hire onto women's studies faculties women who believe that life begins at conception and thus think that abortion is an ending of that life—even though these women would add a dose of diversity to the debate.

In New York in 1991 and 1992 blacks and Hasidic Jews engaged in a violent conflict that absorbed the attention of the entire city. Simultaneously with that, the school system was promulgating its *Children of the Rainbow Curriculum*, which stressed the inclusion of all members of the mosaic so that we could live in a tolerant, multicultural community. The Hasids, however, were not among those mentioned for inclusion in the *Children of the Rainbow Curriculum*, even though you might think that black-Hasidic antagonism would have led some educator to say, "We have to understand the Hasidic culture, which, after all, spans three continents and several centuries." No such comment was made.

In investigating multiculturalism over a period of two years, I have rarely met a multiculturalist ideologue who bothered to learn anything beyond a few heartwarming clichés about another culture, or who even evinced much curiosity about a people other than his own. The ideological multiculturalists are not interested in inclusion or diversity. Indeed, they are so uninterested in ideological diversity that they are among the leading proponents of legislative codes to punish "offensive" speech, thereby helping them in their real goal, which is empowering more people who think as they do. What counts for inclusion in the multiculturalists' world, in short, is not your degree of difference from the mainstream but the extent to which you can present yourself as a sufferer from racism or some other form of oppression. So it is that while multiculturalism takes many forms, it always rests on an analysis of American society that stresses endemic inequity rather than the degree to which the inequities of the past have been eliminated.

From there certain other factors enter the picture. One is a co-optation of the problem of racism, the amount of which can be disputed but the existence of which cannot reasonably be denied, by the ever-proliferating band of other grievance groups. The feminist moral equivalent of racism is sexism, which has been elevated to a point of equal heinousness. For gays and lesbians it is homophobism or heterosexism. For people with disabilities it is what some tender-hearted people call ableism. For other ethnic minorities—or, more properly speaking, for the self-declared spokespersons of these other groups—there is a catchall accusation, Eurocentrism, entailing a supposed cultural narrow-mindedness, intolerance, and xenophobia directed against all others.

There has been great inventiveness in the production of classified, registered, official forms of crimes of the mind, all of them more or less equal in moral gravity and all of them deriving from the domination of society by white men, who are given no credit for having created the sensibility and values that see these things as evils in the first place. This cranky quest for iniquity makes no distinctions. Racism, which would seem to have a certain unique status as an evil in American history, is made equal to sexism as a thought crime, even though men in the West have typically "oppressed" women, in part, by putting them on pedestals, while they have oppressed blacks by hanging them from ropes. This is not to say that sexism has never existed in American life. Of course it has, and it still does. Still, for white women to claim, as a matter of history, a kind of victim status equal to blacks' is to have lost all sense of perspective. Or for homosexuals, who are one of the most affluent and politically powerful groups in American society, to claim an oppression equivalent to that of blacks is a similar misjudgment, motivated, it would seem, by the overall advantages of claiming victim status. All sins are major ones; all are part of the same squalid pattern.

And so the tone of American life, its coloration with the hues of political correctness, derive from a *dérapage*, a skid produced by the legitimate recoil of good people at real racism into a generalized, killjoy ideology of faultfinding and professed victimization. And because these accusations have proved very effective in intimidating opposition, those who use them have been emboldened to use them even more, ever expanding the definitions so as to encompass ever more types of behavior into the spheres of the condemned. Racism and victimization by it are no longer viewed solely as moral horrors to be annihilated; they are sought after, laid claim to, wielded as blunt instruments to cow the intellectual opposition into compliance or silence.

Chapter 7

THE SECRET VICTORY

The year was 1956. A World War II hero named Dwight Eisenhower was president of the United States. Both the Cold War and the Nuclear Age were well under way. Schoolchildren were taught how to hide under their desks with their hands over their heads in the event of Communist attack, while spotters of the Civil Defense Command scanned the skies for enemy bombers. Nonetheless, the country felt good about itself, even though in those years, it bore an unsettling resemblance to South Africa.

The culture reflected the time, or as Joseph Campbell might have put it, the heroes and villains of the moment were, as they always are, embodiments of the things the nation admired and those it feared. Among the best-selling books of that year were *Profiles in Courage*, by future president John F. Kennedy, *The Birth of Britain*, by former prime minister Winston Churchill, Herman Wouk's *Marjorie Morningstar*, and *The Man in the Gray Flannel Suit*, by Sloan Wilson. And at the movies, among the big box-office successes, was the very scary *Invasion of the Body Snatchers*, about an insidious invasion of the earth by seeds that grow into the exact likenesses of people whose souls they will inhabit. *Invasion of the Body Snatchers* has often been interpreted as emblematic of the national dread of Communist subversion, against which constant vigilance, eternal wakefulness, were required—after all, the film's invader "snatches" the body only when the victim goes to sleep.

In the age of multiculturalism, *Body Snatchers* takes on a different symbolism. It came from the era when we were good and the Other was evil. By now, in the movies and in popular entertainment in general, the moral universe of the 1950s has been inverted, and therein lies a chief clue to the as-yet unanswered question of this book: Why now?

In many ways, it would be easier to demonstrate the timing of things if the multicultural revolution had taken place twenty years ago and were being repudiated today. It is strange and paradoxical, in fact, that it has arrived after the various social movements for equality, including the civil rights movement, the women's movement, and the liberation from clandestinity of homosexuals, have succeeded at least enough to have proved the responsiveness of American society to demands for change. Multiculturalism might also have made more sense eighty or ninety years ago, when the uncouth immigrants from Italy, Russia, Ireland, Greece, Poland, and other places began to come in droves, bringing with them their foreignness, their beardedness, their ethnic truculence and religiosity, their jabberings in mysterious tongues, their threadbare costumes, their superstitions, and their lack of experience in democratic self-government. Now all of these people are seen as part of one homogeneous European subculture, which is a sign that the melting pot worked after all. Why then are we only now doing what those people would more logically have done so long ago? Why do we assume that commonality is somehow demeaning when it is exactly commonality that has enabled the great American experiment to work?

More striking still, the embarrassment with our predominantly Western culture comes after the greatest triumph of liberal democracy since the victory over fascism in World War II. The fall of communism and the abandonment of state-sponsored socialism in countries from China to Mozambique is not a victory of Western arms. It is more impressive than that. It is a victory of the essential liberal-democratic idea that has guided the West all along. And so how strange it is that we are celebrating what we think are other "cultures" just at the moment when other cultures are imitating us.

Compare in this regard the America of 1945 with the America of the early 1990s. In both periods the country had just led a triumph of seminal proportions. We had won victories in World War II and in the Cold War. In the first instance we celebrated on a grand scale. In the second we did not. In the year after World War II we wrote novels and made films and wrote histories in which we basked in our courage and sacrifice. When the Soviet empire dissolved in favor of something that it was trying to learn from us, it occurred to almost nobody but a few conservative commentators to find art and drama in the various episodes that led to the victory of our values and our way of life—and conservative commentators have never been very good at art and drama. Instead of celebrating our victory, the country plunged headlong into multiculturalism. If it was not intensifying racism that produced that reaction, if it was not greater-than-ever diversity, what was it?

There can be many answers to this question, one of them based on the old concept of the revolution of rising expectations. The clamor for change comes when change is already taking place, not before it has started. Still, it all goes back to an alteration in the collective awareness that took seed in the late 1960s and grew to flower in the late 1980s and early 1990s. Thirty years ago, something shifted in the national mind. The Vietnam War and the attitudes engendered during that period, the vast disillusionment with the American nature that characterized the elite members of an entire generation, led us to a fault line. For the first time in our history, many of us, especially those headed for the professions, for graduate school, for journalism, the professoriat, the ministry, came to see the United States, its role in the world and its record in history, as more tainted by iniquity than infused with good.

It was a remarkable shift, and a lasting legacy of the spiritual rebellion of the late 1960s, this emergence of an elite generation that came to see a powerful strain of nastiness as a paramount element of the country's essence. That spiritual change lies behind a second element of the answer to the question, why now? It is the empowerment of what were once small voices of protest, who still prefer to be perceived as powerless, but who have come to determine much of the moral tone, the orthodoxies, and the taboos of life in the 1990s. And they like that power even as they deny having it. They have learned to put their opposition on the defensive by accusing it of being the heartless, reactionary establishment, when the truth is that they, in the many domains where they are strong, have become the establishment themselves.

This is the secret victory, the victory that dare not speak its name, since to do so would be to undermine the victors' main claim to legitimacy, which is that they are carrying forward the grand tradition of protest on behalf of the meek.

In 1991, Warner Brothers, the moviemaking arm of the Time Warner media empire, released Oliver Stone's *JFK*, which advanced the theory that the president of the United States, the Central Intelligence Agency, the Defense Department, the Federal Bureau of Investigation, and the chief justice of the United States either engaged in or covered up the assassination of President Kennedy. It also put forward the hypothesis that the murder of Kennedy enabled these plotters and their accessories after the fact to control the national direction from then on (Kennedy, according to Stone's film, wanted to withdraw from Vietnam, and the others wanted nothing to interfere with the imperial American purpose). And so the once-good United States got taken over. The body snatchers were victorious after all. The good emperor Augustus was poisoned and power fell to a new Caligula named Reagan. *JFK* grossed seventy million dollars in the United States alone.

Stone's vision of the leading authorities of the country as coconspirators in a vast plot to defraud the public would have been unimaginable before the 1960s. Other changes in the moral universe, also reflected in the movies, would have been equally unimaginable. The invader from outer space is one reflection of the changes. The cowboy-and-Indian epic is another.

Before the Vietnam War and the transformations of the 1960s, the space creature was typified by the beings portrayed in *Body Snatchers*. In the 1950s and early 1960s the movies showed us here on earth fighting off a wide variety of intergalactic Others, most of whom came in nonhuman form. The title creature in *The Blob* threatened to inundate us with slime. In *The Children of the Damned*, space invaders impregnated women whose children then threatened to take over the earth. The period saw *I Married a Monster from Outer Space*, *This Island Earth*, and *War of the Worlds*. The first is a fantasy similar to *Body Snatchers*, about a race of monsters from an unknown galaxy who take on the form of the humans whose bodies they inhabit. The second has a half-human, half-insect creature that attacks a spaceship whose crew is human. *War of the Worlds*, released in 1953, involves an invasion of the earth by Cycloptic creatures from Mars who are, as the narrator says, "intellects vast, cruel, and unsympathetic." The creatures are unstoppable, even by the atomic bomb. Finally, they droop and die in midattack, done in by bacteria and viruses to which they had developed no immunities back home. The year before *War of the Worlds* there was *The Thing from Outer Space*, about a super-intelligent giant, more human in shape than most of the outer-space creatures but actually a form of vegetable life whose diet consists of human and animal blood.

Playing roles in both of these last two movies is a dramatic character who is open-minded and charitably inclined toward the space creatures, who wants to assume a certain good-heartedness on their part, even believing that they may embody some wisdom in short supply among the earthlings. These characters were ahead of their time in the 1950s in their openheartedness toward Otherness, so it is worth noting that they are treated as irritating fools in these movies. In *War of the Worlds*, the type is represented by a man of the cloth who approaches the spaceship of the invaders, his hand outstretched in a gesture of conciliation, forgetting that the goal of the Martians, which is to seize the earth for themselves, makes them unconciliable. The pastor says, "They are living creatures out there; if they are more advanced than us, they should be closer to the Creator." The good man recites "The Lord Is My Shepherd" as he walks toward the beastly high-tech thing from another planet and is then vaporized by the creatures' matter-destroying weaponry. In *The Thing*, the pro-Otherness character is a scientist who believes we have something to learn from what is, evidently, an intellectually higher form of life. He tries to dissuade the other scientists from their view that the only recourse is to set a trap for the monster and kill it. He makes his approach to the thing, which, uninterested in dialogue or mutual understanding, smashes him to the floor.

It is entirely reasonable to see the 1950s image of the space invader as a reflection of Cold War fears, which in turn were logical enough given the actual existence of a militarized, nuclearized, expansionist communism that had only a few years before taken power in Eastern and Central Europe, North Korea, and China and seemed to be on the march in Indochina. But the space invader as a character in the movies was utterly transformed into something close to the opposite of its 1950s incarnation long before the collapse of communism and of the Soviet Union, and this transformation eerily coincides with the developing consciousness and self-conception of an entire generation.

By the late 1960s, with the civil rights movement and the Vietnam War, we came to think that the menace, the one that, as we used to say then, was dangerous to children and other living things, was no longer the exotic outsider but we ourselves. The science fiction of the late 1970s and the 1980s, revealing this change, inverted the standard fantasy. The new creature from outer space turned from menace to source of superior wisdom. Even though the Cold War was in full swing, our self-conception had changed so much that earthlings and space creatures switched positions in the moral universe.

There was, for example, the pioneering *Close Encounters of the Third Kind*, released in 1977. The visitors from outer space in *Close Encounters*, whose very title suggests the ironic sensibility often given the name "postmodernism," cause a good deal of fright with their high-intensity searchlights and their tendency, born, it seems, of curiosity, to kidnap earthlings. These are an adult's outer-space creatures. But they turn out to be brainy and gentle beings who mean no harm, a long way from the body snatchers.

An even earlier instance of the new space invader form was *The Man Who Fell to Earth* of 1976, in which the singer David Bowie plays not a menace but a lost soul, a postdiluvian stranger looking, as the sociologists might put it, for community, and then being destroyed by the harshness of life among the earthlings. Then there were the various creatures in *Star Wars* and its sequels, which, taken together, form a vision of racial diversity in a decidedly multicultural world. In the *Star Wars* series good comes in many forms—like the mystical Obi-Wan Kenobi, the mechanical R2D2, or the gnomish sage Yoda. Evil, personified by Darth Vader, is a human deformed by those all-too-human characteristics—the Nietzschean will to power, male aggressiveness, the brittle impulse to dominate characteristic of those who do not know how to get in touch with their inner selves, or with the Force.

But it is when *E.T. The Extra-Terrestrial* comes along in 1982 to be the biggest-grossing movie in the history of Hollywood that the space invader as a symbol of good reaches its highest point. *E.T.* is a clarion call to the antiracist ethos, a cinematic lesson in tolerance and cultural pluralism. He is gnomelike, dwarfish, dark-skinned, semireptilian, ungainly, innocuous, sentimental, bug-eyed, scaly. He combines the qualities of Mahatma Gandhi and a lizard. More to the point, he is a twenty-first-century Christ.

Like Jesus, E.T. is mightily unappreciated by the holders of power on earth, who, imbued with the suspicious mentality of the pre–baby boom generation, think that he is of the older genre of the body snatchers, perhaps a carrier of some deadly virus. So the scientists and technicians march around in airtight space suits, making them look far more monstrous than E.T. himself. E.T. spends his last night on earth in a forested glade—a clear reference to the Garden of Gethsemane—striving to communicate with his folks back home. The next day, the scientists and technicians—who play the role that the Pharisees and the Roman centurions play in the biblical version of this story—capture him and stick him behind a prophylactic shield where he dies, temporarily. Only the children, the disciples, the innocents who have no knowledge of intergalactic bacteria and are unprejudiced toward reptilian beings from other solar systems, understand E.T. for what he is: a foil for our own moral blindness, our deep prejudice and racism, our failure to see the evil that lurks inside of us, or to perceive the good within the different. E.T. is resurrected by the love of the children. A spaceship arrives and he ascends to heaven.

There were, to be sure, science fiction films of the 1950s genre made in the 1980s—*Alien* being the most commercially important and probably the scariest of them—and there were some films in the 1950s that were ahead of their time in viewing the earthlings as evil and the space invaders as good. *The Day the Earth Stood Still* of 1951, for example, tells about a delegation from an entente of other planets, an interplanetary U.N., that warns the earthlings that intraearth wars threaten the peace elsewhere in the universe, and if they don't stop, the earth will have to be destroyed.

But even if the period genres are not entirely consistent, it is not hard to see the general drift in the movies' representations of ourselves and of the Other, a change that stemmed from the great intellectual revolution effected by the war in Vietnam. The space invader, the symbol of something that is not us, changes from the devil incarnate to a new Jesus. The earthlings, the beleaguered innocents of the 1950s, are the imperial Romans of the next era.

The passage from *Body Snatchers* to *E.T. The Extra-Terrestrial* is the voyage from conventional acceptance of American norms to the new critical consciousness born out of the real-life dramas of the 1960s. It is a kind of pop-cultural foreshadowing of what happened in the political arena in 1992, when the baby-boomer cohort Bill Clinton took power from World War II veterans like George Bush. We do not perhaps appreciate the fading older generation as much as we should, even though they are, as Peggy Noonan, Ronald Reagan's former speechwriter, has put it, "the great generation that held fast through a bitter depression and fought gallantly in war for a country they never doubted for a second deserved their love." They saved the world against real enemies so that we, the saved, could imagine a world in which the enemies are ourselves.

Appreciated or not, the generation just now passing from the scene was bound in its movies to make the invader from outer space more a body snatcher than a scaly wise man who could turn your bicycle into a flying carpet. There is, of course, much that is heartening in the shift from that generation to another. Indeed, the body snatcher is probably a pretty good illustration of the collective unconscious, which saw whiteness as standard and all other colors as foreign, less than fully human. It is a good sign of the national shift toward greater openness to difference and to genuine participation in national life by minority group members. If the vision that underlies *Body Snatchers* took comfort in a kind of uniculturalism, an ethic of national unity, the vision behind *E.T.* is decidedly multicultural, in the good sense of that word.

E.T. himself bespeaks the supremacy of the values of tolerance, a striving for self-improvement, simplicity, and unpretentiousness (after all, this is an advanced being who wears no clothes, whose heart glows pink when he is moved to strong emotion, and who makes an interstellar telephone device out of a saw blade, a fork, and a television remote control); he is the inverse of our own flaws of complexity, vanity, snobbishness, elaborate materialism, and aggressiveness.

If the space invader has become hero and the earthling the villain, similar inversions have taken place in at least one other cinematic prototype—the cowboy-and-Indian adventure, the classic in this case being Kevin Costner's *Dances With Wolves* of 1990. Never mind that Costner uses a historical event that never happened (the defection of a Civil War cavalry officer to the Indians) and transforms the warlike, scalp-taking, torturing, predatory, patriarchal, male-chauvinistic Sioux Indians into a group that might have founded the Ethical Culture Society. *Dances With Wolves* replaces one myth, that of the brave settler and the savage Indian, with another—the morally advanced friend-of-the-earth Indian ("Never have I seen a people more devoted to family," the cavalry defector says with reverence) and the malodorous, foulmouthed, bellicose white man.

The desire to put the Indian on the pedestal of superior moral awareness defeats even simple truth. In 1991 two American Indians were the subjects of best-selling books. They became icons of the New Consciousness, and they continued to be so even after it was discovered in both cases that their most admirable qualities had been invented for them by white men. One of them, Chief Seattle, became identified with a statement reproduced on posters in practically every multicultural school in America, the statement about "The earth is our mother" and "I have seen a thousand rotting buffalos on the prairie, left by the white man who shot them from a passing train." These quotes reappear every year on Earth Day and form the center-piece of *Brother Eagle, Sister Sky: A Message From Chief Seattle*, which sold 280,000 copies in its first six months in print. The problem is that Chief Seattle's ecological views were invented by a screenwriter named Ted Perry for a 1972 film about environmentalism. Very little is actually know about the real Chief Seattle because he left scant written record of himself, but it is known that he spent his entire life in the Pacific Northwest and never saw buffalo or the prairie.*

The Education of Little Tree and the cult that grew up around him brings into even sharper relief our collective search for new heroes of virtue. *Little Tree*, which was on top of the *New York Times* paperback best-seller list for thirty weeks in 1991, won the Abby Award from the American Booksellers Association, and drew twenty-seven film offers, is supposedly about Native American Forrest Carter's heartwarming Cherokee upbringing, in which white people are depicted as fools and ignoramuses. The evidence is that, in fact, the book was written in the late 1970s as a kind of gag by a certain Asa Carter, a former speechwriter for Alabama's governor George Wallace, a member of the anti-integrationist White Citizens' Council and a founder in 1957 of the Ku Klux Klan of the Confederacy. Even after it was revealed that Carter was no Cherokee but actually a white supremacist, the book remained a *Times* best-seller. A new printing of one hundred thousand copies was ordered by the publisher.†

From *E.T.* and *Little Tree* to Margo Culley, a professor of English at the University of Massachusetts, it is a short but morally very signifi-cant step. In 1990, Culley spoke at a conference organized by some-

---

*I have relied on the account of the Chief Seattle fake in "Just Too Good to Be True," *Newsweek*, May 4, 1992, page 68.

†See "New Age Fable from an Old School Bigot," *Newsweek*, Oct. 14, 1991, page 62.

thing called the New Jersey Project, which is a state-financed program, led by Paula S. Rothenberg, a professor of philosophy at William Paterson State College. The New Jersey Project's goal is, according to its brochures, "to incorporate new scholarship on gender, race, class and ethnicity into core curricula rather than separating it out from mainstream courses." The program gives annual Student Achievement Awards for Excellence in Feminist Scholarship. It holds conferences like the one at which Culley spoke and provides consultants to schools that are "seeking to integrate issues of women and gender, race, class, ethnicity and homophobia and heterosexism into the curriculum." As of late 1991, the New Jersey Project had cost the state taxpayers $1,456,000.

Culley excitedly proclaimed to her audience that the explosion of multiculturalism in the universities was "one of the most rapid, astonishing, profound and far-reaching intellectual revolutions since Copernicus." The move from a "Western and/or Northern Hemisphere–centered world view" is "as astonishing for some of us as learning to think of the sun, not the earth, as the center of our universe."

Professor Culley has certainly lived this latter-day Copernican revolution. She did what she calls "my work in the civil rights movement" and "against the war in Vietnam," and at the same time she became a feminist, and therefore "my story was/is the story of an era." In fact, her particular story, and the assumptions that she carries with her about the values of Western civilization, have to do with academic life, but the story could have taken place in some other domain, like the movies, or journalism, or in philanthropic foundations or the Protestant church. For Culley the exciting thing is how much matters have changed in the academic study of women. In the early 1970s, she said in her New Jersey speech, it was a "struggle" to have papers on women accepted in the major professional organizations. But since then, the number of women's studies courses has increased from a pioneering seventeen in 1969 to two thousand in 1973 and up to twenty thousand courses in 1980. A decade later, it would be just about impossible to count the individual courses, she told her audience, but "over 500 women's studies programs exist and most are thriving." Who could have thought, she said, that at the Modern Language Association, which is the largest scholarly group in the world, with more than thirty thousand members, "the subjects of gender and race have overwhelmed the field?" Who could have imagined that "race and gender issues would be the hottest game in town, or that at times it would seem the only game?"

It might seem odd that someone interested in diversity would so happily proclaim that one perspective has become "the only game" in town, but Professor Culley in fact assumes that within that single game there is fabulous variety, many "perspectives." "Diverse feminisms have extended the boundary of our knowledge," she told her audience in New Jersey. "In the taxonomy of feminisms we find, among others, liberal, cultural, radical, socialist, Third-world, post-colonial, and post-structuralist feminists," she said. Among the others in this diverse phylum are, presumably, Marxist, lesbian, deconstructionist, posthistoricist, and other feminisms. Certainly, there was no point in mentioning Christian or Jewish or Muslim feminists, and Republican or conservative feminists would be oxymoronish.

Professor Culley had other things to say, many of them marinated in the half dozen or so concepts that have become conventional wisdom since the explosion she described began. She spoke of "the importance of subject positions," the "privileging of theory," of the "site of the collision of post-structuralism and feminist politics." She mentioned "gender as a social construct" and "the politics of representation," the "emergent voices of women from the Third World," and how, after she read American Indian autobiographies, white women's autobiography became for her "very specific historically and culturally constructed representations of the white female self."

For those not familiar with this jargon, it might seem to embody something new, when, in fact, it is the standard boilerplate, the prefabricated lingo of academic life. Indeed, it is one of the major conceits of the New Consciousness that a brilliantly "transgressive" (another commonly used word) way of scrutinizing the world is being developed by what is called the new scholarship. And, indeed, there is a great deal that is eye-opening and compelling in literary criticism, history, sociology, and other fields where many scholars are taking a radically skeptical approach to conventional attitudes. Contrary to some critics of the newer academic trends, I find much that is both enjoyable and edifying in deconstruction, in the new historicism, in black studies, and in feminism, where a previously unmapped terrain is being explored by lively minds. The problem is that so much of what is claimed under the banner of the new is actually a stale, simpleminded, Manichaean, and imitative reformulation of that dis-

credited nineteenth-century concept called Marxism, its creases of
great age masked by the lipstick and rouge of a new terminology. It
would be hard to hear a speech at the annual conference of the New
Jersey Project, or at many an academic convention, that did not have
a heavy sprinkling of the phrases and terms of this new language.

There is "dominant discourse," "marginal subjects," the "victimized subaltern"; there are "overdetermined structures of meaning"
and "hegemonic arrangements of power." Open up almost any contemporary academic journal, and you will find phrases like "colonized
bodies," the "vantage points of the subjugated," the "great underground terrain of subjugated knowledge," the "marginalized other,"
which are in contradistinction to the "totalizing metanarratives" and
the "socially produced meaning" of the dominant white-male culture,
represented in the "hegemonic curriculum." Inspired by the ideas
of French philosopher Michel Foucault, the jargon represents the
reformulation of basic nineteenth-century Marxist ideas that have
been borrowed by generations of intellectuals bent on showing that
the world as it exists is the creation (the "social construction") of the
groups that hold power, their ideology (the "dominant discourse")
used to maintain sway over everybody else (the "victimized subal-
terns"). Substitute the new jargon for such older terms as "substruc-
ture" and "superstructure," and you have just about the entire
addition of ideological multiculturalism to already existing Marxist
social theory.

Here, for example, is Rothenberg answering a question about
what she calls "the opponents of a multicultural, gender-balanced
curriculum," namely: "How does the traditional curriculum serve
their interests and perpetuate their power?" Rothenberg's answer is
right out of the sophomore's guide to nineteenth-century dialectical
materialism. "The traditional curriculum teaches all of us to see the
world through the eyes of privileged, white, European males and
to adopt their interests and perspectives as our own," she writes.
Rothenberg is advancing her insight as if it were something new,
when, in fact, all she is doing is replacing the word "bourgeois" or
"capitalist" with the words "white, European males." This tradition,
she continues, "calls books by middle-class, white male writers 'literature' and honors them as timeless and universal, while treating the
literature produced by everyone else as idiosyncratic and transi-
tory. . . . It teaches the art produced by privileged white men in the
West and calls it 'art history.'" Rothenberg continues to say that the

traditional curriculum "values the work of killing and conquest over the production and re-production of life."*

Culley, in this spirit, mentioned in passing that in 1987 she was asked to direct the new general education courses at the University of Massachusetts–Amherst, which involved 1,500 students taking Man and Woman in Literature, "designed to fulfill new University requirements in Social and Cultural Diversity." This is the Paula Rothenberg idea put into practice in the classroom, the teaching of a nontraditional curriculum, and one can well imagine what sort of diversity of thought is encouraged in these classes. Rothenberg has already provided us with her profound social analysis, and as for Culley, she spoke at the conference of the "incalculable harm" done to the country by Ronald Reagan and the need to "maintain a radical intellectual edge in a repressive climate," which is the reason that requirements in social and cultural diversity have been created in the first place. Culley did not explain how, if the climate is so repressive, the number of women's studies programs went from nothing in the late 1960s to being "the hottest game in town"—at times, indeed, "the only game"—twenty years later. She is, however, a bit more honest in making perhaps the most significant claim that can be made on behalf of the bearers of the New Consciousness: "We are here to stay."

Culley, Rothenberg, et al. grow out of the same soil of collective awareness as *E.T.* and the "Ethical Cultural" Indian. But *E.T.* is a benign shift from defensiveness to openness. The Ethical Cultural Indian, while sentimental and historically inaccurate, is perhaps not more sentimental or inaccurate than the cowboy who preceded him. He provides the experience of rooting for the Indians rather than the cavalry, for a change, and I'm ready to see that as a healthy development. The postsixties sensibility often bespeaks the most generously self-critical quality of the American personality, its will to moral perfection, which was put into the soil by our generic Puritan ancestors. What the multiculturalists are saying now is, why leave the job half-done? There is plenty of fault remaining for us to eradicate.

And that argument, of course, is what gives ideological multiculturalism its strategic advantage. Nobody wants to be complacent about injustice, especially when that injustice involves racial and other dis-

---

*Paula Rothenberg, "Critics of Attempts to Democratize the Curriculum Are Waging a Campaign to Misrepresent the Work of Responsible Professors," *Chronicle of Higher Education*, Apr. 10, 1991, page 83.

criminations. But the postsixties, E.T.-ish sensibility did more than create a generation willing to see the fault within itself. It robbed us of our defenses at the same time. It made us prone to *dérapage*. It is responsible in this sense for more than just a bit of noxious but probably not-very-harmful academic silliness à la Culley, Rothenberg, and the New Jersey Project. Bereft of any strong sense of ourselves as embodiments of a great culture and system of values, riven with self-doubt about the worth of our own tradition, we have become defenseless against the extremist claims of multicultural ideology in general. We have become ridden with guilt. We have lost the will to have a common identity, since we no longer have faith that the common identity is morally worthy. We are unwilling to defend complicated truths, whether about Christopher Columbus or the extent to which racism and sexism explain the total experience and status of minority group members and women. We foster an exaggerated sense of aggrievement rather than insist on a degree of responsibility. We are uncomfortable with the notion of standards, because we are prone to the argument that standards and "metanarratives" are one and the same thing—merely ways of seeing the world "through the eyes of privileged, white, European males." And it is all because we are afraid, as Margo Culley might put it, to be found complicitous in the hegemonic arrangements of power. We are subject to the tyranny of political correctness, the dictatorship of virtue, because we have granted the forces of the New Consciousness the right to determine what virtue is.

Professor Culley gets credit for one thing. When she claims to represent "the only game" in town, she is disclosing a truth that the ideological multiculturalists normally keep carefully hidden. The multiculturalist sensibility, which may prevail in the conflicts over values and identity raging across the country, generally does not claim its victory. Usually the upholders of virtue are duty-bound to deny that the victory ever took place. The victory and the simultaneous denial of it explain two things.

First, they answer the question, why now? The bearers of the New Consciousness have, quite simply, arrived at the point of critical mass. They have become capable of determining the moral agenda, of establishing which subjects will get attention, of drawing the iconography of the culture, of getting the new programs and foundation grants, starting the new journals and attracting the graduate students, and, perhaps most important, of exerting just enough intimidation so that certain opinions that run counter to the left-liberal orthodoxy have become virtually taboo, and in many instances (some of them detailed in Chapter 4) punishable offenses. Slowly over the years, the ideological multiculturalism of the Margo Culley variety has been growing in the national petri dish, until, in the 1980s, helped by a reaction against the electoral triumph of Reaganism, it had spread through the entire American polity, affecting a great inversion in American intellectual life. Whereas before the oppressive force came from the political right, and had to do with a particular view of patriotism, standards, and traditional values, the threat of ideological tyranny now comes from the left, and it now has to do with collective guilt, an overweening moralism, and multiculturalism. The danger to such things as free speech and genuine diversity of opinion is no longer due to conservatism; it is due to the triumph of a modish, leftish, moralistic liberalism.

Of course, Reagan won two elections by landslides, and George Bush won one of them. The conservative radio commentator Rush Limbaugh sells far more books and has more listeners than Margo Culley or any other professors at any university. So how could it be that the New Consciousness has come to power?

Limbaugh is a clue to this. His success is the product of a grassroots feeling among many Americans that their values and their self-conception are being assaulted by the liberal elites, and, moreover, that to express their discontent with this would be to expose them as benighted and racist. And they are correct in this. The victory of ideological multiculturalism is not in the numbers or in the polls, because there it would always lose. It is in the penetration of the new sensibility into the elite institutions, in the universities, the press, the liberal churches, the foundations, the schools, and show business, on PBS and "Murphy Brown," at Harvard and Dallas Baptist University, on editorial boards and op-ed pages, at the Ford Foundation and the Rockefeller Brothers Fund, the National Education Association, the American Society of Newspaper Editors, the National Council of Churches, and the Pew Charitable Trusts. In all of them, the sensibility that has fomented the challenge to the American places of memory provides overall guidance. What were once small enclaves of dissent replicated themselves and became so numerous that they became the establishment.

The multiculturalists have won, but their victory depends on their declining to claim it. Since theirs is an antiestablishment rebellion, a victory of virtue, they thrive by maintaining the fiction that they are nothing but small voices struggling to be heard in the louder cacophony of the dominant discourse. Multiculturalism has gained its moral force because of its appropriation of the mantle of the civil rights movement, its jargon and its moral fervor. It appears as the protest of the weak against the Power. It is the battle fought by "inclusion" against "exclusion." It can never admit that it has become the Power, including the power to exclude, even though, in many areas of American life, multiculturalism is the Power consolidating itself.

But how do power holders conceal their strength? How do they dominate the discourse while pretending to be the meek and beleaguered force of rebellion? Multiculturalism, in turning inside out many of the goals of the great civil rights movement of the 1960s, provided a means. It left the new power holders with an establishment to do battle against, the establishment of Eurocentric, racist, whitemale hegemony, and doing so allowed them to cloak themselves in the mantle of the good fight, the moral struggle, the progressive crusade. By dressing themselves in the finery of virtue, multiculturalists gained the power to intimidate and to limit the range of views that are acceptable in our society, even while pretending that they had no power and therefore could neither intimidate nor coerce.

Of course, even Margo Culley does not argue that, since they have won, they can now enjoy the fruits of their victory, bask in the sunshine of their success. The multiculturalists continue to try to expand their influence, to see their visions implemented, and, in so doing, they encounter resistance, create battlefields over which the culture wars are being fought. These battlefields, small and large, are scattered across the United States, but among the hardest fought, and thus most illustrative, were the struggle over the English department at the University of Texas and what I call the battle for young minds in Brookline, Massachusetts, to which we now turn.

PART III

Battlegrounds

All fantasies are fantasies of omnipotence. But then you ask yourself: what happens when one fantasy meets another? There's a duel to the death.

—DANIEL BELL

Chapter 8

THE BATTLE OF BROOKLINE AND OTHER STRUGGLES OVER YOUNG MINDS

Why do they teach us that white people suck?

—Elementary school student from
Brookline, Massachusetts

Ronni and David Stillman are the sort of liberal people that should feel utterly at home in Brookline, Massachusetts, a liberal town in a liberal state, the town where Michael Dukakis lives and sent his children to school and where the population has not voted for a Republican presidential nominee since 1956. The right-thinking people of the town once put a proposal before the town committee that residents' garbage be checked to ensure compliance with the strict local recycling laws. The Stillmans, who make a living writing textbooks for students of French and Spanish and teaching foreign languages at the Harvard Extension School, are from New York, where being a liberal Democrat was practically an inherited characteristic. "In my family," as Ronni put it, "my mother wouldn't talk to me because I supported the Persian Gulf War." David is dark and stocky, and his seriousness is tempered by a self-deprecating sense of humor. Ronni is petite and attractive with bright brown eyes glinting with the passion of her conviction, which sometimes leads her to interrupt her husband, who patiently defers. They are the kind of people who marched in civil rights and antiwar demonstrations in the 1960s, who abhor racism and tyranny.

In the spring of 1989, the Stillmans, whose older child was a sophomore at the public Brookline High School, heard that a demanding and celebrated course, an advanced placement (AP) year of European history, was going to be eliminated by the social studies department on the grounds that the course was "incompatible with multiculturalism."

One course. No big deal. The matter at first did not seem much of a *causus belli*, and the Stillmans never imagined that they would end up in a three-year fight that pitted them and a few allies against the school system, many of the teachers, and quite a few of their neighbors. But their wish to reinstate AP European History turned out to be one of those small things that grew big, feeding on the very bitterness that it engendered, until the couple from Brookline, joined by a few like-minded citizens, was doing titanic battle against the giant force of multiculturalism itself.

It is not, moreover, that they started out hostile to multiculturalism. Like most people first introduced to the idea of greater inclusiveness, they found it a logical extension of liberal ideas. They just didn't quite fathom why AP European History was incompatible with multiculturalism, and they certainly did not understand why, as David put it, "a school would try to improve its overall quality by getting rid of one of its best courses."

The course in question was taken every year by some thirty-five or so students, which is a small minority of the graduating class, including, usually, a high proportion of its best students. It had been taught for eighteen years by the same teacher, who happened to be about the only one in the entire school who was known to be a political conservative, a registered Republican, a fact that, in the context of suburban Boston, made him just a bit suspect.

The teacher, James Dudley, a former marine, was one of the few male teachers at Brookline High who showed up every day in a jacket and tie. Dudley also had a formal classroom and personal manner. He treated school somewhat the way he treated church, which he attends with his family every Sunday. School for him was a special place, a place of serious activity, of hard work, a place not untinged with hierarchy. His formality did not, even in our very informal age, make him unpopular with students. It would not be too much to say that Dudley was revered. College-bound juniors at Brookline would say to each other, "Are you going to do Dudley next year?" meaning, are you going to subject yourself to the rigors of the celebrated AP European History course? Among those that did were three who later became university history professors and another dozen who became high-school teachers.

When they heard that Dudley's famous course had been slated for removal from the curriculum by a 17 to 1 vote of the social studies faculty (Dudley himself was the lone dissenter), the Stillmans assumed that a mistake had been made. They would speak to the proper authorities, and the course would be reinstated. They went to see the headmaster of Brookline High; they met with the head of the social studies department. They were told that AP European History had been eliminated as part of a six-year revision program. It had, they said, come about as a result of a "process," and David remembered reacting negatively to that explanation.

"I hate that kind of talk," he told me. " 'Process.' I mean, what does that mean? Here one of the best courses in the school was being deleted as a result of 'process.' We heard a lot of jargon. They said it was an experiment. They talked about being on the cutting edge of curricular reform. They talked about 'diversity.' 'Global.' That was another term they were using. 'Global.' "

When the Stillmans did not get satisfaction in these early meetings, AP European History began taking on importance not only because it was an excellent course but because it emerged as a symbol, a symbol for what they began to see as the school's lack of concern for academic rigor, its preference for a kind of egalitarian social engineering over old-fashioned meritocracy. They also suspected that the vogue of multiculturalism had overstepped the bounds of good sense, not enriching the curriculum by including non-Western subjects, which they supported, but, in the guise of that enrichment, impoverishing the children by denigrating the West. They began raising questions at school board meetings, which led other parents to be amazed at the school's insistence that the decision about the course would stand, unaltered by outside pressure.

The Stillmans began doing research. They learned (or, more accurately, they reaffirmed) that Brookline High School had since the early 1970s offered courses in African and Asian studies as well as women's studies and other multicultural offerings. A study of the curriculum carried out in 1973 by the nonpartisan Brookline League of Women Voters concluded that students had available to them "a great variety of subjects—such as Black Studies, Women in History, the Urban Experience, Visual Communication, Immigrants & Minorities, the Quest for Peace, and the Economics of Inflation." The league's study said: "Social and ethnic histories have entered the curriculum and the Western tradition no longer dominates. Latin-American, Russian and Asian studies attract large numbers of students." So at least as early as 1973, Brookline High School was "global."

Thus, the Stillmans and their allies felt that the high school had long ago done what the administration said it was now trying to do. They began to hear that other courses, adopted in the interests of a multicultural curriculum, had one-sided political content, so they began trying to find out about those courses too. They discovered that, while the serious study of European history was suddenly "incompatible" with Brookline's approach, various soft and mushy courses, created, it seemed, to give students an amusing and not-very-demanding way of satisfying academic requirements, were compatible. Eventually, after their first efforts to reinstate AP European History were rebuffed, they formed the Committee for Quality Education (CQE), which soon had one hundred members, stationery, and a bank account ($1,500 in donations to start).

The CQE had Ph.D.'s on it, lawyers, university professors, educational scholars. Among the members' friends and sympathizers were celebrated Harvard historians; the editor of the Brookline *Citizen*, the local daily paper; and a Nobel laureate in physics. The CQE requested course descriptions and copies of exam questions from the school, and, when the school refused, the lawyer members of the CQE filed Freedom of Information Act requests in order to get the desired materials. The school authorities felt that such intrusive scrutiny would have a chilling effect on teachers' efforts to be bold and original in the classroom, while the CQE saw the refusal to allow parents to look at the materials of the classroom as an attempt to cover up the blatant politicization of the curriculum. The FOI Act requests were ruled valid and enforceable by the Massachusetts Department of Education. The school then provided some information, which fueled the suspicion of the CQE that a love of social activism, a desire to instill the right attitudes about politics and human relations, and a tendency to see the West in especially negative terms were competing with scholastic rigor at the high school. The decision to eliminate AP European History seemed to them to reflect a prevailing ideology that the members of the CQE found profoundly antiliberal.

"What we found was a conscious perversion, a deliberate sabotage," David Stillman said. The Stillmans and their allies found that the school was guided by New Age "edubabble," as David called it, theories that stressed social conscience and something called moral education, along with peace studies, as much as academic pursuits, and that presented the world through a 1960s prism, whose key concepts were Western racism and Western colonialism. The CQE found written statements of the school's philosophy, which was perfumed with the concept of social activism as the highest goal. The statement of philosophy, for example, blithely affirmed: "Knowledge and reasoning without commitment to action are useless." Mao Zedong could not have put it better.

"The key word is 'diversity,'" Ronni Stillman told me. "That's all we've heard since we came here, diversity. But what they mean by diversity is not diversity of opinion. Diversity means skin color. Diversity in Brookline means different colored people who have been trained to think alike. They treat different opinions with contempt."

This, of course, was not the view of the teachers and administrators of Brookline High School or of the many parents who supported them. There was already plenty of European history in the curriculum, they argued. They wanted to replace AP European History with AP Government, which would have involved a student internship in some local or state agency. More generally, they felt, the change in population and our increasingly interrelated world required that students learn about other cultures. The school, moreover, had to take care of the needs of all of the students, not just the mainly white, college-bound group that "did Dudley" every year. Europe, in any case, was not as important as traditionally believed.

"Is historical 'greatness' reserved exclusively to those individuals who fall within the western traditions?" one veteran social studies teacher, Deborah Quitt, rhetorically asked in a letter to the local newspaper. "Shouldn't students be exposed to historical 'greats' of other cultures? Should Confucius, Buddha, Mohammed, Lenin, and Ghandi [*sic*] be relegated to the back burner because they had the misfortune of not being a product of the European tradition?" Besides, said Quitt, "Eurocentrism has been our greatest deficit in international relations." It may be true, she argued, that the history of England is "critical to understanding the sources of American institutions," but "that of the Continent is absolutely not." The history of the Continent "is not more relevant to American development than is the history of West Africa, East Asia, China, Russia and Latin America." Choices had to be made. In any case, many people felt that the CQE was setting a bad precedent by interfering. Other groups could do the same, some people argued (ignoring the fact that other groups were doing the same, except that the social studies department agreed with them), and thus curricular change could at any time be blocked by organized pressure.

These were, indeed, the issues that had to be resolved. Quitt took some flak from CQE supporters for putting Lenin outside the European tradition and for claiming that Continental European history was no more relevant to American development than West Africa and China (she also misspelled "Gandhi" and probably underestimated the extent to which the principles that guided his action were inspired by Western thought), but she did raise the essential questions that were to be argued out, sometimes quite indirectly, for the next year and a half. Generally, while the members of the CQE in their letters and statements could be forceful, sharp, and sarcastic, and they certainly pursued their cause aggressively, they did focus on what they saw as the faults of the school's position. Many of the statements against them were quite different; they aimed at the CQE's character and motives; they characterized them as members of an extreme right-wing strike force, rather than refute their arguments.

The head of the social studies department, William Hibert, called the Stillmans and their group "self-appointed inquisitors" who "wreaked havoc" at the school; he termed them "rabid citizens" who "could do permanent damage to the system." Deborah Quitt called them "intellectual imperialists." She wrote in one letter to the Brookline *Citizen*: "When people combine education, political savvy, and arrogance, the damage they are capable of wreaking is truly awesome." In a letter to their colleagues, seventeen of the eighteen members of the social studies department (the exception was James Dudley) complained: "As individuals and as a group we have been vilified, ridiculed and slandered." No less a person than the rabbi of the local Reform synagogue (the Stillmans belonged to a different synagogue) preached a sermon in which, without ever bothering to ask the Stillmans their side of the story, he called them and their allies a "small band of shrill knaves" and "master manipulators of media attention" employing the "tactics of intimidation, incitement, dissembling and the invalidation of those who disagree with them." The CQE, the rabbi said, was made up of "a handful of vigilantes whose intellectual terrorism and persistent calumnies and half-truths force those who oppose them into silence and submission."

A flyer announcing a day-long conference on curriculum debates, sponsored by the supposedly nonpartisan Massachusetts Endowment for the Humanities, referred to the two sides in Brookline as "those protesting the curriculum and those fighting the censors." Suddenly the Stillmans et al., who only wanted to put something back into the curriculum, not take anything out, and who had criticized some courses for one-sidedness, were not just critics or dissenters. They were censors. A widely circulated letter from an editor of the Boston *Globe* and his wife to the school headmaster accused the CQE members of behaving like "bullies who, throughout history, have attempted to harass and intimidate intellectual opponents into silence." The writers of the letter said the CQE used "brownshirt type tactics" that "present a clear and present threat to academic freedom and civil liberties." No specific brownshirt tactics were mentioned in this letter. Nonetheless, the Boston *Globe* editor and his wife went on to say that the CQE's methods were "character assassination and intellectual terrorism," and these tactics showed the CQE's "failure to appreciate the heritage of free thought and free speech which lie at the center of this community and this country." They engaged in "vigilante-type censorship" that was in "direct opposition" to "unfettered debate and tolerance for intellectual diversity."

It was odd that these partisans of "unfettered debate" and "intellectual diversity" took the arguments of the Stillmans, which were the only examples of unfettered debate and intellectual diversity around, as "intellectual terrorism."

Is it correct to detect here, even before we've looked at exactly what the Brookline school's detractors actually said, something of the underlying spirit of multiculturalist advocacy, which is that to raise objections to it is not diversity of opinion but a manifestation of evil? In any case, within a few months of the beginning of the Stillmans' first questions about AP European History, the debate in Brookline had, as that Massachusetts Endowment for the Humanities flyer put it, "torn the community apart."

Could all this really have been about one course in European history?

The truth is that Brookline is unusual only because the move toward what is called multiculturalism attracted the attention of a group of highly interested and capable parents who launched a countermovement to oppose it. Across the country in one form or another curriculum revision is taking place to make the schools more "inclusive," more "multicultural," more "gender neutral," "antiracist," and "disability aware," thereby enhancing the "self-esteem" and "critical-thinking skills" of nonwhite, non-Eurocentric students. Much of this no doubt is healthy and enriching. Why not "validate" (that's the commonly used word) the "culture" of every child in a class? Why not make Native Americans the subjects of history, not just the objects encountered in European nation building? My own feeling is that it would be good for all of us to know a bit more about Sojourner Truth and Chief Joseph of the Nez Percé. I absolutely do not oppose validating minority cultures or educating children of European origins to learn more about nonwhites, or making everybody keenly aware that the creation of the United States involved the displacement and slaughter of the Indians and the enslavement of Africans.

Moreover, any evaluation of elementary and secondary education is made vastly more complicated by the fact that there are no villains in the school curriculum debates, or at least none that I have encountered. Education, as it is, is failing millions of American children, especially, but not exclusively, nonwhite children. Many good people have dedicated themselves to striving to reverse this tendency, and for some of these people what is called bias-free, gender-neutral, multicultural education has become a kind of panacea. Perhaps indeed it can help. The problem emerges when what children are is separated from some clear conception of the skills they need to become self-fashioning individuals and responsible citizens, or when they are fed a simplistic, one-dimensional, racially based notion of their identity. When what they learn is determined less by their needs and more by what morally armed groups of adults want in their own battles over image and place in American life, it is then that liberal education reaches the point of *dérapage*.

In Brookline, for example, if the change in images and conceptions was just a matter of greater inclusiveness, there would probably not have been much controversy. Here we encounter another of the paradoxes of late-twentieth-century ideological multiculturalism. As that League of Women Voters study of the Brookline school district indicated, a multicultural curriculum was well established in Brookline as early as 1973. The same is true in many other places. Certainly in textbooks a multiculturalism of inclusion has been a guiding principle for two decades. And so why are the multicultural advocates asking for fundamental change when, in fact, such change has already taken place?

The answer seems to be that the latter-day multiculturalist thrust, while claiming little more than greater inclusiveness, actually aims at two deeper changes: one can be described as simple excess, perhaps distortion, a leaning toward the common multiculturalist sin of making white people and the West the larger-than-life villains of history. Brookline High School in this sense manifested one of the victories already gained by the multiculturalist philosophy: namely that the West cannot any longer be portrayed as superior to other cultures in any way; indeed it must, in a kind of pedagogical redress of the wrongs committed by the pedagogue's ancestors, be presented as worse.

The other change is more subtle: in the past, when the model of assimilation to an American culture prevailed, school was the place where all children would be introduced essentially to the same things, whatever their background or their race. In the present stage of multicultural thinking, the idea is taking hold that different children should learn different things, each group of children having what is presumed to be their own culture reflected back to them, thereby giving them self-esteem and cultural legitimation. A kind of educational separatism, in short, is becoming the goal of the multicultural philosophy.

Bilingual education, for example, is justified in these terms. This program, beloved especially of Hispanic organizations, started nationally in 1968 when Congress passed the Bilingual Education Act as a remedial effort to enable children who did not speak English to learn in the language they did speak, so they would not fall behind the English-speaking children. Since then, it has become a vast effort, spawned a huge bureaucracy, and taken on additional purposes. New York City spends $302.5 million a year on it, according to the *New York Times*. One out of every eight children is put into a bilingual-education program, and a large minority of them stay in it for more than four years. This is true even though in some districts, the *Times* reported in 1993, nearly half of the children in the program were born in the United States. In Brooklyn and Queens there are some twenty schools that offer Haitian Creole as a language of instruction, a language that is not generally used in Haiti itself, where the language of instruction is French. There are public schools in Oklahoma where children are taught in Cherokee. Most important, the program has come to be justified as a cultural necessity, an affirming experience for children who might otherwise experience what one prominent advocate of the approach calls "identity eradication."

This theorist, a Canadian educator named Jim Cummins, has reversed the standard order of things. Bilingual education was initially envisaged, and sold to taxpayers, as a way that children could keep up in their native languages while they learned English. But Cummins, in a book that is a kind of Bible for bilingual programs across the country, argues that the key to success in school is not at all whether children speak English. He is part of that growing coterie, ascendant in the schools of education across the country, that believes in self-esteem as the all-important ingredient leading to academic success. And Cummins links self-esteem not only with bilingual education but with minority-ness itself. Children do badly in school because of their feelings of "shame" at belonging to a minority group rather than to the "dominant group," he argues. For the children to do better, teachers must "consciously challenge the power structure both in their classrooms and schools and in the society at large." Bilingual education in this sense is "empowerment pedagogy."* It is an act of rebellion against white, Anglo cultural domination.

This general philosophy, with its animus against assimilation, is not an implicit part of the emerging educational philosophy. It is explicit, open, out there, standard belief. "The psychological cost of assimilation has been and continues to be high for many U.S. citizens," declares the National Council of Social Studies (NCSS), in Washington, D.C., in its 1992 "Curriculum Guidelines for Multicultural Education." "It too often demands self-denial, self-hatred, and rejection of family and ethnic ties."†

The NCSS is the largest organization in the country devoted to social studies education, with 25,000 members (including institutions) and 110 affiliates in all 50 states. Its guidelines essay cites "research

---

*Jim Cummins, *Empowering Minority Students*, California Association for Bilingual Education (Sacramento, 1989), page ix.

†"Curriculum Guidelines for Multicultural Education," *Social Education* 56, no. 5 (Sept. 1992), page 277.

suggesting that learning styles may be related to ethnicity in some ways," and it declares that simple recognition of cultural difference, a greater degree of inclusiveness, is not enough if we are to achieve the benefits of genuine multicultural education. "Education for multiculturalism, therefore, requires more than a change in curricula and textbooks. It requires systemwide changes that permeate all aspects of school."

That permeation of all aspects of school involves treating different students differently. Here, too, is a change. In the wake of the civil rights movement of the 1960s, when color blindness was seen as an ideal, the assumed injustice done to children of color was that they were treated differently. Now the goal of color blindness is viewed as serving the interests of the "dominant group." Educators should not "dismiss the question of racial and ethnic differences with the all-too-easy cliche, 'I don't see racial differences in students and I treat them all alike,' " the National Council of Social Studies warns. The research shows, it continues, "that if all students are treated alike, their distinctive needs are not being met and they are probably being denied access to equal educational opportunities." Moreover, treating each child differently does not mean treating each child as an ungraspable mystery, a gold coin in the treasure house of individualism. It means, as we shall see, consciously treating them as members of their racial, ethnic, or even sexual-orientation group.

This philosophy explains a great paradox of the drive toward multiculturalism for young people. In 1989, the Commissioner's Task Force on Minorities in New York provoked a new debate about diversity in the schools with the alarming conclusion: "African Americans, Asian Americans, Puerto Ricans/Latinos, and Native Americans have all been the victims of an intellectual and educational oppression that has characterized the culture and institutions of the United States and the European American world for centuries." The task force had a great deal to say about the "dominant culture" and "the people from cultures now largely omitted from the curriculum," who will soon be a majority of the American population. All young people, the task force said, were being "miseducated" because of a "systematic bias toward European culture and its derivatives."*

Could the multicultural animus against "European culture and its derivatives" emerge more clearly than that? Here we have a direct

---

A Curriculum of Inclusion: Report of the Commissioner's Task Force on Minorities: Equity and Excellence (July 1989).

statement that the Western culture is harmful to nonwhite children. And only that belief can make explicable one of the oddest findings of the task force, which was that the textbooks or the curricula concentrate so much on Europe that other "cultures" are neglected. It is as though the task force's members, eager to find "educational oppression" lurking on every page, were remembering the textbooks that they studied when they were in school and assumed that they are the same as the textbooks given to children now.

But it is difficult to look at the textbooks today and to find in them any serious omission of minority groups. Of course, exactly how much space should be given over to multiculturalism is a matter of debate. Perhaps it should be more than it is. Still, there can be no question that a dramatic multiculturalist reform of the textbooks has been under way since at least 1962.

It was in that year that the local branch of the NAACP charged that a history text used in Detroit's public schools portrayed slavery in a favorable light. In response, Detroit withdrew the offending text from circulation and the school board began studying bias in the entire system. Then, as Frances FitzGerald said in a book on the subject published in 1979: "What began as a series of discreet protests against individual books became a general proposition: all texts had treated the United States as a white, middle-class society when it was in fact multiracial and multicultural. And this proposition, never so much as suggested before 1962, had by the late sixties come to be a truism for the educational establishment."*

Women also joined the fray, and by the mid-1970s, every major textbook-publishing company had its lists of "Guidelines for the Equal Treatment of the Sexes" (McGraw-Hill), or "Guidelines for Multiethnic/Nonsexist Survey" (Random House), or "Avoiding Stereotypes: Principles and Applications" (Houghton Mifflin), or "Guidelines for Creating Positive Sexual and Racial Images" (Macmillan). The Macmillan guide, written by Radcliffe College president Matina Horner and published in 1975, warned against the "tyranny of the norm," which "seeks to reinforce upon individuals previously unchallenged but often irrelevant, inaccurate, and outdated stereotypes about what it means to be . . . male or female, black or white, young or old, rich or poor."

The changes in textbooks themselves constituted a revolution in

---

*Frances FitzGerald, *America Revised* (Boston: Little, Brown and Co., 1979), page 39.

the American self-conception, but a revolution that took place before, not as a result of, the current multiculturalist initiative. A quick look at the history of textbook revision shows how rapid and complete this revolution has been.

The most popular text of the first half of the twentieth century, David Saville Muzzey's *An American History*, was first published in 1911. In its several editions Muzzey's book treated blacks only as slaves and hardly even made an attempt to deal with the vast influx of new immigrants from 1890 to 1920, who were seen as utterly different from the Americans in place and not likely to be assimilated. There were shades of multiculturalism in his treatment of women and of Indians, however, but faint shades.

Muzzey, for example, chronicled the protests of women at the denial of rights and opportunities that went automatically to men. He provided a powerful description of the treatment of the Indians, who, he said, "were cheated by rascally government officials, fed on rotten rations, debauched of whiskey, and robbed of their lands." Muzzey, however, portrayed the Indians as primitives and savages. In his 1941 revision, he talked of the treatment of the Indians as "a chapter of dishonor" for the white men, but the Indians themselves, he said, "nowhere advanced beyond the stage of barbarism. . . . They had some noble qualities, such as dignity, courage and endurance, but at bottom they were a treacherous, cruel people who inflicted terrible tortures upon their captured enemies."

Even the great revisionist historian and liberal hero Charles Beard, writing in the prologue to his *History of the American People*, published in 1918, had to explain why he gave so little space to the North American Indians. "They are interesting and picturesque, but they made no impression upon the civilization of the United States," he said, showing a tough-mindedness that would be excoriated now. Anybody who has even flipped casually through a social studies or history textbook today would see immediately how thoroughly any such sentiment has been expunged.

In the 1940s, said FitzGerald, the texts, shedding their Waspy visions of American history, began to stress immigration and the melting-pot ideology, as well as civic virtues and tolerance. In the 1950s, she says, the fear of communism lay behind a "fascination with patriotic symbols" and the duties of good citizenship. Some attention was paid to pictures and short biographies of immigrants. The progress of "the Negro" was presented, but condescendingly. And then in the

1960s began "the most dramatic rewriting of history ever to take place in American textbooks."

This "rewriting," by now more than three decades old, had several key elements: immigrants were no longer treated as separate from "the Americans." There was a host of new subjects treated—urban blight and racial discrimination chief among them. Sections on the civil rights movement were added. Photographs of prominent blacks replaced some of the all-white iconography of earlier texts. The country that the texts "had conceived as male and Anglo-Saxon turned out to be filled with blacks, 'ethnics,' Indians, Asians and women."

By the 1970s, American problems were shown in the school texts to be "running rampant," as FitzGerald put it. Textbooks were rewritten to include blacks and their perspectives on events. For the first time, the American identity and its values seemed uncertain, the iconoclastic questioning of previously accepted icons began. Lewis Paul Todd and Merle Curti in *Rise of the Nation* attempted to reassess Christopher Columbus. Black figures like the eighteenth-century poet Phillis Wheatley and the fugitive slave Crispus Attucks, and Mary Jane Patterson, the first black American to receive a college degree, made their way into the textbooks. The message of the texts of the 1970s, FitzGerald concludes, "would be that Americans have no common history, no common culture and no common values, and that membership in a racial or cultural group constitutes the most fundamental experience of each individual."*

By the 1980s, the question was no longer whether ethnics and nonwhites had been given ample space and positive images, but whether they were being given too much. The sociologists Nathan Glazer and Reed Ueda said that the issue was "whether the growing sophistication of publishers in accommodating to every possible pressure group will lead to a Balkanization of American history, in which every group may get a 'proper' share, but in which the central story, one in which all groups participate, is simply left aside to be assembled as well as possible by the student and teacher."†

In 1983, Glazer and Ueda examined six of the most widely used high school texts. They concluded that, in fact, the central story was still present, that the feared "Balkanization" had not become reality. At the same time, they found that a vast transformation of the focus

---

*FitzGerald, *America Revised*, page 104.

†Nathan Glazer and Reed Ueda, *Ethnic Groups in History Textbooks* (Washington, D.C.: Ethics and Public Policy Center, 1983), page 2.

of the major texts had taken place since the 1920s, when progressive and liberal historians like Beard and Muzzey dominated the field. In every one of the six texts, the total number of pages devoted to blacks and other minorities far exceeded the number of pages given over to ethnic Europeans. Indeed, European immigrants groups got about one-quarter or less of the attention given to blacks, Hispanics, Indians, and others.

Glazer and Ueda found other changes from the progressive days. Ethnic difference, portrayed by writers like Muzzey as threatening to the national fabric, had come to be depicted as good and enriching in the texts of the 1970s. None of the more recent texts spoke of inculcating patriotism as a purpose of education. "Moralism and nationalism are both out of date," the authors concluded. More important for the multiculturalists, Indians, blacks, and other minority groups were no longer presented primarily as victims or slaves but as positive forces in their own right, their achievements in civilization emphasized and their great figures lionized.

By the late 1970s, the textbook publishers had already written into the history books whole sections on the empires of Ghana and Benin, the aim of the text, according to Glazer and Ueda, being "to convince students that indigenous African culture, like American Indian culture, was a substantial human achievement that could have made a great contribution to American society." In the new treatments of slavery, the authors said, "blacks are depicted as active, willful agents, not as a submissive mass." Individual black contributions were amply noted, from Crispus Attucks to Malcolm X. The attention given to discrimination and prejudice in the texts "reduces the stature of the 'white' majority, still the major protagonists of these histories." Because there was very little distinction between immigrant Americans and older Americans, all whites tended to be lumped together, and American history was reduced to a sharp distinction "between oppressors and oppressed." The old racist condescension of the texts of the 1920s had been replaced by "new myths proclaiming the superior moral qualities of minorities, and we find a Manichean inversion in which whites are malevolent and blacks, Indians, Asians, and Hispanics are tragic victims."

Since the 1983 study by Glazer and Ueda, the textbooks have continued to become more and more multicultural. Among the latest trends, for example, is the effort to portray the Other—women, immigrants, blacks, Asians, and so on—in their own words, via their own letters, diaries, and stories. All sorts of nonwhites have been unearthed from historical oblivion and used in capsule biographies. Rather than single narratives, with illustrations, the texts of the mid-1980s are laid out like magazines, with bite-sized pieces of text, history capsules, short biographies set off as sidebars on most pages. In Houghton Mifflin's *History of the United States*, the biographies are of sixty-seven men and twenty-seven women. They include Sequoya (a Cherokee Indian), Olaudah Equiano (a West African slave), Belva Ann Lockwood (the first woman lawyer allowed to argue a case before the Supreme Court), and Mary McLeod Bethune (founder of the National Council of Negro Women).

Another recent textbook, Scott, Foresman's *American Voices: A History of the United States*, opens, not with a statement about American commonalities, but with a declaration of our differences. "Our society reflects racial, ethnic and religious diversity" is virtually the first line that students read. In "meeting the challenges of a multicultural nation," the book goes on, "conflict has been ever present. . . . Racism and sexism have affected more than half the population." The book says that discrimination and prejudice have often "made a mockery of our professed ideas." It informs its readers that "most of the nation's dominant institutions had been controlled by middle-class, Protestant, white males," while "African Americans, Native Americans, Hispanic Americans and members of ethnic groups were largely excluded from the mainstream of American life." And having made oppression and victimization the dominant characteristics of American history, the text provides an official multiculturalist creed:

> For many years people thought of the United States as a melting pot, in which immigrants of various backgrounds blended together into a common American culture. Recently, however, people have been referring to the country as a salad, in which the different ingredients come together in a bowl while still retaining their individual qualities.

Multiculturalism, in short, was the dominant creed well before it came to be called multiculturalism. Why then these claims of an "intellectual and educational oppression" of minorities, these assertions that there must be "systemwide changes that permeate all aspects of school"? This is a difficult question to answer. But one senses that the continued accusation of exclusion, made in the face of the evidence, and the demand for ever greater change is related to at least two factors having little or nothing to do with the educational requirements of children. One is the simple fact that a bureaucracy, once it exists, finds reasons to perpetuate itself. The school-revolution bureaucracy is not an exception to this rule. Second, there is a reason of ideology, a need, arising out of the multiculturalist dogma, to deny that the white patriarchy was capable of making many of the changes that the ideological multiculturalists are demanding. It simply contradicts the multiculturalist political vision, with its stress on oppression and victimization, to believe that such could be the case.

But the tendency of the multiculturalists to step up their demand every time a previous demand has been met also stems from genuine anguish over the real plight of poor American children. The plain fact is that for inner-city kids the advent of standard, post-1960s multiculturalist inclusion has had no magical effect on the disastrous rates of failure, dropping out, and despair, which continue unabated. At the same time, some groups who are also generally poor and distant from European culture have taken to the American school system like fish to water, even though there has been no particular multiculturalist inclusion of them. This is true, in particular, of Asians whose ancestry lies in that broad swath of the earth from Bombay to Seoul—and very few Asian heroes have been written into the curriculum. It is also true of inner-city youngsters in places like the South Bronx, where experiments in core curricula, in mastering an actual content rather than learning how to think "critically," have been put into place.

The multiculturalist dilemma is to justify multiculturalism while accommodating these awkward facts. One thing that the cult of the New Consciousness cannot allow is the notion that certain cultures, certain values, certain ways of behaving, are better than other ways and can help to explain why some groups of children do better in school than others, with or without multiculturalism. Ideological multiculturalism requires that all cultures be equal in value. And since there is inequality of performance, that inequality must be blamed on the system, the oppressiveness of the dominant culture, on identity eradication, on the failure of the system to impart self-esteem. In short, the establishment must still be at fault. It hasn't changed enough. It must be changed even more, which means, in practice, that the very philosophy that has failed to produce results for the children that most need help must be pursued with ever greater vigor.

The scene is the auditorium of the Devotion School, a public elementary school in Brookline. It is October 1990, and a group of teachers has gathered to hear Peggy Means McIntosh, an educational consultant hired by the Brookline school district, talk about new theories in the teaching of children, especially nonwhite and female children. McIntosh is associate director of the Wellesley Center for Research on Women and founder of the National SEED Project on Inclusive Curriculum, SEED standing for Seeking Educational Equity and Diversity, with branches in thirty states and four foreign countries. The purpose of the meeting, the introducer says, is to talk about "practical perspectives on how Brookline educators can think about and plan a multicultural curriculum in our elementary schools."

McIntosh, a shortish, roundish woman with a broad face and a friendly manner, begins with a story. She was recently in Roxbury, she says, referring to Boston's predominantly poor, black neighborhood, where she watched as a young black child attempted to cope with a math worksheet involving the addition of twenty-four sets of three single-digit numbers, like $2 + 4 + 3$.

"She was trying to get these problems right," McIntosh said. "The alternative was to get them wrong." But the girl didn't understand the math involved; she got the first problem wrong and got the others wrong also. Another child, says McIntosh, might have gotten the first problem wrong, but because she did understand the math, she might then get the next twenty-three right. Still, "because of cultural conditioning for her, her best would mean being perfect," and she would have been no happier than the other little girl.

"So this is a situation within the win-lose world in which there's no way the child can feel good about the assignment," McIntosh says.

McIntosh returns often to this theme. The win-lose world, the concepts of "right answers" and "wrong answers," education as competition, as victory or defeat, are key for her. Over and over again, she refers to the faulty paradigm in which children are encouraged to accept the authority of correctness versus wrongness. "It's the either/or, right/wrong, you got it/you didn't, you can be graded high or you can be graded low," she says, adding a key point: You have to "put the child in a lateral relation to her own learning, beyond win-lose. . . . In this case learning is seen not as mastery but as our connection with the world, as we grow and develop as bodies in the body of the world."

McIntosh's audience of schoolteachers listens quietly, respectfully, to this. The teachers watch as their educational consultant makes a sketch, which she projects onto a screen behind her. It is a simple drawing of a mountain with several jagged peaks, in the middle of which is a ladder. It is, McIntosh says, a "pinnacle construction." It shows, she explains, a "part of the psyche filled with ladderlike structures that you feel you must climb while asking, 'How am I doing?' " She writes "top" and "bottom" at the appropriate places next to the "pinnacle construction," and then she elaborates a scheme in which students who are encouraged to engage in the "mastery of something" suffer from an implicit fear of falling off the pinnacle they are made to climb. They experience the fear of falling, of loss, and they are led to be competitive and aggressive. On the other hand, if stress is put on the "lateral" part of the psyche, which involves the simple, everyday matters of life, a kinder and gentler sort of educated person will be produced.

And so, it would seem, there is the dehumanizing vertical or "pinnacled" part of the psyche, preventing even the girl who gets twenty-three out of twenty-four answers right from feeling good about herself, and then the "lateral" part of it. Unfortunately, according to McIntosh, schools have traditionally assumed a pinnacled style of learning, one in which there is a hierarchy of right answers and wrong answers, and, more important, in which competitiveness, aggression, the striving to be best are valued—with the consequent dread of not succeeding and thus falling to the bottom of the mountain. In fact, we need a holistic approach to education, one that will stress not win/lose competition, but the interconnectedness of people and things, the world as network of symbiotic parts and our own place in it—our being "bodies in the body of the world."

"The aim is not to win but to be in the deepest relationship with the invisible elements of the universe," she told her audience.

This might sound a bit New Age guru to some, but in some ways McIntosh seems only to be stating the obvious, namely that learning, even learning how to add three single-digit numbers, should be stimulating, related to the real things of the world, not mechanical, not boring signs on boring paper. There's always a place for imaginative teaching, and the multiculturalists do not have a monopoly on it. Education should not neglect human relations and interconnectedness or even our status as "bodies in the body of the world."

But what Brookline's CQE members, whose concerns about the

high school led them to be curious about elementary education as well, found not so obviously true in McIntosh's presentation was the apparent equivalency she assumes between the do-or-die nastiness of pinnacled learning and learning itself, her dismissal of the concept of mastery of something with the white-male dominator. The black child from Roxbury, after all, needs to know how to add, to get right answers, because when it comes to addition, there are right answers and wrong answers. Being a body in the body of the world does not involve mathematical illiteracy, and learning math does require some confrontation with problem solving if such illiteracy is to be avoided. McIntosh brings no multicultural perspective to this issue, because, in all probability, there is nothing multicultural about it.

Indeed, in her entire hour-and-a-half presentation, McIntosh never does solve the problem of teaching the little black girl how to do sums. She certainly never presents any empirical evidence that different children learn in different ways. She does go on to say that in the so-called lower grades (she doesn't like that word "lower" with its implication of hierarchy, win/lose, right/wrong), the "lateral elements" of the psyche are given their due place. "But as we go up," she warns, getting to one of her main points, "the vertical comes into play and you notice that black achievement disastrously falls off."

Why? McIntosh's theory is at the heart of what might be called postmulticulturalism, the philosophy coming to prevail in public, and many private, schools across America. Black achievement falls off when "the vertical comes into play" because teachers make the mistake of trying to teach black children in the same way they would teach white children, rather than adapting their teaching styles to the "culture" of African-Americans. What this supposed friend of African-American children is saying here, in essence, is that blacks are more tuned in to the "lateral" parts of the psyche, while "climbing, getting ahead," are white values—and that explains why black achievement falls off as the upper grades are reached.

This is the point of ideological multiculturalism. Blacks and whites, boys and girls, other minority groups, have what other educational multiculturalists like to call different learning styles. Black children like to learn cooperatively, in groups, more interactively. White children, especially the boys, are culturally conditioned to learn in a competitive arrangement, to see acquiring knowledge as winning. And since the schools are saturated with the "dominant culture," with white values and what McIntosh calls "invisible white privilege," black children fall behind, and white children surge ahead. The whole structure militates against the success of children of color and girls. It is built to serve the needs of those white boys, "preferably blond white boys," as McIntosh says at one point in her Brookline presentation. That is why things must change.

"Black achievement falls off for both the boys and the girls because the projection onto them is they will not rise up these ladders, and moreover, the language of the ladders is culturally white language," McIntosh says. Moreover, she adds, pointing to the jagged peaks of her pinnacle construction, pinnacled learning "has made a few, especially young white males, dangerous to themselves as well as to the rest of us, especially in a nuclear age."

McIntosh, as she explains all this, elaborates on her drawing. To show the lateral psyche she traces a meandering oblong of connected arrows underneath the pinnacle structure. Then she draws arrows pointing both up and down, presumably to show the interconnections between the vertical world and the lateral one. Her remedy for the ills of elementary education consists of what she calls a One Hundred Year Plan, the goal of which she writes in an epigraph below the connected arrows: "You work for the decent survival of all for therein lies your own best chance for survival." She explains: "It is the way of the future, but it will take 100 years to get there."

In all, it will take five phases, she says, from the most primitive phase—"where you don't study women or people of color or notice that they are absent"—all the way up to Phase V, a century away from us, when education will be "reconstructed and redefined to include us all, and that will be 100 years because it requires a new systemology, a new sense of what knowing is and who knows."

Phase V is so advanced that it is difficult to say exactly what it will be like, according to McIntosh, who only allows that it will "put the lateral in relation with the vertical in ways we cannot yet conceive." And so, for the moment, the highest we can practically go is Phase IV. In this phase, already pretty good, the experience of women and people of color will be taken "as life." In Phases II and III only the extraordinary women and people of color are presented, and they are presented as "exceptions to their kind." In Phase IV, everybody will be validated in their everyday existence.

Of course, Dr. McIntosh has other things in mind for our children as we educate them multiculturally, going from the lower stages to the higher ones. Children will have to be taught about "racism, sexism, heterosexism, nationalism, regionalism, cultural issues," because that will "make children aware of systemic problems inherent in being raised in this culture." Indeed, the implications of a multiculturalism that does not go far enough are actually dangerous. A truncated, incomplete multiculturalism might convey to girls and children of color the idea that they can utterly transcend their group identity and be taken entirely as individuals, no matter what their origins are. This, of course, is false, McIntosh says, since the world is not like that. People will always be taken to be representatives of their group, therefore they should not be removed from their group culture and affiliations, nor shielded from the ways in which racism affects their lives. Instead, she says, speaking of the higher phases of education, new curricula must be invented "where the teacher is not master and the student is a body in the body of the world."

Specifically, though, how is this done? What about the black child who was having problems with her math worksheet? McIntosh asks her audience to give her some ideas for "Phase IV teaching," and, demonstrating the openheartedness of the method, she says she will make no comments or judgments on the suggestions, since that would be to violate the rules, to impose hierarchy, to make it a right/wrong, win/lose, you-got-it/you-don't situation. "When you're going around the table brainstorming in Phase IV pedagogy," she says, "the teacher doesn't interrupt because the teacher is a body in the body of the world of trying to figure out."

Suggestions are made from the audience while Dr. McIntosh beams from the front of the room. After one suggestion, she begins to make a comment, violating her promise not to "impose hierarchy," and then, catching herself, she laughingly names the crime that led her into error—"pinnacling," she calls it. The suggestions involve things such as the following:

- Giving the children the answers in advance and letting them describe how the teacher got there
- Giving the children ten pennies and having them make up different combinations adding up to ten
- Putting them in small groups and having them work out the problems cooperatively

Nothing very revolutionary here, nothing visibly multicultural. More important, there is still no solution to the immediate problem at issue, which is teaching the young black child how to add three single-digit numbers. If the child doesn't understand, what good would it do to give her the answers in advance, or to put her into a group of other children and tell her to solve the problems cooperatively? In the first situation, she still won't understand. In the second, she will most likely passively observe while the children who do understand come up with the answers. Maybe she will be a "body in the body of the world of figuring out," but she still won't get arithmetic, and, in the real win/lose world that she is going to enter, that means that she will lose.

None of the teachers present suggest another solution, the possibility that a teacher might sit down with the girl and try to help her, maybe with pennies, perhaps creating a game in which she has to add up all of Farmer Brown's animals, praising her, and telling her she's great when she gets the problems right. Wouldn't that help the girl's self-esteem more than pretending that she is being nurtured by some dime-store concept of the lateral parts of her psyche, or (to refer here to another common educational concept) to inform her that Africans invented algebra? A strong self-conception does not come from being informed that other people of your race have done well as much as it comes from seeing that you can accomplish things. And after all, we do want this girl to be able to master math, and maybe later, if she so desires, to go to medical school, not to be harmlessly, innocuously noncompetitive even while knowledgeable about "racism, sexism, heterosexism, nationalism, regionalism, cultural issues" and the "systemic problems inherent in being raised in this culture." Is the purpose to give this black child, who needs the public school system far more than wealthier children, the skills and knowledge, pinnacled though they may be, to get ahead, or is it to instill in her a sense of her own victimization?

The members of the CQE were not there for this presentation, but they watched a videotape of it with fascination. Is this what multicultural education is all about? Lateral connectedness? Racism, sexism, heterosexism? They learned that there were other consultants brought in to create a multicultural curriculum. There was, for example, Edwin J. Nichols of Washington, D.C., the director of Nichols and Associates, Inc., which he describes as an "applied behavioral science firm," who upon payment of a fee of $2,454 blessed Brookline with his wisdom. Nichols is the author of an article, "Cultural Foundations for Teaching Black Children," that elucidates the cultural differences, the learning-style differences, between whites and blacks.

"Damage occurs," Nichols writes, "because many educators fail to recognize important cultural differences between Europeans or Euro-Americans and Africans or African-Americans." What are these differences? Nichols breaks them down into three rather arcane categories: axiology, epistemology, and logic. Take axiology, for example.

Nichols says that the European axiology is Man-Object, while the African-American axiology is Man-Man. "The European focus on Man-Object dictates that the highest value lies in the Object or in the acquisition of the Object. . . . The Man-Man axiology," by contrast, "explains why the highest cause of death for Black males between the ages of 17 and 34 is to be killed by another Black Man." How could this be if the value is on the other person rather than on things? Usually, Nichols explains, when a black man has killed another black man it's because the victim "has called me a . . ." "Whatever he called him broke the relationship, which is of the highest value, and life itself then was of secondary or lesser value." Nichols believes, in other words, that African-Americans value their relations with others so much that they kill them when insulted. That's multiculturalism for you.

On it goes:

Epistemology: "Africans know through symbols, imagery and rhythm, while Europeans know through counting and measuring."

Logic: "The European logic system has its basis in dichotomy, by which reality is expressed as either/or. African logic, however, is diunital, characterized by the union of opposites."*

At his lecture in Brookline, Nichols distributed a sheet of paper entitled

Nichols' Model
The Philosophical Aspects of Cultural Difference

---

*Edwin J. Nichols, "Cultural Foundations for Teaching Black Children," in Oswald M. J. Ratteray, ed., *Teaching Mathematics: Culture, Motivation, History, and Classroom Management* (Washington, D.C.: Institute for Independent Education, 1986), pages 10–16.

which lays out his theories in diagrammatic form. He provides, for example, under the rubric "Axiology," the worldview of the various major American ethnic groups:

- European and Euro-American: Member-Object; the highest value lies in the object or in the acquisition of the object.

- African, Afro-American, Native American, Hispanics, Arabs: Member-Member. The highest value lies in the inter-personal relationship between persons.

- Asian, Asian-American, Polynesian: Member-Group. The highest value lies in the cohesiveness of the group.

- Native American: Member–Great Spirit. The highest value lies in oneness with the Great Spirit.

How, you might wonder, does this translate into pedagogy? Nichols is a mite vague on this subject. "It is critical that all teachers not be restricted to only one way of viewing the world, for if only European axiology/epistemology/logic sets are practiced, then only selected individuals will benefit," he says. But what of Dr. McIntosh's little girl from Roxbury? What is the aspect of knowing the African axiology of "Member-Member," or the African epistemology of knowing "through symbols, imagery and rhythm," or the African logic of the "union of opposites" that will help her?

Surely not every teacher in Brookline's schools takes to heart the evident silliness of Dr. Nichols or the airy ruminations of Peggy McIntosh. But one person apparently rather impressed by McIntosh was Patricia Ruane, who, at the time of the AP European History debate, had been Brookline's assistant superintendent of schools, in charge of curriculum, for roughly a decade. In 1990, at a meeting of the League of Women Voters, Ruane said she found the "characterizations developed by Peggy McIntosh . . . very useful as ways to set a general framework and also as a means of commenting on what goes on in Brookline as regards an inclusive curriculum." Ruane talked about "going beyond the traditional white male perspective," and she cited what she called the "pinnacle people" as she summarized McIntosh's five phases of pedagogy. We need, she said, again citing

McIntosh, "a new epistemology, new ways of knowing, so that everyone can really achieve their highest learning potential."

I called Ruane to ask her about this, and she was decidedly not
happy with the fact that members of the CQE had given me the text
of her remarks. There are many ways that staff development takes
place at Brookline, she said. Many consultants with many different
points of view are brought in for meetings, not just McIntosh and
Nichols, so to single those two out is to give a misleading impression,
which, she suggested, is exactly what the CQE wanted to do. Ruane
later sent me a list of consultants who had played a role in the Brookline schools, and it was, indeed, a long list of people, many of whose
viewpoints would have been quite different from those of McIntosh
or Nichols. (It should be noted, though, that Ruane made no reference
to any of these other consultants during the meeting at which she
spoke so highly of McIntosh.) Ruane also noted that the meeting at
which she had spoken of McIntosh had also involved two presentations
by Brookline teachers that showed specific ways of improving teaching
methods. The CQE, she said, failed to distribute the texts of the
teachers' remarks, which, she said, would have showed a sincere and
sensible approach to education, and she accused the CQE of willfully
manipulating the evidence in an effort to make the school look ridiculous. I asked if I could talk to the two teachers, but Ms. Ruane refused
to allow me to do so.

"Shouldn't it be their choice to talk to me or not?"

"No. I'm not interested in burdening them with this. It's been
very painful. People have been feeling very threatened by the stories,
I mean the fiction, that has emerged around this," Ruane replied.

Certainly, Ruane and others in the Brookline school system were
reacting to real changes in a town that was less and less the comfortable
place of upper-middle-class Jews and Irish it had long been and more
and more a place of ethnic and racial diversity. They genuinely and
sincerely felt that changes in educational methods were needed to
keep up with changes in the nature of the student body, and that is
the deep cause of the Brookline conflict.

In years past, Brookline High School in particular enjoyed a reputation as one of the best public high schools in America. Nearly 80
percent of its graduates have generally gone on to college each year,
so it was, almost by definition, an elitist place, though critics of AP
European History use the word "elitist" as a pejorative. Brookline
High was the kind of place where teachers had Ph.D.'s and where

course listings resembled a university catalog. In the late 1970s, there were three full-year courses in American history, a history of the American criminal justice system, American history for foreign students (with individualized help for students learning English). There were two one-semester courses on change in American society ("how change, both non-violent and violent, has occurred throughout our history"), two courses on the immigrant in American life, a semester of Afro-American history in which, the catalog said, "black perspectives will be dealt with to appreciate diversity and understanding current events involving the Black community." There were courses entitled America Through Its Media, America Since 1945, and two semesters of Field Experience in Criminal Justice." Then there were substantial offerings in European history, Russian history, Asian studies, women in society, contemporary Africa, the sociology of the individual, and something called Other Peoples, Other Places, and Us, which included the Eskimo, the Sumerians, and the Navajo. And there was much more.

There is still a great deal. Nonetheless, in the 1970s two things happened. One, the population began to change. By the early 1990s, 13 percent of the student body was Asian, 11 percent was black, and 5 percent was Hispanic. Nearly one-third of the student body came from Russia, Israel, and Asia. Certain courses became segregated by race. So did the bathrooms. An article in *Boston Magazine* in late 1992 caused a stir by describing, among other things, the way students used beepers and cellular phones to keep in touch with gangs outside the school and, presumably, with drug dealers. The Asians did very well. The black children, however, even those brought up in Brookline, tended to be at the bottom of the curve. (The school also accommodated a few busloads of inner-city black children—known as Metco children—brought to Brookline by the greater Boston antisegregation effort.) In a liberal town like Brookline, committed to racial equality and progressive politics, this was particularly disturbing, and so were two lurking menaces: one was the ever-present threat of racial conflict; the other the fear that the kinds of social problems Brookline associated with the inner city of Boston, the gangs, the drugs, the despair of certain groups, were affecting the high school.

It was against this background that the school administration looked again at its multicultural curriculum, and that is the second change. In the social studies department, a task force studied the curriculum and found it to have too many courses, too many electives, but too little focus, little coherence, few consistent themes. After a long study, a new curriculum was put into place, one that, in the teachers' view, would be more responsive to the needs of an increasingly diverse population and more organized around a limited number of themes.

"The social studies department was trying very hard to tighten itself up from a curriculum that was truly all over the place and didn't have a thread of any sort," Ruane told me in my phone conversation with her. "One of the things that the committee did was to look at the range of areas of the world and it saw that an overwhelming majority of time was spent in Europe and there was an interest in broadening that." I asked her if that meant that the United States would still be treated as primarily a development of European civilization, or whether Europe and the West would be just one culture out there, equal with others.

"There's not a single person in the social studies department who doesn't believe that the West is a very important part of what every kid should know," Ruane said. "The West is not just one of several cultures. That's not even the discussion. That's a distortion."

Events in history should be taught "from a variety of perspectives," she said. "It starts with first person, primary sources, and a variety of sources so you are looking at different peoples' telling of an event. It has to do with voice, not somebody's interpretation of events. For example, if you look at colonialism, you want the voices of the colonialists and the voices of the colonized."

To the parents of the CQE who discovered the new curriculum after it had been put into place, what appeared to be happening was a decline in academic standards, an abandonment of the meritocratic principle, the effort to advance a political program via the school, hence a disservice to all the students of whatever race. And if it was a "distortion" to discern hostility to the West in the social studies department, it was a distortion justified by a mounting body of evidence.

Roger and Sarah Blood, parents active in CQE, put it this way in an op-ed piece in the Brookline *Citizen*: "Those who have followed the national debate on curriculum know that 'multicultural' and 'traditional' have become code words for political versus academic priorities in education." Sandra Stotsky put it in the form of a question: "How can you make sure your schools are offering an academically rigorous multicultural curriculum, not political indoctrination into one-sided and simplistic anti-Western and antidemocratic modes of thinking?"

Stotsky, in fact, became a key actor in the Brookline drama. She is a mother of four grown children, two of whom took AP European History with James Dudley. Stotsky, who has written many articles on secondary education in professional journals, noticed that roughly around the time AP European History was removed from the curriculum, something called World in Crisis was put into it. This course was Brookline's version of a trend toward global studies, under way elsewhere, the difference being that while global studies is often a two-year program that touches on the historical development and features of the major civilizations, from China to Mexico, Ghana to Greece, World in Crisis examined three situations—the Middle East, Southeast Asia (meaning the war in Vietnam), and Northern Ireland. More sophomores, about 150, took the course than took the European history course available in the sophomore year. More took it than took African-American, Russian, or Asian history. Stotsky heard that the content of World in Crisis was tendentiously anti-Israeli and anti-Western, so she began to study it. Her basic conclusion: "By the time students finish this course, they have been implicitly encouraged to see all white Protestants, Americans, the British, other Europeans, and Israelis as oppressors of the poor or people of color and to view Britain, America, and Israel, all democracies, as the major oppressor nations of the world."

Indeed, the choice of Northern Ireland, the Middle East, and Vietnam as the only areas of study in the course is rather curious. Why not the Soviet Union in Afghanistan, or 1968 in Czechoslovakia? Why not the Cold War or Khomeini's Iran and Islamic fundamentalism, or the civil war in Lebanon or in Burundi or the dissolution of the Soviet Union, if teachers are interested in portraying the world in crisis?

"The section on Northern Ireland showed the British as the villains, the Indochina part showed America as the villain, then the part on the Mideast ended up implying that the problem was a sinister one of oppression of Palestinians by European colonialists," Stotsky told me during a visit to her home. "It was all to set up the villainy of the West." She continued: "All of the case studies were presented as instances of Western colonialism oppressing Third World peoples."

Deborah Quitt told me the problem with World in Crisis came

from the supersensitivity of Jewish parents in Brookline who saw any criticism of Israel at all as biased and unacceptable. "The question," she said, "is whether it is possible to have anything about Israel at all." There may be some truth to that statement. Nonetheless, the parents of CQE were able to dig up quite a lot of material on the course that did suggest an anti-Israeli, Arabist approach to the crisis in the Middle East. The teacher's guide to World in Crisis, for example, suggested that students view the movie *The Little Drummer Girl* (which is seen as pro-Palestinian and anti-Israeli by many) and then follow up with this: "reading from *Opposing Viewpoints: Terrorism Reader*—an article by Abu Nidal and a response by Jeane Kirkpatrick." The teacher's guide explained: "As these two represent the most radical of their position, they need to be put in context. A follow-up activity asks students to decide if each example of terrorism is justified, and to try to decide on some basic criteria (if any) for terrorism."

One wonders if the students were guided to the conclusion that terrorism is, in some instances, justified. I myself remember an English professor at a conference in Utah once adducing a chic lit-crit definition: "Terrorism," she said, "is a wound in the body of the dominant discourse," and I remember thinking at that time about all the charred and bleeding "dominant discourses" that terrorism had wounded. As for the Brookline curriculum, "the idea," said Robert Costrell, an economics professor at the University of Massachusetts who became president of the CQE, "was to show the two extremes of terrorism, with Abu Nidal and Jeane Kirkpatrick roughly equivalent, so that the PLO seems to be the middle ground."

Stotsky learned of a sophomore class project. It was to organize a mock civil rights demonstration in Northern Ireland, in which students were graded on the banners they created, on their press releases, and on a policy statement on whether to be violent. In World in Crisis, she found questions like this: "Give examples of colonial situations which you have studied this year on Ireland, Vietnam and Palestine. To do so, explain in each area: 1. The colonizing powers in each area. 2. When the colonizing power(s) came in and how they gained power (i.e., trade, missionary work, conflict and war, land purchase, etc.)." Stotsky noted a cloying habit of using the word "Palestine" rather than "Israel," in, for example, this multiple-choice question: "Mecca, the birthplace of Islam, is located in (a) Saudi Arabia, (b) Iran, (c) Iraq, or (d) Palestine."

After looking at the exams, Stotsky and other parents, like the

Stillmans, asked for material on other courses, and there, too, they felt a certain sogginess, a fake kind of democratization, were creeping in. Some, aware of trends at the universities, perceived a downward trickle from higher education sprinkling the young minds of Brookline. There was Women and Society, for example, the purpose of which, according to the 1990 course catalog, "is to understand how gender, race and class act as personal and social forces." The readings were certainly multicultural. There was *Dancing on My Grave*, by the ballerina Gelsey Kirkland (the autobiography, as one critic, Christina Sommers, put it, "of an anorexic, cocaine addicted ballerina"); *Betsey Brown*, by Ntozake Shange; *Sweet Summer: Growing Up With and Without My Dad*, by Bebe Moore Campbell; and, the catalog said, one more yet to be chosen—"either an Asian-American or working class woman's experience." No Jane Austen here either, not even any Virginia Woolf, no George Eliot and Emily Dickinson, but rather a politically correct multicultural offering. It was Stotsky's efforts to get materials on the course from the school that led the CQE, formed in the meantime, to request documents via the Freedom of Information Act. One of the things that Stotsky was allowed to do was go to the school and look at the exams that had been given in a number of courses. She felt that the exams themselves showed the leftist bias of the school. There was, for example, this sly multiple-choice question: "A characteristic of the 13 English colonies was (a) complete religious freedom, (b) free high school education, (c) class distinctions, or (d) universal voting." Of course, class distinctions is the correct answer. The question seems designed to demonstrate that something negative was the sole feature all the colonies had in common. She noted the test item that asked students to identify the "Hellenic epic which established egotistical individualism as heroic." The correct answer: *The Iliad.* The subtext: individualism is egotistical and egoism is a prime characteristic of Western culture, as opposed, apparently, to more communitarian, less selfish, more rhythmic others. Stotsky found this question: "What would you do if you were drafted at 18 to fight in Central America?" An Asian studies question: "What would you do if you were in the military and you were in a situation similar to My Lai? How would you decide what orders to follow?" Stotsky suspected that Asian studies did not include the study of Chinese imperial totalitarianism or the rape of Nanking by Japan. It seemed to have more to do with America than Asia, with a stress on American atrocities, as though they were the whole picture.

While dropping a demanding and serious course on European history, and then fiercely refusing to reinstate the course, Brookline's teachers offered various other courses that the members of the CQE found trivial and silly. There was a course, for example, called the Mind's Eye, which, the catalog copy said, "will grapple with questions such as: How is physics like a fairy tale and does it have a happy ending? Is mathematics more like music or poetry? Does Michael Jordan know more than Albert Einstein ever did?" The course itself seemed rather playful. The problem with it was that it could be taken to satisfy requirements in either math or English and thus seemed to involve a lowering of standards. Another course was Medicine and Society, which, the course description promised, would look into "how people in different times and different cultures understood themselves and others through the looking glass of science and medicine." The course would explore, for example, "what goes on in the mind of a voodoo doctor" and "what life was like in a Victorian mental hospital." This course, the CQE members point out with the relish of vindication, satisfies the social studies, global studies, or the sophomore biology requirement. There was a course called Philosophy East and West that included readings from Socrates, Plato, Buddha, Confucius, Lao-tzu, Locke, and Marx—and then readings from Ayn Rand, Lawrence Kohlberg (a professor at the Harvard School of Education who developed concepts of "moral education" once implemented at Brookline High), Simone de Beauvoir, and the feminist psychologist Carol Gilligan—quite a mixture of the time-tested and the currently fashionable.

There were other things presented by the members of the CQE as signs that a kind of woolly, sixties-style leftism guided the educational program. A group of Brookline teachers, for example, formed something called the Teachers' Circle and published a small newsletter called *The Circle Bulletin*, which seemed devoted to implementing the ideas of Paulo Freire, the Brazilian educator who has guru status within the ranks of multicultural practitioners inspired by his theories of what they sometimes call "empowerment pedagogy."* Education, Freire wrote (in a passage reproduced in the Teachers' Circle's first newsletter), can be "used to facilitate the integration of the younger generation into the logic of the present system and bring about conformity to it, or, it becomes the practice of freedom." Or as two teachers

---

*See the next chapter for more on Freire's influence.

in the Circle asked: "How can we as educators affect [*sic*] change and mitigate the negative effects of schooling that often mirror and reinforce the inequality and oppression that take place in society?"

For Sandra Stotsky, the Stillmans, and others, all of these bits and pieces seemed to explain what they saw as the anti-Western bias of World in Crisis, or the orthodox feminism of Women and Society, and the dropping of AP European History. To other parents, the school more simply was becoming a place where their children were having bad experiences. Sarah Blood remembered when her daughter came home from school and asked her mother not to talk to her because, as Mrs. Blood put it, "she didn't know if what was in her head was my ideas or her ideas." Blood says she began to suspect that something odd was taking place in class. That same daughter took an after-school writing class the sole subject of which seemed to be the nuclear danger. Once she discovered her two daughters whispering together in bed. She asked them why they weren't doing their home-work. "It's no use," one of the girls said. "We're all going to die anyway."

Another parent, Linda Sugarbaker, remembers how one of her five children came home in tears after a Japanese group had come into the school to tell the story of a thousand cranes. In the story, a little girl is dying of radiation sickness because of the American bomb-ing of Hiroshima and Nagasaki. She wants to make a thousand paper cranes before she dies but, tragically, does not meet her goal.

"For weeks my daughter was devastated about how evil the U.S. was, what a terrible country we were," Sugarbaker told me.

On another occasion, during the Dukakis-Bush presidential cam-paign, the subject of abortion came up in her daughter's third-grade class. The teacher asked the children to vote on whether they were for or against. Sugarbaker's daughter was the only child opposed to abortion. She was made to stand in front of the group and to justify her position. "Do you think we really need all these children in the world?" the teacher asked. Another child came home talking of a school session on Greek and Roman civilization and the effects of Judaism and Christianity on the judicial systems of the world today. The teacher asked the children to take out a pencil and put an "X" through that section of the book, explaining that it was unfair to study only Judaism and Christianity and not Buddhism and Confucianism also.

"That was the last straw for me," Sugarbaker said. "If it was a comparative religion course, sure, we should study every religion, but the Judeo-Christian tradition is the basis for a lot in the West. . . .

"There are points of view to every issue," she said, "but what I see happening is that everything is reduced to a single politically correct word that will consume the whole topic. We're reducing people to nonthinkers who will accept whatever the majority wants."

On a corridor at the Hans Christian Andersen Contemporary Schools in Minneapolis is a brick wall decorated with little children's essays on "contributors from many cultures." There are twenty-four of them altogether—two or three scrawled sentences and a sketch or a photograph. Joan Baez is described as a "Hispanic-American, Peace Singer." Jan Matzeliger is "African-American—Invented the Shoemaking machine." There is Alice Pimenthal (African-American—anesthesiologist), Greg Wong (Asian-American—sportswriter), and Nikki Giovanni (African-American—poet). There are three white men also, including the comedian Billy Crystal.

Nearby, several dozen paper fish float on another wall with the legend "What Do I Contribute?" Each of the fish has a little paragraph written by a pupil. For example: "I contribute by being drug free, learning how to make the world a better place, and learning to stop violence, because peace begins with me." Underneath is this inscription: "Klahn Jarboh, and my culture is African American." Among the other "cultures" represented on other fish are Native American, Asian-American, European-American.

Andersen Contemporary—also known as the Andersen Contemporary Schools of Many Voices, "Schools" in the plural because there are three separate divisions in the same building—makes an extremely good first impression. In the heart of one of Minneapolis's largely black neighborhoods, it is a large, clean, concrete-and-steel structure illuminated by skylights and festooned with all manner of banners and slogans and student art. It is a place humming with activity. One day when I visited, there was a student band concert (the band played an adaptation of Tchaikovsky's "1812 Overture," but I was assured there are also African, Asian, and American Indian numbers in the repertoire) and an evening demonstration for parents on methods of "conflict resolution" learned in school by the children. Each class has several designated "peacemakers" who have been specially trained in mediating disputes. They gave a demonstration of their skills to a group of mostly inner-city parents, who were then asked to carry out the same exercise with their children.

I spent two days at Andersen Contemporary, the most thoroughly "multicultural" school in Minnesota, and one of the most multicultural in the entire country. Its student body is about 25 percent American Indian and another 25 percent black. There are smaller numbers of Hispanic and Asian students. About 41 percent are what the school designates "European-American." The school's basic policy is summed up in a clumsy string of letters, MCGFDA, which means "multicultural, gender-fair, and disability aware." In 1990, Minneapolis set up the MCGFDA Task Force, which recommended a new "inclusive educational program" for the entire city. Among its elements, the task force said, would be "special emphasis" on "American Indians/Alaskan Natives, Asian Americans/Pacific Islanders, Black Americans and Hispanic Americans." The task force said that "special emphasis must be placed on the contributions of women." It said, "the program must reflect the wide range of contributions and roles open to handicapped Americans." And it set out seven specific objectives, namely:

1. Students will demonstrate knowledge of, appreciation for, and respect for their own culture.

2. Students will demonstrate knowledge of, appreciation for, and respect for other cultures.

3. Students will have the opportunity at each school site to gain awareness in world languages.

4. School activities will be provided to stimulate participation by a diverse student population.

5. The total school environment will visually and physically reflect the multicultural, gender, and disability diversity inherent in the Minneapolis public schools.

6. Students will demonstrate a positive self-concept and a sense of belonging.

The seventh objective was the creation of a "laboratory school" as a "model demonstration site for implementation of exemplary instructional practices and curriculum." The Andersen Schools, under the energetic and enthusiastic leadership of Principal Barbara Shin, was born charged with the task of pioneering the new MCGFDA way of educating children. As such, what came quickly to be called the Andersen Contemporary Schools of Many Voices was a multicultur-alist's dream come true, a vision of a possible future for a nationally troubled system of public education, though it is certainly not the only possible vision.

Indeed, I have been to other schools where some sort of multicul-turalist vision was being implemented. Going even further than An-dersen Contemporary, for example, are Afrocentric academies established in school systems in several cities, including Baltimore, Milwaukee, Chicago, and Detroit. These schools have been set up in recognition of the painful fact that despite elaborate plans for busing children to achieve school integration, central cities are becoming so overwhelmingly black that there are numerous schools where there is not a single white child. And given that the school's population will, by demographic necessity, be entirely African-American, school administrators, inspired by leading Afrocentric thinkers, have come to the conclusion that a curriculum focused on African culture and on black Americans will impart the pride in black identity necessary for the success of black children.

It is certainly difficult, given the disastrously poor performance, the high dropout rates, and the low reading and math scores of inner-city youngsters, to oppose any well-intentioned effort to try something different. As a white person, moreover, I am extremely uncomfortable trying to assess what will be good for young black children and what will not, or the extent to which the self-esteem of these children will be improved by having role models and historical heroes who are almost exclusively black. The status quo does not leave much to defend. Still, the spread of the concept of Afrocentric education as a subdivision of multicultural education shows the extent to which the post–civil rights ideal of educational integration has waned, while an attempt to create a new form of segregated education has flowed.

During 1991 and 1992, I traveled frequently to Pleasantville, New Jersey, a community adjacent to Atlantic City, where the school system was formulating a new Afrocentric curriculum for a student body that had become well over half black. Specifically, I went to several sessions in which Molefi Kete Asante, the head of the African-American studies department at Temple University in Philadelphia, instructed Pleasantville's curriculum-revision committee in devising an Afrocentric program for the city's children.

Asante is one of the leading figures of Afrocentrism, the founder and chairman of the only university program in America that offers a doctorate in African-American studies. He has published dozens of books on his subject, debated nationally known figures like Arthur Schlesinger, Jr. (who has called Afrocentrism "the use of history as therapy"), and traveled to many towns and cities to consult with school systems eager to create Afrocentric curricula. Asante, who Africanized his name from Arthur L. Smith in 1973, had an early life strikingly similar to that of Supreme Court Justice Clarence Thomas. He was born in 1942 in a small town in Georgia, the oldest boy of a total of sixteen children. He had grandparents and great-grandparents who instilled in him the value of hard work and an education. He went on scholarship to the Nashville Christian Institute in Tennessee; then to Oklahoma Christian College (where he was one of two black students in a total population of one thousand) to get a B.A. in speech. Finally, he went to UCLA, where he was the president of the local branch of the Student Nonviolent Coordinating Committee and where he got a Ph.D. in communication.

As a student in Nashville, Asante joined civil rights demonstrations against White Castle hamburgers, which refused to serve blacks. In 1963, he and a Singaporean friend drove from Oklahoma to Washington, D.C., to be present for Martin Luther King, Jr.'s, great "I have a dream" speech. While in California Asante wrote two books, one called *The Rhetoric of Black Revolution* and the other *Transracial Communication*. During what he now regards as a conventional "Eurocentric education," he became haunted by the idea that something was missing in it for him.

"There were things that would come up in the classroom that would make me say to myself, 'Wow, that can't be right,' things that didn't relate to my experience, to my history or my culture," he told me. "A teacher would talk about the daring deeds of Joan of Arc but he'd never heard of Nzinghe [whom Asante identifies as a seventeenth-century queen of what is now Angola who fought against Portuguese colonizers]. I mean, how could he say that Joan of Arc was more significant as a woman with integrity and leadership than Yaa Asantewaa [a nineteenth-century Ashanti queen who, according to Asante, led women and children resisting British control]. I mean, these were questions that were forming in my head.

"The key point to me," Asante said, "was that I could not believe that African people had never contributed anything to the world. It just didn't sit right with reason. It did not sit right with the intellectual possibilities of any human population. I just could not believe, for example, that there had never been African people who thought about mathematics."

Asante is a man of medium height, round features, café-au-lait color, always dressed in African garb, which he has sent to him from Burkina Faso. He is polite, cordial, energetic, an entirely likable man. My interviews with him at his office at Temple University were interrupted by frequent telephone calls—from students, from conference organizers, from people inviting him to speak or to consult. Among the school systems that have asked him to help create Afrocentric curricula are, he said, Detroit, Baltimore, Camden, Pittsburgh, Hoboken, and Indianapolis. Mild mannered in person, he can be fierce in print. When Diane Ravitch, then a professor at Columbia University's Teachers College, equated Afrocentrism with ethnocentrism and racial fundamentalism, Asante wrote an angry essay in response, accusing her of holding to a "commitment to white hegemony." During his student time, Asante gradually moved toward a belief that, in essence, it was impossible for a black person to be whole in a predominantly white culture, and this is the theory that informs his campaign to create what he calls an Afrocentric education for black children.

"African people were literally moved off in physical terms, but also in psychological, cultural, and intellectual terms by the movement from the continent of Africa to the Americas," I heard him say at a colloquium at Temple. "Three hundred and seventy-four years of being detached, alienated, and dislocated from place, from location, from identity necessitated the movement that we have called the Afrocentrist perspectivist movement, which means that African people are viewed as agents of history, not merely as marginal to the European experience."

Asante's belief, as he put it at Temple that day, is that the very European structure of knowledge "cannot help but reproduce racist thinking." This is because the "Eurocentric perspective" requires that the sources of all knowledge be found in Europe—most often in the Greeks. And so Asante peppers his speeches with arcane references to the Greeks, attempting to show that much of what the Eurocentrists believe to have been invented by the Greeks was actually learned in Egypt, which Asante takes to be the cradle of black-African civilization.

This part of Afrocentrism has been criticized, by Ravitch and

Schlesinger among others, as a school of historical overcompensation, more informed by wishful thinking than accurate, solid scholarship. Nonetheless, Afrocentrism is a booming business, and Asante is one of its leading entrepreneurs. His consulting keeps him constantly on the go. He has written thirty books, the best known of which are *Afrocentricity, The Afrocentric Idea, Afrocentricity: The Theory of Social Change,* and *Knowledge and Afrocentricity.* He has written a slender volume called *The Book of African Names,* designed to help new parents. There are regular meetings and conferences of Afrocentrists. There has been a great outpouring of works, among the most commonly mentioned C. T. Keto, *African Centered Perspective of History;* George Joseph, *The Crest of the Peacock: Non-European Roots of Mathematics;* C. Firth, *The African Background of Medical Science;* Ivan Van Sertima, *They Came Before Columbus: The African Presence in Ancient America* and *Blacks in Science: Ancient and Modern;* Yosef ben-Jochannan, *Africa: Mother of Western Civilization;* Cheikh Anta Diop, *The African Origins of Civilization;* Lerone Bennett, Jr., *Before the Mayflower;* George James, *Stolen Legacy.*

In June 1992, I went to Pleasantville for one of several meetings that Asante had with local teachers. Asante always covers the blackboard with the names of important African historical figures, and distributes background materials that provide information on African achievements in mathematics, in the language arts, in literature, in science, and in other fields. His main point always is that it is inadequate merely to tack on a bit of information about Africans and African culture to an essentially "Eurocentric curriculum." For black children, Africa must be central, not marginal, equal in all respects to Europe, integrated into what children learn at every level, so, for example, when children learn arithmetic, they could be taught to count with African beads rather than, say, Western marbles.

"The majority of African-American students," he said, "sit inside their classrooms but outside the information that's being presented."

As an example of this, Asante talked about the time he spoke at the Harvard Law School to black students who were unable to name a single ethnic group from Africa brought to America as slaves. He then asked the same students to name five European ethnic groups that came to America, and, of course, the students were able to name many more than five. The story, for him, shows the extent to which standard American education alienates black students from what is historically and culturally theirs. Everybody knows about the Irish, the English, the Germans, but nobody, not even the black students, knows about the Ashanti, the Yoruba, the Angola.

The solution, he maintained, is for lessons about Africa and African-Americans to be "systematically infused into the curriculum, in every subject and every theme." During one of his talks in Pleasantville, Asante drew up two tables, the first containing Greek or European names that everybody knows, from Thales to Joan of Arc to Shakespeare. Alongside it, he listed African names, confident that nobody in his small audience would be able to identify Antef or Ptohotep, Yenenga, Ibn Batuta, or Abubakari, even though the second list should, he feels, be as familiar both to black and white children as the first list.

For those who believe that the curriculum has been multicultural for twenty years, Asante reserves a special contempt. "All that means," he said, "is that they've put some African-American people into the content that already exists." At fault is the very structure of knowledge, the basic conceptions of the origins of the sciences and the humanities that sustain what Asante calls elsewhere "white Eurocentric hegemony." And that brought him back to ancient Greece and the "white-supremacist" assumption, arising directly from the Western structure of knowledge, that everything, philosophy and tragedy, science and reason, traces back to the Greeks, while all others are on the margins, even if they are mentioned in a textbook here and there.

At this point, Asante wrote the word "philosophy" on the board, and under it, its component parts, *philo* and *sophia*.

"Philosophy," he said, "is the highest discipline in the world. Philosophy is the product of Greece. It is Western. Europe gave the world philosophy. Confucius had 'thought.' The Africans did not have philosophy. They had myths or religion. The Native Americans didn't have philosophy; they had cosmologies. Philosophy is reflective thinking, rational thinking, and that all begins with Greece.

"Regardless of what you do in the lesson plans, if you have this structure of Greek philosophy being at the origin of things, you will be teaching the white-supremacist curriculum," Asante said. "Reason, according to this dogma, is fundamentally an attribute of the Europeans. It is a Western trait."

The dominant structure of knowledge, Asante continued, began with German scholars at the University of Göttingen in the eighteenth century, the brothers Willem and Friedrich von Humboldt, who invented "the theory of the hierarchy of races." The idea was that the Germans were Aryans, and their racial heritage reached back to the Greeks, who were also Aryans.

Asante then developed a theory of how the "Greek tyranny," the idea that the origins of our civilization were in Greece, was extended to the United States during the nineteenth century. It is seen in such things as Greek Revival architecture, especially in the South, but also in the development of the Greek-letter fraternity and sorority system, and even in secret societies like the Ku Klux Klan. The "Greek tyranny" was especially appealing in the South, Asante said, because the Greeks were a slave-holding people, and thus it nurtured the idea that slavery was compatible with democracy. "In this way," he said, "democracy became something sinister for the African-American."

In fact, said Asante, referring to the words on the blackboard, this whole notion of Greece being at the origins of civilization is nonsense. The very words "philo" and "sophia," the component parts of "philosophy, are not Greek. They do not exist in any Indo-European language." The dictionary of etymology lists the origin of these words as unknown, he maintained. But inscriptions going back to 2052 B.C. in Egypt include a word transliterated as *saba*, meaning "wise," which became *sabo* in the Coptic and *sophia* in the Greek, because the Greeks changed a lot of "b" sounds into "ph" sounds. Later that same word becomes *sufi* in Arabic.

Asante offered the teachers in Pleasantville an Afrocentric version of Greek history. The first philosopher, according to the Eurocentric view, was Thales, who lived around 600 B.C. But in the Afrocentric view, the first philosopher was Ptahotep. Thales himself studied in Africa, Asante said, and so did Isocrates, Homer, Pythagoras, Xenophon, and Plato—all of this supporting the contention of the Afrocentrist scholar George G. M. James that "the so-called Greek philosophy is stolen Egyptian philosophy." According to Asante, the Greeks learned measurement, astronomy, geometry, arithmetic, writing, the calendar, medicine, architecture, law, and the names of the gods all from the Egyptians.

Why is this important? Asante asked. It must be remembered, he said, that Egypt is to African civilization what Greece is to the West. Kemet, or ancient Egypt, is the summation of the African civilizations that preceded it and the origin of the African civilizations that came later.

"If you teach African-American children the same way you teach

white children, you take them out of their culture," Asante said. Right
now, he said, "the African-American brings to the table a damaged
version of the European experience. What I would like to see is a
whole version of the African experience."

The ideas of Molefi Asante and of other Afrocentrists are being implemented in public schools in several cities, from Camden and Pleasantville to Baltimore, Chicago, Detroit, and Milwaukee, where for
the first time in our history, public schools are offering curricula
designed according to the race of the pupils. Perhaps, given the failure
of many young black children in school (and hence, in many cases,
also in life), the Afrocentric experiment is worth a try, though many
of the ideas that are central to the curriculum, the alleged "facts" of
African history, are sharply disputed.

Contrary to what Asante presents as established truths, others
dispute the idea that, for example, Thales, Isocrates, Plato, Homer,
Pythagoras, and Xenophon studied in Egypt, which, in any case, is
only very distantly, if at all, related, in the cultural sense, to sub-
Saharan Africa. Asante himself, though I and my research assistant,
Hilary Dunst, asked him several times, was unable to provide anything more than the flimsiest sketches of the figures from African
history that he says should be familiar to black and white students
alike—figures like Nzinghe and Yaa Asantewaa, or Yenenga (a
founder, either fifteenth or sixteenth century, Asante was not sure,
of the Mossi nation of Burkina Faso) and Abubakari (supposedly a
fourteenth-century king of Mali, but Hilary and the reference librar-
ian at Columbia University were unable to find any reference to
anyone by that name fitting Asante's description). The role of race has
become so important to the Afrocentrist philosophy that there has
been a wholesale effort to attribute black skin to a host of historical
figures who were probably not black.

"The teachers continually drilled into our naive little heads that
ancient Egyptians were black, that Tutankhamen was black, that Cleo-
patra was black, that Carthaginians were black, that Hannibal was
black, and that the triumphs of the Egyptians and Carthaginians were
the triumphs of black culture," a letter writer named D. Jackson wrote
of his Afrocentric education in a Berkeley, California, school of the
1970s. Jackson, whose letter appeared in the *East Bay Express*, was
arguing that, in the end, historical falsification for the sake of racial

redressment provides a soggy foundation for pride. "We should stop lying to ourselves and our children, and stop concocting a false racial resume," he said. "Are we so ashamed of our history that we have to start claiming other peoples' achievements as our own?"

The happy thing about the Afrocentric curriculum is that it appears to involve more than a stress on the centrality of Africa. I visited the two Afrocentric schools that have been created in Milwaukee, an elementary school and a junior high school. The pupils wore uniforms; the teachers believed in discipline and hard work; achievement was expected. One pioneer in the method said he wanted the Afrocentric academies to be like Exeters and Andovers for African-American children, places of prestige and high standards. One can only wish success for this experiment, even as one wonders how much of the curriculum being used stems from the creation of myths presented as disclosures of long-hidden truths.

Andersen Contemporary is different. Afrocentrism is, by definition, not multiculturalism. It is a new form of separate education, now no longer viewed as inherently unequal but, perhaps, as inherently better. Andersen Contemporary, by contrast, embodies a new vision of integrated education, one that is no longer aimed at absorbing all children into a common universe but rather in instructing them in their diversity. Peggy McIntosh believes that in the real world, people of color are going to be identified and treated as such, so to feed them nonsense about color-blindness is to prepare them badly for the real world. Andersen Contemporary seems to have transformed this idea into a complete philosophy of education governing every aspect of the curriculum.

And so with children of different races in the same classrooms, teachers stress what they call the "culture" of each child and of each element in the subject matter. Indeed, difference and diversity take on a fetishistic aspect at Andersen Contemporary. Diversity is not just a goal among others requiring some adjustment of the traditional curriculum. It is the goal, the paramount concern, viewed as more important than everything else, better, higher, deeper, truer. Nothing at Andersen Contemporary is in the curriculum because it has intrinsic merit; it is in there because it represents the Indian culture or the African-American culture or the Asian culture.

"If you study the United States, you're just as likely to study the tribes as you are the capitals," one person announces on a video that the school has prepared for visitors. I met Duane Dunkley, an affable gray-haired Ojibwa Indian man who works as a consultant on Native American matters. He told me cheerfully that he taught the children "stuff you never see in print." Like what? I asked. "Like the power of the medicine man," Dunkley said. "You won't see it in print, but I've seen it in person. My grandfather took the phlegm out of his lungs by using the power of the spirit world." I went into one fourth-grade class where the children were reciting poems. For my benefit the teacher asked the students to tell me each of the poets' names and what she called the poets' cultures. And so the children cried: "Langston Hughes—African-American." The other names were inaudible to me but their "cultures" weren't. The children chanted in unison "European-American" for one poet, "American Indian—Zuni" for the second, and "Asian—China" for the third.

Small children in gaily decorated classrooms with attentive and loving teachers is always a gratifying scene, and Andersen Contemporary certainly has a great deal of charm. My own belief, in any case, is that it almost doesn't matter exactly what subject matter children are taught in such areas as reading and social studies, so long as the specific material is of intrinsic merit. And if, in the process of summoning before young minds a sense of wonder and a love of learning, they can be introduced to a Zuni poem, so much the better. Insofar as the multiculturalist initiative does things like that, it is a good initiative.

Andersen Contemporary did have, to me, a great deal of that flavor of enrichment. For example, children in their reading classes studied a character that they called the trickster, the literary rogue, the mischief maker, and they studied this character across cultures, so that during one stretch of time they did "Br'er Rabbit," learning that that was an African-American trickster story; at other times, they read stories about an Irish trickster, an Indonesian trickster, and an Ojibwa trickster named Winaboojoo who tricked the animals into making the earth. Delightful and stimulating and also multicultural in the good sense of that word.

But then there is a kind of *dérapage*, that familiar skid into ideological excess, into education as compensation for past wrongs, the curriculum as expiation for guilt. Scratch the surface of a multiculturalist curriculum, and there is this worm gnawing away at any notion of American goodness. What emerges is the passion play of victims and oppressors, colonizers and colonized, and an enforced, deterministic identification of one group with white people and the other with everybody else. This, at any rate, is what unfolded for me during my two-day visit.

Early on, I sat down with Barbara Shin and a group of teachers and other school officials who explained the school's philosophy. The key phrase was "different perspectives." The idea is to teach an event always concentrating on how it looked and felt to different groups. The second key ingredient is that every culture is given equal value and equal time so that every child will be validated and supported in his or her own cultural identity. My question here was what allowance was made for what seemed to me the overriding importance of Europe in American history in providing the largest population and, more important perhaps, inspiring our values and our political system.

"Basically it's of equal position" was the answer. "In literature, for example, we have stories from what we call the big five—European, African, Asian, American-Indian, and Hispanic. They help us to be more inclusive."

"The other way that it's done," another person said, "is for an event to be looked at from different cultural points of view. How was this viewed by the Ojibwa, by European settlers, by African-Americans?" Efforts are made also to introduce other languages, not so much as modes of communication but as cultural legitimators.

"We acknowledge that the official language of our country is English," I was told, "but we all understand a plurality of languages. We also acknowledge that Spanish is the second most important language in our nation. We've also tried to instill the Ojibwa language because it's the main native language here. One teacher who is not Ojibwa does math lessons in both English and Ojibwa. It sanctions and legitimates the Ojibwa culture."

I then asked about George Washington and the founding fathers. I asked the questions thinking that certain major events that gave identity to the nation had very little to do with the Ojibwa. Shouldn't history be taught the way it happened, not the way one wishes it to have happened?

"Do you know how it looks to us now?" was the response. "The founding fathers are such a small part of the story," one teacher said. "African-Americans, for example. You can't start with slavery and end with slavery. You have to start with the West African empires; then you have to go beyond the experience of slavery to show, for example, that slavery was foreign to the West African cultures themselves and also that African-Americans were the protagonists of their history both before and after slavery." Then there's the Constitution, one teacher added, which has to be taught from the Algonquin point of view. The teachers showed me a list of books—*Native Americans and the Evolution of American Democracy, Forgotten Founders, Indian Givers*—demonstrating that the Algonquin system of government, the confederation of the five Algonquin tribes, was a model for the framers of the U.S. Constitution.

"The founding fathers," one teacher began. "To me it's unacceptable to see the absence of diversity. When you see the picture of the presidents, it's the homogeneity of it. It's a fact, but it reminds me of the need for opportunities for other citizens. It reminds me of the need to be inclusive.

"Whenever people see something portrayed from one perspective, the message is sent to others: 'You're not included in this.' I don't think we should negate the good works of anybody. It's just that we should include the good works of everybody."

Well, I said, how then does quality enter into the picture? Do you study Shakespeare to illustrate European culture or do you study Shakespeare because his works are sublime? Is the goal to teach children the best that has been thought and said, no matter who thought or said it, or is just about everything chosen to validate some child's ancestral identity?

"I don't distinguish between the two" came the response. "I would say that the greatness of Shakespeare and the greatness of Lao-tzu were in the same domain."

Well, choices have to be made, I said.

"Well, I'm sorry," said Ms. Shin heatedly, "but choices have been made that have excluded a lot of people and a lot of great ideas."

I insisted on George Washington. He was, after all, the first president. There has to be some ordering of the importance of events if there are to be themes to the American identity. There are some events and individuals that exerted greater influence on greater numbers than others and are thus more central to the American experience. One reason we study Shakespeare is because he created the cultural language in which we live. Similarly, not to know George Washington is, simply, to be ignorant.

The answer regarding Washington: "He's acknowledged for what his contribution was, but at the same time, other people are there whose contributions have not been acknowledged."

This conversation took place in what the teachers at the school call the resource room, a large, high-ceilinged library with book-shelves and posters. There were "The Great Queens of Africa." There was a calendar called "365 Days of Black History." There were the "Women of Minnesota," like Susan Frénière Brown, a Mdewakanton Dakota elder, and Ethel Ray Nance, a civil rights activist from Duluth. Nearby were "American-Indian Women in Mathematics," "Famous Black American Writers," and a poster giving mostly satirical names to sports teams—Pittsburgh Negroes, Kansas City Jews, San Diego Caucasians, Cleveland Indians—supporting the contention of some Indian groups that the names of sports teams are offensive to them. There was a map of the Indian tribes of America and a quote from Chief Dan George: "We have taken much from your culture . . . I wish you had taken something from our culture." There were pictures of twenty-one "contemporary leaders," three of whom were white men, the comedian Billy Crystal, the singer Randy Travis, and Ken Burns, the documentary filmmaker, and the rest women and people of color.

Such exhortatory symbols of our multicultural world were scattered all over the school. There was a banner that read: I LEARN THROUGH DIVERSITY. There was a wall display entitled "People Who Make a Difference." There was Eleanor Roosevelt and the golfer Lee Trevino (a Mexican-American). There was Guion S. Bluford, a black astronaut, and Sakokwenonkwas, the chief of the Bear Clan of the Mohawk Nation, and Patricia Harris, a black secretary of housing and urban development in the Carter administration (Carter himself was not there). At the front of the school was the Peace Wall honoring three peacemakers: Martin Luther King, Jr., Chief Seattle (along with a text of "his" environmentalist statement, actually made up by a screenwriter),* and Mother Teresa. I got into a discussion with one teacher about some curriculum materials showing the extent of pre-Columbian African explorers. She told me that there is new research showing traces of African influences among the Aztecs, in northwestern India, in Macedonia, and in China.

The next day I talked with some teachers and students. The first, a middle-aged white man who had taught at the school since long before it had been MCGFDA, admitted to me that he didn't fit in very well. "I'm not an ideologue," he said. "I work with children." Children certainly should have a sense of their personhood, he said,

*See Chapter 7.

and they should learn to be sensitive to and considerate of others, but that can be done without making a fetish of race and ethnicity. "I think we need to say that kids should have an awareness of certain things that we all need to know about, and I don't see that happening here." Instead, what Andersen Contemporary has, he said, is a certain Babel-like confusion. There are no textbooks, no sequence, no structure, more a disconnected jumble of subjects, all of those involving social studies, history, or literature brought into the classroom to demonstrate the diversity of the American population. "There are a lot of speakers invited to the school who put down white people," he said.

The other teachers seemed living proof of his point. I asked a fifth-grade teacher, Lee Ellis, what she taught in social studies. She said that she started with indigenous peoples—the Aztecs, the Indians of the Southwest, the Algonquin. Then she moved to the explorers, "specifically Columbus," she said. "We used different perspectives. Did he discover a new world or was there already an old world? Duane gave us some creation stories," she went on, speaking of Duane Dunkley who had spoken to me of medicine men. "Then we talked about the disasters that happened, how the Indians were wiped out by disease, how they were tricked and taken back to Europe. Then we talked about Cortés and the destruction of the Mayan and the Aztec civilizations. Then we talked about colonization. Why did Europe want to come here? We talked about greed, debts, Christianizing, and the difference between the way the Spaniards treated the Native Americans and the French."

Other subjects covered, Ellis said, included a certain Pedro Ninos, who, she said, was "an African who navigated the Nino." They talked about the slave trade, how Africans were brought here "as chattel, not people, about families being split up, being sold, but also the culture that they brought with them." They talked about the Cherokee Trail of Tears, caused by Andrew Jackson, whom Ellis quoted as saying, "I don't want these Indians here; I want real Americans." "We talked about Sacajawea," Ellis said, referring to an Indian who is making her way into the multiculturalist canon as a guide during the Lewis and Clark Expedition.

What do the children read? Ellis cited *Brother Future*, about a kid from Detroit who is transported back to South Carolina in the 1840s and sees what it's like to live on a plantation. "They don't have a clue yet about how bad slavery was," Ellis explained. Then there is *Sign of the Beaver*, about a white boy lost in the woods and saved by an Iroquois grandfather and boy who teach him how to survive in the wilderness. I asked Ellis what particular historical individuals the children will come away knowing about. She named four black figures, no whites: Crispus Attucks, Sojourner Truth, Harriet Tubman, and Frederick Douglass. Any other figures whom the pupils would see as important?

"I would not say George Washington. I would not say Andrew Jackson. It wouldn't be traditional white heroes. Frederick Douglass might be one. Tecumseh, because he really drew the line in the sand and said, 'Look, we're not going to be pushed off our land anymore.' "

"Why not George Washington?" I asked, my antediluvian concern with the founding fathers pushing to the surface once again.

"I just didn't emphasize him," Ellis said. "I didn't say that he was bad or good. We didn't focus on military strategy; we talked about the formation of the government. It was just that he sort of came to the top.

"I will put stress on Abraham Lincoln," she said as our meeting concluded. "I do think we need some balance. The sentiment in my room is that they don't like Christians and they don't like white people, because they saw what has been done in the name of Christianity and what the white people did to the Indians and the Africans. So I do think we need some balance."

And on it went in similar fashion with other teachers, most of whom confirmed the almost complete absence of white people, especially white men, in MCGFDA pedagogy, except insofar as white people are responsible for the injustices and atrocities that play such a large role in the worldview of Andersen Contemporary. For the sake of thematic consistency I asked a teacher who taught both fifth- and sixth-graders what she taught about George Washington. She answered: "That he was the first president, that he was a slave owner, that he was rich—not much." She then went on to tell me that she did teach about Eli Whitney, and for just a second I thought, finally, a white male. Then the teacher, Katie Diaz, spoiled my illusion.

"They know," she said, speaking of her fifth- and sixth-graders, "that he stole his invention from a woman who didn't patent it."

I asked where she acquired that particular piece of information.

"Another teacher told me," Diaz said.

As I have said, there are no villains in this drama. The teachers at Andersen Contemporary and Brookline, the advocates of Afrocentrism, and the members of the CQE are divided not by their intentions but by the nature of their vision. One group sees unfairness, especially to minority group children; it sees failure, identity eradication, and discrimination, and it wishes to eliminate them. The other side sees lowered standards, politically correct evasions of the truth, and the victim-oppressor theory of American life, all justified by the goal of making things better for disadvantaged children. In the struggle, the staff at Andersen Contemporary and also Brookline have virtue on their side, since they are the ones who are trying to make things better, while their critics often seem to have nothing more exciting to offer than the same old tired solutions to problems that simply do not go away.

The only standard by which to judge any of this, of course, is whether it is good for children and, by consequence, good for the society in which the children will grow up. Does it improve education, make students independent and thinking individuals, instill in them both a love of learning and an attitude of tolerance, and does it give them the best possible preparation for later life? Here is where the confusion comes in. Andersen Contemporary more conspicuously and Brookline more subtly are both striving to advance the causes of social justice in America by making children aware of the sufferings that were unmistakably involved in American history. Is this good for children and for the society? I myself think that knowledge of those sufferings is certainly a good thing. It is when they, and the ethnic politics that underlie them, become the locomotives of instruction, rather than elements of schooling, that education and civic virtue are both harmed, and, at Andersen Contemporary and Brookline, both schools filled with energetic and well-intentioned people whose concern certainly was the well-being of children, they were locomotives, entire freight trains, rushing headlong down the track.

For one thing, there seems to be precious little diversity at Andersen Contemporary. Everything is multicultural ideology, ethnic association, and victimization at the hands of Christians and white people. There is no alternative, no debate, no differing points of view. This is not a school; it is a cult, and it is a cult whose benefits have yet to be proven in practice. There is no proof at all, for example, that there is any educational benefit in choosing books to read or individuals to study because they represent an ethnic group. Children, after all, are very shrewd. Sooner or later they will realize that they have been deprived of the best for the sake of the representative or the politically suitable. Moreover, one question that is never even asked by the multiculturalist ideologues concerns those Asian children, so far culturally from the American mainstream, yet doing so well in school.

Second, it seems that the ideology underlying the MCGFDA program is more likely to nurture a sense of injustice and entitlement than it is to lead to the elusive grail of self-esteem.

Third, nice as it is to be respectful of different ways of doing things and of the many American traditions, the plain fact is that not all "cultures" provide for equal success in the postindustrial, high-tech, bourgeois-capitalist democracy in which we happen to live. This is not a matter of good or bad. It is a matter of preparation for the world as it exists, not as the teachers of Andersen Contemporary might dream it. For children to hear stories about the Ojibwa medicine man is certainly unobjectionable, just as they might read about Babar or Winnie-the-Pooh. It is when the medicine man and modern science get put on the same plateau that confusion sets in.

Fourth, and most important perhaps, the radical form of multiculturalism practiced in these schools and others paradoxically diverts from the deepest lessons that need to be learned about the principles and values that lead to a respect for difference in the first place. The journalist Jonathan Rosen has written about a conversation he had with Lucy Dawidowicz, the late historian of the Holocaust. He asked her whether she thought the Holocaust should be taught to public school students. "I'd feel a lot safer if they learned the meaning of the Constitution instead," Dawidowicz replied.

That is why it is more important for children to know about George Washington than Crispus Attucks or Sacajawea, why one should be primary in American education and the others secondary. Washington was a central figure in the long and painful development of the idea of liberal democracy, which includes within it the concept of the inviolability of the individual, the respect for equal rights under the law, the concepts of equal opportunity and of government as the protector of human rights, not the opponent of them.

Good citizenship involves schooling in those values and in the history of their creation. It also involves respect for the truth, rather than the worship of wishful thinking. And it must include not merely the sense that we are a diverse people, fragmented into many groups, races, religions, and preferences, but that certain values hold us together, and those things transcend the differences among us. It is on those grounds that a place like Andersen Contemporary is a disservice to its children and to its community. As for Brookline, things had not gone quite as bad as elsewhere, but knowledgeable of trends elsewhere in the country, the parents of the Committee for Quality Education waged their fight to avoid the same end result.

In the end, the CQE won its effort to restore AP European History to the Brookline High curriculum. Or, at least, while the CQE parents still have doubts about the predominant philosophy at Brookline, they did succeed in their original goal—but only after a long fight. Ronni and David Stillman began with AP European History. In the fall of 1989, 250 parents and 188 students signed a petition requesting the reinstatement of the course. Around that time, the superintendent of schools, James Walsh, received about forty letters from scholars, Brookline High graduates, and parents urging that the course be reinstated. Among the letters writers: Simon Schama and Stanley Hoffman, both distinguished historians of Europe at Harvard, and Sheldon Glashow, a Nobel Prize winner in physics. Michael Dukakis, two of whose children had "done Dudley," called the AP European History teacher and expressed his support.

Probably, most school committees would simply have heeded the request and put back the damn course, but not Brookline. Well before there was even a thought of founding the CQE, the Stillmans went to a meeting of the curriculum subcommittee, held in late 1989, and found about fifty people in attendance, far more than usual. The Stillmans asked for a vote on reinstatement of AP European History. Dudley himself spoke at the meeting, saying, "This painful episode is part of a larger national trend initiated by those who seek to politicize the curriculum, those who view European history as if it were political indoctrination responsible for what they view as repressive attitudes toward women and minorities." Dudley continued that history "cannot be made to equally employ every sex, class, race, or culture in every age." That is the simple truth, he contended. "To insist curriculum be a species of affirmative action is to return to the damnable superstition equating race and culture." He concluded: "Don't allow the Brookline High School social studies department to be a mere staging area for partisan politics. We know too well through European history that ideology is idiocy, but it is an idiocy, we know too, through European history, that kills."

At the end of the meeting, rather than hold a vote, the subcommittee chairperson, Caroline Graboys, called another meeting instead. The Stillmans were so angry that they didn't attend this second meeting, but Roger and Sarah Blood did, taping it and transcribing the tape. It gives a sense of the depth of the resistance to Dudley's course. At one point a recent Brookline graduate, now a student at Reed College in Oregon, proclaimed that she had not taken AP European History, but didn't feel "that I missed out on anything." In the very next breath, she complained that she did miss out because there was no AP Government at the time she was in high school and therefore did not know how governments work.

"I didn't even know what a prime minister did in Parliament," she said, "or what a parliament meant." It took several speakers before somebody pointed out that had she learned a bit of European history, she might not be as ignorant as she is.

Many members of the social studies department were at the meeting, and a good ten of them spoke. They argued that their decisions had been made carefully over a six-year period. They said that to continue teaching AP European History would only serve the interests of "a very privileged group of students" at the expense of many others. European history is already taught in the sophomore year at Brookline, one teacher added, and students can continue to study more of it in college if they so choose. One quite radical teacher argued that "we must hear the voices of the people that we say we care about teaching," meaning, it seems, the non-Euro-Americans at the school. Their voices, she said, must be heard "not from the oppressive experience of European colonialism, or Europe going out into the world to colonize, to Christianize."

In a kind of concluding statement, William Hibert, the head of the social studies department, said, "The curriculum we have presented to you is consistent with the recommendations of the National Council of Social Studies." He argued for its great inclusiveness and for its "scope and sequence." Then he lambasted the Stillmans and their allies for being "concerned with only a tiny segment of the students that we teach." This "small group of objectors," Hibert went on, "have lobbied and harassed school administrators, teachers, and school committee members," have "provided a disingenuous and fraudulent—I say fraudulent—fact sheet." They "gathered signatures on a petition which deceives its signatories"; they have "defamed members of this department" and "have tried to subvert the orderly process of curriculum development," and "expressed an arrogant contempt for our efforts and our abilities."

A few weeks later, there was a meeting of the full school committee, on December 19, 1989. The room was packed. The debate on AP European History lasted ninety minutes. In the end, a compromise was proposed. Rather than reinstate the course, the decision was to add independent study to the curriculum so, presumably, those students who wanted to study European history would be able to do that. The Stillmans and the other parents who had pressed for the restoration of the course were furious. Not only had the committee ignored the clear desires of all the parents and teachers who had signed the petition for AP European History, but the compromise involving independent study was, they felt, a sham, since that option already existed.

When, after the votes, one of the school committee members then took the floor to propose a budget override, the Stillmans walked out.

"In what other school committee could they kick you in the teeth and then ask you for more money?" David Stillman said. "That's when we created the CQE." And that too is when other members of what came to be called "the small group of angry parents" joined forces, collecting materials on the school, taping events like Peggy McIntosh's "Five Phases of Pedagogy" presentation, raising a bit of money.

A key event came about six months after the Stillmans' early defeats at the school committee meetings. It was the spring of 1990. The CQE members had discovered things like *The Circle Bulletin*, which struck them as evidence of an organized effort to make the curriculum subservient to radical leftist politics. They wrote letters of protest to the school committee and to the Brookline *Citizen*, in one of which they made the mistake of attacking a schoolteacher by name over an article she had written in *Reflections*, Brookline's education journal.

On May 14, 1990, a meeting of the school committee was held that has ever after in the annals of CQE history come to be known as the show trial.

Normally five or six people might come to a school committee meeting. There were four hundred in attendance for this one, held in the auditorium of one of the town's elementary schools. That very day, the Brookline Teachers Association, the union associated with the National Education Association, distributed a pamphlet called *Weathering the Controversy*, which provided advice to the teachers intent on saving their program of reform. It told about the importance of educating staff members about "the vocabulary of the New Right." It said: "Remember, you are dealing with extremists," so there's no point trying to persuade them. They are "censors." It is eliminating their influence with others that is crucial to success, so "be careful to use simple, short words and sentences" and, above all, don't be "inflammatory" or "long-winded."

"Outraged Educators Blast Back" was the headline in the Brookline *Citizen* on May 18, 1990, reporting on the meeting. The auditorium was packed with the supporters of the social studies department who got up one after another to denounce the CQE for conducting a "witch-hunt" of the faculty and of using the tactics of "McCarthyism" and "vigilantism." The specific focus of discussion was a proposal, called Town Meeting Article 47, proposed by some CQE supporters. It demanded "a school environment free of any systematic political, social, religious or historical bias," but a good deal of the anti-CQE anger was due to the terrible blunder that the CQE had made in criticizing a teacher by name. It was the only time such a thing happened, and the CQE paid a big price for it. A school-board member, Kim Michelson, chastised the group for being "vigilantes" rather than just vigilant, the difference lying in "the assumption of ill will" on the part of vigilantes. Robert Costrell of the CQE apologized to the teacher in question and then argued that the real issue was the school's devotion to "values and social responsibility" rather than "reading and writing, math and science." But the damage had been done. To pass Article 47, despite what everybody called its "benign language," would have been an admission of wrongdoing by the school. And so one after another supporter of the teachers got up and lambasted the CQE. The audience hissed those few brave enough to try to defend it. Finally, the meeting decided to take no vote on the article. The members of the CQE, some of whom admit they were too shocked by the virulence of the attacks against them and by the hostile mood in the room, did not take the floor. "We were up against a juggernaut," said Roger Blood, who, along with Sandra Stotsky, had written Article 47.

The CQE was at its lowest ebb. True, they had made a mistake in publicly criticizing a teacher by name. But all along they had been called such things as "rabid citizens," "intellectual terrorists," "vigilantes," "bullies," "brownshirts." It seemed a bit disingenuous to accuse the CQE's members of assuming ill will, or of substituting invective for a genuine debate about the ideas and arguments of their opponents. As parents and citizens, the CQE's members had felt it their democratic right to investigate the quality of education in their town, or, at least, to know what their children were learning. True, they had made some sharp criticisms of what they saw as the reigning philosophy at the school, but the only thing they had ever specifically demanded was the restoration of one course that had legendary status. For that, and for daring to express dissent from the prevailing ortho-doxy, they were accused of waging an "inquisition" and imposing "censorship."

What saved them was a groundswell of support for AP European History and teacher Dudley among the students. Not long after the school board refused to reinstate the course, thirty-five students in the sophomore European history course at Brookline High signed a letter to the *Citizen* in which they praised Dudley ("a marvelous teacher who has opened our eyes to the wonders of history. . . . He has taught us not only history but he has given us confidence in our ability to learn").

The CQE meanwhile learned of an obscure Massachusetts law requiring a school to offer a course of study not already included in the curriculum if thirty students and their parents petition for it. The students carried out the petition drive and got the necessary signatures, working in the face of the evident hostility of many of their teachers. At first, the school administration declared that the petition was nonbinding, since the sophomore European history course was already in the curriculum—therefore the course of study petitioned for was already offered. The CQE and other parents appealed to the legal office of the state Education Department, which decided that sophomore European history and AP European History in the senior year were different courses of study.

On December 18, 1990, the course was reinstated at a meeting of the school committee, but the students' victory was tarnished by a condition: the school committee decided that any student who took both the sophomore and senior European history classes would be required to take a course providing "a non-European, non-American perspective" in order to graduate. That was odd, since nothing stopped students at Brookline from taking all non-Western social studies courses (except for the required year of American history), and they were not required to spend a single minute learning about Europe by way of multiculturalist balance.

"The restriction included in your recommendation is unjust," one junior told the school committee on the night it restored the course. "It unfairly singles out students who are interested in history," the student continued, pointing out that kids interested in biology could take both the sophomore and senior courses in that subject without any conditions. Brookline students are allowed to take four years of such subjects as conservation careers or early childhood development, but two years studying the formation of Europe is too much? The real, unspoken reason for the school committee's condition, the student declared, is that "two years of European history is considered to be 'Eurocentric.'"

Earlier than that, even before AP European History was restored, teachers got an earful from the class valedictorian, who, in the traditional speech, dutifully thanked the teachers for their knowledge, skill, and devotion. Then came a zinger right out of the revolutionary traditions of Europe, a thrust of the lance inspired by the irreverence for authority that is almost an exclusive preserve of Western thought.

"Our gratitude does not blind us to when opinions dominate over knowledge. We resented when our classrooms were politicized. You had no right to indoctrinate us into a unified set of values. We are freeborn individuals and will not sit easy when punished for expressing beliefs contrary to your own. We are not in school to be molded into political clones. We can define our own values and beliefs if provided with the knowledge to make reasoned decisions. Recognize our independence as a compliment, not as ingratitude. If you expect us to respect your values and beliefs, accord ours the same decent hearing."

Chapter 9

THE BATTLE OF TEXAS

You can't teach a man what he thinks he already knows.

—EPICTETUS

The Phi Gamma Delta fraternity house at the University of Texas in Austin has what, given the prevailing campus ethos of the 1990s, might be seen as an unfortunate resemblance to the manor house of an old Southern plantation. It is a white-columned structure of the sort that mere undergrads at a large state university should not be able to afford. Then again, there's a lot of money in Texas and a lot of money at the University of Texas at Austin, which has rich alumni and owns oil wells on land that was granted to it years ago by the state. The University of Texas at Austin is second to Harvard among American universities in the size of its endowment. It is a vast place, occupying 357 acres of prime land inside the Austin city limits, just a few blocks from the Texas state capitol.

The antebellum grandeur of Phi Gamma Delta seemed to confirm certain unpleasant associations of the past when the fraternity came to the center of an incident that shocked the entire campus. In 1990, during Round Up Week, when fraternities hold receptions for new pledges, some members of the fraternity sold T-shirts that showed the body of basketball player Michael Jordan surmounted by what was described as a "Sambo" head. The Sambo, despite being a racist caricature, had once been the insignia of the fraternity, a throwback to that era when homeowners all across America blithely placed statues of grinning black coachmen holding lanterns on their front lawns. The Sambo finally fell victim to more enlightened attitudes in 1987, which was late, but it was abandoned. Why it appeared again on that Round Up Week T-shirt is not known, but the fact that it did took on great importance in campus politics.

The Sambo head at Phi Gamma Delta was one of two incidents that were interpreted to show renascent racism at UT. The other took place at another fraternity house, Tau Delta Tau, and was more blatant. A car parked in front of the fraternity house was spray-painted with the words FUCK COONS and FUCK YOU NIGS DIE. It was never established that anybody at Tau Delta Tau was actually responsible for this outrage. Nonetheless, fraternities, especially all-white fraternities, are widely perceived to be the repositories of much that is crude and offensive in university life. They are supposedly the kinds of places where much beer is swilled, where "date rape" occurs most commonly, and where white boys will be most revoltingly white boys. So, not surprisingly perhaps, when reports of the incidents at Phi Gamma Delta and Tau Delta Tau hit the *Daily Texan*, the school newspaper, the conviction arose that old-fashioned racial hatred was again abroad in the land.

The protests were immediate, vigorous, and far-reaching. According to the *Daily Texan*, more than one thousand students and local residents marched on the state supreme court building, which is a few blocks from the campus, and on one of the fraternity houses to protest what the paper called "a recent outbreak of racist activity on campus." "Hey UT, have you heard? This is not Johannesburg," the protesters shouted. The argument was that the incidents were not the isolated work of a few hateful individuals (even though it seems entirely possible that this was the case) but were rather reflections of the deeper currents of racism that they felt ran through the University of Texas and American society. Marcus Brown, the president of the Black Students Alliance, told the rally in front of the supreme court building that his group wanted to protest not just "these two affronts against black people but also the racist environment which we confront on a daily basis." He said: "Individual acts of racism are merely manifestations of institutional racism. In many instances, 'education' in this institution is designed to relegate people of color to a position of subservience."

Anxious to prevent the incidents from causing generalized tur-

moil, UT's president, William Cunningham, suspended both fraternities to await a "thorough review" of the incidents. In a statement
published in the *Texan*, he said "acts of racial harassment will not be
tolerated at the University of Texas at Austin." Unsatisfied with that,
black student leaders criticized Cunningham for having issued "a lot
of rhetoric," for paying mere "lip service" to the problem of racism,
but doing nothing to eradicate it at its roots or even to punish the
offensive fraternities as groups.

A couple of days later, Cunningham was heckled and interrupted
as he tried to restate his antiracist position in a speech on what is
called the West Mall, a tree-shaded esplanade just below the campus's
main administrative tower. As Cunningham spoke, a few students
crowded around him and, looking over his shoulder, began to read
his prepared text in unison with him, whereupon the president of the
university announced that copies of the speech would be distributed
from his office, and then he retreated, followed by hundreds of students who continued to shout and heckle.

Decidedly, it is not easy being a university president these days,
and the "racial incidents" at UT illustrate the difficulties. Students,
having inherited the legacy of protest and the demand for moral
perfection that came down to them from the 1960s, go on the offensive
with enormous ease. Especially when provided with an emotionally
satisfying pretext—and there is no better pretext than a racial incident—they find it relatively easy to transform the university from a
place where they sit at the feet of people who, presumably, know
more than they do, to a place where they make demands, not only
about what kind of place the university should be, but about what
they should be taught and by whom. University presidents thus have
to deal almost daily with that delicate and combustible substance
made up of the wounded feelings of students and the ideological
objectives of those members of the faculty and administration who
goad the students on.

And so, at Texas, the racial incidents at the two fraternities were
exploited to press an old demand, namely for an ambitious program
for greater diversity and multiculturalism. The program was called
PRIDE, for Proposed Reforms to Institute Diversity in Education.
The principle behind it was that by teaching multiculturalism, which
meant, specifically, courses in what were later called nondominant
cultures and Third World cultures, students would learn to respect
difference. Racial hatreds—as well as such other sins as sexism and

prejudice against homosexuals—would be diminished. At the same time, the self-esteem of minority group members, essential to their success in the majority culture, would be enhanced. This demand, remember, was not simply to make available the study of nondominant cultures, which, in any case, was already available. It was to require that students undertake that study.

One report, issued by the American Association of Higher Education, found that as of July 1991 just under half (48 percent to be exact) of four-year colleges had a "multicultural general education requirement." It's worth thinking about that for a minute. Requirements are those things deemed essential in the acquisition of a liberal education. A student should be introduced, say, to a foreign language, to science, math, some American history, and so forth. Now in what some critics have sardonically called a return to compulsory chapel, half the colleges in the country are saying, in effect, that a certain political attitude is also mandatory, since, as we have seen, multiculturalism is not so much a knowledge and appreciation of other cultures as it is an attitude toward the politics of race and gender. More than seven out of ten vice-presidents and deans surveyed in a random sample of 270 colleges and universities said that they "talk about multiculturalism frequently or continually."*

At the University of Wisconsin, for example, an institution with some fifty thousand undergraduates, the only course required of all students is the one that satisfies the multicultural requirement. The University of California at Berkeley was among the first of many major institutions that went beyond the traditional civil rights goal of opening the doors to racial and ethnic minorities; it requires all students to study those minorities by fulfilling an American Cultures Breadth Requirement. This requirement represented no small change at Berkeley. According to the university's explanatory brochure, some 120 new courses in some 30 disciplines were created to "focus upon how American identity and experience have been shaped and continue to be shaped by the diversity of our constituent cultural traditions."

As colleges and schools across the country have responded to the demands of students and faculty that they adopt changes similar to

---

*Arthur Levine and Jeanette Cureton, "The Quiet Revolution: Eleven Facts About Multiculturalism and the Curriculum," *Change* 24, no. 1 (Jan./Feb. 1992), pages 25–29.

those at Berkeley and Wisconsin, conflicts have resulted between what might be called "reformers" on the pro-multiculturalist side, and "traditionalists" on the other. Those labels, in fact, are misleading, since "reformer" contains a progressive connotation and "traditionalist" an establishmentarian flavor that badly reflects the real points of view expressed in this debate. To be opposed to a multicultural requirement is far from being opposed to multiculturalism itself, though that fine distinction is rarely made. Karen Duban, a lawyer and the wife of an English professor who played a key role in the debates on this issue at Texas, argues for the words "politicizer" versus "nonpoliticizer" to represent opposing points of view, since, she argues, the advocates of mandatory multiculturalism are less interested in educating students than they are in using the educational system to make political changes in society. If, she says, there were a movement across the country to modify curricula to discourage abortion, which would also be aimed at achieving political change, the advocates of this movement would not widely be known as reformers.

It was against the background of this national debate that the racial incidents at the University of Texas in Austin gave new impetus to the demands for change made by the reformers. But what happened at Texas following those incidents has a special drama. One of the efforts to reform the curriculum, to make it more multicultural and more respectful of difference, provoked a conflict far sharper and more enduring than conflicts at most institutions of higher learning across the country. All of the issues involving the challenge to the traditional American culture came into play at Texas, which can be taken as a kind of national laboratory, a crucible for the battle over the American identity.

Linda Brodkey is a friendly, casual woman in her mid-to-late forties, with large, innocent eyes, a breezy manner, a self-deprecating sense of humor, and an air of reasonableness that would seem to disqualify her for the academic barricades. She was born in Hannibal, Missouri, the birthplace of Mark Twain, and went to Western Illinois University—the only place her working-class parents could afford, she says. She served for two years as an English teacher in Senegal and then got a Ph.D. at the University of New Mexico in English language and literature. Her thesis topic indicates that she was a dutiful student: "Linguistic and Non-linguistic Deixis in Academic Prose." While in graduate school she got a job as a writing teacher and loved it. So after getting her Ph.D., she embarked on what seemed like a quiet, unspectacular career as a teacher of writing and rhetoric, of the methods of argumentation and clarity of expression, which is what she did at the University of Pennsylvania, before coming to Texas in 1988.

Alan Gribben, who later became Brodkey's major rival at Austin, followed a pattern not all that dissimilar. Gribben too is a friendly, approachable figure, a mild-mannered professorial type with a full mustache and a lengthy list of publications on nineteenth-century American literature. There is some irony in the fact that his special area is Mark Twain, whose hometown was Linda Brodkey's. Gribben, whose hometown is Parsons, Kansas, and who got his B.A. in English at the University of Kansas in Lawrence, came to Texas long before Brodkey, in 1974. He was a campus leftist during his graduate-student days at Berkeley, a mentor to minority students there. He had tenure at UT, where he was a full professor, and he could have taught there for his entire career if that is what he had insisted on doing. The same is true of Brodkey, who was hired with tenure.

But Gribben left UT in 1991 to go to a smaller place than Texas, in Alabama. In well-publicized charges (summarily, though not convincingly, dismissed as mythomaniac by the chairman of the English department at UT), Gribben says that he was hounded from his department, turned into an outcast, a pariah, because he took a stand in opposition to a proposal of Linda Brodkey's (and, as we will see, before Brodkey entered his life, when he opposed an earlier move to make the English department at Texas conform to trendy multiculturalism). He was shunned in the hallways, uninvited to parties, the target of at least one campus demonstration, persistently labeled a "right-winger" in campus publications (and an "ultra-right-winger" by the very chairman of his department, who disputes Gribben's claims of persecution), labels that do not improve one's standing in the academy these days. Once, he told me, a professor in the Texas College of Business Administration left his card under Gribben's door, so Gribben called him up. "I hoped you would call," he said, "so I would have the opportunity to tell you that I consider you to be a bigoted, racist, Nazi Fascist . . ." Gribben says that he hung up in the middle of the stream of epithets. Twice, he told me, somebody blitzed the English department mailboxes with anti-Gribben circulars. There were 92 faculty members in the department and 182 graduate students. Somehow the offensive circular got into the locked

room where the mailboxes are kept—twice. The informal network
that made Gribben an outcast extended, he says, to some of the
universities that showed great interest in him as a job candidate
(his ostracism having convinced him to look for work elsewhere than
Texas), but then mysteriously lost interest when word spread of his
reputation in Austin.

Brodkey had an easier time of it, even though she, too, she says,
had some very upsetting obscene phone calls from strangers and was
also held up for criticism in articles on the Texas controversy. No
lurid rumors trailed in her wake as she looked for work elsewhere,
and she ended up as the head of a prestigious writing program at the
University of California at San Diego. Still, Brodkey claims that
the persecutory efforts of Gribben and a small number of others
at the university, unopposed by a weak and vacillating university
administration, destroyed her career as a teacher of writing and rhetoric at Texas, made it impossible for her to continue her chosen profession there, and so she too took her leave.

It is not that Brodkey and Gribben were personal enemies, al-
though they did come to say some very nasty things about each other.
Indeed, when the controversy at Texas first broke, they hardly knew
each other, and they virtually never exchanged words even as the
controversy reached its peak. Indeed, the battle at the University of
Texas by no means took place between two people. Brodkey and
Gribben were antagonists in the sense that they personified two opposed positions, with most of the department standing on one side
and a very small, ironically quite diverse, group on the other, until
the positions hardened into stone, wrecking one career and certainly
interfering with another.

What happened? The destructive conflict symbolized by Alan
Gribben and Linda Brodkey centers around what might seem to be
a small and not very significant corner of academic life, nothing more
grand or portentous than the course in composition that many UT
students are required to take as freshmen. Brodkey was commissioned
to revise the course, which was identified in the catalog as E-306.
Gribben raised objections to the changes that she proposed, and he
managed, in part by appealing to the public outside the university,
to arouse enough opposition to the changes to defeat them. That was
the bare-bones conflict between the two teachers.

But the issue grew to engulf the entire university. It destroyed
friendships and produced a file of documents several feet thick. It

received national press coverage at a time when the newspapers and magazines were first discovering what they called political correctness at the universities. It involved both the Modern Language Association and the American Association of University Professors in investigations into whether the criticisms of the revised course, and an eventual decision by the university not to go ahead with it, were violations of academic freedom. In the counsels of academe, Gribben and Brodkey became famous, either as subjects of contempt and derision (Gribben in particular I heard denounced in the speeches of multicultural advocates as loathsome and contemptible) or of admiration and esteem (and, again, Gribben emerged as a hero to the opponents of the New Consciousness).

Brodkey, as I have said, was charged with the responsibility of revising freshman composition. Why a revision? Many agree that at Texas E-306 was taught without any consistent standard, mostly by graduate students earning money as low-level instructors who devised the courses the way each of them saw fit. "The teaching assistants were not being told how to put together a writing program," Brodkey said. "They were not being helped to understand how they should teach writing."

Brodkey believed that she knew how to teach writing. She had years of theory behind her, theory that says, first of all, that writing is something that can be taught, rather than something involving only innate skill or genius. In order to teach writing, however, you need, as Brodkey put it, "to set up a field, a field of information, a big topic." She told me: "You have to set up a discourse, something that creates a universe of tenets so you know it when you're in it and when you're not in it."

In other words, a writing teacher needs a subject that will inspire students to argue, to use rhetorical methods that were set up in other theories going back to the writings of the Greeks on argumentation. And, she said, while we drank cappuccino at a second-floor café on Guadaloupe Street, alongside the UT campus, she wanted a subject that would be unfamiliar enough to students for them to find it challenging, important enough to arouse their interest. That, she said, was how she came up with the new unified subject for E-306, the subject that some at UT found part of an effort by Brodkey and her allies to indoctrinate students in a leftist point of view. The subject was court decisions on cases of civil rights and discrimination. The reading would consist of the texts of court opinions on key cases, these texts, Brodkey said, being a form of expository writing. Students, she said, "could be taught how to read them, how to tear them apart." The course would be called Writing About Difference.

Brodkey outlined her plans in a memo to the Lower Division English Policy Committee on March 20, 1990. This was a few weeks before the racial incidents at Phi Gamma Delta and Tau Delta Tau, but not before the university had started formal discussions of multicultural change. Already, as Brodkey put it in her memo, the faculty senate and the university council, the two main governing bodies at UT, had begun to discuss "the need to educate students on diversity and related topics." Brodkey reminded the other members of the Lower Division English Policy Committee that Dean Standish Meacham had only shortly before formed a Committee on Multicultural Education. She went on to say, "We can make a substantial contribution to the university's efforts." The new E-306 course, Writing About Difference, she announced, had made Dean Meacham "enthusiastic." Then lapsing into the sort of turgid, pretentious prose one hopes Brodkey would have eradicated if one of her freshmen had committed it, she said that she and the head of Lower Division English, Jim Kinneavy, were working on "a pedagogy based on exploratory discourse, appropriate for examining and generating context dependent arguments."

All along, and despite many accusations that the revisions represented a blatant attempt to turn the curriculum into a tool for political instruction, Brodkey and others in the English department who supported her proposed course argued that there was no thought at all on their part to use freshman composition as a means of insinuating a radical view of American society into the tender minds of Texas freshmen. When I visited her two years later during her last semester at Texas, Brodkey was emphatic on that point. She bridled at the accusation that students would have been judged on the political correctness of their ideas. Who, after all, could say that Supreme Court decisions, which would form the bulk of the readings, were radical documents? The subject matter proposed by Brodkey was interesting, important, vital. Students needed to learn to argue points about such sensitive matters as race and discrimination, but they could formulate whatever opinions they wanted about them, she argued. Her goal was to create an environment in which they could formulate and express their views in a clear and compelling fashion—that's all.

"I agree that it's very political," she told me during my visit to Texas, "but not in the way people say it is. It doesn't require you to take any particular position. The purpose is to interrogate everything, including your own ideas. That's why we wanted the theme of difference. It was because we wanted a topic that was important to students and we know that students do this at 3:00 a.m., talking to people who are very like-minded. We wanted them to develop a public language for speaking about a set of issues that they will have to deal with."

Still, the minutes of a meeting of the Lower Division English Policy Committee on April 3 show that Brodkey and her supporters were thinking about multiculturalism as well as about writing skills. "The topic and text," Brodkey said, "would serve at least two important educational goals: first, the entire semester would be devoted to an examination of the difference between opinions and arguments; second, the course would contribute to the university-wide effort to integrate multicultural education into the undergraduate curriculum."

There was an additional element in Brodkey's original proposal that fueled skepticism over her ostensible disavowal of political indoctrination. She proposed to supplement the readings of court cases with a single textbook that would be mandatory in all E-306 classes—and which, indeed, she urged graduate students who would be teaching the class to read over the summer break. The text was *Racism and Sexism: An Integrated Study*, by Paula Rothenberg, the head of the same New Jersey Project that we encountered in an earlier chapter. Even a cursory examination of her book would uncover a clear, eccentric, highly negative view of American life, one emphasizing many of the favorite themes of multiculturalist philosophy, especially the relentless victimization of women and people of color by the white-male power structure. Rothenberg begins with trendy definitions of the prevailing sins, especially that one we have seen cropping up in other debates: "racism = prejudice + power." Sexism, she says, "involves the subordination of women by men." Racism and sexism, those twin insignia of the American experience, are often conscious and intentional, of course, but they can more insidiously be unconscious and unintentional, Rothenberg argues, engaged in by people who passionately believe themselves to be neither.

"One assumption of this book," Rothenberg writes, "is that racism and sexism pervade American culture, that they are learned at an early age and reinforced throughout life by a variety of institutions and experiences that are part of growing up and living in the United States." In one section of her book, she introduces the concept of "oppression" to describe "the pervasive nature of sexism and racism." She speaks of "the profoundly comprehensive and personally crippling impact these two phenomena have on people's lives," and she then presents a series of essays that tend to support her assumptions. The first is a 1937 autobiographical sketch called "The Ethics of Living Jim Crow," by Richard Wright, which is an evocative and powerful description of growing up black in the South and learning the rules of being a black person.

There are dozens of essays, a few of them excellent and important, like the excerpt from Wright, others tendentious and even badly written. Their cumulative effect, not surprisingly, is to depict America not as a place that has striven over the past few decades to knock down the barriers to equal opportunity and to change the way things were when Wright described them roughly fifty-five years ago, but as a place that wallows in such Stygian and unrelenting oppressiveness that it is hard to understand how the all-powerful white male racists and sexists failed to have Rothenberg's book burned and its author sent to prison, much less failed to prevent her from getting taxpayer funds from the New Jersey state legislature to work for the "integration" of feminist scholarship in the school curricula.

One characteristic essay in the book is "Racist Stereotyping in the English Language," by Robert B. Moore, which starts out with this premise: "If one accepts that our dominant white culture is racist, then one would expect our language—an indispensable transmitter of culture—to be racist as well." Moore goes on to give examples of "racist terminology," particularly in the connotations attached to the word "black," as in "blackguard," "blackball," "blackmail," and others whose origin, the author suggests, is in the negative view the dominant white society has of black people.

The article goes on in this vein and is certainly interesting, but it fails even to consider the possibility that there is an explanation of the phenomenon described other than the one based on racism. It does not deal with what would seem to be a crucial historical fact: that most of the words given as examples to prove the existence of contemporary

American racism predate the existence of contemporary American culture. It does not raise the possibility that the symbolism of "black" versus "white" could be naturalistic in origin, having to do with the dark of night and the light of day, rather than with the existence of racial difference. The Chinese language, for example, which evolved in a society with only one race, has similar connotations as English for the words "black" and "white"—black in particular appearing in such Chinese expressions as "black market," "black hand" (a metaphor for an evil person), and "black society" (a literal translation of the Chinese expression for criminal gang).

Still, despite the evident one-sidedness of these essays and of Rothenberg's accompanying explanations, the Lower Division English Policy Committee held a vote on the use of the Rothenberg text, and it passed 4 to 0, with one abstention.

The abstention was important. It was the first glimmer of resistance to the reform from an English department that would in all likelihood have sleepily approved of Brodkey's revision of E-306 had not a small band of dissidents blocked the way. One member of the committee, James Duban, a professor of nineteenth-century American literature and an experienced writing teacher, wondered in a note to Brodkey about the appropriateness of having a single text. Duban, who came to UT in 1977, is a native of Boston and a graduate of the University of Massachusetts who got his Ph. D. at Cornell in American intellectual and literary history. He is what might be called a classical academic liberal—tolerant, reasonable, cultivated, soft-spoken, deferentially polite but firm in his convictions. In his letter to Brodkey he showed appreciation for the "cordial tone of our discussion," but he contended that the graduate assistants who would teach E-306 should have a "variant text." Duban told Brodkey that another member of the committee, John Ruszkiewicz, who was a specialist in the teaching of writing, was unable to attend the committee meeting, but he also had reservations about the single text.

Ruszkiewicz is that rarest of all things in the Texas English department, a registered Republican who voted for George Bush in the 1988 election—though he says that that has no bearing on the way he teaches his course. He is a pale, courtly man who, when moved to the occasion, mines pure veins of eloquence. Two years after these early exchanges, I met with him in his office at UT and heard him give his reasons for opposing the Brodkey revisions:

This was a syllabus that I couldn't teach. Or, at least, there was nothing in all of these readings that I could teach except in an oppositional way. Students who were in the political center or to the right of center wouldn't find anything in that course that reflected their point of view, except for the Supreme Court dissenting opinions, which were rare. I asked: "Are there any readings in the Rothenberg book that are incompatible with each other?" and John Slatin [the committee deputy chairman and an ally of Brodkey] couldn't find one that was. So the students would have had a book in which all the opinions agreed with each other and a teacher who agreed with the book. What does the student do?

At this point Ruszkiewicz shrugged over the obviousness of it all. Rare, he believes, is the eighteen-year-old freshman who would venture into independence in the face of all that authority. For Ruszkiewicz there was a blatant absurdity in the situation, especially given the alleged purpose of freshman composition, which is to teach writing skills, not political ideas.

"All of the readings would have come from a single perspective in a course on argumentation and rhetoric!" he said. "They," he continued, meaning Brodkey, Slatin, and the other advocates of the new E-306 syllabus, "were unable, in a course called Writing About Difference, to come up with more than one perspective. They were apparently incapable of doing what they were asking their students to do.

"It was difference without diversity," Ruszkiewicz said. "They had managed to take out all the differences with their point of view. This was stunning to me. Why didn't they allow one other book? The graduate students would mostly have chosen *Racism and Sexism* anyway, and they would have won, but they were so arrogant and so sure of themselves that they wouldn't allow a single other textbook."

That is true. In a memo to the Lower Division English Policy Committee, Ruszkiewicz complained that "an anthology selected to raise the issue of 'difference' should itself demonstrate an awareness of 'difference.'" It should be a collection of essays "sufficiently diverse to challenge the assumptions of instructors and students alike." This was not the case with the Rothenberg text. Attached to Ruszkiewicz's memo was a list of eight other readers that, he felt, "present a range of social/political issues for classroom discussion."

On April 15, a few days after the racial incidents at Phi Delta

Gamma and Tau Delta Tau had taken place, Brodkey responded to Ruszkiewicz in a memo of her own. She reiterated that the value of the course lay in part in its contribution to "multicultural education," a need, she argued, that had been "underscored by recent events on campus, though I would hope that we do not require overt acts of racism to justify a course in which students would think, read, and write about civil rights, civil rights law, and civil rights cases." A couple of weeks later, on May 1, in a memo spelling out guidelines for the new E-306, Brodkey linked the study not just of difference but of racism and sexism to the encouragement in students of civility and respect for others.

"If students don't begin exploring racism and sexism in college classrooms, then I can't imagine where else in this country anyone is likely to learn how to broach these complex and critical issues—to say nothing of learning how to read, think and write critically about them," she said.

Actually, there are other places to learn how to deal with these complex and critical issues—by reading the newspapers, by going to work, by living in the world. Moreover, there are no doubt many things that students will most likely learn about only in college class-rooms. Brodkey's memos indicated a view of the university as a place for the acquisition of certain perspectives on the world. At times her political agenda shone through her writing like a high-intensity searchlight. Attempting to answer objections to *Racism and Sexism*, she wrote: "I am not compelled by the argument that there are opinions and arguments that would provide a balance to the authors' or that other books would provide 'a wider and more challenging range of opinions.' That's true but moot." She did not choose the Rothenberg text, Brodkey said, because it included every possible point of view but because it was "a way to focus students and teachers on work that has been done on 'difference,' and to give them some time to think about how those who work on and/or live with inequity define, describe and analyze the problems they see."

One of the criticisms of the new theory of composition courses is that it has abandoned such matters as style, grammatical correctness, the poetry of language, on the grounds that such rules serve what is sometimes called a linear, patriarchal logic. And so it is worth noting here that Brodkey, in charge of a program to make better, more precise writers out of University of Texas freshmen, used the verbs "compelled" and "focus" in the dubious ways she did and repeated the word "argument" within seven words of its first appearance in a sentence. It is strange to see a teacher whose very purpose is to show students ways to acquire rhetorical skills, fomenting a clunker like "those who work on and/or live with inequity." But it is unfair to single out Brodkey in this. She is one of many people at the universities who claim to be liberating us from stale orthodoxies of thought, but whose wooden language indicates that she is on a kind of rhetorical automatic pilot, failing to engage in the freshening self-interrogation she claims to want to encourage in students.

Beyond that, it is tempting to see in Brodkey's clumsy, bureaucratic prose a hint of her real purpose. Surely she had nothing against students becoming better writers. Still, it is interesting to see how little there is in her memos about teaching students the fundamentals of written expression, hardly anything about grammar and structure and the use of words. Perhaps teaching these things was taken for granted, and there was no need for Brodkey to say anything about such matters as usage and style. And yet in her reply to Ruszkiewicz, it is the importance of the subject matter that took priority, as she declared that she wanted students to focus on "difference" and on "inequity" to the exclusion of everything else.

It should be noted that E-306 at Texas is taken only by the 40 percent of the entering class that fails to score high enough on a writing test to be excused from it. The course, in other words, is basically a remedial one, aimed at teaching students what they should already have learned in high school—namely correct forms of written expression. Freshman composition, in short, would seem to have a kind of second-class-citizen status among course offerings at Texas, not a program of study that would arouse powerful passions.

Why then did it tear the English department apart? This is not an easy question to answer. The first faculty members to oppose the Brodkey E-306 proposal, with its single-textbook, single-subject philosophy, did so not so much on the grounds that the single subject was a bad subject, or that its choice had been ideologically motivated, but that it was the only subject—and that this was, quite simply, not the best way to teach remedial writing. In August, for example, Jim Duban published an article entitled "A Modest Proposal" in the *Daily Texan* that outlined some of his pedagogical objections to the Brodkey proposal.

"I have come to feel," he said, "that the various *topics* that motivate students to write should receive only passing attention from the instructor, whose primary obligation is to offer freshmen intensive feedback about grammar, style, tone, form, cogency, organization and audience." Duban, in other words, felt that the single-subject approach was objectionable for more than political reasons, that any single subject or single text would have been objectionable. "Different students," he wrote, "sometimes feel inspired to do their best work when writing about different topics." Duban's seventeen years of experience in the teaching of writing, he said, led him to "see no value in politicizing freshman English by restricting the range of issues which students may be allowed to address."

In August 1990, Brodkey released a "tentative syllabus" for E-306: Rhetoric and Composition, Writing About Difference. It was a truly flimsy document, objectionable not only on political grounds, though on those grounds as well, but also on the grounds that there was not much in it. The syllabus covered fifteen weeks of activity. It had seven reading assignments, a couple of them ("How to Write a Review" and something called "MLA Documentation") seemingly nonpolitical. Two of the assignments were essays from the feminist-multiculturalist pantheon. One was an essay called "Making All the Difference," by Martha Minow, a leader in the field of feminist legal criticism; the other, "White Privilege and Male Privilege," by Peggy McIntosh, whose workshop on the "five phases of pedagogy" we saw in the previous chapter. There were additional essays on the struggle of blacks for civil rights (Richard Kluber's "The Spurs of Texas Are Upon You"), on disabled people (Richard Scotch, "Disability as the Basis for a Social Movement"), and on homosexuality (Donna I. Dennis and Ruth E. Harlow, "Gay Yourth [sic] and the Right to Education"), the latter two drawn from academic journals and, no doubt, not easy reading for the bottom two-fifths of the Texas freshman class. In addition, there were readings on court cases involving discrimination and civil rights. That was all—seven readings in fifteen weeks. As for writing, there were ten "script assignments," in which students were asked to write a fragment of an argument, to define a term, or to summarize a point in the readings, in fifty or one hundred words. Two of these script assignments concerned Minow; one, McIntosh; six had to do with the court cases. Finally, there were six "writing assignments," involving longer essays—three of them on Minow, one of them a book review, and two on cases of discrimination. There is not a single word in this syllabus, not one, about problems in writing. It all has to do with the subjects about which the students will write.

In September, offering a "different approach" to E-306, Duban circulated, as a possible basis for an alternative to the Brodkey proposal, a thirteen-page syllabus that he had developed and used during his years as a writing teacher. It asked students to write "persuasive essays about topics of interest to you" or "about topics that I make available for your convenience." Different classes were given over to different techniques and problems involved in writing, like variety in sentences, excessive coordination, passive versus active voice, dangling modifiers, parallelism, wordiness, metaphors, stereotypes, triteness, and others. The class would read various essays, by writers such as Daniel Boorstin, Isaiah Berlin, Arthur Schlesinger, John Kenneth Galbraith, and Joan Kelly, both as examples of good writing and subjects of discussion, even as students wrote their essays and then revised them in light of comments Duban made on their first drafts. Duban's credentials to submit this syllabus were unassailable. In 1981, he had won a five-thousand-dollar President's Associates Teaching Excellence Award for the teaching of composition.

Duban and Ruszkiewicz were not the only faculty members qualified to comment on the Brodkey proposal. Another member of the department with long experience and special knowledge as a composition teacher was Maxine Hairston, who was the coauthor with Ruszkiewicz of a major textbook on writing. Hairston, unlike Ruszkiewicz, was known as a liberal, and she was in favor of multicultural education, including a two-course requirement in what she called "cultural difference." But instruction in multiculturalism was not the purpose of freshman writing, she believed. Indeed, she said, it would be pedagogically harmful if made the center of composition.

Freshmen, Hairston argued in a letter to Meacham, the liberal-arts dean, are too concerned about their grades to express "thoughtful or honest" opinions on such matters as race and discrimination, "particularly if they believe the teacher would disagree with them." She felt that focusing on those subjects would also make minority students uncomfortable in class. They would, she wrote, "not relish having their lives and experiences written and talked about by other students whom they find naive and uninformed." The issues that Brodkey wanted to make the sole concern of the entire course are "extraordinarily complex social and psychological issues," Hairston wrote, and few English department faculty have had the time to develop "well thought out presentations of the material." In short, helping students to become "independent thinkers and confident writers" cannot happen "in classrooms that are politically charged and intimidating to students new to the University."

Comparing the Duban syllabus and the tentative Brodkey syllabus is like comparing a bottle of aged first-growth Bordeaux with some acidic brew served in a plastic container. The fact that the departmental majority preferred that their students drink the latter rather than the former in itself suggests the all too common link between politicization and lowered academic quality. But the alternatives to the Brodkey syllabus were not merely rejected. The reaction against the reaction against Brodkey was, as we will see, one of nail-spitting fury, of an explosion of ad hominem attacks and of paranoid accusations about some vast right-wing conspiracy financed by the reactionary American establishment. It was, in short, a reaction utterly disproportionate to the arguments being made by the opponents of the Brodkey proposal. Why?

Initially, Duban, Ruszkiewicz, and Hairston were arguing from the standpoint of pedagogy. And yet, the controversy over freshman composition stemmed from a deeper difference. At its root, the conflict involved a struggle between two intellectual universes at Texas that had been growing too big for each other for years. One of these universes, represented in large part by the younger faculty members and supported by the chairman of the department, was composed of new ideas that would challenge the status quo, which is characterized by what Rothenberg herself calls the "comprehensive systems of oppression" that operate in American life. In this universe, teaching students to write had become part and parcel of the New Consciousness, of the effort to visualize American society differently than before, to remake the American identity by removing the legitimacy of customary ideas about the country and its history.

As long as the ideas of the younger generation had been restricted to individual classrooms, to papers in the scholarly journals, and to symposia at the regional conferences of the Modern Language Association, the more traditional professors really didn't mind. There is no record that Duban, Ruszkiewicz, Hairston, or Gribben, who, as we will see, was weighing in on the controversy in a more public way, ever opposed the feminist perspectives, the encouragement of cultural diversity, deconstruction, the New Historicism, or any of the other trends sweeping the MLA. Even when Brodkey and company seemed to seize on freshman composition as a way of making their challenge to the status quo a standardized part of the curriculum, her opponents saw the issue as E-306 and E-306 alone. It was only slowly that some of them began to realize that something more than a single course was at stake and to understand that Brodkey, in fact, was a kind of emissary from a different world, which forced her opponents to constitute themselves as a universe in their own right.

It was the pro-Brodkey forces, including some in the English department and a few howling supporters outside of it, who saw in the Duban-Ruszkiewicz-Hairston-Gribben challenge something vastly more important than the fate of a single course. What happened was that the theretofore quiet, almost invisible, effort of the true believers to impose a tendentious political vision on the university was exposed to public view. And, put most simply, they responded, not by answering the pedagogical objections of their detractors, but by trundling out the multiculturalist art of warfare, whose first proposition is to win by portraying the enemy as the face of evil.

The scene was a panel discussion at the enormous convention of the Modern Language Association in San Francisco at the end of 1991. The panel, the second installment of a two-part series of panels, brought together perhaps fifty teachers of composition for a general discussion about many of the questions at issue at UT and elsewhere. Linda Brodkey, having gained fame from the controversy at Texas, was one of the panelists, but neither she nor any other member of the panel spoke a word during the two-hour session. The members of the audience spoke, prompted when one of them told the story of a homophobic paper he had received from one of his students.

The man who raised the issue announced that he was a homosexual and therefore personally affected by the student's offensive remarks. The question was: What to do in such a situation? Should the matter be brought up privately with the student? Should the paper be read in class for comment?

Various members of the audience at the MLA had different reactions to the problem of dealing with homophobic prejudice and hatred in the classroom. As the conversation wore on, however, a striking absence became (to borrow a rhetorical device quite trendy in the academy) present. While there was much said about combating racism, sexism, and homophobia, one thing that almost never came up during the entire panel discussion was student writing and how to make it better. In his "Modest Proposal," Duban had warned that by focusing on writing topics, rather than the techniques of writing, the teachers of writing would fail to impart to their students the lessons that they really needed to succeed in life. The conversation at the MLA panel never touched on such matters as the poor writing of many college freshmen or ways to impart to students some sense of the beauty and power of language, of how to turn to advantage that remarkable instrument called English, enriched and refined over the course of centuries. All of the talk centered on politics—on how to combat the evils of society in writing classes.

What I had stumbled on, I learned later, was a meeting of the members of the club of what is sometimes called critical literacy. This accident led me to a new discovery when, a few weeks later, I arrived at the University of Texas to look into the battle over freshman composition. I realized that Linda Brodkey and her E-306 accomplices were in a sense a branch of a larger national movement implanted in Austin, one of whose major goals is to transform writing teachers into proselytes of the New Consciousness. What the composition teachers did was apply the social theories, mass-produced at places like the MLA, to the teaching of writing. Whereas in the good old days of freshman composition you learned classical form, organization, the hazards of dangling clauses, of mixed metaphors and malapropisms, of hackneyed phrases, of clichés, and of the need to use words like "compel" and "focus" correctly, now you would learn how writing itself is implicated in the struggle for power.

The operative term, "critical literacy"—a counterpart to what is called critical legal studies, which is very big at the Harvard Law School and other prestigious institutions—is a part of critical theory in general, that word "critical" another of the many code words adopted by the multiculturalist movement. Actually, "critical" means heavily influenced by the economic determinism of Karl Marx. The main notion of critical legal studies is that the law, while appearing to be a neutral and impartial set of rules, actually functions to help maintain the domination of society by the dominant group. Critical literacy holds that reading and writing do pretty much the same thing. Or as C. H. Knoblauch, a professor of English at the State University of New York at Albany, put it: it demonstrates "the extent to which people with authority to name the world dominate others whose voices they have been able to suppress."

Critical literacy was what some of the members of the Texas English department, previously so innocent of all of this, discovered once, propelled by the conflict over E-306 to go to the library to do academic combat, they started reading up on the main journals in the field of composition, *College English, Rhetoric Review, College Composition and Communication*. Nobody should be condemned to reading much of this stuff, which is turgid, repetitive, and extremely self-satisfied, but both John Ruszkiewicz and Maxine Hairston, one a conservative, the other a liberal, eager to learn more about the new currents of thought wafting about their field, read through reams of it, each of them producing papers on the way the teaching of writing had been captured by politics. Ruszkiewicz's is entitled "Critical Literacy and the New Forcers of Conscience." Hairston's is "Diversity, Ideology and Teaching Writing." Both mined many characteristic and incriminating nuggets from the literature in the field:

> The context of writing is inescapably interactional and finally power structured or political.—Carolyn Ericksen Hill, Associate Professor of English and Director of the Center for the Teaching and Study of Writing, Towson State University, Maryland

> The pursuit of self-evident and unquestioned goals in the composing process parallels the pursuit of self-evident and unquestioned profit-making goals in the corporate marketplace. —James Berlin, Professor of English, Purdue University, West Lafayette, Indiana

> [We have to teach] an expanded notion of rhetoric that understands language as the site of struggle over socially produced meaning.—Lester Faigley, Director, Division of Rhetoric and Composition, University of Texas–Austin

> All teaching supposes ideology; there simply is no value free pedagogy. For these reasons, my paradigm of composition is changing to one of critical literacy, a literacy of political consciousness and social action.—James Laditka, Instructor in Writing, Mohawk Valley Community College, Utica, New York

> [Standard English is] an instrument of domination by the privileged.—James Sledd, Professor Emeritus, Department of English, University of Texas–Austin

> It is of course reasonable—if that is what we believe—to try to inculcate into our students the conviction that the dominant order is repressive, that they should feel angered by the injustices

done to others, that an emancipatory vision should be formulated, and that its praxis should be exercised.—Charles Paine, Graduate Student, Department of English, Duke University, Durham, North Carolina

[Those of us] who try to make a pluralistic study of difference into a curriculum are calling students to the service of some higher good which we do not have the courage to name.—Patricia Bizzell, Professor of English and Director of the Writing Program, College of the Holy Cross

We can affirm the freedom to dissent radically in the classroom by refusing equal time to ruling powers.—James R. Bennett, Professor of English, University of Arkansas–Fayetteville

Those who occupy the best positions a discourse has to offer would have a vested interest in maintaining the illusion of speaking rather than being spoken by discourse.—Linda Brodkey

There is much plain boilerplate in this. These are the phrases that fill up the pages of Modern Language Association writing these days like boulders in a ditch. Fancy and specialized as the writing is, however, critical literacy is not very complicated. It means that language is not a neutral something that is available in equal measure to everybody, or even that it is consciously used and shaped by an author to reflect reality. Language is a creation of society that serves the holders of power, enabling them to maintain that power by controlling the very way in which thought and ideas are expressed—even while, of course, giving the impression that the way things are, the status quo, is entirely rational, inevitable. Thus, for example, the rules and regulations in writing that have traditionally been taught mirror the rules and regulations of a society dominated by white men. The grammar of language mirrors the grammar of political hierarchy. As Ruszkiewicz summed it up: "Traditional writing instruction can only reproduce the status quo." It inhibits change, keeps women and minorities in their inferior places, favors that "linear, patriarchal logic," which is really only the logic of the dominant class, race, and gender.

The idea seems ridiculous on the face of it, since the great historic challenges to power and authority have been based on the same mastery of language and rhetoric that, the critical theorists hold, perpetrates the power of the dominant culture. One of the reasons for the triumph of Martin Luther King, Jr., is that he was a better

rhetorician than his opponents. Still, all you have to do is leaf through
the pages of the journals in the field of writing and you will see the
critical literacy argument everywhere. Open, for example, to the first
article in the first *College English* of 1990, and you will see "The
Sublime and the Vulgar," by Karen Swann, identified in the article
as an assistant professor of English at Williams College. Swann has
clearly mastered the standard MLA prose style, whose purpose, in
my somewhat-jaundiced view, is to show the writer's profundity by
the use of a very complex and elusive jargon, sentences like: "But the
discourse on the sublime promotes an anti-critical, affective mode of
engagement with power which turns a perception of the arbitrariness
of things to the advantage of at least certain representational forms,
as the subject becomes oriented to the shape or figure for its own
sake, in the register of aesthetics." Swann, I think, is saying that the
ruling class uses the idea of standards as a way of maintaining their
power against what they see as the vulgar masses—the masses these
days being, says Swann, "the feminists, minorities and Marxists."

In the next volume of the journal, a piece on black women writers
reminds us of an article of faith: even if black women writers sometimes portray black men as violent, as rapists, as criminals, we should
all remember that "the ultimate source of black women's oppression
is white racism, which also victimizes black men." That may be true,
but what is it doing in *College English*? A regular section of the
journal is called "NCTE to You," NCTE being the National Council of
Teachers of English, which publishes *College English*. The notes in
the first issue of 1991 are devoted to excerpts from speeches at an
NCTE conference in Baltimore, held in November 1989.

The first speech excerpted is by Anne E. Berthoff of the University
of Massachusetts, her subject being "Paulo Freire's Liberation Pedagogy." Here is a brief spark from a large flame. Freire, a Brazilian
campaigner for peasant literacy who was once exiled from his country
for fourteen years by the military government, is the author of a book
called *The Pedagogy of the Oppressed*, which serves as a cult classic
for the advocates of critical literacy. Freire believed, as Berthoff points
out, that it was not enough to teach oppressed peasants to read,
because if they merely read the discourses of the dominant culture,
they would be unable to liberate themselves from their oppressed
position. They had, as Berthoff puts it, to be taught "words directly
connected to peasants' everyday survival concerns." By doing so,

Freire "involved them in talking and thinking about their situation—acts which led them to discover that their misery was not God's Will."

Berthoff is explicit in her belief, which seems, judging from NCTE, to be widely accepted, that writing teachers in the United States should, as she puts it, "adapt Paulo Freire's theory and practice to our own courses," there being, it would seem, no qualitative difference in the condition of feminists, minorities, and Marxists in American society and the oppressed peasantry of South America. Berthoff says: "We have ways of transforming our society which are neither violent nor millennial." The important thing in this work of transformation is "To see to it that cultural literacy is not equated with lists of facts." No, "liberation pedagogy," she says, means "reading the world and reading the word." It means that literacy must be united with a "consciousness of consciousness," meaning, it would seem, an awareness of oppression and the need to do something about it.

Other speeches: the poet June Jordan tells the conferees that the universities are places that reflect the "national power structure" and are, as *College English* summarizes it, "out of touch with the needs of a racially and culturally diversifying citizenry." Jordan is quoted as saying that universities were deemed to be good insofar as they were unicultural. "The more people your standards of admission could reject, the more people of cultures . . . other than your own that you could exclude from your core curriculum or patronize, the better the school," she says. Having a good education meant knowing *King Lear* but nothing about "the prayers, chants . . . the unified perspectives of Native Americans." But, she confirms, times are changing, since "some of us have looked into the future, and we have seen that the future will not be white, or spoken or written in standard English."

A lot of this, both the speeches and the scholarly articles, involves a kind of applied Marxism, the creation of a connection between what Marx called the structure and the superstructure. The structure in this case is the power of the white race and the male sex; the superstructure is the language, the grammar, the rhetorical methods used to maintain that power. This is true. The analysis of the use of language as an instrument of social order is not far-fetched; nor is it original. Incorrect grammar excludes people just as bad manners do. It was not an accident (as the Marxists, including current Marxists, love to say) that slaves were prevented from learning to read and write. George Orwell's Newspeak is a language of totalitarian control, and so is the language of China's *People's Daily*, and so too was the use of Latin rather than the vernacular as the language of literature in medieval Europe. Newspeak and the *People's Daily* channel thought, limit consciousness, anesthetize the brain. Medieval Latin limited access to knowledge, kept it in the hands of the reigning theocrats.

What is actually kind of funny is the failure of the critical theorists to see the extent to which they are the ones now captured by a thought-channeling jargon, how their corrugated-iron constructions imprison them in petrified dogma, utterly unattached to any actual experience of the world. Still, it is not difficult to see the simplistic appeal of the theories of critical literacy in contemporary America. They provide an explanation, a startling vision of the world for those who feel that they have been excluded from the full benefits of American life, or who feel that they have suffered from prejudice. The problem with the theory of critical literacy is not that it is entirely wrong and useless. The problem is that, like so much of the multiculturalist thrust, far too much is made of a few useful insights. They are stretched too thin, stated with exaggeration, immoderation, proclaimed to explain everything, and brought into the service of an eccentric, certainly disputable, vision of the nature of American life whose main premise, only modestly caricatured here, is that there is little to distinguish late-twentieth-century America from eleventh-century theocracy.

No doubt, the students in the bottom two-fifths of the class at Texas need help writing with greater power, with more imagination, with more accuracy. Anyone who has seen freshman writing might assume that freshmen need help with the basics—bad grammar, incorrect word usage, wordiness, clumsiness of expression, prefabricated jargon that substitutes for thought itself—more than with some radical vision of American society. They also, frankly, need to know why it is more helpful, especially when time is limited and choices have to be made, to know *King Lear* than Native American chants. To assure them that their nonstandard English is just as good as standard English is to doom them to a cruel fate, because once they get out of college, they will find that it is not as good—even if the tenured, salaried, retirement-pensioned, and medically insured teachers who inculcated them with that nonsense still have their positions at the university.

"I and other professors across campus see an inconsistency between imbuing students with a hope for economic and political equality of opportunities while denying these students a foundation of writing skills essential for success," Duban wrote in his "Modest Proposal."

Put another way, students need to be taught the tools of success to rise up in the lousy patriarchal hierarchy of American life if they are to avoid continuing to be its victims. Anybody who wants to empower them will teach them how to outdo the patriarchy at its own game. That is how the excluded have always succeeded in American life, by slugging it out in the ring of achievement, and prevailing over an establishment too decadent, too complacent, too well fed for the fight. To tell students that the key to empowerment is to demand respect from the dominant culture is to deceive them.

In May 1990, months before the debates about E-306 became public, a bombshell landed in the middle of the Texas English department. It was in the form of an article in *Texas Monthly* by Gregory Curtis, who is now the magazine's editor, in which he asked, "Did you hear about the party with the flag burning?"

Curtis explained, by way of background, that the English department is one of the largest and most powerful at UT precisely because students from all departments have to take courses in it to graduate. He reviewed its recent history, its division into two groups—one made up of "older and more established professors who believe in traditional literature and traditional teaching," the other comprising younger people "who see in literature a 'tool of oppression,' as a typical phrase goes, and teaching as a way of proselytizing for their gender, their race, or their radical—most often specifically Marxist—political beliefs."

The younger members of the faculty, Curtis wrote, had a party at the end of the previous spring term at which each person was supposed to bring something Texan to burn. In the background of this was the emotional debate then taking place on the Supreme Court's decision affirming the constitutionality of flag burning. Indeed, here and there across the country American flags were being burned in celebration of the Court's action. And so at that junior faculty party, a fire was started around midnight on the street outside the home of the host. Texas road maps were thrown into the fire. Some graduate students contributed papers by professors they did not like. Finally, as Curtis described it, "in went a Texas flag, which, despite some determined but comical efforts, would not burn completely."

The flag burning was only one incident that Curtis cited in an article not intended to portray the English department radicals in a favorable light. The attitude that led faculty members to engage in acts of anti-Texas symbolism governed classroom teaching as well, he wrote. He reported on one student known to him who signed up for a sophomore survey of literature, another UT requirement, to find the professor announcing that the students in her section of the course would "read only the works of women from developing countries." Then, describing an incident that had aroused much talk in the English department, he mentioned the Hispanic professor who, as a member of the English department executive committee, tried to have his own sister, getting her Ph.D. at Texas, hired for a full-time job on the Texas English faculty. The University of Texas does not hire its own graduate students, so the sister was rejected, whereupon the Hispanic professor claimed that the refusal had been made for political and ideological reasons. A special meeting of the entire department was held "to try to avert any charges of racism."

It was into this harmonious environment that Alan Gribben entered the nascent controversy about E-306. Indeed, in his article, Curtis seemed to have had Gribben in mind when he described "an intense whisper campaign that has now spread outside the University of Texas to other schools" centering on a professor, unnamed by Curtis, "who is hardly racist or sexist in any rational meaning of those words."

A couple of years earlier, Gribben had been the only faculty member to vote against the proposed creation of a master's program in ethnic and Third World literatures, an ideological crime that had unleashed the first accusations of his alleged sexism and racism. Up to that point, Gribben, who was forty-nine years old in 1990, had had an entirely solid and respectable academic career. In a world where publishing in scholarly reviews is the most important criterion for success, he had clearly done well. His list of books, articles, and conference papers is a closely spaced six and a half pages. He is the author of the two-volume *Mark Twain's Library: A Reconstruction*, along with thirty-six scholarly articles and twenty-four book reviews, many of them on Twain. In the two years leading up to his political problems in the department, Gribben, as he put it in a letter to his chairman, "earned a 92 percentile rating in the College exit surveys of students." It seems hard to believe that members of a major department of the humanities where, supposedly, the values of tolerance and respect for difference are being taught would embark on a campaign of innuendo and ostracism over a simple negative vote regarding a new M.A. program, but that is exactly what Gribben says happened.

Minutes of the meetings on the Third World course indicate that Gribben wanted to have two votes, one on the Ph.D., which he favored, and one on the M.A., which he opposed. His argument was that the master's degree was too low a level for that degree of specialization. Students, he argued, should be better grounded in the American and European canon before venturing down less explored paths. He also thought, as he once wrote to me, that the pairing of "Third World" with American "ethnic" literature was "amateurish." Certainly that combination, though almost universally accepted, is more a political demand that all of the "oppressed" forms of expression be put into the same category, than a conclusion regarding some essential commonality between the two.

In any case, thoughtful as Gribben's objections to the course were, some of those dwelling in the superheated atmosphere of the UT English department saw them as nothing less than a right-winger's fury at the invasion of the New Consciousness, at the audacity of putting ethnic and Third World literature on the same plane as the classics of European and American books. But there is no indication that the scholar of Mark Twain (he who remarked "Soap and education are not as sudden as a massacre, but they are more deadly in the long run") held to such outmoded views. And, in any case, as Gribben well knew it would be, the entire proposal, including the M.A., was adopted by a vote of 41 to 1. (As Huck Finn might have put it: "Hain't we got all the fools in town on our side? and ain't that a big enough majority in any town?")

What happened as a result of Gribben's sole negative vote is a matter of one person's word against another's. Gribben says that his ostracism began. It was then that anonymous pieces of hate mail appeared in all of the 274 mailboxes in the English department. His salary increases for two years were 0.75 percent a year. His graduate students, he says, were pressured into dropping him as their dissertation adviser. Some of Gribben's faculty colleagues, like Duban and Ruszkiewicz, confirm that Gribben was indeed shunned, that many people became frightened even to be seen talking to him in the

corridors of the English department. After about a year, Gribben
decided to appeal to his colleagues for an end to his pariahdom, and
he begged for mercy at a meeting of the Graduate Studies Committee,
of which he was a member. Immediately afterward, he and his wife,
a Chinese-American named Irene Wong, and his two children all
went to the Christmas-season holiday buffet. "It was like walking into
an iceberg," Gribben said. "Irene saw how people stepped back from
me and turned away. We laid our plates down and walked out, and
as we did so, the crowd opened up to make way for us, as though we
were lepers.

"I don't know if you've ever seen anybody cut out from the herd,"
Gribben told me. "You can take it for a few weeks, but after a while,
you just can't take it anymore."

Perhaps if Gribben really was a conservative, his treatment would
have pained him less. The fact that he viewed himself as a liberal,
as someone repelled by the very idea of the right wing, made his
punishment even harder to bear. And so in plaintive memos of five,
six, or more pages, each written to the dean, Standish Meacham,
and to Joseph Kruppa, the English department chairman, Gribben
catalogs the injustices being done, asks for redress, recounts his liberal
history.

"Believe it or not," he writes in one memo, he was arrested during
an incident he refers to as the "Third World Strike" at Berkeley when
he was a graduate student there in the 1960s. At Berkeley too he was
chosen to "mentor" the new African-American teaching assistants,
"owing to my reputation as someone unusually sympathetic to their
needs." And now, he says, "here I sit, as the 1990's dawn, with my
departmental and community image in shreds, cast as a supposed
enemy of the very causes and people I have championed." In another
letter, he recounts how one student "came to me in tears and reported
that she was 'under so much pressure' from graduate students and
faculty members that she would have to replace me as her Ph.D.
dissertation supervisor." He says that his reputation as a sexist and a
racist, built up through innuendo and rumor, pursued him when,
finding his ostracism at Texas intolerable, he began to look for employment elsewhere. "Numerous schools," he said, put him on a short list
of candidates "and then mysteriously dropped my candidacy at the
point of inquiring among my present colleagues about my departmental reputation." At one midwestern school, he reports, following tele-

phone calls to Texas, some female members of the department threatened to quit if Gribben was hired.

Kruppa, when I visited him in Austin, gave me a prepared statement on Gribben portraying his claims of persecution as unfounded. Kruppa addressed the claim that Gribben's graduate students had been pressured into abandoning him. He didn't have many graduate students in the first place, no more before his negative vote than after, Kruppa said. The department chairman's statement is a three-page typewritten manuscript with an additional three pages of supporting documents (principally an account of Gribben's teaching load from 1983 to 1991, showing that his academic duties continued more or less as they had been before the famous vote) attached. There is nothing in it about rumors and innuendo, about low salary increases, about charges of racism and sexism or being shunned in the hallways. Gribben, Kruppa said, tried to "elevate one person's skewed vision of the world into a general principle, into an evaluation of a complex and varied English department." Along the way he "has tarnished the reputation of a fine department and the hardworking individuals within it."

Kruppa's arguments notwithstanding, it is certainly a little odd that a scholar could have an untroubled tenure in a department for fifteen or sixteen years and then suddenly, with a single vote, run into serious trouble. But as the *Texas Monthly* pointed out, Gribben was living in a rapidly changing environment, during which time what might be called the MLA liberation army was sending its cadres out to the hinterlands to spread the message of poststructuralism, of feminist scholarship in its several varieties, of the new historicism, social constructionism, gay and lesbian studies, Marxism, ethnic and Third World studies—in short, all of the various regiments in the army of ideological multiculturalism. The new Ph.D.'s coming up in the best universities tended to be in these new fields, so the hiring at Texas was decidedly in the direction of the New Consciousness.

Since 1985, twenty-four new faculty members were hired in the English department. Nineteen of them, by one insider's analysis, belong to one or another of the schools of thought in what might be called the MLA cult. "If you go out to the best graduate schools and hire the candidates that most people are after, they're going to be working on the cutting edge, not on the things I was working on in graduate school, which would be anachronisms now," Kruppa told me, adding that when he was in graduate school in the 1960s doing a dissertation on John Donne, he had never heard of deconstruction, didn't know that there was such a thing as feminist criticism or other "new critical approaches." The field, he said, is much more exciting now. There has been "a very healthy transformation of the profession." He is heartened by the "different voices being heard now," by the "discourses that we simply didn't hear when I was in graduate school." But it would be a mistake, he said, to characterize the Texas English department as leftist. "The department is famous for its diversity in the fullest sense of the word," he said. "There are some people on the extreme left and a few on the extreme right, but most of the faculty falls into the large middle," Kruppa said. "I think the nature of the department has been seriously misrepresented by the opponents of E-306, especially by one person," he concluded.

That "one person" was Gribben, who, having learned of the new proposed E-306, and not concurring with Kruppa about the great "diversity" of the Texas English department, saw in it a politically motivated assault on the humanities in the making. His eye, like others, caught on the title of that single textbook recommended by Linda Brodkey, *Racism and Sexism*. Gribben was also concerned that the new course, which was a university-wide requirement, was being rushed through by the English department without the usual scrutiny by the curriculum committees or the creation of trial sections that, in his experience, accompanied even lesser changes than the one being proposed for E-306.

Important in this is that in May, a month or so after Brodkey's original memo, Kruppa and Brodkey had put out a press release to the local Texas media announcing the new course and its philosophy. Even though E-306 was a university-wide requirement, there had, at this point, not even been a vote on the course by the entire English department faculty, much less the full faculty senate. Nonetheless, there were Brodkey and her chairman already announcing publicly that from now on students in E-306 "will read and write about landmark court decisions on civil rights and affirmative action." The Rothenberg text will provide "supplementary readings" in order, Brodkey was quoted as saying, "to steady students with respect to the topic of difference."

In the past, the press release said, students might read George Orwell's "Shooting an Elephant" one week, and then "write a persuasive essay on colonialism"; another week they might read Ralph Waldo

Emerson's "Gifts" and then write an essay on the author's "literary technique." The problem with that old approach, the press release said, was that the various essays had "no thematic relation." The new course will have a common theme, Kruppa announced in the press release, but the change is also a "side effect" of "the ever-increasing necessity for Americans to understand the social implications of differences in race, ethnic background, age, gender, sexual preference and religion."

Kruppa and Brodkey seemed aware of some criticisms that might be leveled at the new course, in particular that it might, as they put it in the press release, be seen as "an indoctrination to the liberal point of view" and that students will lose something in the removal of those classic essays that used to make up the readings in the course. In fact, in proclaiming the "side effect" element in their proposed revision, Kruppa and Brodkey implied that "the liberal point of view" certainly did guide the proposed change. Still, they hastened to deny what they had just implied. There would be no indoctrination, said Brodkey. "The question that will be addressed in this class is not 'What is your position on racism or sexism?' but 'What do you have to support your argument?' " And as for the classic old essays, she contended, nothing will be lost. "I don't think anybody's going to miss those old saws at all," she was quoted as saying, presumably referring to such "old saws" as "Shooting an Elephant" (my own point of view on this is that every paragraph of "Shooting an Elephant" is worth vastly more than the collected works of Paula Rothenberg).*

An obvious question could certainly be raised at this point, namely: What could be more important than showing students in a writing course just how good writing can be? What could be better than inspiring them with a few great examples of argumentation and style? Brodkey's casual dismissal of the likes of Orwell and Emerson and her apparent preference for academic cant shows her to have a certain tin ear when it comes to literature. Still, while it is hard to see any value in her position on the "old saws," she does hit upon a truth with regard to indoctrination. After all, even eighteen-year-olds, while perhaps not very knowledgeable about the major civil rights decisions of the Supreme Court, are not tabulae rasae on which any extremist ideology can be inscribed at will. Students are pretty savvy at detecting efforts at indoctrination. Brodkey herself makes

---

*Is it belaboring a point to note that a "saw" refers to a proverb, a piece of conventional wisdom, not to a classic essay like "Shooting an Elephant"?

this point. Talking with me in 1992, she said, "It's naive to think that people twelve years of age or older believe anything just because you say it to them."

The fact remains, however, that a student's ability to resist indoctrination does not justify your effort to go ahead and try to indoctrinate anyway. All the freshmen in Brodkey's E-306 would have had to support their arguments was the stuff in Paula Rothenberg's putative sociology text along with, presumably, the unbiased opinions of the acolytes of critical literacy who volunteered to teach the new course. Students were not going to be freely expressing themselves on Sunday afternoon football or Communist oppression but on racism and sexism. Beyond that, as one law professor at Texas, Douglas Laycock, who reviewed the cases included in Brodkey's syllabus, noted: "If the reading materials and the instructor are tilted to a particular view, it is illusory to say that the bottom half of our freshman class will be able to create good arguments for a different view."

Gribben noted all of this about E-306, but he acknowledges that his decision to step into the debate was also accompanied by a hope: that by calling attention to the way things were being done in the English department with E-306, he might get senior administrators to see that that was the way things had been done to him after his vote on the Ethnic and Third World Literatures program and maybe to use their power and influence either to end his ostracism or to transfer him to another UT campus. And so, on June 18, 1990, he took a fateful step. He had a short, three-paragraph letter published in the *Daily Texan* in which he declared that "without even pausing for a vote," the English department "will start explaining to presumedly benighted UT students how they ought to feel about issues of ethnicity and feminism."

"After I wrote the letter to the *Texan*, I really thought they would say 'Let's talk,' " Gribben told me—"they" being Kruppa and other administrators who, up to that point, had ignored his pleas for help. "I really had the sense that it might open things up," he said, his tone that of a man who now recognizes the foolishness of his optimism. "I thought it might bring them to the point of saying, 'Let's talk about your situation. Let's talk about the department.' But it didn't."

And when it didn't, Gribben decided a week later to send a second letter, this one to the local newspaper, the Austin *American-Statesman*, which in May had run an article on the new E-306 based on the Kruppa-Brodkey press release and had followed that up with an editorial praising the new course. "The largest required course at the University of Texas at Austin—English E-306, rhetoric and composition—has now fallen prey to the current mania for converting every academic subject into a politicized study of race, class and gender," he wrote. He mentioned Rothenberg's "slanted sociology textbook." And he reported that students "will begin having their social attitudes as well as their essays graded by English Department instructors in what has to be the most massive effort at thought-control ever attempted on the campus."

It is fair to say that from this point on and for the next year or so the English department at UT became a battleground. One element intensifying the conflict was the national press coverage that freshman composition got at UT. The *New York Times* ran a stringer's piece in its weekly "Campus Talk" section that gave a straightforward account of the controversy. In September, the nationally syndicated columnist George Will lambasted E-306 as an illustration of a nationwide phe-nomenon—"political indoctrination supplanting education." Along the way, there were sarcastic articles about E-306 by John Leo in *U.S. News and World Report* and by Jonathan Yardley in the Wash-ington *Post*, Yardley praising Gribben for his "courage" and terming Brodkey's plan for E-306 "a consciousness-raising indoctrination in politically correct attitudes toward racism and sexism and any other ism that might happen along."

Well before this national press attention, several developments came in rapid succession at UT. First, the Rothenberg text was dropped. Kruppa explained the decision to the press this way: "A lot of people had trouble with the book because it had weak material and we were only going to use a small part of it." In her conversations with me, Brodkey explained matters differently: "We dropped the Rothenberg book because of the difficulty of coordinating the readings with the court cases," she said. Kruppa told the press that a new syllabus would be developed for E-306 that would retain the Writing About Difference idea. There would, he said, be a packet of materials, including court cases, a few essays from the Rothenberg book, and some other, as yet unspecified readings.

Whatever the reason for dropping Rothenberg, the fact is that by then other faculty in other parts of the university (whose students would also have had to take the revised E-306) were letting senior administration officials know that they saw the course as biased. And so dropping the Rothenberg text, which happened at the end of June, was a way of chopping off the most blatantly political branch of the proposed composition program without really changing its essential political thrust. Still, in mid-July, fifty-six members of the UT faculty published a petition in the *Texan* complaining that the proposed E-306, even with the Rothenberg textbook taken out, "distorts the fundamental purpose of a composition class." Some of the departments unhappy about the new course let it be known that they would teach their own writing classes rather than have students attend what they saw as mandatory political-sensitivity training in E-306.

On July 24, 1990, Dean Meacham, responding to these pressures, announced that the new E-306 would be postponed for one year to allow more time for debate. Meacham had earlier been a supporter of the course, though he supported it in principle and had not actually known of its precise contents. He announced his decision after a meeting at which the university's president, William Cunningham, was also present, along with Joseph Kruppa. One person at the meeting said that the president made it clear that the senior administration at Texas was not ready to do battle with an aroused public, skeptical alumni, and a dubious faculty on that particular issue.

But the postponement—which was seen at the time as exactly that, a postponement, not a cancellation—hardly put the E-306 matter to rest. Indeed, Brodkey was still the chairperson of the Lower Division English Policy Committee, and she continued to work on her revisions. She produced her proposed syllabus for the course even after Meacham's decision, figuring that it would be put into effect the following year. The English department itself was still powerfully influenced by the advocates of the New Consciousness, and just as equally as ever distrusted by the traditionalists. Meacham's interference with the English department's autonomy to decide the content of its own courses was highly unusual. It was to be the basis for the counterattack by the supporters of E-306, who began soon to contend that a vicious, well-financed conspiracy by the extreme right had intimidated the university administration into capitulating to the critics of E-306, thereby violating standard academic procedures and posing a threat to academic freedom. Indeed, the fact is that the most intense and outrageous part of the battle was about to begin.

For some months in the fall and winter of 1990 a small cutout of a paid advertisement in the *Daily Texan* was kept on display in a glass case outside the English department office. It was a petition published in the newspaper and signed by forty members of the English department faculty, including Chairman Kruppa. The first paragraph of this document, entitled "A Statement of Academic Concern," reads as follows:

> WE, the undersigned members of the English faculty, protest the continuing attacks on the professional integrity of Professor Linda Brodkey and other members of the Lower Division English Policy Committee. We take particularly strong exception to Geoff Henley's ungrounded speculations (Daily Texan 10/10/90) about Professor Brodkey and the Committee's motives in proposing the revised syllabus for English 306. We deplore and condemn ad hominem attacks and misrepresentation at the expense of genuine intellectual debate.

This collective response to a student journalist's article in the *Texan* is certainly a strange document—strange not only because of the last sentence, which does not actually mean what the forty professors of English apparently want to say. More important, here is roughly half of the faculty of a major academic department not only bothering to defend a colleague against a student's attack and to chastise the student for what they regard as an intemperate expression of opinion, but then displaying that chastisement for months in a glass case, as though it were a copy of the university's treasured Gutenberg Bible. It happens that a couple of months earlier, James Duban, the American literature specialist who was among the first to protest the Brodkey revisions, was embroiled in a scandal that helps to put the faculty's response to Henley in perspective.

Duban, who struck me as a mild, polite, entirely temperate person, happily married to Karen Duban and the devoted father of their three children, was accused by a female faculty member of sexual harassment. It happened this way: Duban had seen a petition that was being circulated in the English department in which the signers, again including Kruppa, had deplored the "unprofessional manner" in which opponents of Writing About Difference had "misrepresented the substance and aims of the course." Duban was upset over those words "unprofessional" and "misrepresented," which he felt, as an opponent of the new course, made him out to be both lacking in dignity and a liar. The document was, he understood, being circulated for signatures, and so he tried to call its sponsors to let them know of his concern. He left a message on Ramon Saldivar's answering machine, Saldivar being one of the people circulating the petition.

Duban waited to hear from Saldivar, but when he had not done so by around ten-thirty or eleven o'clock that night, he called the home of a married couple, both of whom were on the English faculty and both of whom were also involved in the petition. This was Kurt and Susan Heinzelman, enthusiastic backers of the new E-306. Duban says that he apologized for the lateness of the call and asked if he could speak to both of them on the phone at the same time, but Susan Heinzelman replied that her husband was not feeling well and could not come to the phone. Duban and Ms. Heinzelman then talked for some minutes and Duban warned her that if the petition as it then read was published, he would consider it defamatory and libelous and would take whatever steps he could to protect his reputation. Then a couple of weeks later, Susan Heinzelman was quoted in the *Texan* accusing Duban of sexual harassment. Heinzelman's argument: "When a full professor calls up an untenured lecturer who's a woman at 11 o'clock on a Friday night and threatens her with a libel suit, that's sexual harassment."

When I asked Susan Heinzelman about this accusation, she said that the *Daily Texan* reporter, who also called her up rather late at night, had misquoted her. She had said "harassment," not "sexual harassment," she told me, arguing that when a full tenured professor threatens a junior nontenured professor with a lawsuit, harassment is taking place. She added that her being a woman did have something to do with the charge. "I felt that gender played a part in it," she said. "Harassment is in part constituted by the difference in power between one gender and another."

Heinzelman, who made no public effort to rectify the misquotation at the time, seems to be saying that what Duban did was indeed sexual harassment; it's just that she did not call it that. In any case, I asked others about the sexual harassment charge, and the argument in general was that since Duban outranked Heinzelman and could thus cause her damage in her career at Texas, the accusation of sexual harassment was justified. Duban was creating a "hostile environment" for a woman, and according to one of the criteria established by the Equal Employment Opportunity Commission, that alone supports the accusation of sexual harassment. This, for example, was the way Brodkey explained the matter when I raised it with her. So did

Kruppa. Neither of them seemed to have been informed of the fact that Heinzelman had been misquoted in the newspaper and had not made a sexual harassment charge at all.

The incident, which upset Duban greatly, came across to me as a standard element in the English department's response to the critics of the revised E-306. Here after all was Duban with seventeen years of experience teaching composition and the author of "A Modest Proposal," which had politely questioned the proposed new course for its pedagogical inadequacies—and what was the response of his colleagues? Rather than reply to his arguments, they seized an opportunity to let fly one of those charges of sinfulness that have the same effect on campuses these days as charges of being a Communist or a fellow traveler had two generations ago. In short, they smeared him. And, of course, that is what forty members of the English department did with Geoff Henley also, though instead of accusing him of sexual harassment, they labeled him as the purveyor of a more general sort of sleaze.

I asked Kruppa: If Duban was guilty of sexual harassment against Heinzelman, what kind of harassment was involved when forty professors publicly and in print and over a period of several months attacked a mere undergraduate?

Kruppa's answer was twofold. First, he said, a full professor has more power over a lecturer than a group of professors has over an undergraduate. This, I agree, is technically true. The undergraduate is not seeking a salary increase or tenure. Still, I am not sure how many twenty-year-olds would be entirely unfazed by the mass attack of the better part of an entire department. It did seem to me that Henley might have felt the English department to be a hostile environment.* Then Kruppa, a stylish, trim man in his fifties, with longish hair and a graying upside-down "U" of a mustache, said that to understand the faculty's response to Henley you merely needed to see how nasty his articles were. "Read his pieces," Kruppa told me. "They are not argumentative pieces. They are vicious personal attacks. The ones on me I didn't respond to because they were so scummy."

Well, I did read the Henley piece that elicited the faculty's petition against him. It begins with a summary of the Nigerian playwright

---

*Henley, it so happens, was unfazed. I met him for lunch at a student hangout, and he generally laughed off the English department members. I told him that Kruppa had assured me that the department had great "diversity." Henley's reply: "Oh, yeah, they're very diverse. They've got Marxists, deconstructionists, five varieties of feminists, new historicists, ethnic studies, and Third World studies types—very diverse!"

Wole Soyinka's *Play of Giants* (a nice multicultural touch, I thought), in which Soyinka parodies African dictators for wanting to place a giant statue of themselves at the entrance to the United Nations and then brutalizing "those who do not support their cause or admire their statue." Soyinka might have had Brodkey and her restructuring of E-306 in mind, Henley says, given that she "is imposing her own image to glorify the efforts of marginal factions." Brodkey, Henley writes, has waged "a campaign transcending dishonesty." Given the "incredibly biased nature of the readings," a student would have to be "incredibly brave" to dissent from the views presented in the course, he says. "No one would want to risk being labeled a racist or misogynist."

Whether or not this article was "vicious" and "scummy" is perhaps a matter of opinion, though I must say that I found it to be a pretty good piece of rhetorical expression. In fact, Henley's article represented something of a minority point of view in the student press, which was generally critical, not of Brodkey, Kruppa, and their supporters, but of Gribben, Duban, and Ruszkiewicz. During the summer, Gribben had been denounced at a campus rally called by the president of the student body to protest his opposition to the new E-306. According to the *Texan*, one member of the faculty, Kim Emory, spoke at the rally about "Gribben and company's hyperbolic and hypocritical attacks" on E-306. Another member of the English department, Barbara Harlow, said: "We need to recognize that there are academic death squads operating on our campus." It should be noted that Harlow signed the anti-Henley petition, a document that called for "genuine intellectual debate."

That was only the beginning of the assault on Gribben and company's integrity, motives, and professionalism. A student publication, *The Polemicist*, published a lengthy account of the E-306 affair called "Chronicle of a Smear Campaign: How the New Right Attacks Diversity," in which Gribben and others are accused of "hysteria," of perpetrating "diatribes," of being "wild-eyed," et cetera, none of which moved any of the English department defenders of "genuine intellectual debate" to complain about ad hominem attacks against some of their own. The faculty members who engaged in the debate on the side of E-306 gave some good examples of viciousness and scumminess of their own. In an article in the *Daily Texan*, a philosophy professor, Douglas Kellner, wrote an attack on the attackers of E-306, the first two paragraphs of which contain these phrases: "the reactionary right," "a well-orchestrated right-wing offensive," "a few conservative

English professors," and "a national right-wing group." The epithets "right wing" and "reactionary right," applied to people who, in an America of Patrick Buchanan, David Duke, and the Moral Majority, could be considered right wing only in the context of a university, appeared thirteen times in an article of nineteen short paragraphs. So did the phrase "McCarthyist tactics" and "thought police," a manner of expression that was deemed "vicious" when it appeared as "thought control" in one of Alan Gribben's letters. When the original plan to implement a new E-306 was postponed by the UT dean, Brodkey darkly suggested that if some students took the move as an example of institutional racism at Texas that would be pretty understandable. "I'm afraid of the message it's going to send out to the minority students," she told the *Daily Texan*. "I'm afraid that the message may be that the lives and intellectual histories of these students is of no interest to the University."

Kruppa himself was not always a model of dispassion. He told the Houston *Post* that opposition to E-306 was spearheaded by "two right-wing faculty members." Some of them, he said, "are ultra right-wingers who are members of the National Association of Scholars," the National Association of Scholars being a nationwide group of generally moderate to conservative views that is seen as the Great Satan by the academic left. On another occasion, Kruppa furthered "genuine intellectual debate" by talking of "a campaign mounted by a few zealots." He attributed the defeat of E-306 to "misrepresentation and misinformation on the part of a few people of bad intentions." In my interview with him, Kruppa told me: "A small group of people took it [meaning E-306] to the media and made it a media event for their own purposes." He seemed to forget that the first people on campus to take E-306 to the media were he and Brodkey in their press release on the new course, which is what led to the favorable editorial in the Austin *American-Statesman*, producing Alan Gribben's three-para-graph letter to the newspaper. Kruppa did not sign a petition criticizing himself for making ad hominem attacks rather than engaging in genuine debate.

Another point is worth making with regard to the student Geoff Henley. It could certainly be said that here was a young man doing exactly the sort of thing that was supposed to be encouraged by E-306, making an effective argument. Henley's article in the *Texan* showed none of the clunky syntax, the trite, pedantic jargon or the imitative usages of Linda Brodkey and her allies, who at times seem better qualified to take freshman composition than to teach it. But, then again, Henley was not a student in a composition class so he got no grade for his essay, and that's probably a lucky thing. Over and over again Brodkey, Kruppa, et al. maintained that different viewpoints would be encouraged in their E-306. Maybe that is true, but judging from the response of forty members of the English department faculty to Henley's article, it is hard to imagine that he would have been graded solely on the quality of his writing, and not at all on the content of his ideas.

In the end, the Brodkey E-306, even in the form it took after Rothenberg was dropped and the reading list was revised, was never put into place at Texas. Eventually, after a half year of battle, Brodkey and all the members of the Lower Division English Policy Committee resigned, even though the English department, by a secret ballot vote of 46 to 11, had given the committee a vote of confidence. When I saw her later, she told me that the committee had been maligned by Gribben in the press and left unsupported by the administration, so there was really no point in pressing on. Looking back on the whole incident, she said that she found that she was overwhelmed by events. Faculty from other departments expressed opinions on what she felt should have been an English department matter. The administration, in declining to support the department, sided with the course's critics.

"And then," she said, "Alan Gribben, who wasn't at the faculty meeting at which we talked about the course, came up with these letters to the Austin *American-Statesman* saying that we were going to indoctrinate kids. I think it was over at that point. I mean, I can't imagine a professor making a statement like that without having a lot of evidence.

"I guess he really believed that we were going to be indoctrinating students," Brodkey said of Gribben. "I don't really know him. He never came to my office or called me on the phone. He never said 'I'm really worried about what you are doing, Linda, and I want to talk to you.' I wasn't surprised that he was opposed, because there had been rumors, but I was surprised about the letters he wrote." Brodkey felt, moreover, that Gribben's public questioning of her motives, and his charge that she was engaged in "thought control," were outrageous. "It is a serious allegation to make against a colleague, and I see it as an extraordinarily irresponsible act. It's to take real liberties with your colleagues' lives, professional as well as personal."

Brodkey said that after E-306 began getting publicity in the local press, she began receiving hate mail and obscene phone calls—men saying things like "I'm going to shoot your cunt off" and "I'm going to cut off your nipples, you dyke." Around that time, she says, she was not feeling well. Strangely, she said, she received one postcard expressing the wish that she die of disease, even though she had told very few people about her health.

The charge that most upset her, she said, is that her goal was to impose her own politics on students. She believes that faculty members who claim that their own courses are free of politics are deluding themselves. She held to the point of view that politics permeates everything. To teach a traditional course is implicitly to support the political status quo. She identified herself as a "progressive," meaning she believed that the status quo "doesn't work." But she maintained that her critics "confuse my personal politics with my classroom role. I am left wing," she said. "I do have strong ideas. But I also think I know the difference between what I believe and what I feel is my responsibility in the classroom."

"I was a maverick liberal who unknowingly took on an entire network of enforcers," Gribben told me in a letter, written after he had left Texas and was settled into his new job in Alabama. The passage of time had not dimmed his outrage at the slander he felt he had to suffer because he had flouted the reigning orthodoxies of UT's English department. Certainly, he is not persuaded by Brodkey's claims to have suffered as much from the controversy as he did. Brodkey, after all, is still a featured speaker on the academic-conference circuit, where she continues to talk about "difference" and to be a leader in the critical literacy movement. If anything, her move to San Diego, where she is the head of a whole college-level program, not just a department, represented a bureaucratic step upward. She does not seem to have been punished because of what happened to her at Texas.

Gribben feels that Brodkey's charge that he was "irresponsible" and took "liberties with his colleagues' lives" is reminiscent of the tactics used by the pro–E-306 forces all along. True, he took the anti–E-306 side to the public, but Brodkey, Kruppa, and others in the debate gave interviews and made statements in the public debate as well. Put into juxtaposition with the threatening and obscene calls and letters she reports receiving, it insinuates that Gribben, by writing his views on E-306 in the newspaper, was somehow responsible for the expressions of hate directed against Brodkey, but this is certainly not true.

"You look at your feet when somebody makes those arguments," Gribben told me. "What can you say? It stops the debate." In fact, Gribben feels he took no "liberties" with Brodkey's life. Austin, Texas, and the university are very liberal communities. They do not correspond, Gribben says, to the redneck clichés regarding Texas harbored in the minds of easterners. Gribben, in arguing that Brodkey was politicizing E-306, was not inviting verbal violence against anyone. And, he feels, Brodkey's suffering from anonymous verbal assaults was certainly no worse than what he suffered from students and faculty members right there on the UT campus, in the student newspaper, at academic conferences, in speeches, transforming him from the "maverick liberal" he was into a symbol of the evil racist establishment. I remember once hearing Houston Baker, later the president of the Modern Language Association, speak of Gribben at a conference at the University of Michigan in October 1991. "Gribben was a radical at Berkeley," Baker said. "That didn't stop him from writing vicious articles in the *Daily Texan* and from really distorting the truth in terms of what had happened with the committee on E-306."

"They created me for their own purposes," Gribben told me. I had asked him why he bore the brunt of the radicals' attacks, while, for example, John Ruszkiewicz, a self-identified conservative, had not. "I believe that without foreseeing what would ensue, I had threatened them," he said of those who attacked him, "and I didn't even mean to threaten them as much as I did. It was unnerving for them because I set an example for other liberal-minded people who were agonizing over the increasing politicization of their departments, so I was a bad example." Ruszkiewicz, as a conservative, Gribben argues, was, paradoxically, less of a threat because his views would have been more expected. Ruszkiewicz, along with Duban and Hairston, were also either members of the Lower Division English Policy Committee or members of the writing faculty, so, unlike Gribben, it was harder to accuse them of evil behavior when they were dealing with a matter officially within their purview. Still, Duban, feeling isolated and uncomfortable in his department, took a job elsewhere in Texas; Hair-ston retired early. Only Ruszkiewicz of the department's four E-306 dissidents remains at Texas. He, it should be noted, has become associate director of the new Department of Rhetoric and Composition, separate from the English department.

One of the most disturbing things about Gribben's case is that none of the major academic organizations, those supposedly watchful for freedom of expression, took up his cause. Indeed, they took the other side in the Texas battle. We have seen Houston Baker accusing Gribben of "distorting the truth." It happens that shortly after that, in 1992, the year that Gribben, his life made all but impossible at Texas, moved to Alabama to start a new life, Baker became president of the thirty-thousand-member Modern Language Association. Well before that, the MLA had played a modest but interesting role in the UT controversy. A year after the revised E-306 was rejected, the MLA published a statement in its newsletter, which goes out to its members, entitled "Postponement of Course Raises Academic-Freedom Issues." The MLA's Committee on Academic Freedom and Professional Rights and Responsibilities, having read about the controversy on E-306, decided to look into it, the newsletter said. It gave a brief account of "the facts," an account that left out the content of the course that Brodkey was proposing. It concluded "that pressures from parties outside the university, like the National Association of Scholars and columnist William Murchison [who writes for the Dallas *Morning News*], may have played a role" in the decision to postpone the course.

The newsletter said "may have played a role," rather than "did play a role," so it is only offering a conjecture. Still, it offered no substantiation for this conjecture, other than the fact that there were people outside the university arguing that E-306 as conceived by Brodkey was a bad idea. The newsletter made no mention of the opposition inside the university, such as the threats of departments to offer their own writing courses if E-306 were adopted, or the petition signed by fifty-six faculty members opposing the Brodkey proposal. Then, again with no evidence offered to back up another bit of conjecture, the newsletter concluded that "the character of the debate on the Austin campus and throughout the state suggests that incomplete, inaccurate and distorted information may well have contributed to decisions affecting the course and the faculty members responsible for it." The truth is, the MLA statement goes on, that "at every stage the course design called for students to read arguments and court decisions on all sides of the controversial issues being discussed."

What is remarkable about this document is not only its blithe assumption that opponents of E-306 misrepresented it while those who supported it told only the truth. The MLA also assumed, again, it seems, on faith, that the E-306 proponents created a course in which "all sides of the controversial issues" would have been discussed. As we have seen, Linda Brodkey forthrightly acknowledged that the textbook initially proposed for the course did not present "all sides" at all, but that fact, she said, was "moot."

Another organization, one disposing of considerable prestige, also entered the dispute. This was the American Association of University Professors, founded about three-quarters of a century ago and known for its vigilance about threats to academic freedom. The AAUP's president, Barbara R. Bergmann, who teaches economics at American University in Washington, D.C., read about the E-306 controversy in the national press. She also received a copy of something called "An Interim Report on the Attack on English 306 and the National Association of Scholars," an anonymous, fifteen-page, single-spaced document put out by a previously unheard-of group, the Ad-hoc Committee on Subversion of University Autonomy.

This document, which could reasonably be accused of putting out "distorted information," came out at the height of the E-306 debate and advances the usual conspiracy theory, namely that E-306 was killed by "a series of right-wing institutions backed by equally right-wing foundations." The aim was a "roll-back" of multiculturalism that "explicitly targets not only multicultural elements in courses, such as the revised E-306, but all feminist, gay, minority and ethnic studies as well as non-academic programs designed to provide space of support for minority groups of students."

Since none of the opponents of E-306 ever said anything about "feminist, gay, minority and ethnic studies" (and since the president of the National Association of Scholars at UT had, when he was dean, instituted a women's studies major some years before), it was hard to see what was so explicit about the goals of this right-wing conspiracy. In any case, the document, which was widely distributed around the University of Texas in the weeks after the revised E-306 course was postponed by Dean Meacham, refers to such elements in the picture as the "inflammatory letters" that Alan Gribben sent to newspapers "around the state," thereby setting off "the whole hysterical smear campaign" involving "a carefully planned and well-financed operation with a national agenda," for which the anti–E-306 individuals at Texas were the "shock troops."

To her credit, Professor Bergmann called Douglas Laycock of the UT Law School and asked him for his informal view of the matter. Laycock told her in a long return letter that she had read "an extreme version of one side of a complex dispute." He offered some opinions, calling the Rothenberg book, for example, "truly awful . . . riddled with factual errors," and flawed by its tendency of "relentlessly pre-senting the view that all is evil in America." By choosing it, the proponents of the course had forfeited their credibility, he said. Most important, Laycock, a long-term member of the AAUP who once campaigned together with Bergmann for equal pensions for female academics, dismissed the idea that any question of academic freedom had arisen. "The power of committees to impose a common syllabus on individual instructors is not an academic freedom right," Lay-cock wrote. Academic freedom is "a right of individuals," not of committees.

Bergmann, however, persisted in her inquiry. She had noted, she told me, that it was unusual for a dean first to express support and enthusiasm for a course planned by a department and then, suddenly, to withdraw his support for it and, in effect, kill it via a postponement. It was possible, she felt, that outside pressures on the university, pressures that the administration had refused to resist, had led the dean to his action. And, if that were the case, as she put it to Laycock, "might not there be a justifiable concern about the climate for aca-demic freedom at Austin?"

A good question. Bergmann tried to interest the staff at the AAUP, particularly the staff of Committee A, which is concerned with aca-demic freedom, in investigating the situation at Texas. Ernst Benja-min, who is the senior permanent member of the AAUP staff, got together a committee to look into E-306 and a few other matters. Originally, the intention was to visit several campuses and to prepare a report, but the committee did no such thing. What it did do, indeed, well illustrates the reflexes of major portions of the academic establishment. It used the occasion of a putative inquiry into events at UT to issue a proclamation on another subject entirely.

As Bergmann told me, the committee visited no campuses. It met for a single day and then issued a report, not on Texas or any other university, but on the subject of political correctness, which, for a few weeks, was something of a national media event. *Newsweek* had published a cover story brandishing the concept of the campus "thought police." *The New Republic* had written negatively about left-wing intimidation on campus. I myself had written an article in the *New York Times* headlined "The Rising Hegemony of the Politically Correct," which reported on the power on campuses of a kind of leftist orthodoxy. The campuses were in a tizzy about all the publicity. The allegedly politically correct were in an especial tizzy, accusing the press of sensationalism, of conducting a witch hunt, of manufacturing a nonexistent terror. And so the AAUP committee, supposedly considering the imbroglio at Texas, ended up making a pronouncement on political correctness in entire agreement with the PC point of view.

The statement, published in the AAUP's journal, *Academe*, accused the critics of PC of "sloganeering . . . name calling" and "irresponsible use of anecdotes." Their real motivation was an "only partly-concealed animosity toward equal opportunity and its first effects of modestly increasing the participation of women and racial and cultural minorities on campus." In other words, the AAUP, which is a body of university professors supposedly committed to the primacy of the disinterested quest for the truth, did not bother to look into the merits of the anti-PC arguments. In essence, the committee agreed with that Ad Hoc Committee on Subversion of University Autonomy that had charged the opponents of E-306 with wanting to roll back the gains of feminists, gays, and minority and ethnic group members at universities. And in framing the argument in that way, of course, the AAUP committee proved the power of the very force whose existence it denied. Once you have attributed to your opponents the motive of opposing "the participation of women and racial and cultural minorities on campus," you suppress debate without ever having to counter the actual arguments of the other side. You also illustrate the very tactic whose use you claim is highly exaggerated by the media.

I asked Barbara Bergmann about the committee's statement on PC. Perhaps, she replied, "it went a little too far in attributing bad motives to those who are raising the PC issue." But Professor Bergmann then went on to agree with its underlying spirit. "I think there is an attempt by the right wing to silence those who feel oppressed and who are protesting their oppression," she said.

In the end, the AAUP never formally investigated Texas, and it is just as well. It might have found, as I did, that the opponents of E-306 had a better complaint about violations of academic freedom than the proponents did. Certainly, as he packed his bags and left for his new job, Alan Gribben might have thought so. Gribben, however, was not likely to think that if he brought a complaint to the AAUP, it would get an impartial hearing.

"The last twelve years have loosened the tongue of racism and made it less unrespectable to say things that hurt other people, to make other people feel bad," Bergmann told me.

We started this account of conflict at the University of Texas with the question of race and racial conflicts, and we will end it on the same subject. In the battle between the two universes in Austin there were powerful echoes of the surrounding debate about race. It was rarely explicitly thus—though Brodkey did at times explicitly make that link. But there is little doubt, in my mind, at any rate, that much of the moral fervor with which the campaign in favor of E-306 was waged stemmed from the belief that changing the curriculum, making it deal with "difference," would advance the battle against racism and for inclusion. The issue was seen in those terms by many outside the university as well. Bergmann, for example, feels that "new scholarship," the demand for diversity, the stress on the oppressive and unfair aspects of the American experience, are justified as part of the battle against racism. She thinks that when the charge of racism is made on campuses across the United States, the charge is justified, as are demands that racism be combated by fundamentally changing the university's intellectual program.

But is the charge true, and does it matter? Certainly there is plenty of evidence that racism at UT is not endemic but aberrational. While the battle over E-306 was at its height, the president of the student body, who had won her office by getting 54 percent of the vote in a secret ballot, was a black woman and a firebrand named Toni Luckett. How could it be that a place so deeply drenched in racism and sexism had elected a person like her?

Then there were those two racial incidents on campus that spurred so many to action to combat the racist scourge. To many, particularly to black students, the incidents proved the existence of a deeper, albeit usually hidden, racism at Texas. These students, after all, were a minority among a largely white majority. All students of whatever race tend to be insecure about themselves, worried about their ability to compete, hoping to find that they belong. But the black students, many of whom are admitted by policies of racial preference, and often come from poorer families, arrive at Texas tenderer than most. Given that, when somebody scrawls FUCK YOU NIGS DIE on a car parked outside a white-columned fraternity residence that already resembles a plantation manor house, it is easy to see how cries of "institutional racism" result, along with demands for hate speech codes, for mandatory racial-sensitivity sessions, and for more courses on ethnic and Third World literatures, which are, presumably, antidotes to the Western culture that produced racism in the first place.

At Texas there was an effort to find out just how racist the institution was. Mark G. Yudof, the dean of the law school, headed a nine-member Committee on Racial Harassment that listened to all who wanted to testify before it and, without giving details about the specific incidents reported, concluded thusly: "Many speakers felt that they had experienced racism, resulting in deep feelings of personal anger, distress and isolation. . . . Various examples of racial harassment, both subtle and overt, were related." The committee recommended that students or faculty who commit racial harassment be disciplined, and it took great care in its definition of "racial harassment," trying to avoid the fate of some hate speech codes that were so vague and all-embracing that they were rejected by the courts. Texas used the definition of "racial harassment" as "extreme or outrageous acts or communications that are intended to harass, intimidate, or humiliate a student or students on account of race, color or national origin and that reasonably cause them to suffer severe emotional distress."

The committee also created a race-relations counselor, whose duties would be to receive complaints of racial harassment and help victimized students deal with attacks against them. In late 1993, after nearly three years, thirty cases had been handled by Curtis Polk, the race-relations counselor. They involved such complaints as those against the white male student who started speaking with a peculiar accent when some Asian students blocked his view at a performance; the Asian student who used the word "nigger" when he handed a fifty-dollar parking fine over to a black clerk; the woman who remarked to her Jewish office mate that "Jews are stingy." Polk said that all but one of these matters were handled via mediation, generally involving some calm discussion with the offending person and often a face-to-face meeting between the perpetrator and the victim. But only one case, involving a student who sent racial epithets over a global computer network, actually led to disciplinary action.

What are we to make of these incidents? Certainly, many instances of racism are not reported. Among those that are—such as the time in 1992 when, according to the *Daily Texan*, racist graffiti were found in some bathroom stalls—many probably do not come formally to Polk's attention. The thirty cases that did—meaning on average ten cases a year, or, on a campus of fifty thousand students, one case per five thousand students per year—do not, in my view, indicate the existence of an epidemic of racism that needs to be combated by transforming the curriculum. Appointing a sensible race-relations counselor to handle incidents that do arise seems to be an adequate way of providing relief for students and others who feel that they have been victimized.

Whatever the figures on racism, however, there is clearly the perception that racism exists, and it is not difficult to perceive why that is the case. "There are very few overt incidents," Yudof told me, speaking of actual racial harassment. "What happens is that when white Americans see events as these they say that they are anomalies; they're terrible but they are anomalies. When a black student sees them, he says, 'This is the tip of the iceberg; they don't really want me here; they don't respect my culture.' What impressed me was not the total number of complaints, but that the worldview of these groups is so totally different."

And so, given that assessment, what should a faculty do? The fatal flaw in the Kruppa-Brodkey approach lies in the belief that changing the basic premises of liberal education is going to ease racial tensions and increase multicultural understanding. Here is the *dérapage*, the point at which the civil rights impulse sends the locomotive off the tracks. The very educational values that led Texas from being an all-white, segregated, and quite conspicuously racist institution, which it once was, to one in which a black woman can be elected student-body president are the values that are corrupted when identity politics and group rights become the guiding principles of the classroom.

The English teachers said that E-306, and greater stress on "multi-cultural education," would have the result of reducing the allegedly rampant racism that existed at Texas. But almost the entire debate took place without any evidence whatever either that racism was rampant or, even if it was, that the proposed changes would do anything at all to reduce it. Do English professors really believe that telling people in a classroom to be racially sensitive will actually make them so? And, in the end, is turning a course of study into what many will see as an effort in political indoctrination going to improve anybody's understanding of difference?

George Santayana once said, "Fanaticism consists of redoubling your effort when you have forgotten your aim." He may have been wrong about that. At Texas, the bearers of the New Consciousness did not forget their aim. Santayana should have said: "Fanaticism consists of redoubling your efforts even when what you are doing cannot accomplish your aim."

Epilogue

THE EMPTY FORTRESS

Things could have been worse at the University of Texas, and in Brookline too. In both places the forces of politicization in education were held at bay. But as we have seen, the "emanation of virtue," in the Robespierrean sense, triumphed in other places. Certainly the forces of virtue have become extremely powerful, capable of joining the battle at any time and in any place, of deeply affecting life in places as far apart as newsrooms and elementary school classrooms.

What will happen next?

On the one side, the forces of the New Consciousness are on the rise, and, as George Orwell once pointed out, to be on the rise is an end in itself. "The object of power is power," he said in *1984*. "One does not establish a dictatorship in order to safeguard a revolution; one makes the revolution in order to safeguard the dictatorship." Certainly, this is true of the dictatorship of virtue. It is propelled by so many forces. There is post-1960s disillusionment; there are rising expectations; there is a general inclination in liberal-democratic societies to find fault in the large historical forces, rather than in individual acts of irresponsibility. There is the normal human propensity toward a foolish zealousness. There is the yearning for community that the sociologists are always telling us about. You read the journals with their boilerplate about "genuinely oppositional education," and you sense that much of what is politically correct stems from a desire to win the admiration of the rest of the New Consciousness cohort, to belong to the club. And there is also the American infatuation with the new. Susan Haack, a professor of philosophy at the University of

Miami, explained to me the power that novelty has in academic life. "If somebody submits an idea saying that she, or he, is going to do research that radically changes how we look at our world, how before everything was masculine and white and bourgeois, then that generates excitement. If somebody, more reasonably, comes along and says, 'I'd like to look into this, and I think that in doing so I might make a modest change in our vision of things,' that generates less excitement. The first is far more likely to win a research grant than the second."

Above all, perhaps, the New Consciousness senses that it is gaining power, and that alone is reason for its existence in the first place. Indeed, to come close to power takes a good deal of the risk out of an enterprise that presents itself as inherently risky. The fact is that assaulting the establishment, declaiming against the racism and sexism of society, reiterating the approved phrases about oppression and exclusion, promising to uncover previously neglected worlds, these require not a jot of courage these days. These are the sanctioned activities of the counterestablishment, the gestures and idioms that gain approval and lead to good opportunities, to jobs, to prizes, to book contracts, to prominence in American life. It takes no bravery to be a multiculturalist. There is no risk in smashing the icons. There are millions of dollars in foundation grants available for people who claim they are doing so. Linda Brodkey felt that she had to leave the University of Texas in the wake of the E-306 controversy, but in her field of composition and rhetoric, Brodkey is comfortably ensconced in what has become the mainstream. Alan Gribben, who left Texas also, is not.

Indeed, courage is now required to transgress the dictatorship of virtue. That is perhaps the greatest of the multicultural–politically correct victories. The upholders of the dictatorship of virtue have put the other side on the defensive.

It might not last. I sense that a lot of the enthusiasts of the New Consciousness are like the Red Guards of China's Great Proletarian Cultural Revolution. They will be swept along by their zeal and enthusiasm for quite a while, wreaking considerable damage during that time. They will impose the characteristics not of real but of ideological multiculturalism: they will replace the truly inspiring notion of greatness with the tepid concept of representativeness. They will push people to adopt, not a personal philosophy, but ethnicity, race, or sex as the principle of personal identity. They will exalt racial and sexual rage over reason. They will cover us over with a thick glue of piousness, which, in turn, will smother argument. They will undermine the quest for objective truth with a riot of subjectivities. They will turn almost anything that they do not like into one of the new cardinal sins—racism, sexism, sexual harassment, homophobia—and they will try to punish those who commit those sins. They will confuse knowledge and an appreciation of other cultures with cultural chauvinism, the superpatriotism of the small group. They will turn reading into an exercise in ethnic boosterism and the cultivation of "self-esteem," forgetting Kafka's admonition that a book should be "the axe that breaks the frozen sea inside us." And then their immoderation and mindlessness and the fact that they do not fulfill basic needs will get the better of them. The pendulum will swing eventually in the other direction.

Much of that will depend, however, on the courage of the bearers of the sometimes unspectacular but, in the end, always precious liberal tradition. In the late 1940s and the 1950s, a group of liberal thinkers, including such giants as Irving Howe, Sidney Hook, George Orwell, and others, realized that the liberal tradition was being sabotaged by a movement of Higher Virtue, known as the class struggle. It was represented, unfortunately, by a totalitarian power and defended by an intellectual class operating not so much out of the conviction that it was an unblemished good, but out of the fear of handing over a victory to the class enemy by admitting those blemishes. The liberal idea was almost plundered by these enablers of the totalitarian idea. The type was well represented by the French philosopher Jean-Paul Sartre, who, when asked to explain why he did not expose the faults of Soviet communism, replied: *"Il faut pas désespérer Billaincourt"*—we must not discourage the workers at the Renault factory at Billaincourt from waging the class struggle. There will always be a bit of excess, Sartre was arguing. It should not deter us from pursuing the cause of the people.

It was certainly a painful choice for the true liberals to declare their rejection of Sartre's argument and to uphold the principles of democracy and liberty as the paramount principles. They did so at a time when the fabulous panaceas of state control and class struggle had a certain glamour. Those who insisted on speaking the truth and on defending liberalism as a universal value, not, as the far left would have it, as an instrument of capitalist power, suffered a certain banishment from the ranks of the virtuous.

Afterword to the Vintage Edition

A few months after the hardcover edition of this book went to press, a federal judge in New Hampshire named Shane Devine decided in favor of J. Donald Silva in his lawsuit against the University of New Hampshire. Silva had been dismissed after a three-decade teaching career, when a sexual harassment judicial panel found him guilty of creating a hostile and intimidating environment for students in one of his writing classes. Judge Devine ruled that the university had violated Silva's First Amendment rights, and he ordered New Hampshire to reinstate him immediately and to pay him his back salary and his legal expenses—a total that probably cost the university around $300,000, including its own legal expenses. At first, the trustees threatened to appeal, saying at a press conference after the ruling that the decision was a threat to "true" academic freedom. Given the ridiculousness of the charges against Silva, it was hard to imagine that the university could have won had it done so, and that probably had something to do with its decision to drop the matter. Still, despite the court's apparent vindication of Silva, there was no sign that any of those who had accused him in the first place believed they had made a mistake.

"No one admitted, either publicly or privately, that anything wrong had been done," said Chris Balling, the physics professor who served as one of Silva's advisers while his ordeal was underway. Showing the absence of remorse, the administration and its faculty supporters continued to press in the University Senate for an expanded speech and harassment code of the sort that, one might have thought, had been thoroughly discredited by the outcome of the Silva case. The code clearly had been used in a political way, not to curb speech that amounted to harassment or injury, but to punish speech that was merely unpopular, that transgressed the sensibilities of the new Victorians on campus. As of this writing, the debate was still underway at New Hampshire, but it did not appear that the faculty had the votes to get the expanded code through.

Meanwhile, in Texas, Alan Gribben, who moved to a teaching job in Alabama after conditions in Texas became unbearable for him, put a case for reinstatement in letters to the university's new president, Robert M. Berdahl. His request was denied. In New Jersey, after lobbying by the National Association of Scholars, the state legislature voted against appropriating any money for the New Jersey Project, the organization whose aim was to foster "new scholarship" on women and minorities. The group's founder and director was Paula Rothenberg, who, it will be remembered, was the author of *Racism and Sexism: An Integrated Approach*, which was for a time the sole textbook proposed for use in the revamped Texas freshman composition course. After the cutoff of funds by the legislature, however, the Republican governor of New Jersey, Christine Whitman, dipped into her own discretionary funds to enable the New Jersey Project to continue.

One of the other things that continued, or grew in magnitude, was the institution of sensitivity training, which was extended to many new organizations, including the *New York Times*, where I work. The training at the newspaper was generally viewed by at least some who attended as silly, perhaps annoying, but not very harmful, at worst a waste of time. The well-intentioned philosophy of group determinism, the rose-colored stereotypes about group identity put forward by the outside facilitators hired to train the staff of the world's greatest newspaper in the new realities of our diverse world, did not appeal to some of the trainees who, after all, were among the brightest and most savvy people around. Elsewhere, however, diversity training was getting a worse reputation even as it was accepted more and more widely as a normal part of life. The newspapers carried one report of "cultural diversity" training at the Federal Aviation Administration during which male air-traffic controllers were required to run a gauntlet of women who fondled them and made comments about their sexual parts. I don't know if some men might have enjoyed this fondling, though, certainly, it would have been fatal to admit it if they had. The point of the session was to enable men to understand what it is like to be a woman and to be sexually harassed by a man.

Meanwhile, many of the trends described in the preceding pages continued. In September 1994, Harvey Sperling, the headmaster of the University School of Milwaukee, happily announced in a letter to parents that "Our theme this year is *inclusion*." The inspiration, Sperling announced, came from the national SEED project, based at the Wellesley College Center for Research on Women, which has encouraged the Milwaukee school to "explore issues of inclusion, multi-culturalism, and gender, among others, as they are encountered in our daily lives and in the literature." The SEED Project, of course, is the brainchild of Peggy Means McIntosh, whom we have met at a workshop for teachers in Brookline, Massachusetts, discussing "pinnacled learning" and "lateral learning" and the need for the schools to teach "racism, sexism, heterosexism, nationalism, regionalism, cultural issues." McIntosh, who was the subject of a laudatory front-page profile in the *Wall Street Journal*, continued to expand her influence, while the liberal education establishment pressed an appreciation of what it calls "diversity" as the key to better education.

The plan of eight towns in western Connecticut, for example, lists "enhance diversity and awareness of diversity," as one of its four goals. A group of seventy-five people "from various racial, ethnic and socioeconomic backgrounds" met to suggest "how quality and diversity might be improved in our schools." In other words, we not only have to improve quality. Diversity has to be improved also! Several recommendations were made: "Curricula must reflect a belief that students' educational experiences will be substantially enhanced through exposure to various races, ethnicities, cultures and socioeconomic groups" is the sentence of the plan listed next to the word "Content." But what, it might be asked, of people who do not hold to this belief, which is, to say the least, of dubious validity? Next to the word "Attitude" was this sentence: "Diversity must be stressed as a social resource through the use of diversity training techniques and programs." Then there was "Strategy: We must employ teaching techniques, academic programs, and extracurricular programs that are designed to allow actual interaction among students from diverse socioeconomic and cultural backgrounds." The plan continues in this vein for twenty pages, but what is it? It certainly sounds more like a political program, an effort to have every group given its pride of place, than an educational one. It sounds like the substitution of a kind of social therapy for real lessons and real learning. Needless to say, the plan has the usual verbiage about "role models" and "self-esteem." It asks teachers to pay attention to questions like "Whose knowledge do we use?" and "Whose knowledge has been historically excluded?" (Note in this a shift from the idea that different groups have different "perspectives" to the notion that they have different "knowledge.") The plan further asks teachers to make sure that "all cultures" be "given credit for their contributions . . . to the discipline."

There were also continued incidents of the sort that I recounted in the "Notebook" chapter of this book and showing the sensibility that has come to be known as political correctness in action. A certain Laura Bennet Peterson, denied tenure at Suffolk University in Boston, sued the university for violating the Americans With Disabilities Act. The university had refused to give her more time to satisfy the publishing requirements even though she suffered from chronic fatigue syndrome. In Corpus Christi, Texas, a fourteen-year-old girl sued administrators of both the National Science Foundation and Texas A & M University when she was barred from participating in an environmental study program called Planet Earth. NSF funding guidelines had restricted Planet Earth to blacks, Hispanics, and Native Americans, the logic being that "future environmental scientists . . . must come from all of the racial and ethnic groups present in our society." At the California State University in Chico, Joseph R. Conlin, a history professor of twenty-eight years standing, wanted to make fun of an administration memorandum that discouraged sexual relations between faculty and students. Conlin had noted that around the same time that the memo was distributed, an argument was raging over the use of university office space. Professor Conlin decided to exercise his free speech rights by writing a parody in the form of a memo proposing that the space be used for "innovative student-faculty conferences" and be furnished with a water bed.

Whereupon, Jacqueline Barnhardt, a history professor who had been appointed by the university to handle sex harassment problems, protested Conlin's little joke, saying in a letter distributed around the campus that Conlin's letter was not only "vulgar," it also violated sexual harassment laws by making some female students feel "unwelcome." She told a reporter for *The Chronicle of Higher Education*, which reported on the "fractured" department at Chico State, that Conlin stormed into her office after she wrote her complaint and demanded that she bring formal charges against him if he had indeed violated any rules. Conlin also wrote to Barnhardt, telling her (again, according to *The Chronicle of Higher Education*) that she used to be a "fat, jolly, harmless cipher," but had become a "nasty, scheming, back-stabbing bitch." Whereupon Barnardt did sue Conlin, charging him with "intimidation, coercion, and threatening, frightening behavior," all of which, she said, was motived by "gender bias, hatred, and retaliation." Another member of the department, Charles L. Geshekter, responded to a letter that Conlin had gotten from Barnhardt's lawyer. Geshekter's letter, *The Chronicle* reported, ended with the sentence: "I got two words comin' your way: 'Shut the f__ up.' "

The incident did not seem to indicate any particularly distinguished behavior on the part of the male professors who were sued. It did nonetheless illustrate a main point about the dictatorship of virtue, which is that acrimoniousness itself has now become a matter for litigation. Professors Conlin and Geshekter seem to have been trying to subvert the prevailing sanctimoniousness by being intentionally outrageous and offensive, making the point that, in debate and in exchanges of opinion, boorishness and intemperance are not to be confused with criminal offenses. When they were formally charged in Barnhardt's lawsuit with "gender bias, hatred, and retaliation," they seem to have proven their point.

Across the country in Pennsylvania, according to R. Randy Lee, writing in the *Wall Street Journal*, the state Human Relations Commission, the Realtors' Association, and the Pennsylvania Newspaper Publishers' Association agreed on a list of "unacceptable" words in real estate advertisements. Numerous words were banned, the idea being that phrases like "ocean view" could be offensive to the blind or "master bedroom" to women (the implication here was that the word "master" stood for the male and his dominance over the female). Mr. Lee reported that the Fair Housing Council of Suburban Philadelphia filed lawsuits against landlords and three newspapers demanding damages in excess of $1 million. An ad for a "rare find" in Chester was pulled after it was called "racist." The argument here was that the house was located in a largely black area, so the "rare find" phrase suggested that blacks rarely live in nice houses.

In short, in the year since *Dictatorship of Virtue* was published in hardcover, many incidents, small and not so small, reflected the conflicts engendered by the ongoing debate about the American identity. Conflicts over what are called "places of memory" in Chapter 2 were sharp and acrimonious. The Smithsonian Institution in Washington, D.C., after months of accusations and counter-accusations, essentially scrapped a planned exhibition on the end of the war in the Pacific. The exhibition, in the view of its critics (and I agreed with them), showed the post-sixties American habit of self-incrimination (and the belief in the Other as the incarnation of superior wisdom and morality) by exaggerating the fault involved in the dropping of the atomic bomb on Japan, while diminishing Japanese aggression, wartime atrocities, and the number of American casualties that were prevented when it became unnecessary to invade the Japanese mainland. Shortly after the fracas at the Smithsonian, the Japanese parliament approved the text of an ambiguous statement that amounted to a refusal to apologize for the suffering caused by Japanese aggression in World War II. What a wonderful illustration of multiculturalism! The Japanese culture does not permit a national apology even when one would seem, in light of such incidents as the rape of Nanking, to be due. In Judeo-Christian America, we want to apologize even when we have done nothing wrong. An equally sharp debate took place over several months in 1994 and 1995 when the National Center for History in the Schools released a report outlining what students should learn about American history in grades five to twelve.

The standards certainly were demanding. Students needed to know a great deal in order to meet them—probably a good deal more than most of them actually would know upon graduating from high school. The national standards were not, contrary to the view of some conservative critics, akin to a radical multiculturalist document. They represented no "dumbing down" of the curriculum. But the standards did, to me at least, mark the triumph of the multiculturalist sensibility in several ways.

First, there was a conspicuous attention to the roles of the various "victim" groups—women, blacks, and Indians—at every stage of history. The formation of the country, for example, was presented as a meeting of three civilizations, each of them treated as of equal importance—the West African, the Indian, and the European. The very idea that the European influence was not only the victorious one but was responsible for creating the institutions and values by which Americans continue to live was present in the standards only by implication. Second was the acceptance of what the standards called "multiple perspectives," a phrase right out of the multiculturalist handbook whose actual meaning is: There is no truth, there are only the conflicting visions that come from membership in a group. And so, for example, the section on the Civil War was divided into three parts, the first two of which consisted of what might be called the traditional subject matter. The first part concerned the causes of the war, the different systems and ideologies of North and South, the growth of the Republican Party, the existence of slavery as a factor in the conflict. Second was the actual course of the war itself, the different resources of the two sides, innovations in technology, and the nature of the political leadership of the Union and the Confederacy, the actual battles and how they shaped the course of the conflict. In this section, there was already a requirement to know "the position of the major Indian nations during the Civil War" and "the effects of the war upon these nations." Then the third part called for students to understand "the social experience of the war," specifically "the treatment of African American soldiers in the Union army and Confederacy," "the causes and consequences of the New York City draft riots in July 1863 and the irony of African Americans fighting for liberty and democracy at Fort Wagner a few days after the outbreak of violence against blacks in New York City," the role of "different perspectives" on the curbing of civil liberties during the war, the "roles of women on the home front and battle front," and "the human cost of the war."

In general, while the standards were far better than what was being taught at, say, the Hans Christian Andersen Schools of Many Voices in Minneapolis (see Chapter 8), there was an underlying theme visible in the first section of the standards, known as "Era 1: Three Worlds Meet (beginnings to 1620)." It was that West Africans and Native Americans lived in harmony with each other and with nature until the white Christian Europeans came along sowing the havoc and despoilation associated with the colonization of the New World. Is it wrong? No. Indeed, the cost of the creation of the New World is a part of our history, which should be understood by all of us. But is it the main element of the story? Again, the answer would appear to be no. In my view, at any rate, the main story would be the gradual unfolding over time of the liberal ideas enshrined in the Declaration of Independence, and the creation on the North American continent of the greatest prosperity under conditions of the greatest degree of liberty for the greatest variety of people ever in the history of our planet. That is not the main thrust of the history standards, though those themes are present for teachers who want to extract them. More conspicuous is the curriculum as a political compromise worked out among the various racial and sexual interest groups.

But, it might be argued, there has been, since *Dictatorship of Virtue* was first published, a major shift toward the right in American life, a sweeping victory of the Republicans in the midterm elections of 1994 that swept conservatives like Newt Gingrich and others into power. Doesn't that indicate a turning of the tide, that the forces of multiculturalism have been defeated at the polls and sent reeling into defeat?

Indeed, I find myself feeling that, yes, in some areas there has been a turning of the tide, or, at least, an ebbing of it. Press reports on the prosecutorial practices often associated with the quest for "diversity" revealed that there had been for some time a dark, inquisitorial side to multiculturalism, and some of that has diminished. There is, in some places, a greater awareness that the word "diversity" has been used to impose a single, correct opinion. Cornell University's resident adviser training no longer uses gay safe-sex films. At the University of Pennsylvania—where a new president, Judith Rogan, formerly provost at Yale, took office in 1994—some of the worst practices have ceased. The behavior code under which Eden Jacobowitz was prosecuted in the famous "water buffalo" incident (Chapter 3) was abolished. The mandatory freshmen reading program became less overtly political—one year, for example, the selections included some works by the English playwright Tom Stoppard, so the previously monochromatic themes of race and gender took on some variation. Jacobowitz himself ran for the undergraduate assembly and emerged as the single highest vote getter. The mood has shifted at Penn, according to some faculty members, in part because Rogan very early on put out the word that all students at Penn would have equal treatment regardless of race or sex, and that there would be no prosecutions because of the content of opinions expressed on campus.

There has also been the growth of a kind of anti-PC movement, especially on the universities and among women's groups, so that dissenters from the liberal orthodoxy, who previously had no place to go, can now find support. That does not mean that the fortress has been found to be empty, but that the society is more divided on the issue of multiculturalism than it was before. What has not changed is the bureaucracy of virtue whose mission—to redress the effects of past and alleged present discrimination—gives them a vested interest in tribal warfare in America, as well as in hyperbolic presentations of the putative iniquity of the civilization of the West. At Yale University, a gift of $20 million from the Bass family of Texas, which envisioned a special program in the study of the West, was returned, supposedly because the donors were demanding too much academic control. In truth, the Bass family demanded no control until its members finally became exasperated by four years of procrastination by a university administration clearly nervous about instituting new programs in Western studies during this era of multiculturalism. Remember how the former dean at Yale, Donald Kagan, was shouted down in 1990 when he made a speech to incoming freshman urging them to make the study of the West central to their education. Imagine that the Bass donation had been made for a new program in African-American studies, or women's studies, or Hispanic studies or in gay and lesbian studies. Imagine further that the university, claiming to be nervous about academic independence, sent the money back. First of all, one cannot imagine that because it would never happen. But if it did happen, imagine the outcry that would have been provoked on campus. When Yale, which is in a financial crisis, turned back $20 million for the further study of the West, there was barely a peep of protest.

The point is that multiculturalism as an adversary culture remains dominant within the elite institutions. Its assumptions are unchanged: that there is no single national culture but several cultures defined by race and ethnicity; that all cultures are equal and all cultures made equal contributions to the American civilization; that the ineradicable ingredient of American life is its oppressiveness and unfairness to women and minorities; that the country is changing its nature and we must make radical changes to be prepared for the new "diversity"; that instilling ethnic and racial self-esteem is the main task of education; that the remediation of attitudes about race and gender (and sometimes the prosecution of those attitudes) should be ever more important goals of our society. Multiculturalism in this sense is an ideology that is unaware of itself as an ideology. It is presumed to embody virtue, and virtue needs to brook no opposition. In reality, however, multiculturalism is not virtue. It is a new entitlement, being presented as virtue as a way of forestalling opposition.

There is something else occurring that has to do with the continued tribalization of American life. The elections of 1994, in which just under two-thirds of white men voted Republican, was—correctly, I believe—construed as a rebellion (or, as it was more commonly put, a "backlash") against the liberalism that has prevailed for the past two decades. It was an expression of annoyance at Bill Clinton's post-election promise to "make the government look like America," which was correctly perceived by many white men as a call to replace merit with non-maleness and non-whiteness as a qualification. In California, as of this writing, two obscure academics have created the California Civil Rights Initiative, which is a movement to put on the state ballot a constitutional amendment that would ban all preferences, targets, and quotas based on race and sex. In other words, it would require schools, the government, and employers to return to equal opportunity and non-discrimination, rather than equality of result and differential treatment, as the operative principles of civil society.

But the very power of this rebellion signalled in its way the triumph of multiculturalism, because it saw white men behaving, in essence, in the way the multiculturalists said they behaved—as a racial and sexual group with their own sense of grievance and victimization and their own racial and sexual interests to defend. In short, the election showed a powerful resentment against some of the programs supported by multiculturalism. And it provided a hint of what American multiculturalism will mean in the future. We are going to be a nation ever more fractured along group lines, with each group supposedly grounded, not only in its own separate interest, but in its own, separate-but-equal culture.

The demographic trends, so gleefully heralded by the multiculturalists as a welcome end to the white male hegemony and as requiring new respect for what they call "diversity," are deeply troubling when seen in the context of this accelerated tribalization. The multiculturalists, as we saw in Chapter 5, have exaggerated the speed and extent of demographic change, but they are correct in pointing out that sometime, perhaps around the middle of the next century if current trends persist, the United States will have no ethnic or racial majority. White males, the only large group in the country that does not benefit from some kind of preferential treatment, will number less than 25 percent of the total.

The American nation is a complicated and elusive creation. It is a kind of mongrelization of the original Anglo-Protestant migration that reached the New World in the seventeenth century. It is a black and white amalgam, but one whose shared political values came from Europe. Never mind that in the public schools of New York, students are taught that the Iroquois Confederation is what gave the Founding Fathers the idea for the Federal system established in the Constitution. That is just one of the remedial myths created by the curriculum of ethnic politics and self-esteem. It is our identity as individuals in a modified Western polity that has enabled the great mongrel nation called the United States of America to function. Martin Luther King, Jr., did not call on ancient African customs to lead us toward his vision of a more just society.

But what will come now? Multiculturalism is what the writer Peter Brimelow, in another context, has called an assault on the nation, or, more correctly, on the idea that we are a nation, with a common culture and common political values. If indeed we are heading toward a society of greater ethnic and racial diversity, the notion of nationhood, the sense of common bonds, needs strengthening. To attack it as illegitimate is to dilute the very substance that has enabled us to achieve our status as a unified and functioning nation.

To stress our differences, rather than our similarities, is to put the proven formula at risk. But multiculturalism portrays the common bond as a trick devised by hegemonic Eurocentrism. Multiculturalism is a license for people to make demands on the government and on each other on the basis of different group identities. It therefore must put a premium on difference. And stressing difference as the essential ingredient of a society has been more than risky in many other countries. It has led directly to calamity.

JUNE 1995

Acknowledgments

Index

Acknowledgments

This book is the product of two years of full-time work and the help of many people and organizations. I am grateful to Max Frankel and the editors of the *New York Times* who gave me a leave of absence so I could carry out the project. The Freedom Forum Media Studies Center, housed at Columbia University, awarded me a residential fellowship for the 1991–92 academic year. I owe a special debt of gratitude to Everette Dennis and the members of the Freedom Forum staff for the many ways in which they helped me. The Smith-Richardson Foundation provided me with a six-month stipend and a research grant to cover some of my expenses, and when I had used that up, the Lynde and Harry Bradley Foundation stepped in with similar support. I want especially to thank Devon Cross, Heather Richardson, and Michael Joyce for their encouragement and their friendship. I am also deeply indebted to Jeffrey Paul and Fred Miller of the Social Philosophy and Policy Center for the many ways in which they supported my work. In no instance did any of my benefactors ever ask to see a sentence of the manuscript or to know the direction that my research was taking. The opinions, the point of view, and the facts, as well as any errors that may be found in these pages, are my responsibility.

There are others who provided their wisdom and guidance. Jim Sleeper read the whole manuscript and made numerous valuable suggestions, and I am deeply grateful to him. Others who provided a special degree of guidance, information, or access are Alan Kors, Michael MacDonald, Christina Sommers, Mary Lefkowitz, Ben Mora, Dianne Monroe, Steve Balch, Laurie Bernstein, George Mitchell, and Gilbert Sewell. I want to express special thanks to Claudia Kalb and Hilary Dunst, my research assistants at different points in the writing of this book, both of whom routinely carried out missions that I gave them thinking they were impossible.

There are others, including those I will not mention by name, who told me their stories or gave me permission to witness their meetings, their classes, their conferences, their workshops. I am grateful to many people in Brookline, Massachusetts, and Austin, Texas, who took part in conflicts that I describe in Chapters 8 and 9. It is clear where I came down on these conflicts, but I am grateful both to those with whom I agreed and to those toward whom I was skeptical, since almost everybody, whatever side of the issue they were on, agreed to talk to me.

Others who extended me similar courtesies are at the University of Pennsylvania; at Temple University's Department of African-American Studies; at the Hans Christian Andersen Schools in Minneapolis; in the Afrocentric academies and on the public school board of Milwaukee; and at the University of California at Santa Cruz, the Philadelphia *Inquirer*, the New Jersey Project, the National Association for Multicultural Education, Rethinking Schools, Griggs Productions in California, Tulin Diversiteam, Inc., in Philadelphia, and the Community Board of Astoria, Queens.

My agent, Kathy Robbins, has been steadfast in her support and shrewd in her judgments, as always. And then, of course, there is my friend and editor, Jonathan Segal, who provided his usual scrupulous attention, his criticisms, his good humor, and his excellent company. This is our second book together. May there be more.

Index

CULTURAL LITERACY
What Every American Needs to Know
by E. D. Hirsch, Jr.

In this forceful manifesto, which engendered a nationwide debate on educational standards, Professor E. D. Hirsch, Jr., argues that children in the United States are being deprived of cultural literacy: a grasp of fundamental information that would enable them to function successfully in contemporary society. Thus, even if a student has a basic competence in English language, he or she has little chance of making it in the American mainstream without knowing, for example, what a silicon chip is, or when the Civil War was fought.

NONFICTION/EDUCATION/0-394-75843-9

BEYOND THE BURNING CROSS
A Landmark Case of Race, Censorship, and the First Amendment
by Edward J. Cleary

Does our abhorrence of racism allow us to ban certain forms of speech? This simple yet subversive question lies at the heart of the historic *R.A.V. v. St. Paul* case. When Edward Cleary agreed to defend a white teenager who had burned a cross on the front lawn of a black family, he did so even though he loathed his client's beliefs. In *Beyond the Burning Cross*, Cleary persuasively argues why any law that proscribes expressions of racism is as dangerous as one that bars protests against it.

CURRENT AFFAIRS/LAW/0-679-74703-6

Available at your local bookstore, or call toll-free to order:
1-800-793-2665 (credit cards only).